SvDenys

&12

47467

D1435967

ST ALBAN'S COLLEGE, VALLADOLID

MICHAEL E. WILLIAMS

St Alban's College Valladolid

Four Centuries of English Catholic Presence in Spain

C. HURST & COMPANY, LONDON
ST. MARTIN'S PRESS, NEW YORK

First published in the United Kingdom by
C. Hurst & Co. (Publishers) Ltd.,
38 King Street, London WC2E 8JT,
and in the United States of America by
St. Martin's Press, Inc.,
175 Fifth Avenue, New York, NY 10010

ISBNs
Hurst: 1-85065-019-5
St. Martin's: 0-312-69736-8

Library of Congress Cataloging-in-Publication Data

Williams, Michael E., 1922–
    St. Alban's College, Valladolid.

    Bibliography: p.
    Includes index.
    1. St. Alban's College (Valladolid, Spain)
2. Valladolid (Spain)––Church history. 3. Catholics,
English––Spain––Valladolid––History. I. Title.
BX920.V357W55 1986   207'.4623   86–17787
ISBN 0–312–69736–8

ACKNOWLEDGMENTS

The author of a work of this kind incurs many debts. Over a period of years many books and articles have been read and conferences attended. Discussions with friends and colleagues and even chance meetings have all helped to furnish facts and form judgments.

But not all the assistance is anonymous. In the first place, thanks must go to the College of St Alban at Valladolid for its hospitality and to the Rectors John Ryan and Ronald Hishon for their help and encouragement and for giving me access to the Archives. Gratitude is also due to archivists in the United Kingdom: Miss Elizabeth Poyser of the Archdiocese of Westminster, Fr George Bradley of the Diocese of Leeds, Fr John Allen of Salford, Fr Mark Dilworth, O.S.B., of the Scottish Catholic National Archives; Fr Michael Sharrat of St Cuthbert's College, Ushaw, and Fr Francis Edwards, S.J., who let me consult his forthcoming life of Robert Persons.

I am greatly indebted to Ronald Cueto of the University of Leeds for guidance on matters of Spanish ecclesiastical history. Martin Murphy kept me informed of his researches into the history of St Gregory's College, Seville. Of those who read part or whole of the manuscript and offered suggestions I should like to make special mention of Eamon Duffy, John Short and Bishop Thomas Holland. Dawn Marshall put the whole work on a word processor, and Canon Nicholas Rothon made the arrangements with the publisher. To all I wish to express my sincere thanks.

Trinity and All Saints College,   M.E.W.
Horsforth, Leeds
Spring 1986

ABBREVIATIONS

Unless otherwise stated, footnote references are to the archives held at St Alban's College Valladolid as described in Appendix B.

Anglia	Stonyhurst, Anglia A.
Anstruther	*The Seminary Priests: A Dictionary of the Secular Clergy of England and Wales, 1558–1800*, 4 vols.
CRS	Catholic Record Society Publications (Records Series).
CSP	Calendar of State Papers.
DNB	*Dictionary of National Biography*
E.S.	Publicaciones del Departamento de Inglés, Universidad de Valladolid.
Foley	*Records of the English Province of the Society of Jesus*, 8 vols.
Simancas	Archivo General de Simancas.
Tierney Dodd	Dodd's *Church History of England*, with notes, additions and a continuation by the Revd M.A. Tierney, 5 vols.
UCM	Ushaw College Manuscripts.
VEC	Archives of the Venerable English College Rome.
WCA	Westminster Cathedral Archives.

CONTENTS

PLATES

between pages 82 and 83

Principal street frontage of the College (after restoration)
The patio
Interior view of the Chapel dome
General view of the Chapel
The Martyrs' Corridor
The Refectory
Portrait of St Ambrose Barlow
Portrait of St Henry Walpole
Extract from the College register for Thomas Benstead
Our Lady Vulnerata
The High Altar of the Chapel
The 'Big Library'
The modern working library
The communications studio
The Country House at Viana de Ceya
In the Chapel of the Residence at Sanlúcar de Barrameda.
Portrait of Monsignor Edwin Henson
The belfry of the College Chapel

INTRODUCTION

There have been several attempts to write a history of St Alban's College.[1] Many of these are related to lawsuits where it was necessary to establish certain claims by appealing to historical evidence. Frequently these are examples of special pleading and thus lack the breadth and objectivity desirable in a true history. However, as long ago as 1606 an official history was ordered by the Father-General of the Society of Jesus. The visitation of 30 April 1613 recorded that nothing had yet been done about it, but it would seem that the project came to partial fulfilment in the *Annales Collegii Anglorum Vallisoletani* attributed to Father John Blackfan, S.J., a former student, which was probably written 1619–20.[2]

However, there are records that predate the *Annales*. The *Liber Alumnorum* begins in 1589 and continues to 1677, where it breaks off with the expulsion from the College of Titus Oates. After this date, several pages are missing, but there are a few entries for 1756–8. Philip Perry, the first secular Rector, began a new register and diary in 1768, which continued after his death up to 1797. When John Guest was administering the College, he not only resumed the Register from 1848 but also filled in the intervening years from other sources in the College Archives so that there is in fact an unbroken, although imperfect, record of students from 1589 to the present day. In addition, the *Liber Primi Examinis* 1592–1623 contains the names and particulars of students entered up on their arrival at the College as part of the process for scrutinising candidates and so detecting spies and other undesirable characters. In 1930 the then Rector, Edwin Henson, published *The Registers of the English College, Valladolid, 1589–1862* for the Catholic Record Society.[3] This work, which is based on the records mentioned above supplemented by other archival material, takes the story up to the time of John Guest. Henson's introduction, which he intended to be 'no more than a vague

1. E.g. Perry on the origins of the College, Series II, *legajo* (hereafter L) 8; Guest notes on the history. Series III, L21; Allen on the history, Series II, L25.
2. Published privately by Manresa Press, 1899. The revised *Annals* are to be found in the Appendix to CRS, 30, pp. 263–72.
3. CRS, 30. The passages from the *Liber Primi Examinis* printed here often give the family background of the students of 1529–1623, and are thus important for the student of social history. Unfortunately, such a study is outside the range of the present work.

background for the registers with a list of Rectors and of all the English superiors', provides a valuable outline of the College's history.

At the Albanian Society meeting of 1893 a suggestion was made that Michael Burns should write and have printed the 'Lives of the Martyrs and Remarkable Members of St Alban's College'. In the following months Burns drafted a plan for a history of the College from the beginnings up to his own time, and designated certain individuals whom he thought would be able to write on specific topics. Nothing seems to have come of this project, although the idea was revived when Burns became Rector, and in 1921 Robert Smith, parish priest of St Joseph's, Nelson, Lancashire, published a 31-page pamphlet *Gleanings for a History of St Alban's English Catholic College*. In 1980 William J. Gaffney had his 280-page book *Elizabethan Students: The story of the English College of St Alban, Valladolid, Spain* privately printed. The present work is a revival of the idea of a general history of the College in readiness for its fourth centenary in 1989.

The College of St Alban, Valladolid, is the sole survivor of several former colleges and residences at Seville, Madrid, Sanlúcar de Barrameda and Lisbon, which inevitably enter into the story from time to time. Peter Guilday set out to write about *The English Catholic Refugees on the Continent, 1558–1795*,[4] but he never progressed beyond the first volume and was not able to give his attention to English Catholics in the Iberian Peninsula. Since his day our knowledge of post-Reformation Catholicism both in England and in Spain has greatly increased, and in writing of this institution on foreign soil it is essential to keep in mind these wider contexts. To appreciate the history of St Alban's some knowledge of the Church in Spain as well as in England is necessary, and this in turn requires an understanding of the secular history of these two countries. It is this aspect that takes the present work outside its domestic area of concern since it has something to say of the connections between English and Spanish Catholicism over the four centuries from 1589.

The story begins with the founding of English colleges in Spain at Valladolid and Seville. They were opened after those at Douai and Rome, and once established they quickly developed their own distinctive character. The attitude of Philip II towards ecclesiastical institutions, their administration and finances, meant that Valladolid was never a charge on the Holy See and relations with Rome were conducted through the Spanish crown. Generous support was given by the King,

---

4. *The English Colleges and Convents in the Low Countries, 1558–1795*, vol. 1, London, 1914.

but the College depended very much on alms raised from the faithful in Spain. Spanish superiors were part of the price Father Persons had to pay for the initial arrangement with the King. Although this ensured an efficient administration, the Spanish fathers were not always able to provide the students with a training suitable for work in England.

The expulsion of the Jesuits from Spain in 1767 divides the history of the College into two parts. From this date the establishments at Valladolid, Madrid and Seville were united into the one College at Valladolid, and the English secular clergy assumed the administration. Because of their dissatisfaction with the Spanish Jesuits, they were eager to take charge, but they were soon confronted with an unfamiliar situation. The expulsion of the Jesuits was not the result of a petty rivalry among Catholics but part of a larger plan of the Bourbon monarch Charles III and his principal ministers to establish a closer link between Church and state, especially in all matters relating to education. In effect the new Rector, Philip Perry, had to direct his establishment in accordance with the ideals of the Catholic enlightenment. However, this situation did not last; the *ancien régime* crumbled, and during the Peninsular War law and order collapsed in both Church and state.

The Rectors now assumed a heavy responsibility. If the College under the Jesuits can be said to have worked according to a system (regular visitations, change of superiors, answerability to the Provincial), from the nineteenth century its very existence depended on the calibre of the Rector alone. With no financial help from Rome or the Crown, he had to manage affairs as best he could. During the varying fortunes of the restored Bourbon monarchy he had to cope with the claims of royal patronage and periodic anti-clerical legislation. At the same time he had to satisfy the Bishops in England. His appointment was dependent on them as well as on the King, and he relied on them to provide him with students. At the best they did not interfere, and at the worst they grumbled but found it difficult to remove him. If they accused him of being out of touch with England he could reply that they were not aware of the conditions in Spain.

The College never lost its Englishness. Often it had to assert this to keep its identity and so escape the penalties of the law. But on these occasions there was no doubt where its sympathies lay. This is most apparent during the Second Carlist War and the Franco uprising. Its anti-republicanism in the 1930s had little to do with the royal patronage, but stemmed rather from the unhappy experience of the Church during the First and Second Republics. Patriotism was often an issue. In the early days not everyone at Valladolid supported Persons' Spanish policy, some finding it to conflict with their loyalties as Englishmen. During the Peninsular War Spaniards and Englishmen fought together for the country's Independence. But during the Second World War support of the Allied cause brought its problems from both Church and state.

St Alban's is a seminary, and so its main task is to train men to serve as priests on the English Mission. From this point of view its golden age was in the first thirty years of its existence; more than twenty of its students were martyred, five of them and one Vice-Rector (minister) are Canonised Saints. Since that time it has continued its task but often in conditions of great difficulty. Although seminaries have been established in England since the end of the eighteenth century, it is only since the Second Vatican Council that the question of the maintenance of the colleges abroad has been raised seriously. Criticism that the College was not preparing students for conditions in England has existed since its early days, and this was directed mainly at the studies at S. Ambrosio. However there was no discussion about the need to segregate clerical students from the world for a period of formation; even those studying in their homeland were cut off from family and friends. But priestly formation and training are now under review, although at the time of writing the degree of isolation is not yet determined.

However, the seminary training had a positive aspect in that students were exposed to influences that would help to foster their piety and prepare them for future pastoral work. During the days of persecution in England, Catholic Spain provided such a climate, and one of the purposes in securing the residence at Sanlúcar de Barrameda was to give newly-ordained priests experience of ministering in a Catholic country. But the place of Catholicism in Spain has changed over the years, and after the end of the Franco period conditions for the Church are much the same as in any other modern secular state. This, together with the ease of communications between the two countries, means that there is less contrast than in the past between living as a Catholic in Spain and living as one in England. The demands of Christian witness in the two countries are very similar. But differences remain, and perhaps the experience of a different tradition and cultural expression of Catholicism can widen the horizons of those preparing to serve the Church in England.

PART ONE
THE COLLEGE UNDER THE JESUITS

1

FOUNDATIONS: HOW THERE CAME TO BE ENGLISH COLLEGES IN SPAIN

During the reign of Elizabeth I the number of Catholic exiles on the continent increased. Many of the English foundations of religious orders of men and women found refuge in the Low Countries, within easy reach of England yet in relative safety since they were under the protection of the King of Spain.[1] It should be remembered that their presence abroad was not of their own choosing; they were there because of the religious persecution at home, and most of them regarded their exile as temporary. They looked forward to returning home when their country had healed the breach with Rome. In the mean time they wanted to preserve their own identity, and they had little desire to mingle with foreigners more than was strictly necessary.[2] They deliberately chose to lie low and not attract the attention and curiosity of either the local inhabitants or (as was not infrequently the case) government spies from England. In consequence, a researcher into their history has to be prepared to find only sparse documentation in contemporary records. This isolation was to remain a characteristic of their way of life throughout their sojurn abroad despite inevitable concessions to certain demands from ecclesiastical and civil authorities.

In 1559 a new university was established at Douai to promote the Counter Reformation in the Spanish Provinces, and the town soon became a centre for churchmen and scholars. In 1568 the exiled English scholar William Allen with the support of Philip II founded an English

---

1. For a list of English foundations on the continent see P. Guilday, *The English Colleges and Convents in the Catholic Low Countries 1558–1795* (vol. 1 of *The English Catholic Refugees on the Continent 1558–1795*), London 1914, p. 40.
2. This gregariousness of the English exiles accounts for the continued existence of national colleges. Belonging to an international religious community did not find favour with either the authorities in England or with those who studied abroad.

College there.[3] There is some disagreement about his exact intentions,[4] but among them certainly was that of enabling English Catholic academics to enjoy the benefit of a collegial life in a university town, something now denied them in their own country. In addition, he wanted to form a body of learned priests capable of restoring the Catholic religion in England when circumstances would permit. The College was not originally an establishment exclusively for the training of priests, nor did it envisage sending the priests it did produce back on a mission to convert England from heresy. It was simply a matter of making provision for a future restoration of Catholicism; this was considered certain, the only doubt being as to the exact time it would take place. In the event, the spiritual objective of training the clergy became the predominant purpose although the other side was never lost sight of, and Douai College expanded downwards so that it began to cater for the education of boys up to university level.

However, only ten years after its foundation Douai College ran into trouble when the Catholic exiles were forced to leave the country. Camden maintains that this was due to an arrangement between Elizabeth I and the Governor of Flanders,[5] whereas Dodd suggests it simply resulted from fear of English spies and the general unpopularity of the English residents.[6] The College was not included in this order directly — because the decree applied only to those who could bear arms and so university professors and children were exempt — but the citizens of the town made things extremely difficult for the College since the English Catholics were associated with their hated Spanish protectors.[7] As a result of this anti-Spanish nationalism, the College had to transfer to French territory, and set itself up at Rheims in 1578.[8] But hopes were

3. T.F. Knox (ed.), *The First and Second Douay Diaries*, London, 1878; E.H. Burton and T.L. Williams (eds), *Third, Fourth and Fifth Diaries*, London, 1911; CRS, vols 10 and 11; E.H. Burton and E. Nolan (eds), *The Seventh Diary*, London, 1928, CRS, vol. 28; P.R. Harris (ed.), *Douai College Documents*, 1972, CRS, 63.

4. A.C.F. Beales, *Education under Penalty*, London 1963, p. 110.

5. W. Camden, *Rerum Anglicarum et Hibernicarum Annales* (ed. Thomas Hearne), Oxford 1717, p. 296.

6 Dodd's *Church History of England* with notes, additions and a continuation by the Revd M.A. Tierney, London 1839, vol. II, pp. 162–6.

7. A contemporary account of the expulsion of the English from Douai in 1578 speaks of the supposed fidelity of the English to the King of Spain. WCA 2, 9.

8. The move took place on 22 March 1578 and the buildings at Douai continued to be used as a junior seminary where only students too young to bear arms were allowed to live.

not very high of settling permanently in France since the English were not popular there either, and it was by no means clear at this time whether France would throw in her lot with the Catholic or the Protestant powers. So there was a constant search for an alternative site during the fifteen years that the College was at Rheims before it eventually returned to Douai.

From Anglo-Saxon times there had been a hospice in Rome to cater for pilgrims from England.[9] At this time it was on a site it had occupied since 1362, but with the change in religion in England, pilgrimages became rarer and the building was largely occupied by priests ordained under Mary Tudor and now in exile. The plan was to change this hospice into a College, and after initial objections from the residents who did not wish to be disturbed from their comfortable life of inaction, there eventually emerged in 1579 a seminary to supplement the work of Douai/Rheims in the training of priests. By this time, however, it had become clear that the restoration of England to the old faith could not be expected in the immediate future, and so the new Roman English College was from the start a missionary enterprise. Unlike Douai it was never a school for the laity, and the policy was not to wait until the tide turned but to send the students back after ordination to work in England, knowing full well that they would probably meet with arrest and death. This change in policy — 'Today rather than tomorrow', as Protomartyr Ralph Sherwin put it — provided a new challenge and a rallying point for English Catholics, and more and more young men applied for admission to the seminaries at Rheims and Rome, attracted by an active and dangerous ecclesiastical career.

It is at this point that the story of the Spanish foundations begins. The College at Rheims had a somewhat precarious existence, and when Pope Gregory XIII died in 1585, Rome began to have its share of troubles. The new Pope Sixtus V removed the papal subsidies from all the colleges in Rome as part of an economy drive, and so it was not possible for the College there to admit all the students who were applying for entry.[10] Eyes turned to Spain because of its geographical position. Up to this time

9. F.A. Gasquet, *A History of the Venerable English College, Rome*, London 1920; M.E. Williams, *The Venerable English College Rome*, London 1979.

10. In September 1584 the Cardinal Secretary of State had reprimanded Allen for taking more students at Rheims than he could support, CRS, 39, pp. lxviii–lxix. For the complaints at Rome concerning Gregory XIII's munificence, see R.M. Wiltgen, 'Propaganda is placed in charge of the Pontifical Colleges', *Sacrae Congregationis de Propaganda Fide Memoria Rerum* 1/1 (Rome, Freiburg, Vienna 1971), p. 486.

the normal route from Rome to England and the Low Countries was through the Mount Cenis pass, Lyons and Paris, but with the intensification of the religious wars in France, alternative routes had to be found. One of the most popular of these was across the western Mediterranean from Italy to Spain, then across Spain to Bilbao or another northern port and then by sea to England either direct or by way of Ireland.[11] Moreover, it was sometimes too dangerous to cross directly from the Low Countries to England, so that the journey home also had to be the long way round, via Spain.

It is not clear when the first English students arrived in Spain. The earliest record found so far is of a petition for help addressed on 24 October 1588 (a few weeks after receiving the news of the defeat of the Armada) to the Ayuntamiento of Valladolid from fourteen English and Irish students and priests exiled for their faith, who had been living there for more than a year.[12] Valladolid, though no longer the permanent official court capital as under Charles V, was the third largest city in the kingdom and the most important centre of communications in the north, so that travellers to any of the northern coastal ports would pass through it.[13] It contained numerous monasteries and churches, and was still the home of the Supreme Court and the Inquisition. Its University made it a natural meeting place for scholars, and the town now had a reputation for Catholic orthodoxy. In the 1580s the University had established new chairs, and pre-university studies were encouraged by the success of the Jesuit College of S. Ambrosio. Many of its citizens were rich as well as pious and it seemed an obvious place to win sympathy and influential support for the English Catholic cause. However, the first recorded connection between the College at Rheims and Spain is the departure from Rheims on 10 November 1588 of William Cowling,

11. J. Bossy, 'Rome and the Elizabethan Catholics: A Question of Geography', *Historical Jnl.*, VII (1964), pp. 135–42; see also CRS, 39, pp. xxxix–xlii, for Persons' residence at Rouen and the difficulty of crossing to England.

12. T. Morrissey, S.J., 'The Irish Student Diaspora in the Sixteenth Century and the early years of the Irish College at Salamanca', *Recusant History*, 14, pp. 242 f., mentions Irishmen in Valladolid since 1582. But according to CSP, Domestic Series, Addenda, 1580–1625, London 1872, p. 37, John Donne, a spy, was present in Valladolid on 18 August 1580. See also Mary Bridget Blake, 'The Irish College at Salamanca, its early history and the influence of its work on Irish Education', unpubl. MA thesis, University of Liverpool, 1951, which gives names of Irish students in Spain before 1580.

13. B. Benassar, *Valladolid au siècle d'or*, Paris 1967; and 'Valladolid en el Reinado de Felipe II' in *Historia de Valladolid*, vol. 3, Valladolid 1981.

Gerard Cliburn and Francis Lockwood for Spain.[14] As all three were already ordained priests, their journey could hardly be in search of a place to begin their studies, so they were either compelled to make this long detour because of the impossibility of crossing directly to England from France,[15] or they were following up some Spanish contact and were perhaps seeking alms for the seminary at Rheims and even perhaps an alternative site for a seminary. But shortly after their departure, on 23 and 24 December, Henry Duke of Guise and his brother the Cardinal Archbishop of Rheims were assassinated and new fears arose for the future of the Rheims College. Not only was the Guise family its chief protector and benefactor in the kingdom of France, but there was now renewed anxiety lest there should be an alliance between Henry of Navarre and Elizabeth of England, which would certainly bode ill for any English Catholic in France. Some sort of decision about sending students from Rheims to study in Spain must have been made early in 1589. On 8 May 1589 Henry Floyd (Deacon), John Blackfan (Subdeacon) and James Bosville, M.A., set out from Rheims for Spain via Nantes and Bilbao, and two weeks later Dr Still (sometimes called Stillington), John Fixer and Thomas Lovelace did likewise with the intention of becoming professors and taking charge of the students. It has been suggested[16] that Philip II was believed to be more prepared to support an establishment in Spain than to increase his benefactions to Douai; but any hesitation in deciding to establish a College in Spain can be explained by the fact that it was an unpropitious time for the English to visit the country.[17] On 25 April, La Coruña had been sacked by the English and on 25 May a force had landed at Lisbon as part of the campaign in support of Dom Antonio, Prior de Crato and claimant to the throne of Portugal. Antonio did not gain popular support, which is hardly surprising in view of some of the concessions he had made to

14. Knox (ed.), *Douay Diaries*, p. 221. Exactly how the College at Valladolid came into existence is not certain. Henson, CRS, 30, pp. vii–xvi, discusses the documentation at length, and the account given here agrees substantially with his reconstruction of events.

15. This is in fact suggested by D. Rogers in his Introduction to the Gregg Press reprint of Diego de Yepes, *Historia de la Persecución de Inglaterra* (1971).

16. J. Hicks, 'Father Persons SJ and the Seminaries in Spain', *The Month*, CLVI, p. 417.

17. The correspondence between the Nuncio in Spain and the Holy See testifies to the anxiety felt in Spain concerning the raids on Spanish shipping by Francis Drake and the fear of an invasion of Portugal. Jose de Olarra Garmendia and María Luisa de Larramendi viuda de Olarra, *Correspondencia entre la Nunciatura en España y la Santa Sede. Reinado de Felipe III*, 7 vols, Rome 1960–7.

England, which included a promise to appoint English Catholic exiles to vacant Bishoprics in Portugal.

Elizabeth was gratified by the patriotic stance of some of the Catholics at the time of the Armada crisis, and hoped that such a recompense would divert their attention from the situation at home and give them an incentive to remain in exile.[18] Such happenings as this did not inspire Spanish confidence in English Catholics and thus it is understandable that these groups of English students arriving in Spain fell under suspicion of being spies.[19] Floyd and his companions were arrested at Burgos but eventually released, and they reached Valladolid and joined up with Cowling, Cliburn and Lockwood. Meanwhile two other students, Henry Sherrat and John Gillibrand, had arrived in Spain from England by way of Ireland. They were intending to go to Rheims, but an English Franciscan they met at Bilbao recommended that it would be better for them to proceed to Rome and join the College there. Passing through Valladolid on their way to the Mediterranean, they met the six Rheims students and threw in their lot with them. They secured lodgings near the Convent of Santa Clara and began to attend the lectures at the Jesuit College, since at this time Still and his companions, their destined teachers, had not yet arrived in Spain. Their financial position improved when John Cecil[20] arrived on the scene. He fell in with the Rheims students at Valladolid and they secured the patronage of a wealthy Spaniard, Don Alonso de Quiñones; so that by July 1589 there were at Valladolid three Rheims priests, three Rheims students, two students from England and John Cecil — not counting any others who had been resident in the town since 1587 or earlier.

It is at this point that the principal character in the story of the

---

18. *The Notebook of John Southcote, D.D.*, CRS, 1, pp. 97 f.

19. H. More, *Historia Missionis Anglicanae Societatis Jesu*, and J. Blackfan, *Annales*, both give an account of the vicissitudes of these early parties in their journeys to Spain.

20. Cecil had become a Catholic while at Oxford, had studied at Rheims and then proceeded to Rome where he was ordained. When William Allen, the founder of Douai College, was created a Cardinal in 1587 or early 1588, he was sent by Allen to Spain perhaps with the intention of starting a College there. His later history is somewhat controversial. From the state papers it is evident he was a double agent in touch with his namesake in the English government from as early as 1588. Together with John Fixer, he was arrested on his return to England in the spring of 1591 and he divulged much information concerning the Catholic exiles. CSP Domestic Series, Elizabeth, 1591–4, London 1867, nos 160, 168, 169, 179, 180, 181. Also CSP Salisbury MSS., vol. IV, no. 104. See also *DNB*, vol. XXII (Supplement I, 1901), p. 403. Anstruther, I, p. 63.

founding of the College makes his appearance. About the same time as the first group of priests left Rheims November 1588 — the Jesuit Robert Persons left Rome for Spain. He had already visited Spain in 1582 when, with the backing of Gregory XIII, he had begged alms for the College of Rheims; this time he was sent by the General of the Order, Claudio Aquaviva, on a special mission to accompany José Acosta.[21] The Jesuits in Spain were in dispute with the crown and with the Inquisition, who wished to control their activities, whereas they wanted freedom of action and to be answerable only to Rome.[22] Persons took the opportunity of his interview with the King to ask for further financial assistance for the Rheims College and for the College in Rome of which he had recently been Rector. He was also anxious to obtain the King's permission for English Jesuits to become members of Spanish Jesuit houses. It is not easy to ascertain the exact connection between Persons' journey to Spain, the students' journey from Rheims, and Cecil's journey from Rome. Blackfan[23] says that Persons, while still in Rome, had written to Fr Barret, Rector of Douai/Rheims, suggesting that students should be sent from Rheims to Spain,[24] but it should be noted that Persons arrived in Spain early in 1589, probably before any students had yet arrived from Rheims.[25] But by the summer he got to know of the existence of this community at Valladolid. He had an audience of the King on 13 July, and on 22 July wrote from Madrid to Creswell in Rome saying that he had obtained letters favouring a new seminary to be founded at Valladolid.[26] An order-in-council dated 22 July 1589 granted

21. A. Astrain, *Historia de la Compañía de Jesús*, bk. II, Madrid 1912–25, chap. XIV, pp. 491 f.
22. This matter of the relationship of the religious houses to the Crown extended beyond the dispute with the Jesuits; it would affect the government of any future seminary in Spain.
23. Blackfan, *Annales*; also H. More, *Historia Missionis Anglicanae Societatis Jesus*. Astrain, op. cit., bk. II, chap. 2, pp. 254–6, says that Persons discussed the founding of an English seminary in Spain with Aquaviva before leaving Rome. However, the Spanish edition of *A Relation of the King of Spain's Receiving* suggests that the foundation was not premeditated. Cf. Henson, CRS, 30, x.
24. D. Bartoli, *Dell'Istoria della Compagnia di Gesù. Inghilterra*, Turin 1825, bk. V, chap. 2, using extracts from Greene's *Collectanea P*, says that on 28 April 1589 Persons wrote to Creswell from Alcalá about sending some English Jesuit students to Spain, saying that the Spanish Jesuits would maintain them. So there seemed no explicit intention of founding a seminary.
25. Persons seems to have had an audience of the King late in January or early February. He reports it in a letter of 17 Feb. 1589 (letter from L. Hicks to E. Henson, 16 June 1931, in the Valladolid archives).
26. Persons circulated a work *Información que da el Padre Personio : . . . . acerca del Seminario*

permission to beg alms throughout 'our kingdoms' for a period of four years;[27] and following this, on 24 November, two of the priests of this new community, Cowling and Cliburn, received permission from the Cardinal of Portugal to solicit alms for four years when they arrived in Lisbon. Such a permission gave hope of financial security that was a necessary prerequisite to any future foundation.

In addition, the English students received official permission to reside in the town, and they were placed under the care of the local ecclesiastical superior, the 'Abbot' of the Collegiate Church[28] and the Rector of the Jesuit College. At first the 'Abbot' was opposed to the presence of young men from a country steeped in heresy, and because of the Jesuit connection the Inquisition was also antagonistic.[29] Persons' friends at Court won the day for him, but the royal order that the Hospice of Saints Cosmas and Damian[30] be put at the disposal of the priests and students was refused by the priest in charge, and eventually property was obtained on the site of the present College. There were many offers of help in these early days, including that from Francisco de Fonseca, Lord of Coca, who more than once offered his castle at Coca with its large estates as a residence for the English students.

After the concession to beg was granted in mid-July, events moved swiftly. The first book of accounts recording the names of the first benefactors begins on 1 August and the College Roll, *Liber Alumnorum Collegii S. Albani*, begins on 1 September.[31] John Cecil is the first name in the Register, and seven others are also entered under this date — considerably fewer than the total number of students in Valladolid at this time. Cliburn does not appear although the other two ordained priests, Cowling and Lockwood, do. There is no record of the

---

de Valladolid, dated 1 Sept. 1589, giving publicity to his project, showing the need for a seminary and dispelling rumours about English spies. Federico Esquíluz de Latierro, 'La Fundación del Colegio Inglés de Valladolid', *E.S.*, pp. 131–77.

27. Persons also secured help from two prominent English Catholic exiles at the Spanish Court: Jane Dormer, Duchess of Feria, and Sir Francis Englefield.

28. Valladolid was not yet an episcopal see, but was under the Bishop of Palencia; thus the head of the collegiate church was in effect the ecclesiastical superior.

29. The Inquisitor Juan Vígil de Quiñones was one of those most opposed to the College, cf. F. Esquíluz de Latierro, op. cit, p. 147.

30. 'El Abad de Valladolid a Su Majestad', 5 Aug. 1589. See Simancas E166, Mod.85, f. 133, for the later history of this house see Angel Benito y Durán, 'Monasterio de San Cosmé y San Damián de monjes Basilios', *Hispania Sacra*, vols 31–32 (1978–9), pp. 201–83.

31. St Alban was venerated by the recusants both as protomartyr of England and as a layman who suffered death for giving refuge to a priest in his house.

fourteen English and Irish students who had been given assistance by the Ayuntamiento in the previous October, and this has led some[32] to suppose that there was another College, an Irish one, in the town. However the new English College had become so well organised within this short time that when Still and the two other prospective teachers from Rheims eventually arrived in October, their services were not needed since arrangements had already been made for the students to be taught at the Jesuit College of S. Ambrosio which they had already been attending before the Persons' arrival.[33] In a letter to Dr Barrett at Rheims on 28 October 1590,[34] Still said that at first the fathers 'wanted nobody but themselves and their scholars in this College'. But there was a steady supply of scholars arriving from Rheims, not all of them prospective Jesuits. In the same letter Still wrote: 'For the College we have two large houses with a garden between, but we shall be put to stabling if you send us any more. The habit is a black cloth gown, such as you wear, for without a habit no College in Spain can stand.'

Although he was the founder of the new College, and had assumed overall responsibility for English Catholic affairs in Spain, Persons did not become one of its superiors. From the beginning the Rectors were Spanish Jesuits, although the Father Minister was usually English. There was some 'sorting out' of the students to be done, and some, being considered unsuitable for Spain, were sent to other seminaries.[35] Persons rapid success in overcoming obstacles and opposition suggests that he had the full backing of the King. Whatever may have been the views of Acosta and the General of the Society concerning the relationship of the Spanish Jesuits to the Crown and the Inquisition, Persons perceived that there was no future for an English seminary in Spain unless it were under the control of the King in some way. This was a matter of the King's overall religious policy and had little to do with the College being

32. H. More, *Historia Missionis*, bk. V, no. 3, is supported by E. Hogan, S.J., *Ibernia Ignatiana*, Dublin 1880. L. Hicks in a letter to Henson, 29 June 1931, says: 'I wrote to the Irish S.J. concerned with the history of the Irish Province and he has replied that there were a good number of Irish students at Valladolid in 1588 and even in 1585, and that what More says is clearly demonstrable by contemporary documents still extant. . . . He has not told me the documents, but I can take his word for it, as he is very careful and an extraordinarily well-informed man.'

33. Dr Still went to Sanlúcar de Barrameda.

34. CSP Domestic Addenda, 1580–1625, p. 311.

35. William J. Gaffney, *Elizabethan Students of the English College of St Alban, Valladolid* (privately printed 1981), p. 56, relates the dismissal of students by Persons, and the disagreement with Henry Walpole, to Persons' pro-Spanish political views.

intended for Englishmen. This fundamental principle may well have influenced not only the appointment as Rector of Bartolomé de Sicilia,[36] a close friend of Philip II, but also the non-employment of Still and his colleagues as professors, and the removal of certain students from the College, and the disagreement with Henry Walpole. In addition, the appointment of Spanish superiors in the new College assuaged the Inquisition's fear of English unorthodoxy.[37]

Following the concession by the King, the students from time to time made begging expeditions throughout the Peninsula. We have referred to Cowling and Cliburn going to Lisbon, and a little later John Cecil and William Warford went to Andalusia whence they brought back glowing accounts of Seville. The generosity of its people, and its closeness to the sea and hence easy communications with England, made it a promising site for a future college. There were already English priests at Seville at this time, and in 1591 twelve set out from there for the English Mission, including eight who had previously spent some time at Valladolid.[38] Persons was not unaware of the situation in the south, because he had wintered there and ministered to English galley-slaves at Puerto de Santa María, but with Valladolid still in its infancy he did not judge it wise to open another seminary so soon.

However, there was another English centre in the south at Sanlúcar de Barrameda.[39] At least since the time of Henry VIII there had been an English church in the town dedicated to St George and cared for by a confraternity of English merchants. With the change in religion and the falling off of trade between the two countries the confraternity was in decline, and it made over the house and church to Persons as a residence for English priests; money for rebuilding the church was given by the King and the Duke of Medina Sidonia. Persons saw it as a place where the newly-ordained priests could exercise a ministry, under normal conditions in a Catholic country, before departing for the rigours of the English Mission.

By now the number of candidates for the seminary in Valladolid was rapidly increasing. The first news of the seminary at Valladolid seems to have reached England as early as 7 October 1589. Francis Lombard met Richard Fowloe in Bilbao, who told him sometime before 2 September:

36. Henson, CRS, 30, pp. xvii–xviii. Bartolomé de Sicilia was only ordained priest in 1589, but had a capacity for managing money matters and was connected with the Duke of Albuquerque and the Duke of Medinaceli.
37. J. Cordara, *Historia Societatis Jesu*, part 6, vol. 1, bk. 2, 1750, pp. 107–8.
38. See *Annals of the English College Seville*, CRS, 14, p. 4.
39. See Appendix F for Sanlúcar de Barrameda. Cecil had been at Sanlúcar in 1587.

'Father Persons and other English students had obtained leave to have a free College at the King's charge at Valladolid for all English that would come.'[40] In Elizabeth's proclamation of 1591 against the seminary priests the College at Valladolid was mentioned by name, and this publicity helped the recruitment to such an extent that with seventy students accommodated within its walls not only was it necessary to launch an extensive building scheme,[41] but the need for another college become pressing. Financially Valladolid was sound since Spanish Catholics of all classes had responded generously to the calls on their charity.[42]

On 25 April 1592 the Papal Bull of Foundation was published declaring the College to be immediately subject to the Holy See and was empowered to grant degrees in Arts and Philosophy equivalent to the Universities of Oxford and Cambridge. But although the College was made subject to the Holy See, neither it nor the one in Seville became a Pontifical College in the sense of being maintained either wholly or partly by an annual papal subsidy. The finances did not come from Rome.[43] In the early summer of 1592 the King of Spain paid a prolonged visit to Valladolid and on 3 August accompanied by the two Princes including the future Philip III) visited the College officially and was received in great style in the refectory, then still incomplete.[44] He received addresses of welcome from the students in ten languages.[45] This royal visit was a feather in the cap for Persons who now had no difficulty in obtaining from the King official letters of commendation for a second college to be situated in Seville.

40. CSP, Domestic Addenda, 1580–1625, p. 288. CSP, Venice, 1581–91, vol. 8, p. 471. In the *Noticias y Avisos de Inglaterra* (Series II, L6) it is reported from London on 20 August 1591 that seven or eight priests had arrived from Spain and that others are said to be on their way from a seminary 'recently instituted by His Catholic Majesty in the town of Valladolid'.

41. The *Libro de Gastos* (Series II, L13) reports extensive building in July 1592 and in the days preceeding the King's visit.

42. See chapter 5 for a general treatment of the contributions made by Spaniards to the finances of the English College.

43. When Propaganda Fide was established in 1622 the College never became subject to it, although when the oath originally imposed on the English College in Rome — to prevent defections to the Jesuits — was extended to all Pontifical colleges (both inside and outside Rome), this was made to apply to the Colleges in Spain also.

44. The story of this visit is told in *A Relation of the king of Spain's Receiving in Valladolid, and in the English College of the same town, in August last past, of this year 1592*, Antwerp 1592. Yepes, in his *Historia de la persecución de Inglaterra*, made use of a Spanish version of this work. Another royal visit was made in 1600 by Philip III and his consort. See p. 62 below.

45. The languages were Greek, Latin, Hebrew, Spanish, English, French, Italian, Flemish, Scottish and Welsh. In 1600 an address was made in Cornish as well.

Speed characterised the beginnings of the Seville foundation, like Valladolid. Permission was granted in August and St Gregory's College was opened on 25 November with fourteen students, some being recruited from St Alban's Valladolid and the others coming from Rheims.[46] The College was to be administered in a similar way to Valladolid — a Spanish Rector and an English Minister, with the students attending lectures at the Jesuit College of S. Hermenegild. On the Feast of St Thomas of Canterbury, 29 December, the chapel was solemnly opened and there were the customary celebrations in chapel and hall. On 15 May 1594 the seminary was confirmed by the Pope and placed under the protection of the Holy See, its governance was assigned to the Jesuits, and Cardinal Allen was given the same position of oversight and control as he already had over St Alban's.

But Persons was not finished yet. Spain and Portugal had been united under the one crown since 1581, and Lisbon was not only an busy international port but also a suitable point of embarkation for England and thus a useful listening-post for news from England and the North of Europe. About this time (the date can not be exactly determined) Persons founded a Residence there — which, however, he did not wish to develop further into a seminary. There was already an Irish College in Lisbon[47] and a second establishment from the British Isles might have resulted in friction between the two communities as had happened in Rome between the Welsh and the English at the English College.[48] In addition, despite the excellent sea communications between Lisbon and the rest of the world, the landlines between Spain and Portugal were no better than they are today, and because Persons needed to travel a great deal between the English foundations and communities, it was decided at this time not to found a college in Lisbon. However, Persons did gain support from the Cardinal-Viceroy of Portugal, the Archbishop of

---

46. For further information about the Seville College, see Appendix E. An account of the beginnings of the Seville College (as well as of the Sanlúcar Residence) can be found in *News from Spayne and Holland conteyning an information of English affayres in Spayne with a conference made thereupon in Amsterdame of Holland. Written by a Gentleman travelour borne in the Low Countries, and brought up from a child in England unto a Gentleman his friend and oste in London*, Antwerp 1593 probably the work of Persons.

47. Thomas Morrissey, S.J., 'The Irish Student Diaspora in the Sixteenth Century and the early years of the Irish College at Salamanca', *Recusant History*, 14, no. 4 (Oct. 1978), pp. 242–60. Eventually a seminary was established at Lisbon (see below, p. 38) but the College of SS. Peter and Paul, Lisbon, always remained under the control of the secular clergy and had closer links with Douai College than with the English colleges in Spain.

48. M.E. Williams, *The Venerable English College, Rome*, London 1979, p. 5.

Lisbon and the Duke of Braganza for an annual pension towards the upkeep of the Residence.

In the following year, 1593, Persons established a College in the Low Countries at St Omer.[49] This was to provide schooling for English Catholic exiles, but it had a connection with the Spanish seminaries in so far as it was intended also to provide and encourage vocations to the priesthood and so aid recruitment to the Iberian colleges. Something of the alarm created in government circles by this activity of Persons can be gathered from the letter of 2 February 1597 from Henry Twetchbourne, S.J., to Thomas Derbyshire, S.J., stating that there are 70 scholars at Douai, 120 at St Omer, 80 at Valladolid, 63 at Seville and 65 at Sanlúcar. There are also two residences 'fitted for our mission in Lisbon'.[50]

Thus within only four years Persons had established a network of colleges and residences in Spain to provide priests for the English Mission.[51] There were already priests and promising students in the Peninsula and there was popular support from the Spaniards for the Catholic cause in England, but his achievement lay in realising that no ecclesiastical enterprise was viable in Spain without active support from the King and the *placet* of the Inquisition, which would mean making concessions in the day-to-day administration of the Colleges and so co-operating with the Spanish Jesuit Province. Persons' friendship with the General, Claudio Aquaviva, gave him confidence and strength in dealing with the Spanish Province. The possible difficulties of this situation were secondary compared with the pressing need for seminaries on friendly foreign soil. France and the Low Countries were politically unstable, and Rome was in financial difficulties. All hopes for the provision of future clergy rested on Spain. Persons' own conviction, since 1582 at least, had been that without Spanish help England would never return to the old faith, and this identification in his mind of the causes of Catholicism and Spain was perhaps the reason for his success with Philip II. We shall see how, early in the history of the College at Valladolid, some of these implications began to unfold.

---

49. H. Chadwick, S.J., *St Omers to Stonyhurst*, London 1962; H. More, *Historia Missionis*, bk. 6, 9, trans. by F. Edwards and published as *The Elizabethan Jesuits* (London 1981), p. 305. Referred to hereafter by the English title.

50. CSP Domestic Elizabeth, 1595–7, p. 356. These figures seem inflated; see below, p. 21, for discussion of numbers in the college.

51. The College of St George at Madrid was a later foundation (1611) and owed its existence largely to Joseph Creswell, see below, p. 29.

2

YEARS OF PROMISE AND FULFILMENT, 1589–1613

Father Persons and the Spanish cause

Some later writers[1] have considered that the founding of seminaries on the continent was unwise. According to their view not only would it have been possible to establish colleges 'better suited to our genius' at home, but the existence of colleges abroad worsened relations between the government and Catholics and created suspicion of intrigue with foreigners against English interests. Persons was a favourite target for accusations of treason. These views put forward with some vehemence in the nineteenth century, were associated with a small but significant body of Catholics who objected to the growing ultramontanism in England. Most modern accounts, however, assume that the foundation of the colleges abroad was the only means of preserving the faith in England, and of maintaining the supply of priests there.[2] But Persons' work in Spain involved him in negotiations with Philip II, and even in his own day he was violently opposed by some Catholics who did not consider that there was need for so close an alignment with the cause of Spain.[3] From the 1580s Paget, Morgan, Grately and Chisholm, the exiled Bishop of Dunblane, were among his opponents,[4] and when the *Book of Succession* appeared in 1594, the rift within the Catholic body became more marked. However, the only aspect of these controversies that concerns us here is the effect Persons' support of the Spanish claims had on the colleges in the Peninsula. For him the supply of clergy for

1. E.g. J. Berrington is his 'Introduction' to *The Memoirs of Gregorio Panzani*, Birmingham 1793.
2. For those taking the other view, see L. Hicks, 'Father Persons, S.J., and the seminaries in Spain', *The Month*, CLCII, p. 194.
3. A. Pritchard, *Catholic Loyalism in Elizabethan England*, London, 1979, esp. chapter IX.
4. Tierney-Dodd, vol. 3, gives the origin of the hostility of Charles Paget and Thomas Morgan to Persons, Appendix XIII, pp. lix-lxvii, and Appendix XVIII, pp. xciv-xcviii. For Edward Grately cf. G. Anstruther, 1, p. 135, and P. Caraman, S.J., *William Weston: Autobiography of an Elizabethan*, London 1955, pp. 238–41.

England, the establishment of seminaries in Spain and the political future of the English monarchy were all connected; he had a singleness of vision shared by many of his contemporaries like those who put the 'bloody question' to Catholics after the Armada. To be pro-Catholic meant to be pro-Spanish, and to be pro-English meant to be anti-Catholic. But Persons was unaware of how many Catholics did not accept this simplification;[5] in Rome the majority of students at the English College were anti-Spanish, and they complained that their Jesuit superiors leant too much towards their country's enemies. Given the troubled times in the Netherlands, Douai College could not be entirely devoted to the cause of Spain. But Persons did not consider these views to be anything more that those of a minority, and a dangerous minority at that.

The failure of Catholics in England to rise in support of the Armada was not taken seriously enough — as the sure indication which it was that the views of Catholics at home were not identical with those of the continental exiles among whom Persons worked. In 1596 he sent English priests from Valladolid to Lisbon, with the intention that they should act as chaplains with the Spanish invasion fleet that was being prepared; their landing in England would be a sign to the people that the Spanish forces were bringing back the true priesthood to their shores.[6] This naivety is in contrast to his astuteness in summing up the position of religious institutions in Spain *vis-à-vis* the Catholic Monarchy. At Valladolid it was not easy to express anti-Spanish feelings even if one had them, but John Cecil was not the only former student who became attached to the anti-Spanish party. Despite the initial fear experienced when news reached England of the founding of the colleges in Spain,[7] it

---

5. Somewhat later, on 21 March 1596, Persons wrote to the King of Spain that without the assistance of the Spanish Crown there could be no hope for reform of the bad government in England or for the extirpation of heresy from that land. In Persons' mind, at least, the 'stirs' in the English College in Rome were associated with the anti-Spanish faction that gained ascendancy after the death of Allen in 1594. He urged the need for the creation of a new English Cardinal to combat the likes of Owen Lewis, Thomas Throckmorton and others 'who rejoice in the defeats of Spain and refuse to greet the Duke of Sesa' (the Spanish Ambassador in Rome). He wanted Philip to refuse to support the founding of a Scots seminary in Flanders, since the Scots preferred their own King to succeed to the throne of England (Series II, L 1, nos 25 and 27).

6. CSP, Domestic Elizabeth, 1595–7, p. 364.

7. *News from England*, 20 August 1591. The information that the heretics are most keen to capture priests coming from Spain is reported in *News from England*, 16 May 1592.

does not seem that the support given by Persons and Creswell to the Spanish cause made any noticeable difference to the colleges. Gaffney attributes this to the influence of Henry Walpole.[8]

From the point of view of the students, there is no clear evidence that their residence in Spain made them less or more hostile to the idea of a Spanish succession in the English monarchy; political questions of this sort were not in the forefront of their minds. Their destiny was to return to England to work on the Mission, and profession of the old faith was regarded as treason irrespective of any connection with Spain. The persecution varied in intensity during the reign of Elizabeth, and it did not abate when James came to the throne: although encouraged by the Treaty that was concluded with Spain, the hopes that James's accession would benefit the Catholics did not materialise. In fact, all that the Treaty did was to signal the end of a serious Spanish interest in supporting a Catholic rising in England, and Philip III's Ambassador in London warned his master against trusting the account of the situation given by pro-Spanish English Catholics.[9] In general, that situation was unchanged; Catholics continued to be persecuted, and former students continued to be martyred whatever political changes might have occurred. Rather than suffering distress from having studied in Spain, the main anxiety for students in these days arose from the factions within the Catholic body in England.[10] Even the Gunpowder Plot left little mark on College history. When Guy Fawkes and John Wright (Catesby's agent) visited the Spanish court in 1603, they encountered a cooling of interest in Spanish intervention on behalf of the English Catholics. There were no longer any grounds for thinking that the English Colleges in Spain would serve any useful political purpose, such as being a training ground for pro-Spanish clergy.

---

8. Ibid., p. 55. Henry Walpole, after two months in Seville, arrived in Valladolid in early 1593 and became Minister, but he left after six months due to some difference with Persons. Walpole had been present at the martyrdom of Campion and was to suffer a similar fate himself. At his trial he affirmed his loyalty to the Queen and spoke of his differences with Persons. Although five future martyrs were students in Spain while he was a Superior, his presence at the colleges would seem to have been too brief for him to have exercised the influence that Gaffney attributes to him.

9. A.J. Loomie, 'Guy Fawkes in Spain: The "Spanish Treason" ', in a special supplement of the *Bulletin of the Institute of Historical Research*, Nov. 1971, p. 63.

10. For attitudes adopted by former students at variance with the Jesuit point of view, see below, pp. 38, 40 (note 16), 42, 45.

Administration of the College

Although the College was administered by the Spanish Jesuits, care was taken in the early days to employ some English fathers on the staff. Persons had overall responsibility for the Spanish seminaries, and he was soon to be made Prefect of the Mission, which gave him charge over all the English colleges administered by the Jesuits as well as those members of the Society engaged on the English Mission.[11] This was a Jesuit appointment made by the General, but it did mean that he had a measure of control over the secular clergy in so far as they were being educated at Jesuit establishments. During his lifetime, Cardinal Allen worked closely together with Persons, seeing eye to eye with him on most matters including politics. But when the Cardinal died in 1594, the secular clergy lost their leading spokesman and many of them felt suspicious of the behaviour of Persons.[12] When Bartolomé de Sicilia, the first Rector, was recalled by the King, Pedro de Guzmán succeeded him with Father Flack as Minister, but Persons did not find it a suitable appointment,[13] and was relieved when Juan López de Manzano replaced him in July 1590. One of the most distinguished of the early Rectors was Rodrigo de Cabredo, who after a period as confessor became Rector in 1591 at the age of thirty-three. It was he who set up the College financially, freeing it from debt and putting the accounts in order (from this date the *gastos* and *recibos* were kept in two different books), and in 1593 Persons requested Aquaviva, the General, to allow Cabredo to remain in Valladolid.[14] Eventually he was sent to Peru as Provincial, but he kept in touch with English affairs in Spain, corresponding with Fr Peralta, the Rector of St

11. *Officium et Regulae Praefecti Missionis in Seminariis Anglicanis qui in Hispanis et Belgio Societatis Regimini subsunt.* Dated 16 April 1598, the rules were ratified in 1606. H. More, *Historia Missionis: The Elizabethan Jesuits*, pp. 298–307. The arrangement proved difficult to both parties. Not only did the English students resent having Spanish Superiors, but the Spaniards felt that they did not have full control since the Prefect of English Mission was directly responsible to the General and could use the revenues of the English Colleges for the Mission. See T.M. McCoog, S.J., 'The Establishment of the English Province of the Society of Jesus', *Recusant History*, vol. 17, pp. 121–39. The appointment of Persons as Prefect was ratified by the Nuncio to Spain, WCA, 5, no. 92.
12. In 1594 efforts were made to have Persons created a Cardinal, but Persons resisted this as he felt that such a promotion would remove him from close contact with the English scene as had been the case with Allen.
13. Letter to Creswell, 24 June 1590. CRS, XIV, p. 21.
14. Astrain, vol. IV, p. 750.

Gregory's College in Seville.[15] González del Río, his successor as Rector, was an unfortunate choice and he was replaced in 1596.[16]

Shortly afterwards Persons left the Peninsula at the behest of Aquaviva to take charge of the College in Rome, and Joseph Creswell, who had been assisting him in Spain, assumed control of the Spanish colleges. Like his predecessor, he kept in close touch with the Spanish royal court. Creswell was more abrasive than Persons, and his period of office was not without its crises, but when he eventually left for Flanders in 1613, a period of College history ended. There were no dominating personalities of the quality of Persons and Creswell left in Spain, and after the death of Aquaviva in 1615 the Spanish Jesuits began for various reasons to exercise more control over College affairs.

The English scene as viewed from the seminaries in Spain

The intelligence service of the Jesuits was extremely effective. Correspondence was maintained with England, and from various papers still extant[17] we can form some idea of the situation as it would have appeared to the students who were shortly to return to their own country. Because the intensity of the persecution varied according to both locality and season, up-to-date information was essential. For example, in 1590 there was news from Brussels of a slackening in the search for priests, but the next year a dispatch from London recorded the arrival of seven or eight priests from Spain and reported the annoyance of Queen Elizabeth on discovering that four disguised priests had actually been questioned and then released without their identity being discovered. The capture of Robert Southwell, S.J., was reported,[18] as was the escape of John Gerard

---

15. Cabredo was recipient of a letter from Peralta, relating the life and death in England of Luisa de Carvajal.
16. Del Río governed very autocratically; he entertained guests at College expense and antagonised the English Fathers — see Persons to Creswell, 16 Jan. 1596: 'The end he seems to have set before himself was to play lord and master, entertain his friends and stroll about with a following of students like a retinue of honour. He had begun to make accusations against us to Fr General.' It was this experience of Del Río which led Persons to promote the appointment of a Prefect of the Mission to have full authority, even over Rectors. I am indebted to Fr F. Edwards, S.J., for this information, which is contained in his forthcoming *Life* of Persons.
17. *Noticias y avisos de Inglaterra, 1590–1647*, in Series II, L6.
18. Dispatch from London, 26 July 1592.

from the Tower.[19] A former student wrote to Persons from London on 1 October 1593; '*La voz de los seminarios de España suena mucho por acá y alcança muchas oraciones y bendiciones devotas de los católicos a su Majestad Católica.*' News of the arrest and imprisonment of former students reached Spain,[20] as did that of the martyrdom of Fr John Almond,[21] Fr Thomas Maxfield,[22] Fr John Maxi,[23] Fr John Boste[24] and Fr Thomas Holland.[25] But it was not only Catholics who suffered. News from London on 20 August 1591 announced 'another tragedy for men of a different spirit'. Three Puritans saying they were prophets got up on carts and declared they were sent by God to preach the truth; all spoke ill of the religion and government of the Queen, 'reprehending her for her trust in the Archbishop of Canterbury and cavalier Hatton, the Chancellor of the Kingdom'. The informant concluded that the heretics warring between themselves, Catholics were even more resolved to prove the truth of their religion, and every day increasing numbers of people were giving up heresy. The late 1590s were marked by a food crisis in Europe, and the lack of bread caused riots in England, especially among the poor. To add to the confusion in the apocalyptic last days of Elizabeth, signs were seen in the heavens. On the Feast of St George in 1591 strange phenomena could be observed in the sky in the county of Norfolk two hours before sunset. The news from London on 23 June included a diagram of the way in which three suns had appeared in the sky. In 1593 a girl in Winchester fell into a fifteen-day sleep and on awakening said she had had a vision and that Queen Elizabeth would die the same year. In 1597 mysterious lights were seen in a deserted field near Gloucester, and in 1598 there were lights in the sky at Cockermouth. Such reports were not uncommon in this period as readers of Shakespeare will be aware, but it is remarkable to find them reported in the same documents as news of arrests, imprisonments and deaths.[26]

19. Dispatch from London, 19 Oct. 1597.
20. That William Atkinson and Thomas Paliser were imprisoned in England was reported by a Jesuit father from Flanders in 1597.
21. An account of 1612 in English and another in Spanish is to be found in Series II, L2.
22. L3, cf. CRS, vol. 3, p. 30 (1616).
23. L3 (1617).
24. Sent by John Cecil to Persons (1594), CRS, vol. 5, p. 285.
25. L3 (1642).
26. Similar accounts of portents and wonders are related by Pedro de Ribadeneira, *Historia Eclesiástica del Cisma del Reino de Inglaterra*, bk. III, chapters VI and VIII.

The journey back from Spain to England

The journey to England was often long and hazardous — longer than one to the Indies, as one report had it.[27] This was because detours had to be taken, and there was always the risk of being captured at sea by enemies of the country to whom their ship belonged. The students and priests travelled in disguise, as soldiers or merchants or even cabin boys. They received travelling expenses, known as *viaticum*, for their return home after ordination; this was a grant from the King of Spain and it was maintained for most of the College's existence.

Before leaving for England they were given priestly faculties for hearing confessions, imparting blessings and so on from the Prefect of the Mission. Several of these documents are to be found in the Archives, which suggests that it was too risky to carry them since they would be identified as priests if arrested. An example of the sort of journey the students could expect is to be found in a letter of William Warford written to Persons from Amsterdam, 15 May 1591.[28] He wrote from the house of a priest with whom he was staying at Haarlem that although the general government of the area was in the hands of heretics, Catholics could expect a good reception at Haarlem and Amsterdam. He had been promised a passage on a ship to Newcastle, the master of which was a Catholic and knew that he was a priest but he had just received news that another ship sailing direct to London was available. This likewise had a Catholic master who had contacts with German Catholics in London. Warford gave Persons useful information to pass on to priests returning to England this way in future. They should be careful not to dress in a way that could make them appear Spanish, and they should avoid using English names; Irish, Scottish German or Polish, or any other national names were preferable. This was because an English name immediately attracted attention, since all Englishmen are considered either great heretics or determined Catholics, and both the one and the other of these things have a danger of their own on these roads.'

27. Creswell. See J.R. Fernández Suárez, 'Joseph Creswell: al servico de Dios y de su majestad católica (1598–1613)', *E.S.*, Sep. 1978, pp. 47–83.
28. Warford was ordained priest in Rome and was sent back to England with John Cecil via Seville. Three years later in 1594 he returned to Rome and became a Jesuit; he died at Valladolid in 1608. His name figures in the list of Seville students, CRS, 14, and it is possible he was one and the same as Walter Morgan, who is mentioned below, p. 28. Several copies of his letter are to be found in Series II, L1, which suggests that contemporaries were also interested by it.

The students

A list of the dioceses of origin of the students coming to the College between 1589 and 1603[29] shows how representative the College was of the whole of England. However, as a prelude to the account of how the first students fared under Persons and Creswell, further details need to be remembered. Between 1589 and 1613 the registers record 326 entrants to the College. At the beginning, recruitment was mainly from Rheims or Rome, so that the first students had already begun their ecclesiastical education elsewhere and came to Valladolid to complete their studies and be ordained, and between 1592 and 1598 about forty students went from Valladolid to help establish the new College in Seville. Of the 326 entrants, 177 returned to work on the English mission: some of these went directly from Valladolid, while others passed on to other colleges first before arriving in England. There were forty-five deaths in the College, 1591 being a particularly bad year when Persons himself fell ill and had to be removed to the College of S. Ambrosio for proper nursing. There were several transfers of students to other colleges, mainly Douai, because of ill-health — the years 1611 and 1612 seem to have been the worst for illness. Of those returning to England in these years eleven were martyred including St Henry Walpole, S.J., who, though never a student, spent some months in Valladolid on the staff.[30]

It is hardly surprising, in view of the administration of the College, that a number of students joined the Society of Jesus. Sometimes this was before ordination and meant that they left the College for the novitiate; sometimes they joined after ordination, but this did not necessarily mean that they were lost to the English Mission. A good example is John Blackfan, the probable author of the *Annales*. He was one of the first batch of students in 1589; he became a Jesuit after his ordination in 1594, but remained associated with the College until 1610, thus providing a

---

29. Given in A.J. Loomie, S.J., *The Spanish Elizabethans*, New York 1963, p. 237. An account of everyday life in the College at this period is given in Appendix A.
30. Walpole was martyred at York in 1595. The others were Ven. Thomas Benstead (*alias* Hunt), the College student protomartyr (Lincoln, 1600); Ven. Roger Filcock, S.J. (Durham, 1600); Ven. Thomas Palaser (Durham, 1600); Bl. Mark Barkworth, O.S.B. (Tyburn, 1601); Bl. William Richardson (Tyburn, 1603); Ven. Robert Drury (Tyburn, 1607); St Thomas Garnet, S.J. (Tyburn, 1608); St Edmund (or Ambrose) Barlow, O.S.B. (Lancaster, 1610); Ven. Roger Cadwallader (Leominster, 1610); and St John Roberts, O.S.B. (Tyburn, 1610). For a full list of College martyrs, see Appendix C.

valuable link with the early days. He was imprisoned on his return to England, exiled, returned to Spain for a short period as Rector of St Alban's, and eventually returned to the English Mission where he died. Altogether in this period sixty-one students are recorded as having joined the Jesuits.

It is difficult to ascertain how many students were in the College at any given time or even what the average number was. From the Registers the figures work out at between 30 and 60 in any given year, with an average roll of 38, but from other sources the numbers are much higher; Persons in 1591 says that the roll at Valladolid 'will shortly reach 60'.[31] A 1599 account book mentioned 70. The highest figure seems to be for 1603: '*La razón del gasto tan excessivo de este año sobre los demás ha sido la porque ha avido en esta casa los ocho meses de año a pie de cien personas.*'[32] This may mean that 100 individuals passed through the College and not that all were resident at the same time. It could also be that the higher number in these reports includes Jesuits whose names would not find a place in the College records.[33]

St Alban's and the Benedictines, 1599 and 1603

This movement towards the Jesuits, unlike a similar development at the College in Rome, did not seem at this time to occasion much resentment at Valladolid. But dissatisfaction among the students showed itself in a large-scale 'defection' to the Benedictines. The attraction of English seminarians for the Benedictine Order seems to have begun in Rome, for after the departure of Robert Sayer from the *Venerabile* for Monte Cassino in 1588, five other students followed him in 1591–6. Although the general impression is that they left that College quietly, they seem to have made contact later with those students who were opposed to the Jesuit superiors; but the number of defections in Rome waas never very high.[34] However, in 1596 Mark Barkworth arrived in Spain from Rome

31. Persons to Creswell, 15 July 1591. CRS, XIV, p. 22.
32. *Gastos* 1, f. 180: 'The reason for such excessive costs this year has been that for more than 8 months there have been approaching 100 people in the House.'
33. That there were also Jesuits in residence seems clear from the visitation records, which make a distinction between '*los nuestros*' and others. In 1596 '*los nuestros*' were not allowed to play chess, either among themselves or with the alumni, and in 1598 they were not allowed to play ball or other games with the students. Moreover, penances and correction for faults were not to take place in the refectory.
34. The best account of the students who joined the Benedictines is David Lunn, *The*

to continue his studies at Valladolid; he soon applied to join the Benedictines in Spain, but was advised by them to spend some time first as a missionary in England. He left for England in 1599 but stopped en route and was received as a novice at Irache. Soon after his arrival in England he was arrested and made his profession as a member of the Order at his martyrdom in 1601. But an interest in the Benedictine vocation began at Valladolid before news of this martyrdom reached the College.

In 1599 John Bradshaw persuaded the prior of the Valladolid monastery of S. Benito to receive him as a novice,[35] and during the same year five other students left the College for the Benedictines. The Jesuit superiors became alarmed, and accused the monks of soliciting vocations; they were not only anxious about losing students from their own College but they also feared that the monks might be admitting candidates to the religious life with insufficient scrutiny. They were also anxious lest the English government would infiltrate spies into the monastery — with some justification since it was known that the government was anxious to deflect candidates from the English Mission and stir up ill-feeling between the religious orders. A rumour had been circulating that one of the early recruits to the Italian Monte Cassino Congregation, Anthony Martin, was a paid spy. Persons was informed of these events at the College, and he replied in a letter from Rome to Blackfan and Floyd. After referring to similar cases in France and Rome of students finding their vocation in a religious order, he advised the superiors at Valladolid to act calmly and prudently, concluding:

My good father, *quid mihi est in coelo vel ab hoc quid aliud volo super terram* for all our labours for these youths, but only *ut fiat de eis voluntas Dei*? If God Almighty will have them priests that is our first end, to make them good priests for England. If he will have them religious men of what order soever within his Church *hoc etiam deputabimus in lucrum* that he calleth them to a state of more perfection, so they go orderly and godly to so high a vocation. If he will have any lost or cast away between them both or by disorderly behaving themselves, in either of these states, who are we that can resist this judgment?[36]

Perhaps due to Persons' good advice this crisis passed, but three years

---

English Benedictines 1540-1688, London 1980, pp. 19–26; 57–61. There are two contemporary accounts — that in Blackfan's *Annales* and Fr Leander Jones' *Responsio pro Monachis Anglis*.

35. Luis Rodríguez Martínez, *Historia del Monasterio de San Benito El Real de Valladolid*, Valladolid 1981.

36. Series II, L1, 23 Aug. 1599.

later in 1603 there was further trouble. This time, the occasion seems to have been a dispute between the students and the superiors which resulted in six students fleeing from the College and being received at S. Benito. The *Annales* maintain that there were riots at the College due to visits made by the Benedictines with a view to enticing students to the order. But other accounts say that Father Creswell physically intervened when a student priest came to blows with other students, and as a result of this six alumni fled to the Benedictines.[37] At any rate, Creswell appealed to the King to have the six fugitives sent back to the College. The matter was referred to the Consejo;[38] the Nuncio, who was reputed to be favourable to S. Benito, received the interested parties in audience, and the Rector of the College, Pedro Ruiz de Vallejo, protested that the Pope was really to blame since it was he who had given permission for the Benedictines to send priests to work on the Mission in England. As a result of this outburst the Rector was relieved of his duties and a new superior was appointed. Creswell continued to pursue the matter by complaining of the conduct of the Prior of S. Benito to the Spanish President-General of the Order, Alonso de Corral.

For the significance of these events in 1599 and 1603 to be appreciated, it is necessary to bear several points in mind.[39] As long ago as 1594 there had been negotiations for the Benedictines to become engaged in the English mission,[40] and their case was supported by those who saw them as a possible 'third force' — neither seculars nor Jesuits — and thus untouched by the rivalries developing among the English Catholics. For many Englishmen the thought of the return of the Benedictines had an attraction, since it recalled the story of Pope Gregory sending St Augus-

37. See Lunn, op. cit., pp. 58–9, for an assessment of these events; also G. Sitwell, 'The Foundation & Recruitment of the English Benedictine Congregation', *Downside Review*, vol. 102, pp. 51–4.

38. 'Consulta del Consejo de Estado sobre la Fuga de 6 colegiales de San Albano al convento de S. Benito, 21 Ag. 1603', Simancas, *Estado*, L2511.

39. The total number of students who joined the Benedictines does not seem to have been as large as is sometimes stated. Blackfan puts the number at 25, and he is followed by A.C.F. Beales, *Education under Penalty*, London 1963 p. 81, and Bede Camm, *A Benedictine Martyr in England . . . . John Roberts, O.S.B.*, London 1897, p. 134. Lunn thinks that this is an error of transcription, and that the real number was 15.

40. Having conceded the mission verbally, the Pope made his final decision on 5 December 1602, and on 20 March 1603 faculties were formally granted. By 1603 students needed no enticement; the Benedictines had sent their first missionaries to England, and with the death of Elizabeth there were renewed hopes of a restoration of monasticism there (Lunn, pp. 25–6).

tine to convert the English people as well as reminding them of the contribution made by monasticism to English life before the Reformation. But the Benedictines had their own reasons for re-establishing themselves; if England were to become Catholic again, the question of the ownership of the monastic property that had been secularised would arise. Persons outlined in his *Memorial*[41] his vision of a future Catholic England, but he did not think it convenient to return the monasteries to the Benedictines since there were so few English members of that Order. Consequently, there was a fear among the monks that the Jesuits intended to appropriate this property for themselves. But as for the students in Valladolid their attraction towards the Benedictines was not an attempt to escape from their missionary oath since it was their full intention to return to work on the Mission in England and not to remain for the rest of their lives in a Spanish monastery.

How was all this viewed by the monks of S. Benito? Originally founded in the fourteenth century as a monastery of strict observance, by the end of the sixteenth century it had reached a position of eminence and was assisting the reforms promoted by the Catholic Monarchy. The Spanish Congregation, under the influence of Counter-Reformation ideas, was becoming more activist, and in 1598 a licence had been obtained from Philip II allowing Benedictine monks to go on the missions in America. Hence the acceptance of English postulants who desired to spend their lives working among the persecuted Catholics in their own country can be seen as a further extension of this tendency. From an early stage, however, it was realised that this was but a temporary measure until the English monks should have a novitiate of their own. But the Valladolid students were not only motivated by the positive ideals of the Benedictine way of life; there was also dissatisfaction with life at the College. In 1599 there was a severe outbreak of plague which made it necessary for forty students to be sent to Valverde, the remaining twenty staying on in Valladolid; and the following year there was dissension between, on the one hand, Fr John Floyd and Fr Michael Walpole and, on the other, Fr Creswell and Fr Anthony Hoskins, which led Persons to write to Creswell on Tuesday 26th 1600: 'These young English Fathers of ours, being quickly put in Government after their noviceship and studies, run into danger, if they be not looked unto.'[42]

41. *A Memorial of the reformation in England.* This appeared in MS. in 1596, and as it was read daily at dinner at St Alban's and probably also in Rome, its contents would be well known although it was not printed till 1690.
42. Anglia, II, p. 61.

But apart from the recurring complaints about climate, over-strict discipline, over-crowding and lack of recreation facilities,[43] a new factor emerged in 1601. The court took up residence in Valladolid, and with it came Joseph Creswell. The presence of the court raised anxiety about spies, through whom information concerning students in Spain might reach England, causing their families to suffer in consequence. In fact, Persons considered removing the College from Valladolid to Salamanca.[44] The advent of Creswell was to upset the delicate balance between the students and the Jesuits and between the English and the Spaniards; indeed he had something of a reputation for upsetting people. In 1593 there were plans for removing him from Spain, but his designated successor William Holt died before he could take office.[45] A former Rector of the English College in Rome, Creswell had administrative ability, and his knowledge of English affairs across Europe made him a valuable adviser to the Spanish King.[46] His subsequent history involved him in complaints about the prodigality and fanaticism of the Spanish

43. See Lewis Owen, *The State of the English Colleges in Foreign Parts*, London, 1626, pp. 51–67, concerning Valladolid. A hostile but fairly accurate account.

44. '*Pues aunque quedando en Valladolid se procurara con todo cuidado de no ofender al dicho embajador, o a su gente: todavía siendo herejes los más dellos, o políticos y espías los quales todos tienen muy mala voluntad a los seminarios y a nuestra sagrada religión, se a de creer que procurarán por todos los medios posibles de malear alguno de los estudiantes si pueden, a hacer daño a sus parientes en Inglaterra descrubiendo quiénes son. Y finalmente se duda que aurá una contienda perpetua con ellos si queda el Colegio en Valladolid aunque de la otra parte también avrá sus difficultades en passar el Collegio a Salamanca.*' Persons to King (no date), Series II, L2, 10. Translation: 'Although staying in Valladolid one would be careful not to offend the said ambassador or his people; nevertheless, most of them being heretics or political, and spies who have no goodwill towards the seminaries and our sacred religion, one can only believe that they would seek by all means possible to play upon the students so as to harm their relatives in England by discovering their identity. Finally, it is doubtful whether there would be a perpetual struggle with them if the College remained in Valladolid, although on the other hand there would be difficulties in transferring the College to Salamanca.'

45. J.H. Pollen, 'Troubles of Jesuits and Benedictines at Valladolid in 1603', *The Month*, 1897, pp. 581–600, and 1899, pp. 233–48; Bede Camm, 'Jesuits and Benedictines at Valladolid 1599–1604', *The Month*, 1898, pp. 364–77. For Creswell, see A.J. Loomie, *The Spanish Elizabethans*, pp. 182–229. J.R. Fernández Suárez, 'Joseph Creswell: Al servicio de Dios y de su Majestad Católica (1598–1613)', *E.S.*, Sept. 1978, pp. 47–83, treats of Creswell's activities at court on behalf of English exiles in Spain.

46. Creswell in 1599–1600 advised Philip III to make war on England: '*No fue más gloriosa para Godofredo de Bullón la empresa de Jerusalen que será ésta para V. Majestad*' A.J. Loomie, 'Guy Fawkes in Spain', *Bulletin of the Institute of Historical Research*, Supplement, Nov. 1971.

Rectors of St Alban's and quarrels with his fellow English Jesuits in Spain. When the riot broke out in 1603, it was his intervention that resulted in the subsequent flight of the students to S. Benito, and it was he who took the matter further by appealing to both the King and the Abbot-President of the Spanish Congregation.

Further unrest, 1607 and 1608

Creswell may have been a source of contention while living in Valladolid, but it was his absence that occasioned the next bout of unrest involving the students at St Alban's. He was called to Rome in August 1605 to report on the trouble with the Benedictines, and for the next few years spent many months away from Spain. In 1606 the court returned to Madrid so that his power-base was no longer in the same city as the College. An outbreak of plague in 1607 meant that no new students came to the College that year,[47] and in August the students were moved to write to Persons complaining about the changes that had been introduced into College discipline since the departure of Father Creswell.[48] They said that the Spanish Jesuit Provincial had ordered the 'divines' (theology students) to attend at S. Ambrosio — where they had lessons — every Sunday so that, apart from the few vineyard days, they had to hear lectures or engage in the academic exercise of 'conclusions' on every day of the year, and as a result their health had suffered. The 'divines' had refused to obey the order until they heard from Father Creswell, but they were told it had nothing to do with him. Despite an appeal to the Provincial on his Visitation, their complaints had been ignored and hence they were now writing to Persons for help. Twenty-seven students signed the letter; the four who thought it would be prejudicial for them to sign were in accord with the majority opinion.

Persons was able to discuss the matter with Blackfan who was also in Rome at the time, and he wrote his reply on 18 September. He said that the health of the students gave him cause for concern, and he had therefore written to the Rector and Minister to see that a good infirmarian was appointed. As to attendance at lectures, this was the first time he had heard of complaints, but he went on the explain that he and Creswell only had authority on matters concerning the English Mission, the

47. Thus repeating the situation of 1601.
48. CRS, 30, pp. 90–5.

government of the College being the responsibility of the Provincial and the Rector.[49] Even Father Richard Walpole, the English Jesuit at St Alban's, was only spiritual director and so not a superior, and so he could not interfere. We do not know the result of this letter, but on 29 August 1608 Persons wrote to Walter Morgan who had recently arrived from Seville. He, like Walpole, was not a superior, but Persons asked him to assist some of the students who were in danger of being expelled for bad conduct. It seems that the Pope had heard of trouble at the College and given orders to Cardinal Bianchetti, who was in charge of English affairs, to have them put out of the house. Perhaps this related to the Benedictine affair and the representations made to Rome, but it might also have been this matter of attendance at lectures. A further letter of the students, with twelve names attached, reached Persons in Rome. Apparently sickness had struck the College, Father Walpole had died, the Rector was ill, and the Father Minister was running the College. In a letter of 14 October 1608, Persons tried to make peace: he asked why they were so aggrieved with the Minister — had he not provided them with meat, drink, clothing and other necessities? He exhorted the students to bear with their superiors, and warned that the College would be discredited if stories of disturbances got abroad. When they left England, had they not resolved to suffer in God's cause? They must realise that these dissensions were the work of the Enemy of mankind. He told them he was going to send Blackfan back to Valladolid to help them in their trouble, and his arrival seems to have eased matters. In the same year too, an agreement was reached concerning the Benedictine affair.[50] In this 'accord' the Jesuits were told to see to it that the alumni obeyed the rules of 1600, but they were not to prevent students of their colleges from entering the Benedictine or any other order approved by the Holy See. For their part, the Benedictines were not to invite or entice pupils of Jesuit colleges even to become oblates. Neither the Jesuits nor

---

49. In fact, in May the previous year, 1606, there had appeared three documents from the General, Aquaviva, laying down regulations for the Prefect of the Mission and the Rectors and Superiors of the English seminaries conducted by the Society. *Officium et regula Prefecti Missionum tam pro missione Societatis dirigenda, quam pro Seminariis Anglicanis quae Societatis regimini subsunt, iuvandis. 15 Maii 1606; Quaedam a Rectoribus Seminariorum Nationis Anglicanae quae Societatis curae subsent, observandae. 16 Maii 1606; Instructiones et ordinationes observandae a Praefecto et Vice-Praefecto missionis Anglicanae pro eadem missione melius dirigenda. 18 Maii 1606.* Series II, L2.
50. *Rules of Accorde made by His Holiness betwixt the Society and the Order of St Benedict,* L2 (no. 31), also L12.

the Benedictines were to compel anyone who had entered their order to go to England before the end of a year's novitiate and before other requirements had been met according to their constitution. Moreover, no Abbot or Rector could order his subjects to go on the Mission without the previous consent of the Provincial, Superior or Visitator. Both were warned not to meddle in politics, but to look to the conversion of souls.

One of the results of the Benedictine incident was that the Jesuits were confirmed in their view that there was a lack of proper facilities for encouraging and training English aspirants to the Society of Jesus. Many excellent students had become Benedictines when they might have become Jesuits. This was a reappraisal of the former view that only the malcontents joined the Benedictines. About this time serious plans were made for acquiring a suitable place for a novitiate.[51] In 1610 there was another brief scare when some students joined the Dominican order, but unlike the previous defections to the Benedictines this was resolved without any great secession of students. Also in 1610, one of the last links with the early days was broken when Blackfan left Spain for Flanders. Persons continued to correspond with Spain, although his health no longer permitted him to travel. He died in Rome in 1610. In his last days he had assumed the role of peacemaker, seeking to act as intermediary between the students and their Spanish superiors. Thus he lived to see one of the less fortunate consequences of his otherwise successful negotiations with Philip II for the founding of English Colleges in Spain.

The founding of St George's College, Madrid[52]

An important part of College administration was to secure future solvency by means of obtaining bequests. The English Jesuits, by reason of their contacts with exiles in Spain and in the Low Countries, were able to gain many advantages for the College and for the Society. Persons, Creswell and Blackfan were executors of such distinguished personages as Sir Francis Englefield (died 1569), Nicholas Baldwin (died 1597), Colonel William Stanley (died *circa* 1600) and Sir Albert Bluet (died

51. *Concerning the English Novitiate at Watten*, 6 Feb. 1605, L2 (11).
52. Edwin Henson (ed.), *The English College at Madrid, 1611–1767*, CRS, 29, especially the Historical Summary.

1612).[53] As executors they not only had to contend with claims of relatives and household, but also had to decide whether bequests were made to the Colleges of Seville and Valladolid as such, or to the Society that administered them. It is in this context that the foundation of the last of the Spanish colleges, St George at Madrid, has to be considered.

While the court was at Valladolid, the King's surgeon César Bogacio was on friendly terms with the Jesuits at the English College, and on returning to Madrid he decided to found another college there on the lines of St Alban's. Thus on the feast of St Ignatius in 1610, he made a deed of gift to Father Joseph Creswell, Prefect of the English Mission, of houses in the Calle del Príncipe. He changed his will, formerly in favour of the Convent of Augustinian Recollects, and the new seminary became his sole heir. One of the reasons he gave for this new college was the sicknesses suffered by students at Valladolid[54] and the desirability of having a place in Madrid where students could become acclimatised before passing on to other colleges. To begin with, there would be twelve English students with a Rector and other superiors, but it was envisaged that this would grow and become a larger house of studies. If at any future time England were to be converted to Catholicism and so have no need for its seminarians to study abroad, then the Jesuit Provincial and the person in charge of the English seminaries in Spain would, with the approval of the Father General and the Ambassador of the Republic of Lucca (Bogacio's home town in Italy), have the option of applying the College to whatever use they deemed of greatest service of the Church. It becomes clear from this that Bogacio's intention was that this College, like that of Valladolid, would be administered by the Jesuits. However, complications soon arose. Creswell had also to see that obligations already entered into by Bogacio concerning a dowry and gifts to certain nuns, and a bequest to his servant, were met. Moreover, the cost of converting houses into suitable accommodation and providing a chapel had been seriously underestimated. Some of the houses in question were occupied by court pensioners who contested the will.[55]

Creswell was aware of these problems, but he hoped that the King would free him from some of the obligations and that he would be able to raise money for any additional expenses. On 21 October 1610 four

---

53. Series II, L5.
54. There was a serious outbreak of sickness shortly afterwards in 1611–12, and the advisability of moving the College away from Valladolid was discussed.
55. Don Alonso de Arceo of Valdepeñas said that the houses were not Bogacio's. The Secretary of the Royal Council of the Indies had lodgings there and refused to move.

students arrived from Valladolid, and St George's Seminary can be said to have begun that day. The following March, receiving news that the twelve students for whom they had asked St Omer were about to arrive, the four students from Valladolid were sent back. On 24 April the twelve arrived from St Omer together with Father John Thompson, who was to act as their master.[56] At this time the Jesuits had not yet formally accepted the College, and so Creswell as Prefect of the Mission nominated Thompson as Rector. The newly arrived students in Madrid 'kissed the hand of Our Lord the King', and Creswell was careful to secure as well the approval of Giovanni Antonio Caetano, the Papal Nuncio in Spain. A Brief for the erection of the Seminary with twelve students, a Rector and other officers, was given on 23 December 1611,[57] and a Bull of Paul V of 3 July 1613 exempted the Rector, students and property from the jurisdiction of the Archbishop of Toledo placing them immediately under the Holy See. From this date Creswell became more and more involved in the Madrid College, and Valladolid and Seville took a subordinate place in his thoughts. But what happened in Madrid is important for understanding the reasons for Creswell's eventual departure from Spain and the relationship of the Spanish Jesuits to their English confrères.

There was opposition from the start to the new Seminary in Madrid, principally because it was situated in the capital city. There had been similar objections to St Alban's when the court was resident at Valladolid. The reasons for this were the unsuitability of students living in proximity to a court atmosphere and the danger of spies being infiltrated into the College so that students might be recognised when they returned to England. The objections were not all from the English Catholic side; many Spaniards did not trust the College because it was thought that it might harbour English spies. In fact, the council of State resolved that the establishment should be transferred to either Ocaña, Salamanca or Alcalá, but Creswell was able to secure the suspension of

---

56. Thompson, a former student of St Alban's, ordained in 1590, had joined the Jesuits in 1598. The names of the first students are given in CRS, 29, pp. 10 and 85. In fact Creswell bound himself to have twelve students by 1611 or earlier, because if this condition were not fulfilled (even if the King had not been able to free the houses from the court pensioner or for any other reason), then the will was null and void. Hence his haste.

57. This was after T. Owen, S.J., Rector of the English College in Rome, had written to Cardinal Branchetti stressing the importance of sending the papal brief quickly because of the time condition imposed in Bogacio's will. V.E.C. Archives, *Scritture* 6(12,1).

this decree. However, Creswell's activities were creating trouble on a much wider scale. He circulated a series of pamphlets in Spain that gave a lurid picture of the persecution Catholics were receiving in England, and King James was so annoyed when he heard of it that he complained to his fellow-monarch, the King of Spain.

So another attempt was made to have the College removed, and Creswell remarked that English Catholics would be scandalised if they discovered that they were now being persecuted in Madrid as they were in London. He was assured that the Spanish King would continue to look after the College wherever it was, and the Jesuit Provincial was asked to order Creswell to remove to Alcalá. He did in fact rent a house there, but he himself had to return to Madrid almost immediately because of a lawsuit regarding the original bequest. There now arose the question whether the College could legally be transferred in this way. The College buildings were empty of students, but in order to maintain the claim on it students from Valladolid and Seville were invited to make use of it and stay there when visiting the capital. There then arose another objection, this time concerning the ownership of the chapel now that the students had removed to Alcalá. After a serious fire — whether through an accident or by arson is not clear — the chapel was rebuilt from alms begged by the fathers and from the executors of Bogacio. The general impression given was that the property belonged to the Jesuits but this was not true since they had never formally accepted it. The Rector was an English priest and it was the English fathers, particularly Creswell, who were involved in the affair. To resolve the dilemma, the General was consulted and it was decided that the English fathers were not to consider the property as theirs until the General had accepted it on behalf of the Society; they were forbidden to say Mass in the chapel, and were to leave all control to the Rector.

However, the English government was equally opposed to the new Seminary, and had been spreading unfavourable reports about Creswell through its Ambassador; also, a powerful faction at the Spanish court, led by the Duke of Lerma, distrusted the English exiles.[58] Furthermore, Creswell had been a friend of the German Jesuit Richard Haller, confessor to the Queen, Margaret of Austria, and although both Haller and the Queen were now dead, it seems as though this friendship had been at the root of Lerma's dislike.[59] So it was that the General removed

58. See Loomie, *The Spanish Elizabethans*, pp. 224–5.
59. This is suggested by A.F. Allison, 'The Later Life and Writings of Joseph Creswell, S.J. (1556–1623)', *Recusant History*, vol. 15, no. 2, Oct. 1979, p. 80. Queen

Creswell from Spain to the Low Countries.[60] Creswell's departure meant in effect the end of the English College in Madrid as a seminary on the lines of Valladolid. Quite apart from the objections raised against its being in Madrid, there was no real need at this time for another seminary. So in 1614 Fr John Thompson,[61] with nine students who had now completed their course of philosophy, arrived at Valladolid from Madrid or Alcalá. They were welcomed by the fathers, and Thompson began to teach at St Alban's. There was only one class now attending lectures at S. Ambrosio and thus Thompson's advent helped to solve the problem arising from the continual objections of the English students to the teaching there.

Philip III now wrote to the General asking him to appoint an English Rector at Valladolid. The Spanish Jesuits were up in arms against this, but the General agreed with the King, and so it was that in 1614 Fr William Weston, S.J., was appointed the first English Rector. This was a somewhat surprising reversal of the agreement Persons had considered essential when the College was founded, and even only two years earlier such a turn of events would nave seemed highly unlikely. On 3 September 1612, Fr T. Owen had written from Rome to Fr John Clare: 'Of English superiors there is no likelihood in those provinces. Father General understandeth our case and is likely to live to help us many years by God's holy assistance, yet in this point he giveth no hope; and hath such good reasons, as is not convenient to reply any further, but helps ourselves with the best we can get though not of the nation.' Perhaps the removal of English students from Madrid, the departure of Creswell and the fact that Persons was now dead, had induced the General to make this concession.

Margaret visited the College at Valladolid on more than one occasion, see below, p. 62.

60. One of the accusations against Creswell was that he had tried to convert Francis Cottington. Cottington was associated with Spain for many years. In 1605 he was in Madrid as a clerk to the Ambassador, Cornwallis. A brother of his had become a Catholic and was for a time a Jesuit novice in Rome, but he died in 1602. At several stages in his diplomatic career, Cottington himself was thought to have become a Catholic. He left England when the Commonwealth was established, and settled in Valladolid; he made bequests to the College and was buried there in 1652. Later his body was taken back to England and buried in Westminster Abbey, 24 June 1678.

61. As to Thompson and how far he can be identified with Goodrich alias Harper, see CRS, 29, p. 368. H. Chadwick, *St. Omers to Stonyhurst* (p. 52), tells us that John Thompson was one of the aliases of Fr John Gerard, S.J., so it may have been a common alias. It is more likely that Thompson can be identified with student no. 26 in the College Register. See also J. Simón Díaz, *Historia del Colegio Imperial de Madrid*, vol. I., Madrid 1952, p. 574.

3

THE SEVENTEENTH-CENTURY CRISES OF THE ENGLISH ESTABLISHMENTS IN SPAIN, 1614–1677

Although various influences conspired to secure the removal of students from St George's, Madrid, the complaints that Spanish superiors were unable to understand the needs of English youths at last bore fruit, and for a little over three years there were English Jesuit Rectors at St Alban's, Valladolid. The first of these was the distinguished confessor of the faith, William Weston[1] but he died after less than a year in office and was succeeded by Anthony Hoskins,[2] Prefect of the English Mission and superior of the English seminaries in Spain. But the wave of ill-health that had struck the College two years previously returned during the summer holidays, and Hoskins died after only a few months as Rector. So it was that John Blackfan, who had become a Jesuit after being one of the first students at Valladolid, was ordered to leave Brussels and come to Valladolid as Rector. By now the superiors at the College were all Englishmen, and the students attended lectures in the house and did not go to the Jesuit College of S. Ambrosio. The English character of the College was now being made very clear, but when the Duke of Lerma learnt of the situation from the one remaining Spanish lay brother, he told the Jesuits that there had to be a Spanish superior, and the students were ordered back to lectures at S. Ambrosio. When the students refused to obey, the King intervened, writing to the Provincial that there should be no changes made to the former customs of the College. So the original

1. Weston had spent 17 years in prison for his priesthood. For his history see *William Weston: The Autobiography of an Elizabethan*, translated from the Latin by Philip Caraman, London, 1955. John Morris, *The Troubles of our Catholic Forefathers related by themselves* (2nd series, 1875), includes 'The Life of Father William Weston, S.J.', which is based on a 1689 transcript by Fr Christopher Greene of a writing of Fr Persons. See also the Life of Fr Weston, written in Spanish by Peralta, Rector of the English College, Seville. Weston was a contemporary of Peralta.
2. Foley, vol. IV, pp. 392–4. It was during Hoskins' Rectorship (August 1615) that St Alban's paid back to St Omer all the *viáticos* up to the current year. *Gastos* 2, f.14.

arrangement entered into by Persons and Philip II was restored.[3]

But there was now nobody of the calibre or authority of Persons to win over compliance with the situation, and the fortunes of the College began to decline. Four or five students ran away in 1617,[4] and in 1619 there were further departures and expulsions.[5] Some of the English members of the staff were replaced by Spaniards and later, in 1623, an instruction of the General formalised this by declaring that the Spanish Provincial and Rector were to be the superiors of the English fathers and of their Seminaries.[6] Whatever may have been the case previously, the control of the Spanish Jesuits over the seminary at Valladolid from 1617 onwards was one of the factors in the decline of support for the establishment from England. Although the English Jesuits remained responsible for the recruitment of students and the sending of ordained priests back to England, there was continual criticism that the clerical training in the College was done by people ignorant of the conditions under which their students would subsequently have to labour. While it is true that there were individual English members of staff, this was not sufficient to end the complaints.

In fact, the situation was aggravated in another respect. Often it was the Father Minister who was English, and he became involved in financial transactions following on bequests and other gifts, which often proved an embarrassment to the College. There is not much doubt that this was a sad time for the College, when it became less responsive to the requirements of the pastoral clergy at home. But in spite of this, the College was not isolated from the religious issues of the seventeenth century; in fact, one of the troubles was that it became ever more deeply involved in the divisive politics of the Spanish court.

---

3. Cordara gives an account of the 1617 troubles in *Historia Societatis Jesu*, part 6, vol. 1, bk. II, pp. 107–8 (1750). The appointment of a Spanish Rector, Francisco de Benavides, was made by the General, Vitelleschi.

4. *Registers*, students nos 352–356. In the original register there are deletions and scoring of the names.

5. Students nos 363–367.

6. CRS, 29 p. 212. This is connected with the fact that in 1619 the English Jesuit Mission had become a Vice-Province. The English Jesuits could now appoint their own superiors for the College at St Omer, since their houses in Belgium were now part of the new Vice-Province. But this was at the cost of their Colleges in Spain, which were now ceded to the care of the Spanish Provinces. However, the new arrangement did remove something of the anomaly referred to above, p. 17, note 11. The Spanish Superiors no longer felt impeded in their office by the Prefect of the English Mission.

Maladministration in Madrid

An essential feature of the history of St. Alban's in 1614–69 was the deep involvement of the English Jesuits in St George's College, Madrid, and the reputation they gained by their administration of that property. Long after there had ceased to be English Rectors at Valladolid, indeed right up to 1669, the Madrid College remained under English Jesuit control, and this conflicted with the claims of the Spanish Provincials over English Colleges in Spain. After the departure of the last students from Madrid for Valladolid in 1614, the English fathers moved to the Colegio Imperial, the chief house of the Society in Madrid, where one priest and an assistant had as their main business the securing of pensions belonging to St Omer and administering the estate of the College of St George. The College property was now empty, and in order to put it to use, students from Valladolid or Seville visiting the capital were accommodated there. On such an occasion some students from Valladolid spending part of the summer there presented a deed of security which charged Madrid with the obligation of paying a *censo*, which Valladolid claimed to have taken out in favour of Madrid.[7] This trick perpetrated by four youths passing themselves off as superiors seems only to have been discovered many years later in 1645, and it resulted in litigation between St Alban's and St George's which lasted until 1735.[8]

The plausibility of this story increases as one learns more about the administration of St George's, which seem to have been extremely haphazard. In 1622 the Spanish Jesuits wanted to exchange St George's for their Casa Profesa in the Calle del Prado, but Father Forcer, the administrator of St George's, refused the offer, claiming that such an exchange was contrary to Bogacio's deed of bequest. It seems that at this

---

7. The *censo* was for 2,000 ducats from Beatriz de Chaves. Series I, L15. For some explanation of the *censo* system, see below, p. 68.
8. Edward Risley seems to have been an energetic Procurator at St George's. Anxious to clear up the financial situation and profiting from the fall of Count Olivares, he made claims on behalf of the College. This zeal brought him into conflict with St Alban's, since St George's had been paying a *censo* to Ignacio Noble (the heir of Beatriz de Chaves), which really belonged to the Valladolid College. In a letter to the Rector at Valladolid, 7 November 1646, he claimed that the *censo* was obtained in 1616 after the College had been closed and at a time when Madrid was in no need of money. So Valladolid could not claim to have undertaken this obligation on behalf of St George's. Throughout the dispute, Valladolid always maintained that the sole reason for accepting this obligation was to relieve the poverty of the Madrid College. See CRS, 29, esp. pp. 283–91. Madrid Archives, vols 15 and 32.

time Forcer was contemplating structural changes with the idea of turning the property into a Jesuit establishment. Already money intended for the setting up of a Jesuit Novitiate had been diverted to St George's by Creswell.[9] A little later, in 1626, in order to escape from the obligation of supporting a court pensioner in one of the houses left by Bogacio, Forcer gave Count Olivares, the Chief Minister of the Realm, the patronage of the College and this powerful figure secured the desired exemption. On the death of Olivares, the Duke of Medina de las Torres claimed the patronage, and after contesting this Father Sankey, the Administrator, was obliged to give him possession in 1656.

A little while afterwards a further crisis developed. Although the College had no resident English priest, a sacristan was employed to look after the chapel and say Mass there, and in 1659 the Duke of Medina de las Torres obtained a title for Don Aquiles Napolitano who had performed this duty for the previous thirty-three years. Sankey maintained that the Duke had exceeded his powers, as had the Vicar of Madrid in giving his approval, and in 1659 dismissed Napolitano. There was an appeal to the Consejo, who ordered an inspection of the College accounts. Aquiles' petition of 1660 included accusations against the whole Jesuit administration of the College. He said that the will of Bogacio had never been fully carried out, that Masses were not said with the money bequeathed for that purpose, and that the chapel was not cared for by the College, leaving the sacristan to provide for its entire upkeep. Sankey at first refused to reply, saying that he was only answerable to the Nuncio and to the Holy See. This same year the Procurator moved from the Imperial College into the property at St George's and assumed the title of Rector, thus securing the possession of the property now that the sacristan had been dispossessed. Sankey's plea of exemption from inspection was rejected by the Consejo, and he was made to produce his accounts. His figures did not agree with those presented by Ignacio Noble for the Procurator Fiscal, and so his goods were ordered to be sequestrated. Sankey himself was removed from office, and Father Kendal was put in charge.[10] This took place in 1663. Two years later Aquiles was ordered to be restored to his post, but this only took effect in 1668, by which time Antonio de Monsalve was

---

9. On 29 Oct. 1620 there was a written statement by Creswell at Watten to the effect that he had used 11,399 ducats out of 15,386 destined for the Liège Novitiate to pay the obligations of Cesar Bogacio regarding the Madrid College on 21 Nov. 1613. Madrid Archives, vol. 32, p. 4, and vol. 12, p. 52.

10. For Sankey's defence, see Madrid Archives, vol. 22, p. 28.

appointed Superior, and in 1669 Pedro Ortiz de Moncada became the first Spanish Jesuit Rector of St George's.

Thus the English Jesuits lost their control of the College due to accusations of bad administration. The English Fathers for their part never accepted these charges; they maintained that from the start the Bogacio will was an impossible burden and that anything good emerging from Madrid was due to the zeal and industry of the Jesuits. Thus a great wrong had been done them. The arguments are not always consistent: as we have seen, Risley maintained that the College in Madrid was not in any financial difficulties once it had ceased to be a seminary. Cabrera, on whose account much of the above depends,[11] was of the opinion that the Jesuits did in fact acquire property in order to provide an income that could not be obtained from the Bogacio bequest. Whatever the exact details of the case, St George's provided a perpetual anxiety to the Jesuits both in Madrid and Valladolid, and in 1652 there was talk of amalgamating Madrid with St Alban's and later in 1673 of amalgamating it with St. Gregory's in Seville. Moreover, the story of St George's helps to make it clear why the Spanish Jesuits were determined to remain in control of the College in Valladolid.

The College of the Secular Clergy at Lisbon

Another event that has to be considered for its effect on the fortunes of St Alban's was the founding of the College at Lisbon, where there had been a residence for priests since the time of Persons.[12] It would seem that this house, like other similar establishments, was at the service of the English Mission in general and not exclusively for the use of members of the Society. As to English priests in Lisbon, we know that Nicholas Ashton, a secular and former Valladolid student, was Rector of the Residence in 1597 and acted as visitor to foreign ships on behalf of the Inquisition. He seems to have been the first to acquire property with

11. Juan de Cabrera was Rector of St George's, 1718–27. For the information of his successors he wrote *Resumen Historial del Seminario de Ingleses de S. Jorge*. This is to be found (with translation into English) in CRS, 29.
12. Tierney-Dodd, vol. IV, pp. 123–33. Its exact location in Lisbon is not known. It might have been near the Jesuit church of S. Roque, in which there is a memorial erected in 1626, to the English Catholic exile Francis Tregian, of which the inscription refers to the body being discovered incorrupt the previous year — Tregian having died in 1608.

the intention of founding an English seminary. He is said to have died about 1605.[13] William Newman arrived in Lisbon from Seville in 1609 and became Superior of a house owned by the secular clergy; like Ashton he earned his keep by working for the Inquisition. But the English Jesuits also had an interest in Lisbon. Since 1611 at the latest they had been acting as trustees and managers of property in Valladolid and Madrid owned by the Brigittine nuns now resident in Portugal, and priests made fairly frequent visits to Lisbon from Valladolid.[14] In 1621 Blackfan, the Superior of the English Jesuit Mission, accused William Newman, the resident secular priest in Lisbon, of handing over to the Dominicans or Seculars, a house destined for a seminary run by the Jesuits. In his defence Newman said that it was only after he had accepted the gift from Dom Pedro de Coutinho that the founder explicitly excluded the Jesuits from the administration of the future Seminary. Blackfan said that the Jesuits had been negotiating for years to set up an English seminary in Lisbon, which was the reason why they had established a residence many years ago. The Jesuits presented their own case as to why, if there were to be a seminary in Lisbon, it should be under their care.[15] They argued that Jesuit control of the Lisbon seminary would ensure the appointment of Portuguese Superiors, and these, by reason of their greater sense of discipline and firmness in the Catholic faith, would ensure a better quality of priests emerging from the College than English secular Superiors would do. They said that George Blackwell, the Archpriest in England, was a laxist who allowed English Catholics to attend Protestant churches, and who was also careless in the selection of candidates for the priesthood. Special caution was needed in Portugal because of the many English heretics living in Lisbon. These opinions were similar to those voiced at the time of the founding of St Alban's and were part of the reason why in the end it was put under the control of the Spanish Jesuits. However, in the case of Lisbon they were disregarded; the conditions laid down by Pedro de Coutinho were observed, and following on the permission of King Philip (among whose titles was now that of King of Portugal), papal approval was

13. There is a difficulty here. If Ashton died around 1605 (Anstruther), how could he have bequeathed (Dodd) property to Newman, who did not arrive until 1609 (Anstruther)?
14. Series II, L9. Letter from Brigittine Joseph Foster to Jesuit Thomas Sylvester, 22 Jan. 1611.
15. Series II, L3, 7.

given in 1622, although no Rector was appointed till 1626.[16] The first
students were recruited from Douai and reached Lisbon on 14 November
1628.[17] As to the anxiety of the Jesuits concerning the orthodoxy of a
college run by the seculars, this was somewhat allayed by placing the
College under the Inquisition and the Inquisitor-General, which was
achieved by Blacklow on a mission to Madrid in 1631.[18] Although not
explicitly intended as a rebuff to Valladolid, the founding of a new
college within a comparatively short time after the failure of Madrid, and
at a time when recruitment was beginning to fall at St Alban's, could
easily be interpreted as a falling-off of support in England for the Spanish
seminaries that were administered by the Jesuits.

The marriage of the Prince of Wales and factions within English Catholicism

Any change in the diplomatic relations between Spain and England was
scrutinised for the effect it might have not only on the religious situation
in England but more especially on the position of the English Catholic
exiles in Spain. Following the Treaty between England and Spain in 1604
an Anglo-Spanish marriage was mooted in 1611. Charles Cornwallis was
sent to Spain to ask the hand of the Infanta Ana on behalf of Henry,
James I's eldest son. When Henry died, Charles, Prince of Wales, took
his place as the intended bridegroom but now of the Infanta María. The
negotiations went on for several years with varying enthusiasm, but
there were obstacles on both sides which in the end were to prove insur-
mountable. However much King James may have favoured such an
alliance, there was opposition from the Puritans and from Parliament

16. The first President was Joseph Harvey or Haynes, a relative of John Bennet, the
    agent for the English secular clergy in Rome. Bennet had warned that the Jesuits
    were trying to establish a seminary in Lisbon. Harvey was appointed by Bishop
    Smith and all the Chapter on 4 August 1626. See G. Anstruther, 'Historical
    Letters', *Lisbonian Magazine*, vol. XXX, no. 2, p. 45.
17. M. Sharrat, 'Douai to Lisbon', *Ushaw Magazine*, vol. 86, pp. 7–23; vol. 87, pp.
    30–41, 22–35; vol. 88, pp. 16–25; vol. 89, pp. 18–26. The history of Lisbon College
    belongs elsewhere, but it should perhaps be noted that the college was very
    conscious of being a daughter of Douai. Although Ashton, Newman and Harvey
    had been students at Valladolid, the links with St Alban's were not close. Indeed
    Lisbon College provided the secular clergy with some of its most out-spoken anti-
    Jesuit polemicists, like Blacklow and Sergeant. For documents concerning the
    foundation of Lisbon, see Tierney-Dodd, vol. 4, Appendixes LI-LIV.
18. *Ushaw Magazine*, vol. 89, p. 25.

since the Spaniards insisted that a pre-condition for such a match would have to be a relaxation of the laws against Catholics in England. The Spaniards too were not wholeheartedly in favour of the marriage, even though safeguards might be made concerning the freedom of the Infanta to practise her religion and bring up the children as Catholics. Some felt that the Catholic Monarchy would be weakened and diluted by assuming into itself Protestant blood — as would happen even in the unlikely event of Charles being converted to Catholicism. In any case, a papal dispensation would be necessary and the Spanish theologians took a hard line in demanding concessions from the English monarch.[19]

In 1621 Pope Paul V and King Philip III died within months of each other but the negotiations continued. There was encouragement from Rome where Cardinal Ludovisi, the Cardinal Protector of England, favoured the marriage. Although up to this point the connection of the College in Valladolid with these matters was remote, the prospects of such an alliance were naturally dear to those who, like the Jesuits, had an interest in bringing England closer to Spain. Then in 1623 George Villiers, Duke of Buckingham, conceived the idea of taking Prince Charles with him on a visit to Spain, and on his way to Madrid Charles visited the English College at Valladolid. Apart from a reference in the account books,[20] we have no details of this visit and it would be unwise to attach too much importance to it. On his return journey to England after six months in Spain, the Prince again passed through Valladolid but there is no record of his having visited the College a second time. In England many were relieved that he did not return with a Spanish bride, and although in November 1623 Urban VIII granted the dispensation for the marriage, it was no longer in the interests of either country to pursue the matter further, and in 1624 the English Parliament formally agreed to the breaking off of negotiations with Spain. Had the marriage taken place, the Spanish seminaries might have had a different history; although, as it turned out, the subsequent marriage of the heir to the throne did have an effect on the College.

Other European powers had not looked with much favour on the prospects of an Anglo-Spanish union, and French diplomatic activity was rewarded by the marriage in 1625 of Charles to Henrietta Maria, the

---

19. Rafael Rodríguez-Moñino Soriano, *Razón de Estado y Dogmatismo Religioso en la España del XVII*, Barcelona 1976. The Spaniards had not forgotten Henry VIII's repudiation of Catherine of Aragon, the brief marriage of Philip II and Mary Tudor, and the execution of Mary Queen of Scots.

20. It was for expenses in hiring musicians for the Prince's visit.

younger sister of King Louis XIII of France. This switch in political alliances had its effects within the Catholic community in England since it gave encouragement to the francophile element among the secular clergy and those opposed to the Jesuits.[21]

In 1623 Pope Gregory XV decided to restore some measure of episcopal rule to England. The misgivings in the Curia about this decision seemed justified when the new Superior, William Bishop, appointed a Chapter without first consulting Rome. After only a year in office Bishop died. It was French pressure that persuaded Rome not only to appoint a successor, but to nominate Richard Smith, a man who was likely to support the new alliance and French interests among English Catholics. Smith had wide experience. He had studied and taught at Rome, Valladolid[22] and Seville, and was thus a product of Jesuit seminary education. He had then taught at Douai with the seculars, and in 1610 had been a member of the mission to Rome voicing the grievances of the secular clergy. He too began to feel bitterness about the Jesuits, and in 1611 he settled in France where he was instrumental in founding a college in Paris for English seculars. Known as the College of Arras,[23] it was a house of study for writers of controversy. For thirteen years he was a member of Richelieu's household and remained faithful to the Cardinal after his disgrace in 1617. Because at this time the Nuncio in Paris was responsible for Catholic affairs in England, Smith, although in exile, was at the centre of power, and his antipathy towards the Jesuits was noted by the young Nuncio, Bernadino Spada, with favour. Among his other supporters were Thomas Rant, the Agent for the English secular clergy in Rome, and Pierre de Bérulle, the influential founder of the French Oratorians, a keen supporter of the English marriage, and no friend of the Jesuits.

The Chapter set up by William Bishop was governing the Church in England, *sede vacante*, but was unaware of these connections; it is hardly likely that the members would have welcomed a move that might alienate not merely Spain but also the Colleges in Spain, Portugal and the

21. A.F. Allison, 'Richard Smith, Richelieu and the French Marriage: The Political Context of Smith's Appointment as Bishop for England in 1624', *Recusant History*, vol. 7 (Jan. 1964), pp. 148–211.

22. Smith's name occurs more than once in the *Libro de Gastos*. Eight pounds of *cabrito* were bought in May 1598 to celebrate his '*acta*' (graduation), and in July there were further celebrations in his honour. In October 1598 he received a *viaticum* of 200 reales.

23. Tierney-Dodd, vol. IV, p. 123.

Netherlands. Smith was appointed titular Bishop of Chalcedon, responsible for the Church in England. In the event his administration was a turbulent one in which the matter of episcopal jurisdiction, Church government and relations with Rome all came under discussion.[24] But a pattern had been set that was to last through the reign of Charles I. Although Smith was forced to leave England and reside in France in 1631, English ecclesiastical affairs were managed by the Chapter, which was not on the whole favourable to the Jesuits. At the court Queen Henrietta Maria's chaplains were Capuchins and the presence of a Papal Agent in London attached to the Queen's court did nothing to help matters *vis-à-vis* Spain. The Pope, Urban VIII, was favourable to France, and his Legate in England, Gregorio Panzani,[25] in reporting back in 1634 remarked on the strong pro-Catholic feeling at the court and the opposition to Catholics from the Puritans and Parliament. However he could not forbear from adding: 'If we had neither Jesuits nor Puritans in England, I am confident a union might easily be effected.' The presence of this anti-Jesuit and anti-Spanish feeling did not make this a particularly good time for anyone sympathetic to Spain or the Society — this was a contributory cause of the decline of the Spanish seminaries from this date. What is more, as we see below, this anti-Jesuit faction had its representatives in Madrid.

Student disturbances, 1636

The year 1636 was marked by intensive diplomatic activity in London.[26] George Conn arrived as Papal Agent at the Queen's court, and his reputed Spanish sympathies were expected to influence Catholic attitudes towards the Thirty Years' War. Meanwhile, for the first time since 1619, there was a recurrence of trouble among the students at St Alban's which in 1636 reached such a pitch of violence that the police were called in. According to two documents of the time,[27] one from the

---

24. A.F. Allison, 'A Question of Jurisdiction: Richard Smith, Bishop of Chalcedon, and the Catholic Laity, 1625–1631', *Recusant History*, vol. 16, S2 (Oct. 1982), pp. 111–45.
25. Panzani was the first Papal Agent, and his aim was to settle the dispute between the seculars and the regulars. In 1636 he was replaced by George Conn, who returned to Rome in 1639 to be succeeded by Carlo Rossetti.
26. Caroline M. Hibbard, *Charles I and the Popish Plot* (Chapel Hill, N.C. 1983), pp. 38–71.
27. Series II, L3. The letters are partly printed in CRS, 30, pp. 150–2.

Rector and the Superiors and the other the draft of a letter to the General, it all happened as follows.

A certain Edward Veles or Velez (perhaps Veale or Wells) arrived from Lisbon on 8 June 1634. He had completed his philosophy, and was sent to Valladolid by a father of the Society, who believed him capable of a Public Act in theology to study that subject there. (These final oral examinations, given in the presence of the whole university; were a privilege reserved for the very best students.) He made good progress and was ordained the following year. But almost immediately he put himself at the head of the Lancashire students and became quarrelsome with the rest of the community. One particular incident prompted an intervention by the Rector, who ordered Veles, according to the customary procedure to confess his fault and make satisfaction to the aggrieved party.[28] This the student priest refused to do and, together with three other Lancastrians, provoked further trouble. The Rector went to report the matter to the Provincial, but on his return found that the four students had left the College. One of their companions said that Veles had told him he was leaving of his own accord because he did not want to be expelled. It would appear that Veles had appealed to the Bishop of Valladolid, but because the English Seminary was not within the Bishop's jurisdiction the matter was referred to the Nuncio in Madrid. The Nuncio and the Provincial were both persuaded to agree that Véles and the other three students should return to the College, but before accepting them the Rector wanted confirmation of this decision from the Provincial himself; he did not think that the Nuncio had any rights in the matter since it was the King who was patron of the College.

On enquiry it was discovered that the Nuncio's order was only provisional, and that Veles was to be received back by the Rector only while the case as to whether or not the punishment had been just was being examined. One of the points at issue was how far the students, since they were not religious, were bound by the customs of the Society: did the rules bind under sin? However, the Rector continued to maintain that according to the Bull of Clement VIII the Nuncio had no power to admit anyone in the Seminary, since this right belonged to the Provincial. The students, on the other hand, agreed with the Nuncio, and despite the protests of their Superior they performed a ceremony of clothing Veles once more in the College gown. The Senate was informed and imme-

---

28. The Jesuit rule of fraternal correction was challenged by many at this time, the Dominicans saying that it was against the Gospel. See Astrain, bk. 1, chap. IX, vol. V, p. 191.

diately sent a minister of justice to defrock Veles and eject him from the Seminary. There was a fight during which the police's rod and insignia of office were broken, but Veles was ejected and some of the other students fled to Madrid once more. On arrival they found that the Nuncio was no longer favourable to their cause as he had been warned by the King not to meddle in Seminary affairs. Meanwhile the Senate of Valladolid banished Veles from the town and its surroundings, and the two other Lancashire students were warned that if they did not behave they would have to suffer the traditional ignoming of being led round the town on a donkey.

There is more to this incident than may appear at first sight, since Veles had made contact in Madrid with English exiles inimical to both the Jesuits and the cause of Spain. In a note appended to the statement made by all the superiors, the Rector gave as one of the reasons for refusing to receive back Veles: 'He has imbibed the spirit of Missington which is against the Society and the Spanish Crown.' Missington, or Maddison, a former student at Valladolid, had been since 4 November 1619 Agent for Douai College in Madrid[29] or, as the Rector put it, 'Agent for the Bishop of Chalcedon [i.e. Richard Smith] who wears on his heart the Lilies of France'. That Veles and his companions were consorting with the court of France and with Cardinal Richelieu, the Society's greatest enemy, was a grave accusation. 'If this faction is to enter the seminary then it is like putting France into Spain.' Thus it is hardly to be wondered at that the King had to reprimand the Nuncio. The Rector stated: 'Cardinal Borgia said that even were Veles right he must not be allowed back, and that the Rector by admitting him would do disservice to His Majesty.' He went on to say that anyone doubting the true situation should refer to Don Carlos Coloma, sometime Ambassador to England, since he would be able to give particulars of the faction operating in England against the Society, and of how the Society did not enjoy the protection of the Queen of England because it is Spanish.

Whether or not it was the exact truth that Missington was representing the Bishop of Chalcedon in Madrid, it is clear from this incident that the Jesuits in Spain were highly sensitive to the strong body of Catholic opinion in England — represented even in Madrid itself —

---

29. See Anstruther, vol. 2, p. 207, under 'Edward Maddison'. Missington had also been consulted by Pedro de Coutinho concerning the founding of the English College in Lisbon, and since 26 May 1626 had been acting as his procurator in Madrid. WCA, 19.114 and 20.11.

that was unfriendly to them because of their loyalty to the Spanish crown.

The students, 1614–1677

We should now, seek to assess how, in these difficult years, the College performed its main task of preparing priests for the English Mission. After the departure of Creswell for the Low Countries in 1614, the intake of students maintained itself until 1617[30] when, as a result of the conflict between the English and the Spanish over the government of the College, there were no new recruits. From 1618 onwards recruitment continued, but at a reduced rate. There were no new students in 1620, but fifteen in 1621. The yearly intake for the rest of the decade was: 3,10,0,8,1,6,0,7. Of the fifty entrants between 1620 and 1629, nineteen were ordained for the English Mission (one died after ordination), eleven joined the Jesuits, two became Benedictines, one a Dominican and one a Franciscan; eight died in College before ordination.[31] From 1630 onwards the recruitment was much worse — 0, 0, 11, 0, 8, 0, 11, 6 — and between 1638 and 1640 there were no students in the College at all. Of the thirty-six in this decade ten were ordained, two became Jesuits, one joined the Brigittines, three went to other seminaries and five died before ordination. To keep a correct perspective it should be remembered that it was in 1635 that France entered the Thirty Years' War against Spain, which affected the supply of students from the Low Countries to both Rome and Spain. Most of the new students came from St Omer — if not straight from the school, then at least using the College there as an assembly-point. The annual letters of St Omer for 1636 speak of a new and more expensive route to Southern Europe.[32] No longer was it possible to sail direct from Calais, but students had to return to England first and then proceed by sea to Spain; those going to Rome had to cross Spain to the Mediterranean and then take ship.

The Jesuits cannot be blamed for the decline in numbers at this time;[33]

---

30. Fourteen in 1614, eleven in 1615 and thirteen in 1616. Registers, CRS, 30.
31. To add to the difficulties of the College authorities, epidemics were frequent in seventeenth-century Valladolid due largely to the bad state of the water supply. See *Historia de Valladolid IV* ('Valladolid en el Siglo XVII'), pp. 38–9.
32. H. Chadwick, *St Omers to Stonyhurst*, p. 150.
33. 'Owing to the evil times and the consequent sufferings of our English Colleges at Valladolid and Seville, no students had been sent to either place' (Foley, vol. VII,

in fact they began to reorganise their admissions in view of the new situation. In 1640 there was a large intake of twelve and they now began to accept students every other year, thus ensuring reasonably-sized classes to the advantage of both students and professors. Of the thirty accepted in 1640, 1642 and 1644, sixteen were ordained for the secular priesthood and seven became Jesuits. After matters had not improved in the 1650s, a new system was introduced in 1663 whereby one class of students was accepted and taken through the whole course up to ordination, and only then was another class admitted. So new students were only accepted every seven years. The years from 1645 to 1677, when the registers were mutilated, saw the admission of forty-six students, nearly all of whom were ordained priests: twenty-five became seculars and eleven joined the Jesuits.

Although not numerous, the students who were ordained from Valladolid during these crisis years were of no mean calibre, and according to the reports made at the frequent visitations by the Provincial, life seems to have been fairly peaceful and well-ordered. The Veles incident was by no means typical. There were references to complaints that the studies at S. Ambrosio were not always suited to future missionaries in England, and to the need for more 'controversies', but this complaint has been made at most periods of the College's history. However, former students were not found wanting when it came to the test. A number were put to death for the faith: Ven. Arthur Bell, O.F.M. (entered St Alban's 1615), Ven. Edward Richardson or Bamber (1625), John Smith or Harrington (1625), Ven. Thomas Whittaker or Starkie (1634), Ven. Thomas Downes or Bedingfield (1636), St John Lloyd (1649) and St John Plessington (1660).

In this period the College harboured one of its most infamous alumni, Titus Ambrose (*vere* Oates), one of the ten students admitted in 1677. He arrived at the College on 1 June 1677 but was expelled on 30 October the same year. His departure signalled a new turn of events in the fortune of Catholics in England.

---

pt. 2: Annual Letters of St Omer 1653). For the ruinous state of the finances in Castile in 1643–59, see Antonio Domínguez Ortiz, *Política y Hacienda de Felipe IV*, Madrid 1980.

4

FROM THE POPISH PLOT TO THE EXPULSION
OF THE JESUITS FROM SPAIN, 1678–1767

After entry number 538 — '*Titus Ambrose vere Oates venit cum praedictis et ob pessimos mores post 4 meses ejectus, factus est infamis apostata . . . .*' — there is a break in the registers. Nicholas Porter, the Minister of the College in 1764, noted that several pages were missing for which he could offer no explanation. The original registers have a few entries for 1756 and 1758, and then come to an end. A new register was only begun by Philip Perry, the first secular Rector, when he arrived in 1768. The intervening years 1677–1768 for which there is no record were researched by John Guest, who in 1868 compiled a list of the students who had been in the College; he made use of books of account and other documents, but naturally the information is imperfect. In his introduction to CRS, vol. 30, Henson also fills in some of the events of these years from other sources. As it happens, the Lisbon archives are imperfect for the years 1667–1710,[1] and there is a break in the records of Douai College for 1676–1692.[2] But where Valladolid is concerned, the question arises as to whether the missing pages contained anything to do with the Popish Plot given the fact that Oates was resident in the College for a time.

Oates arrived on 1 June 1677 and a few months later was expelled '*ob pessimos mores*'. He left the College on 30 October accompanied by a post-boy, and we have an account of his journey back via Torquemada, Burgos, Pancorbo, Saracho to Bilbao, which records such things as Oates not going to Mass on the Sunday but attending it on All Saints Day — this was part of the testimony sent to London a year later, 21 November 1678, in order to refute some of the statements he was then making.[3] Jane Lane, in her biography of Oates,[4] implies that there were

1. See Anstruther, 3, p. ix.
2. The Sixth Diary is missing, and although there are notes preceeding the Seventh Diary and covering 1689–1715 (printed in CRS, 28), there is no full record for 1654–1715. Also Astrain, vol. 6, notes a lack of documentation in the Spanish Jesuit archives during this period. There is no extant correspondence between the Provincial and the Father General, and the annual letters are missing.
3. Series II, L3. Further information about Oates may be found in John Warner, *The History of English Persecution of Catholics and the Presbyterian Plot* (ed. T.A. Birrell), CRS, 47 and 48. Also J. Kenyon, *The Popish Plot* (London 1972), chap. 3.
4. Jane Lane, *Titus Oates*, London 1949.

no other students in Valladolid while Oates was there, but this does not seem to have been the case. There had been a long period from 1671 when there had been no new entrants, but there were students in the College at this time and it was after four students returned to England on 3 February 1677 that the College, according to what was then customary procedure, was ready to accept a new class. Ten students including Oates were accepted to begin their studies in 1677. The Rector was Father Manuel de Calatayud and in his account of the building of the new church which took place at this time, he refers to an unexpected gift sent by Fr John Newport[5] via Titus Ambrose (*vere* Oates) continuing: 'On the strength of the letters of the said Newport and of the Provincial of England, I admitted him, very much against the grain though it was. I kept him in lay dress all the time until the Students' mission on St Luke's Day, October 18th. Little more than a month went by, and he was in such a hurry to begin his mischief that I was obliged to expel him from the College. He was a curse. What I went through and suffered from that man, God alone knows.'[6] But even after his expulsion, Oates kept in touch with the Jesuits and was received at St Omer.[7]

Oates and Valladolid: Some unsolved problems

Like all other Catholic institutions, Valladolid was affected by the activities of Oates. Two of his classmates, Charles and Francis Langhorne, were sons of Richard Langhorne, one of the victims of the plot who was executed at Tyburn while they were still students in Spain.[8] Former students martyred at this time were St John Lloyd and St John Plessington, while others like Thomas Downes (or Bedingfield) and Thomas Molyneaux died in prison and others were either imprisoned or hunted,[9] but none of these was at the College while Oates was there.

To understand how Oates came to be received in the College, even for so short a period, one has to be aware of the climate of Catholicism in England at this time. The Catholic community was declining not only

5. *Alias* Charles Keynes, *Cobbet's Complete Collection of State Trials*, vol. VI, London 1811, col. 1436, G. Holt, S.J., *The English Jesuits 1630–1829*, CRS, 70, p. 137.
6. *Principios y Progressos de la milagrosa Fábrica de la Madre de Dios Injuriada* (Calatayud's account of the building of the Chapel).
7. H. Chadwick, *St Omers to Stonyhurst*, pp. 184–210.
8. See Anstruther, 3, pp. 127–9, for a full account.
9. See *Registers* (CRS, 30), students nos 512,486,503 and 517.

on account of the repression of the penal laws but also because the Holy See seemed reluctant to provide an ecclesiastical superior to succeed Richard Smith, now in exile in France. The clergy showed a lack of discipline, morale was low and, even if they did not fall into the vices of drunkenness and lechery, they were often condemned to a life of idleness. Dependence on the gentry meant that the clergy were often simply providing a service to the dwindling number of Catholics and not concerned with the evangelisation of the masses. Despite the complaints about the unsuitability of the studies at S. Ambrosio, only a few priests in England did in fact engage in controversy with Protestants. The great vices were boredom and laziness, which proved an attraction for the less zealous, and many priests flocked to London in the 1660s and 1670s including eccentrics and impostors from France and Ireland. Among such, as Aveling remarks,[10] Titus Oates would pass almost unnoticed. When the Jesuits befriended him, they need not have been ignorant of his previous history of expulsions from Merchant Taylors School, from Gonville and Caius College at Cambridge, and from his chaplaincy on a frigate bound for Tangier. Perhaps by contemporary standards Oates was genuinely converted to Catholicism. But to assert that he went to Valladolid as a spy or to infiltrate the Jesuits is perhaps to attribute to him more decisiveness and commitment than is characteristic. Oates was a shameless liar, as his subsequent history showed, and he proved an embarrassment to the enemies as well as the friends of Catholicism. But plots and rumours of plots were in the air, and Oates did not originate them, but simply exploited them to his own advantage. Although the Catholics feared the Puritans, they did not always realise that their own position caused anxiety in others. At court there were a number of Catholics, most notably the Queen and the Duke of York, and it was hardly to be wondered at that Catholics began to fantasise and dream about a restoration of Catholicism. A paranoia affected the whole nation. A state of emergency was declared in London, and there were rumours of landings of invasion forces at various ports. The Jesuits bore the brunt of this hysteria; between 1678 and 1681 nine were executed, twelve died in prison, and three others met their death as a result of the 'Plot'. The arrest and martyrdom of the Provincial, Thomas Whitbread, left the Society without a leader. The General appointed John Warner, Rector at Liège, as Vice Provincial but he was forbidden to travel to England. Those Jesuits who did so were often arrested and imprisoned.

10. J.C.H. Aveling, *The Handle and the Axe*, London 1970, pp. 204–21.

Most Catholics soon realised that the Jesuits were not the culprits as popular opinion held them to be, but there were some who openly sided with the government.[11] However it was perhaps the European connections that caused the most worry to Protestants, and Oates' visit to Spain is still shrouded in mystery.[12] One of the assertions, consistently denied at the College, was that he had visited Madrid or indeed spent any time away from St Alban's.[13] Oates, on the contrary, maintained that he had been sent from Valladolid to Madrid and had there taken part in a discussion with John of Austria on behalf of the Catholics in a plot to murder King Charles. Oates gave a description of John of Austria which was far from the reality, and the judgment of history has been against him. He clearly did not meet the people he claimed to have met in Madrid,[14] but although there was no truth in a Spanish involvement in a plot to kill the King, a claim to have visited Madrid touched a sensitive nerve. Charles II's Ambassador was Sir William Godolphin, and there was a rumour that he had become a Catholic; this was denied at the time, but Oates maintained that Godolphin was involved in the Spanish plot to kill the King — hence the importance of that visit to Madrid. When persecution did break out in England as a result of the Oates plot, Ronquillo, the Spanish Ambassador in London, gave considerable help to the persecuted English Catholics, showing that although the situation had changed since the beginning of the century, there was still a fellow-feeling among Catholics of the two countries. This was far from reassuring to the Protestants. Godolphin's subsequent history does nothing to clarify matters: he did become a Catholic, remained in Spain and left his money to the Church, the Jesuit Edward Meredith administering some of the estate. The legacies were contested not only by his own family but also by the secular clergy.[15]

---

11. The most notable of these was John Sergeant. Trained at Lisbon College, he was not only a writer of controversial works and an apologist for Catholicism, but was also one of the few Catholics who upheld the legality of the oath of allegiance and was reputed to have delated Jesuits to the authorities for not showing their loyalty in this way.
12. Edward Coleman, secretary to the Duchess of York, was engaged in correspondence with the French Jesuit Père Lachaise, and was eventually put to death for treason. There were other correspondents with Lachaise, cf. Anglia, VI.
13. See Warner, 112, CRS, 47.
14. J.P. Kenyon, *The Popish Plot*, p. 80.
15. For Godolphin, see *DNB*. His family contested his will, claiming that on his deathbed he 'was surrounded by friars, priests and Jesuits' and 'was influenced to

College life in Spain

Remarkably, despite the intrigue and turmoil surrounding the Oates plot, day-to-day College life was very little affected — less so than was the case with the other colleges abroad. Kenyon's remark that damage was done to the European bases of English Catholicism because the flow of alms from England was interrupted by the plot[16] scarcely applied to the Spanish foundations. They had never relied on England for alms, and even the fact that St Omer was now in French territory as a result of the war was no disadvantage, since Louis XIV agreed to maintain a royal pension. Thus the main source of recruitment of students to the colleges in Spain was assured.[17]

Compared to the frenzy of life in England, College life at St Alban's was well ordered and placid.[18] Visitations by the Provincial occurred regularly, and there was the customary change of superiors, Rectors usually ruling for three years and then being replaced. The community comprised three or four Jesuit fathers and three lay brothers, and there were between six and nine students for the secular clergy. Officers were appointed each year on St Luke's Day, and the small number of students meant that every student had a particular task to perform in the house — for example, as bellringer or music master, or in charge of recreation. From the book of *Gastos* it can be inferred that there were three big feasts during the year: St Alban's Day, the Immaculate Conception and the Feast of St Francis Xavier. These days were celebrated with special music for which singers were hired, and there was a banquet, and the celebrations took place even when there were no English students in the

---

consent to an act before a public notary on or about May 30th 1696, whereby it was signified that four persons named therein, Don Matías de Escobar, Abbot of the Basilians, Gerónimo Guerrero, Procurator General of the Jesuits, Don Baltasar de Cabredo a secular priest, and Don Antonio de Cendoya, a lawyer; were to be his *testamentarios*.' The family succeeded in obtaining a private act of William III that his property should not be used for superstitious purposes (10 William III, 9 April 1698). On 18 July 1699, the Cámera Apostólica passed judgement in favour of the English College in Rome against family claims. A burse for a West Country student was held at the VEC. See VEC, *Scritt.* 11, 12; 17, 1–15.

16. T.H. Kenyon, *The Popish Plot*, p. 241.
17. H. Chadwick, *St Omers to Stonyhurst*, pp. 179–201.
18. In 1737 James Dodd sent a memorial to Bishop Stonor containing complaints about the Jesuit administration in his student days in the 1670s. He does, however, praise the good discipline and schools of the Jesuits, WCA Old Brotherhood, MSS., no. 130 (this is a transcript in Philip Perry's hand).

College. Since the early seventeenth century, July and August were spent at Portillo. A house was purchased in 1675, and was used until Dr Perry bought Viana in 1770. The College chapel, rebuilt in 1679, was further adorned by the completion of *retablos* for the side-chapels in 1700–2. In the following years repairs were made to the College property, and during the long absence of students between 1739 and 1756 there was extensive rebuilding; this began in 1744, and it would seem from the amount of materials acquired that the College was totally rebuilt from cellars to roof. The refectory and sacristy with their ceilings and plaster mouldings date from this period, as does the main wooden staircase and its banisters. The library too was built at this time. All this had long been needed, but money had not been available. Why it was available now is not clear, since there is no book of *recibos* for this period of College history.

Recruitment of students

The pattern was now established whereby students were accepted (usually coming from St Omer) every seven years. They were taken through their seven-year course of philosophy and theology, and only after the studies were completed and they had returned to England was another class admitted. Thus of the eight who entered in 1685, three left in March 1692 for the Mission, five having left previously *re infecta*; and only in November 1692 did the new students arrive. This pattern was not always followed, but it was the case with those who left in February 1701; they were only replaced in October of that year. These went through the course and the last of them left in 1708 and in October of that year seven new students arrived. But when the last two of that year's intake left in 1713, there was a break until 1718. The reason for this gap is explained[19] by the fact that the Spanish King was at war and so withheld payment of the accustomed pension. The last of the class of 1718 had left by June 1724, but there was a further gap before new students arrived in November 1726; when these had completed their course in 1733, more arrived later that year, but when this intake left in 1739 there was a long period until 1756 before they were replaced. The 1756 students left in April 1763 and in October the last five students to be educated under the Jesuits arrived.

19. By Father Solana in 1725, Series II, L4.

The College policy of accepting students in this way was quite deliberate, and when the Rector of St Omer wrote to the Rector of St Alban's offering students, he used an almost stereotyped formula.[20] The shortage of vocations in England and the unwillingness of anyone outside St Omer to support the College because of its Spanish Jesuit superiors, were contraints and in these circumstances the restriction of entry to only once in six or seven years had several advantages. The superiors had only one class to deal with at a time, so their education and formation could be more methodical. The students were isolated from their predecessors and successors thus automatically eliminating criticism and dissent in the College such as might arise from changes in customs or precedent. The Visitation reports bear this out, and there are several glowing accounts of the peace and harmony in the community.[21]

There were financial advantages too. Budgeting was easier if one could plan ahead knowing that not more than seven students would have to be accommodated for the next six or seven years. When these were ordained and successfully launched on the Mission, admission of a new class would depend on the state of the finances — hence the gaps when new students were not admitted. Savings were made; in 1693 at the Visitation, there was a considerable sum of money in hand, and the Provincial ordered that 3,000 ducats should be invested in a *censo*. On the other hand, in 1711 it was noted at the Visitation that there was a decrease in income because many annuities were not paid, leading to a period between 1713 and 1718 when no new students were admitted.[22] But although there were some years when there were no students at all (and the longest gap was 1739–56), there was a continuity. There were always Jesuit priests and lay brothers resident, and although not able to support students, the College was a going concern and there was no question of having to close completely.

Although efficient from the point of view of discipline and finance, the

20. The letter of September 1718 printed in CRS, 30, p. 182, is almost the same in form, *mutatis mutandis*, as that of Sept. 1710, found in Series II, L4.

21. For example, the Visitations of 14 June 1696; 12 Feb. 1699; 20 March 1700; 1 March 1703; 13 May 1725; 16 May 1734; 14 Jan. 1762.

22. The Visitation of 13 May 1714 explicitly attributed the absence of students to lack of funds. Similarly the visitation of 22 Feb. 1716. A letter from Charles Walmesley of Liège to the Rector of St. Alban's, 24 Sept. 1717, says that he has not the number of students that the Rector requires, so rather than 'divide the numbers' he will hold them back until they can be increased in the following year. But in Feb. 1718 the Rector was told at the Visitation that he had to make a greater effort to obtain students.

system was not likely to please the ecclesiastical authorities in England. The number of students returning was small. There was not a large wastage, and in fact the proportion of ordained priests to those who had begun the course was high, but the Vicars Apostolic could only expect students from Valladolid every seven years. According to Guest's register for 1689–1763, forty-four were ordained and sent to England. If this is measured by the number of years covered — seventy-four — it is a very poor performance, but compared with the actual entry classes, (8) it is creditable. However, of the forty-four ordained priests, eighteen subsequently became Jesuits and of the twenty-one who left the College before ordination, five left to join the Society. At times it looked as if the superiors of St Omer chose students to go to Valladolid because they were prospective Jesuits. A letter of 1 April 1692 from St Omer to St Alban's recommends six students for philosophy at Valladolid, to begin in October; they were, it said, 'worthy to become Jesuits; they nearly all want to be.' Later, in July 1725, the General gave a ruling that the students of the College did not need a dispensation from their oath in order to enter the Society, and from then on we find several students joining the Society.[23]

Complaints

A serious development took place when the General, Francisco Retz, wrote to the Rector of St Alban's on 2 July 1735 with the news that a complaint against the College had been lodged at the Congregation of Propaganda Fide. The two main charges were that in former times priests had left the seminary for the English Mission every year, whereas they now did so only every seven years, and moreover the students were not receiving proper preparation for the Mission; there had been cases of 'depraved customs' and frequent apostasies. The General had repudiated the charges, but he now asked the Rector for a list of the names and dates of those who had left the College in the last forty years, with an explanation of why there were so few, and for any information about the charges

23. This was also the period when students arrived from Maryland. Andrew White (no. 110 in *Register*) had founded the Maryland Mission in 1633. He was joined by John Gravenor (or Gregory, no. 204) and George Pole (no. 497) sometime in 1665. In 1692 two students arrived from Maryland (544 and 545) and another three (598, 599 and 600) in 1756. For the Maryland Mission see T.A. Hughes, S.J., *History of the Society of Jesus in North America*, London 1910, vol. I; Foley, vol. III, pp. 320–400.

of a decline in academic standards and a lessening of zeal. The replies were to be clear, concise and in Latin.

The Rector, Pedro José Solana, drafted a somewhat evasive reply.[24] He said that having scrutinised all the books since 1633 he had not found any record of students completing their curriculum, being ordained and being sent back to England after a year. Rather, missionaries were sent from St Omer to do a seven-year course and only then return to England. He appended a list of students who had completed their studies, been ordained, and sent to England since 1677. He could not deny that in the early days a great number of students were sent on the Mission, but this was because so many were admitted to the College. In the early days the College could rely on the annual income from the Founder, and on the munificence of prelates and pious nobles. Now that this charity has cooled off, the College could only support eight or ten apart from the Jesuit fathers and brothers and this was the reason why students only came to the College every seven years. The students attended lectures at S. Ambrosio and followed the same course in philosophy and theology as the Jesuit students, attending the same lectures. They worked during vacations, and they had conferences and days of recollection. Many of their professors had been in Rome and said that the St Alban's alumni were as well instructed as those in Rome. If there was any blame, then this must be attributed to the incapacity of the pupils and not to the negligence of their masters. Equal care and diligence was taken to see that the alumni advanced in virtue. Their formation was almost the same as 'our' scholars. They spent half an hour's meditation in the morning, attended Mass, had two *examens* (examinations of conscience) each day, said the rosary, had half an hour's spiritual reading in their rooms, and their life was governed by bells. Each year they had eight days' spiritual exercises, they went to confession, and they received Holy Communion every Sunday and on the Feasts of our Lord, our Lady, the Apostles, the Saints of the Society, St John the Baptist and St Joseph. They had no communication with lay people and so neither invited visitors, nor paid visits themselves, outside the College. When they went out, they all went together accompanied by the Father Minister. Hence any defections later on could not be due to faulty upbringing or negligence on the part of the superiors but only to the fragility of human nature.[25]

The Rector's reply is simply a statement on the college routine, and

---

24. 10 Aug. 1735. L4, 30: Spanish Draft, 34: Latin Draft. Transcript 14.
25. See also CRS, 30, pp. xxxvi–xxxvii.

does not tackle the question of whether such a way of life was suitable for those preparing for the English mission. The English bishops can hardly have been reassured when four years later the College was again empty of students and so remained till 1756. The cause of this new break in admissions was once more financial, but the absence of students was used to put the College buildings into a state of good repair.[26]

The final crisis

In 1762 there came a further blow when St Omer's College was seized as part of the growing campaign in France against the Jesuits. This raised the question of how St Alban's could continue with even its meagre flow of students now that its chief source had been supressed and handed over to the English secular clergy to administer. The Rector of St Omer sent an urgent message on 25 July 1762 to the Rector of St Alban's, begging him to receive a new class for philosophy, even though there were still theologians in the College who had not yet completed their course.[27]

Further bad news arrived the next year. Father Nicholas Sanderson wrote from London on 11 June 1763 to the Rector[28] saying that the English secular clergy were trying to dispossess the Society of the College at Valladolid, just as they had already done with St Omer. They had appealed to both the Pope and Propaganda Fide. Their case was that St Alban's was founded for the secular clergy alone, and that therefore no sutdent should join a religious order. But they had a special grievance concerning a priest and a deacon who had just arrived from Valladolid, who wanted to join the Jesuit novitiate. The Bishop whose subjects they were lodged an appeal in Rome, and appealed as well to the Nuncio in Madrid.[29] It was because of all this that Sanderson had been

26. An estimate for these repairs, 12 March 1748, is in Series II, L4, 44. See also Visitation, 10 Dec. 1747. *Gastos*, 26 (1753–67). Complaints about specific students from the Jesuit-run colleges, including Valladolid, were lodged by the VAs in 1713 and 1714. WCA, 38, 71 and 74.
27. The Rector of St Alban's did not accede to this request, and it was only in Oct. 1763 that six new students arrived accompanied by Nicholas Porter, the newly-appointed Minister, to replace those who had left in April. They travelled via London having completed their humanities at Bruges.
28. Series II, L4, 73. See CRS, 30, pp. xl and xli.
29. This appeal revived the old question of the oath and its binding force after ordination. R.M. Wiltgen, 'Propaganda is placed in charge of the Pontifical Colleges' in *Sacrae Congregationis de Propaganda Fide, Memoria Rerum*, 1/1, pp. 483–505.

instructed to write to the Rector requesting him to appeal to the King or to some other high personage like the Queen Mother. He was also to send a copy of the rule drawn up by Persons and an account of the foundation and history of the College to Mr Francis Scarisbrick at 'Government House, Bruges' and to Mr Cornelius Murphy in 'Queen Street, London'.[30] At the end of the letter Sanderson reported somewhat gleefully that the priest and deacon at the root of the trouble were already safe in the novitiate at Watten.

The Rector sent an account of this letter to Clemente Recio, the Provincial of Castile, who replied that to place the Seminary under the seculars would indeed mean its extinction; but, he added, the English Bishops were correct in their objection, and the English Provincial ought to have forestalled the charge. The Rector also wrote to Father Francisco Nieto,[31] a former Rector of the College, who advised him that because the dispute was about students joining the Society after having taken the oath, the best thing to do would be to adduce proof that there was no evidence for any student trying to join the Spanish Province. This could easily be done as the Book of *Viáticos* contained the names of all who had returned to England. In fact any desire on the part of students to join the Spanish Jesuit Province had always been rebuffed. Nothing was done in the Seminary to induce them to become Jesuits 'except in a general way', and the College could not be held responsible if former students became Jesuits afterwards when they had returned to England or Flanders. Such a decision would hardly be surprising among those who had spent seven years in an orderly Jesuit community and then saw at first hand the zeal of the Jesuit missionaries in England.

It was a case of the Spanish administrators of the College feeling that their responsibility was over once they had sent the ordained students back to England. There was no case of students, during their stay in Spain, leaving the College and not returning to England, unlike the situation in the early seventeenth century when there were defections to the Benedictines. This observation was not quite accurate since they did not consider the many cases where students left the College to join the Jesuit novitiate. They made their case rest on whether any students, *after ordination*, joined the Jesuits and remained in Spain. Such a position was unassailable, but it was not what the Vicars Apostolic were concerned

---

30. Francis Scarisbrick and Cornelius Murphy were Jesuits. See G. Holt, CRS, 70, pp. 173 and 221.
31. Letters of 3 and 31 Aug., L4.

about. However, by placing responsibility on the English authorities for any who had joined the Society, they not only discomfited their confrères but also touched on a weak point in the seculars, namely their lack of zeal and discipline in England as compared with the Jesuits.[32] It was this, they argued, that caused priests to desert the seculars. The English Jesuits, having had the responsibility placed on them for any who might join the Society, made their position plain to the Rector of St Alban's. As a general rule, the students they sent to Valladolid from St Omer were already disposed towards entering the Society, and if they had thought that the College oath would militate against this, they would never have consented to go to Valladolid in the first place. Nathaniel Elliot suggested that the students should appeal to the King, but the General intervened and ruled that they should be informed before leaving St Omer that they would be bound by an oath to return to England after ordination and would work as members of the secular clergy — with the result that no one who had taken the oath would be able to join the Society. In the light of this ruling no appeal was made to the King.

But it was now the turn of the students to express their view on the matter.[33] They disagreed with the General: they did not believe that the oath imposed a ban on joining a religious order. At this the General modified his position, saying that what he had said was his private opinion of what was the case, and that he had no intention of imposing any new obligation on them. The students' viewpoint was conveyed to the Nuncio, who replied in much the same vein as the General: if the students did not want to take the oath, they had to leave the College. Should they wish to join a religious order after ordination, then this would be possible if their Bishop in England allowed it; but, like the General, the Nuncio wished to cover himself, since he added that this was just his private opinion and that the decision would have to be made by Propaganda Fide.

By now the dispute had been going on for two years, and in the light of all this uncertainty the students had not yet been asked to take the

32. While this correspondence between the Rector and Nieto was going on, the Nuncio wrote to the Bishop of Valladolid asking for information about the College oath.

33. It was the five students who arrived at the College in Oct. 1763 who were concerned in this matter. The General had made it clear that any ruling would not be retroactive and would only have implications for the future. One cannot help wondering whether it was the Jesuits in the College who were inspiring the students to protest against this new interpretation of the oath.

College oath. As the appeal to the Nuncio had failed, the question of an appeal to the King was again considered. The General consented on condition that the affair should be left to the students themselves and that no member of the Society should have a hand in it.[34] Clearly it was in the interests of the Jesuits that an appeal should be made to the King, because the English Province did not want to be deprived of possible new recruits, as would happen if the oath were interpreted in the way the seculars intended and which the General did not completely reject. On the other hand, the situation of the Society in Spain was such that the King, through his ministers, would not willingly make concessions to the Jesuits, whereas an appeal by students on behalf of the Jesuits might help to persuade him that there were some people who sided with the Jesuits. On 15 February 1766 the Provincial, Francisco Javier Idiáquez, gave the students permission to go to Madrid and present their case at court. But there was another delay; the students wanted the seminary to pay the cost of the journey and so the matter was referred back to the General.

Matters quite suddenly came to a head. There is in existence the text of a letter addressed to the King concerning the oath, but it is doubtful if it was ever presented because the oath was imposed on the five students on 22 June 1766. Three refused to take it, and so a passage was arranged from Bilbao to Flanders and they left Valladolid and joined the Society. The two remaining students, Buller and Addis, took the oath and so were allowed to stay.[35] Francisco Texerizo, a former Rector, writing to Antonio Miguel Santiesteban on 20 July 1766 expressed his sorrow that the other students had not taken the oath since they would have been very useful missionaries.

Thus at the beginning of the academic year 1766–7 there were only two students, and future recruitment looked bleak. The source of new blood was no longer at St Omer, and the interpretation of the oath that now prevailed seemed to exclude any students coming to Valladolid from Jesuit-run colleges.

34. Letter from Provincial to Rector of St Alban's, 9 Sept. 1765.
35. Buller took the oath but also signed a declaration to the effect that, having taken it, he would still consider himself free to join a religious order. CRS, 30, p. xlvi. See below, p. 77.

5

THE COLLEGE AND SPANISH CATHOLICISM

Although founded for the benefit of the Catholic Church in England, the College of St Alban, Valladolid, is also bound up with the history of the Church in Spain. The most interesting aspect of this link is the personal and religious one which brought together individuals of the two nations in a common religious bond. Two stories from the early days illustrate this.

The Vulnerata

The early years of the Colleges in Spain were marked by hostilities between the two countries, including several naval engagements between the English and Spanish fleets. Each country had plans for invading the other, and in 1596 the Earl of Essex led an expedition to destroy the Spanish fleet that was assembling in Cadiz harbour.[1] English sailors sacked the town on 21 June. From one of the churches a statue of the Virgin and Child was dragged into the street, hacked and mutilated. What was left was a figure with sabre cuts on the face, part of the nose and mouth missing and both arms reduced to stumps, and all that remained of the Infant was a tiny foot attached to the Mother's knee. But after the outrage this remnant of the statue became the object of a particular devotion, and the *Adelantado* (Captain-General) of Castile, the Count of Santa Gadea, and his wife took it back with them to Madrid and gave it an honoured place in their oratory. In 1600 Father John Blackfan, the Procurator of the English College at Valladolid, was in Madrid on business and, learning about the statue, approached the *Adelantado* and his wife with the idea of obtaining it for the College. They were most reluctant to part with it, but Father Creswell organised a petition among the English students: 'It is just that the English Catholics should disclaim the injuries which the English heretics have

---

1. *Recebimiento que se hizo en Valladolid a una imagen de Nuestra Señora*, Madrid 1600. Pedro de Abreu, *Historia de Saqueo de Cádiz por los Ingleses en 1596*, 1866, chap. XIII: 'Imágenes ultrajadas por los Ingleses', reprints a contemporary account.

offered to our Lady, and should serve and reverence the image which they have abused. [. . .] Our respect to it will be greater and more sincere than the irreverence which they manifested to it.' The Countess of Santa Gadea, wife of the *Adelantado*, replied in a personal letter that she had agreed to comply with the request, but before parting with the statue she wished to have made for it a golden crown, a rich mantle and a veil to cover the disfigurement. She herself escorted the image to Valladolid and a solemn entry was made into the town; from the Church of the Discalced Carmelites outside the gates it was taken in procession on a litter lent by the Queen of Spain, escorted by twenty-four English students bearing lighted tapers. At the door of the Cathedral the statue was formally received by the Canons of the chapter and the clergy. There was an all-night vigil and, after High Mass the next day, the Feast of the Nativity of Mary 8 September, another procession in which the confraternities, the religious orders, the clergy and the people took part. A large crowd waited outside the English College, and in the chapel were the Queen and her retinue; she was the first to pay homage to the statue in its new home[2] — an encounter as the contemporary record puts it, between 'the only Queen of Heaven and the only Catholic Queen on earth'. After hymns in Latin and English the proceedings came to an end for that day, and the College dined at the Queen's expense.

On each of the following nine days there were various ceremonies including one in which the Rector and academic staff of the University took the leading part. The concluding ceremony was performed by the Bishop of Valladolid who bestowed on the statue the title of Santa María Vulnerata (the Wounded One). Not only did it become an object of veneration for the students and a boost to their missionary zeal, but it also attracted the devotion of the local people. Cures and miracles were attributed to it,[3] and it became a serious rival to that other image, the

---

2. The King and Queen (Philip III and Doña Margarita) arrived in Valladolid on 19 July, and on 20 Aug. visited the English College. For an account of this visit, see *Relación de la Venida de los Reyes Católicos, al Colegio Inglés de Valladolid, en el mes de Agosto Año de 1600 y la Colocación y Fiesta hecha en el mesmo Colegio, de una Ymagen de Nuestra Señora Maltratada de los Herejes. Dirigida a la Santíssima Señora Infanta de España Doña Isabel Clara Eugenia por Don Antonio Ortiz*, Madrid, 1600. The reception of the Vulnerata consequently occasioned the second visit of the Queen to the College in the space of a few weeks. The King was in Madrid when the statue arrived in Valladolid.

3　E.g. Sept. 1618, Oct. 1622, 1631, 1642. Juan de Villafañe, *Compendio Histórico en que se da noticia de Las Milagrosas y Devotas Imagenes de la Reyna de Cielos y Tierra,*

Virgin of S. Lorenzo, the patron of the city (today in the convent of Santa Ana). From 1663, the Sunday within the octave of the Feast of the Immaculate Conception was celebrated as the Feast of the Vulnerata. The Jesuits gave full encouragement to this devotion, and when Fr Manuel de Calatayud became Rector in 1671, a difficult time in College history, he decided to build a larger and more magnificent church for the Virgin. He has left us accounts both of his travels throughout Spain begging money and gifts of jewellery, and of the construction work on the church and the ceremonies when it was opened in 1679.[4] The writer's piety towards the Virgin and his accounts of miraculous intervention, on the one hand, and his somewhat caustic remarks about the lack of generosity of the townspeople and some of the religious orders, on the other, provide a piquant contrast. However, there is no doubt about the splendour of the end-result of Calatayud's begging. The octagonal church designed by the Jesuit Pedro Matas is not only wide and spacious, but has six rectangular side-chapels which contain magnificent examples of Valladolid polychrome sculptured wood, completed in 1702. High up on the walls of the central octagon are eight seventeenth-century paintings showing the story of the translation of the Vulnerata from Cadiz to Madrid and thence to Valladolid.

The contributions for the new chapel came largely from Spaniards,[5] and it was built as much for the use of the town as for the College. In the succeeding years it received many gifts and offerings, and the continued existence of the College through the times when there were few and sometimes no English students is partly explained by the need to keep in being this Spanish shrine with English connections. Public devotion to the statue continued into the nineteenth century, and during the 1840s, as a public statement against the anti-clerical legislation of Mendizábal and Calatrava, the ordination of an English student (John Guest — destined to become Rector of the College) was held in the chapel at a

---

Salamanca 1726, devotes several pages to the Vulnerata and miracles worked through her intercession.
4. *Principios y Progressos de la Milagrosa Fábrica de la Madre de Dios Injuriada. Translación de la Milagrosa Imagen de nuestra Señora La Vulnerata a su nuevo templo — Año de 1679. A 22 de Octobre* (The beginnings and progress of the church of the miraculous statue of the Mother of God, Our Lady Vulnerata. Translation of the miraculous statue of our Lady Vulnerata to the new shrine. 22 Oct. 1679).
5. In the eighteenth century Perry, the first Rector who was a secular priest, wrote into the *Register* beside certain students' names the donations they had sent from England for the new church. See nos 513, 522 and 528.

time when other ordinations were forbidden in Spain on the grounds that there was an over-supply of priests. This event occasioned an outburst of popular Catholic piety directed towards the Vulnerata. The statue remains today in place over the high altar.[6]

Doña Luisa de Carvajal

We come now to the second story. Among the devout Spanish Catholics of Valladolid at the time when the Vulnerata was installed was Doña Luisa de Carvajal y Mendoza.[7] She was one of the rich and pious ladies who undertook to dress the image. As with many other townspeople over the centuries, her devotion to the image was associated with a regard for the former English College students who had suffered in England for their religion. She had read of the martyrdom of Edmund Campion and his companions in a letter she had received from a relative, the former Spanish Ambassador in London, Don Juan de Mendoza. But she was most affected by the account (translated into Spanish) of the life and death of Henry Walpole, who had been on the staff of St Alban's for a short time. Her confessor, a Jesuit, introduced her to the English fathers at the College, and she took up residence in a little house nearby. Like many of her contemporaries, she was much inspired by harrowing details of torture and death, and she conceived a great desire to travel to England and offer her services to former students who were now missionaries in their native land. She had already donated money towards the foundation of a novitiate for English Jesuits in Flanders,[8] and when the

6. Although crowned, the Vulnerata no longer wears a mantle or veil, so the full mutilation and disfigurement are clearly visible.

7. El Licenciado Luiz Munoz, *Vida y Virtudes de la Venerabile Virgen Doña Luisa de Carvajal y Mendoza, su jornada a Inglaterra, y successos en aquel reyno*, Madrid 1632; Lady Georgiana Fullerton, *The Life of Luisa de Carvajal*, London 1873. Of more direct interest to the College is the letter which Fr de Peralta, Rector of St Gregory's, Seville, wrote in 1614 to Fr Rodrigo de Cabredo, former Rector of St Alban's and at the time Provincial in New Spain. Written shortly after Doña Luisa's death, it tells of her life, labours and death in England, and gives an account of the posthumous honours accorded her at the English Colleges of Seville and Valladolid. The College also possesses a life of Doña Luisa written by Fr Michael Walpole. See also Camilo M. Abad, S.J., *Una Misionera Española en la Inglaterra de Siglo XVIII*, and Doña Luisa de Carvajal y Mendoza, *Epistolario y Poesías*, Biblioteca de Autores Españoles, vol. 179. There is a full-length portrait of Doña Luisa in the bottom corridor of the College.

8. See above, p. 37 (note 9), concerning Creswell's use of this money.

peace treaty between England and Spain was signed at the beginning of James I's reign, she set out for England taking with her what remained of her fortune. On arrival she studiously avoided the Spanish colony in London, but found that English Catholics were suspicious of her, and afraid to receive an unknown Spanish woman into their houses. Eventually, at the request of her family in Spain, she was traced by the Ambassador, Don Pedro de Zúñiga, and persuaded to lodge in the embassy itself, where she would be free to visit English Catholics in prison or otherwise in need of help.

When the scare following the Gunpowder Plot had quietened down, she rented a house of her own where she used to entertain.[9] As a Spanish subject there was no question of her being put to death, but on several occasions she was in danger of being deported. Once, after addressing the crowd in Cheapside — she defended the Catholic faith and tried to convert the tradespeople from heresy — she was arrested and taken before the justices of the peace. In her halting English she began comparing King James favourably with Queen Elizabeth, but in so doing she entirely misjudged the mood of the time, since James was not at all popular. Her long black dress and far from pretty features led some to believe that she was a man — a priest in disguise — and she was committed to prison. She begged not to be sent to the common gaol in deference to her sex — the judge replied that she had no need to fear for her virtue as she was so ugly that no man would lay a hand on her. She was eventually released, since at the time Lord Burleigh was anxious not to offend the Spaniards, and returned to her house, her entertaining and her good works of assisting needy Catholics, supplying them with spiritual reading and encouraging young men and women who believed they had a vocation for the religious life by putting them in touch with religious houses on the continent. At Spitalfields she established a small religious community devoted to prayer and almsdeeds, and was again arraigned, this time by the Archbishop of Canterbury, and put in prison. Once more she was released by the good offices of the Ambassador, the Count of Gondomar, but this time she was compelled to reside in the Embassy and negotiations began to return her to Spain. She wrote to the Duke of Lerma to plead with Philip III to allow her to stay, but during this correspondence she died, on 2 January 1614, aged

9. When Robert Drury, a former student at Valladolid, was in prison in 1607, Doña Luisa visited him and discussed the position of Catholics towards the Oath of Allegiance of 1608 (Gaffney, p. 170).

forty-eight. She had wished her body to be taken to Flanders and be buried at the new novitiate she had helped to found, but instead it was returned to Spain by sea and rests today in the Convent of the Incarnation in Madrid. She left behind several religious poems and other writings and, although miracles were reported as a result of her intercession and the cause of her beatification was revived at the beginning of the twentieth century when Cardinal Merry del Val was Secretary of State, very little is heard of her today.

Doña Marina de Escobar

A further link between Spanish and English Catholicism in the seventeenth century was Doña Marina de Escobar. A native of Valladolid, she learnt through her confessor, Fr Luis de la Puente, S.J.,[10] of the troubles afflicting the Catholics in England. At the request of her spiritual directors, she recorded her visions and dreams, and these were incorporated in a *Life* written by Fr de la Puente and completed by Andrés Pinto Ramírez.[11] We read there that she held all nations of the world in her heart, but especially English Catholics.[12] Hearing of the persecution from her conversations with English Jesuit fathers, she was filled with a great desire to help them by alms and prayers. Among her visions of the 1620s was one of visiting England, where she saw a house full of Catholics who were debating whether to leave their homes and farms and make their way to Catholic lands. However, the doors of the house were firmly bolted. Then there was a knock at the door, which caused them to utter sad cries; they did not realise that it was the angels who were knocking. When they opened the door, the room, hitherto dark and gloomy, was flooded with light. They were filled with joy and wished to be crucified by the wicked king and the heretics, along with Christ. On more than one occasion Doña Marina compared the persecution in England with that of Spanish Christians by the Moors; but whereas the Moors only held bodies captive, the heretics were in search of men's souls. But Doña Marina prayed for the conversion and not the destruction of the heretics. On the Prince of Wales's visit to Spain in

10. La Puente was resident at S. Ambrosio and a frequent visitor to St Alban's. His own cause for beatification was introduced in the eighteenth century.
11. *Vida Maravillosa de la Venerable Virgen Doña Marina de Escobar natural de Valladolid, sacada de lo que ella misma escrivió de orden de sus Padres Espirituales*, Madrid 1665.
12. Bk. 2, chapters 13,14,15.

1623 she was only in favour of a marriage if it meant his conversion, and when later, she heard of Charles' death on the scaffold, she was most impressed by the ways of divine justice.

Conclusions

By way of a conclusion to the first part of the history, it is time to discuss the characteristics of these Colleges in the Peninsula which distinguished them from other English Catholic establishments abroad. Although at the beginning, Spain was of strategic importance geographically since it lay on the route from Rome to England and the Low Countries, this position was almost entirely due to the difficulty of crossing France during the wars of religion. Afterwards, when Spain ceased to be on the main line of communication, it had other advantages; its secluded situation provided a better opportunity for quiet study and prayer, and it offered a freedom from civil disorder such as could not be found in France or Flanders.

But these seminaries were also situated in the heartland of England's great political rival, Spain, and the close connection between religious and political issues meant that the protection afforded them by the King of Spain could be a liability when their loyalty and patriotism came to be considered. But there is no evidence that the fact of having studied in Spain ever became, of itself, the basis for a charge of treason. A reason for this is perhaps that although tied to the Spanish monarchy for protection and support, the Colleges would not have survived without the goodwill of the Spanish people. There was hostility to the English nation not only on political but also on religious grounds, and initially the English students were distrusted as spies of a foreign and heretical government. Yet in the end it was due to alms begged throughout Spain that the Colleges were able to become financially viable. Fellow religious feeling of Spanish Catholics for English Catholics overcame any political repugnance, and this Spanish zeal for the spread of the Catholic religion — which was inspired by the King — continued to support these institutions even when there was no longer either desire or expectation of defeating England in war. This link lasted through the years when neither Spain nor England was interested in each other's affairs. There is a parallel between the students and their benefactors. The students, however divided among themselves politically about the role of Spain, agreed as to their calling as missionaries. There was a mutual sharing of religious values that over-rode other more nationalistic motives.

What was the nature of the support given by the Spaniards? The provision by the King and his Council of *viaticum* money for the return journey to England after ordination was maintained almost without interruption, and was not only a practical help but an effectual demonstration of Spain's commitment to provide priests for the English Mission. Of the other benefactions, there were, first, regular monetary gifts of between 2 and 200 ducats a year, a pressing need for the college when, as very often happened, benefactors fell in arrears with their payment.[13] Secondly, there were offerings for Masses, especially annual foundation Masses.[14] Thirdly there was property.[15] Property bequests took the form not only of straightforward gifts of land, houses, farms and so on, but more often of *juros* and *censos*. According to the system operating in this part of Spain, many of the people of Valladolid lived off income they received from those paying what amounted to a perpetual mortgage on their property holdings. It often happened that the College would be given such a *censo*, which meant that it was now entitled to collect this annual rent for itself. This was not an unmixed blessing since there would be times when the tenant was unable to pay, and as the seventeenth century progressed, inflation whittled away the value of this income. Fourthly, the College was granted certain exemptions from tithes (*diezmos*) due to such bodies as the Cathedral Chapter and the University. However, this exemption was liable to be challenged, and it had always to be defended. Finally, in order to encourage prompt payment of donations and to introduce a personal note that related to the main missionary purpose of the College, there was introduced in 1602, at a time when the court was at Valladolid, a system of sponsorship. The *Lista de los Señores que tienen alumnos por hijos en este Colegio Inglés* attached named benefactors to named students. Thus the Duchess of Cea and the Patriarch of Valencia were supporting Fr William Evans; the Countess of Villamediana, Henry More; the Count of Olivares and Don Juan de Tassis, Richard Baynes; Don Antonio de Toledo and the Duke of Lerma, Edmund Worthington; the Duke of Infantado and the Count of

---

13. *Recibos y Gastos*, 6, notes in 1612 those falling behind in payment.
14. Annual Masses were said for King Philip II, Cardinal Quiroga Archbishop of Toledo, Doña Marina de Escobar, the Chapter of the Cathedral of Palencia, Don Pedro López de Ayala Conde de Fuensalida, and the Duke of Sesar. Series I, L5.
15. Don Alfonso Quiñones helped in the purchase of houses and Don Francisco de Reynosa provided furniture. Francisco Sarmiento de Mendoza, Bishop of Jaén, gave 600 crowns a year. Blackfan, *Annales*.

Oropesa, James Pollard; the Count of Lemos and the Duchess of Alba, William Shelley; Gregorio de Tapia and the Bishop of Tarragona, Stephen Chapman.[16]

The less wealthy also supported the College, mainly through their gifts and offerings to the Vulnerata. This link with the people both at the financial and the spiritual level meant that although the Colleges were an English enclave in a foreign land, as were all the overseas English establishments, there was in effect less insularity here than elsewhere.[17] Although the students were all English or Welsh, and often had Englishmen as superiors, the Rector was a foreigner, a Spanish Jesuit; in this St Alban's was different from other Colleges. This was a condition laid down by Philip II, and except for a very short period it was strictly adhered to. The students attended lectures at the Spanish Jesuit College, and the English College was subject to a regular visitation, not from a delegate of the Holy See but from the Spanish Jesuit Provincial who made the decisions about the appointment of confessor, spiritual director, Minister and Rector. This link with the Society ensured that the College, for better or worse, would not be on the periphery of Spanish Catholicism. Although Valladolid was one of the more important towns in Spain at the end of the sixteenth century, it had not the cosmopolitan character of Rome where there were national colleges other than the English one. Neither did Castile resemble the Low Countries where there were many English religious houses in exile. At this period the Scots had not yet arrived in the town, and St Alban's was the only foreign college there, which meant that in its early days it was surrounded on all sides by the popular Catholicism of the last days of Philip II. The condition and practice of religion were not all that different from what the students believed to have prevailed in England before the Reformation and it was this ideal they were hoping to see restored. In contrast to Rome, there was no Papacy to give the

16. The full list is in CRS, 30, pp. xx–xxi. Series II, L2.
17. There are also examples of Valladolid's connections with other English institutions. Although a College for the secular clergy and administered by the Jesuits, former students not only joined orders such as the Dominicans and Franciscans (including the O.F.M. martyr Francis Bell) but were instrumental in the foundation of the English Benedictine Congregation. Furthermore, it fell to the Jesuits at the English College to administer property in Valladolid on behalf of the Brigittine nuns who had fled successively from England to the Low Countries and then to France, and were now established in Lisbon. J.R. Fletcher, *The Story of the English Brigittines of Sion Abbey*, South Brent, Devon 1933.

impression of living in an extraordinary or unique situation. Unlike Douai or Rheims there were not even the occasional heretics apart from those at the English embassy. However, it was precisely this Spanishness of the College that was to bring about a decline in support from home. More than the other colleges on foreign soil, Valladolid suffered the fate of the exile who accommodates too much to his temporary home.

PART TWO
THE COLLEGE UNDER THE SECULAR CLERGY

6

UNDER NEW MANAGEMENT, 1767–1771; THE COLLEGE AND THE EUROPEAN ENLIGHTENMENT

The expulsion of the Jesuits from Spain and the reopening of the College

For a long time the Vicars Apostolic had been dissatisfied with the running of the three English Colleges in Spain. Very few students were going back as priests to work in England. Valladolid had been closed to students during the rebuilding in 1739–56, and since its reopening only five priests had returned for work on the Mission. It was an extremely small community of five Jesuits, five students and three servants. In 1763–4 there was trouble because some students were unwilling to take the missionary oath; these went to St Omer and subsequently joined the Society.

It was in 1767 that the disaster which had already overtaken the Order in Portugal in 1759 and France in 1762 occurred in Spain. On 27 February there was a decree of the King empowering the Count of Aranda[1] to expel the Jesuits from the Kingdom, and on 1 March an instruction was issued on the procedure to be undertaken by the Royal Commissioners in their confiscation of the Society's property. All this was under strict secrecy, and on 20 March Aranda sent sealed orders, which were not to be opened until 2 April, to the mayors of every town in Spain. The King's pragmatic sanction for the expulsion of the regulars of the Company of Jesus from the Kingdom, the occupation of their temporalities, and the prohibition of their re-establishment at any time in the country, was dated 2 April 1767. Accompanied by a detachment of

---

1. It was not Aranda so much as Campomanes who was the predominant influence in the suppression. For the full story see J. Cejudo and T. Egido (eds), *Pedro Rodríguez de Campomanes. Dictamen Fiscal*, Madrid 1977.

troops and witnesses, Andrés Saenz Díez y Durango went to the College on the night of 2 April and took possession.[2] An inventory was made, and when this was completed by 13 or 15 August, Juan González López, Secretary of the Holy Office in Valladolid, became Administrator. On 7 July passports had been issued for the two students and the fact that there were students, however few, did indicate that Valladolid, unlike Seville and Madrid, could claim to be a living College.

Although executed suddenly, the suppression of the order in Spain was not entirely unexpected and the English bishops had had experience of a similar event in the seizure of the College at St Omer in 1762 when France expelled the Society; as a result of that measure St Omer was now under the rule of Douai and the seculars. Thus the English Bishops approached the Ambassador Extraordinary of Spain in London Prince Masserin sometime in early summer of 1767,[3] pointing out that the three Colleges in Spain belonged to the Catholic Church in England.

On 29 June the King's Secretary of State Grimaldi[4] wrote to Masserin of the results of the enquiry into the Colleges with the following information. The three English colleges certainly existed; the College at Madrid had had no students for several years and the revenues were being taken by the Jesuit province of Toledo; a similar situation existed at Seville; at Valladolid there were two students but there were complaints that the Jesuits did not present them with a dogmatic and pastoral theology that was useful for the Mission in England; the examination into the foundation and hence into the ownership of these colleges would proceed; and the English Bishops were allowed to use the mediation of France in their dealings with Spain. The letter was sent to the English Bishops on 21 July, and on the 26th Challoner, Vicar Apostolic of the London District, spoke to Masserin thanking the King for the action, which was 'truly worthy of a Catholic Monarch'. Challoner also took the opportunity to complain of the maladministration, which had meant that at that time there was only one secular priest in the whole of Great Britain who had been a student in the Colleges in Spain. He went on to

2. Not 22 April as stated in CRS, 30, p. 192.
3. Felipe Victorio Amadeo Ferrero de Fiesco, Prince Masserin, Marquis of Crevecoeur, Grandee of Spain, born Madrid 11 October 1713, was nominated Ambassador in England in Feb. 1763, and remained there till 1777. A Morel Fatio, *Recueil des Instructions donnés aux Ambassadeurs et ministres de France*, XII bis: Espagne, vol. 3, Paris 1899, p. 285, speaks of him as having all the spirit of intrigue and pliancy of an Italian.
4. Jerónimo Grimaldi, Marqués de Grimaldi (1706–89), of Genoese origins, succeeded Wall as Minister of State in 1763, resigning in 1776.

expound the need for students to study humanities there, and because the funds were insufficient to cover expenses, the King was asked to establish an annual pension. A further suggestion was that there should in future be one College rather than three, and because Valladolid had the best climate, it was this College that should continue while the revenues from Madrid and Seville were used to support it. The King consulted with his Council[5] on 8 September and the decision was communicated in a letter from Grimaldi to Masserin on 14 September. The three colleges would be merged into the one establishment at Valladolid; all the rents and foundations from Seville and Madrid would be united to those of Valladolid. The clergy of England could, immediately and without publicity,[6] send ten students with a priest as Rector, another priest as Professor of Dogmatic Theology and Polemics, and a third for Humanities and Latin, following the pattern of the English Colleges at Douai Lisbon and Rome. Care should be exercised in choosing the Rector; he was to be an Englishman resident either in England or abroad; but he was to be someone unlikely to attract persecution or jealousy from the British Government, whose whole concern would be to conserve the Catholic religion. 10,000 pesos would be available through the Royal Bank for the cost of travel out to Spain. The decision made by the King and Council closely followed the suggestion made by Challoner's guidelines for staffing. The qualities of the Rector and the need for discretion are clearly from someone in touch with the English situation, but the decision was a royal one and the generous travel allowance was an act of magnaminity by the King. Even though the claims of Challoner and the English Bishops were recognised, they were not the absolute masters of the College and without the King's action the College would have been lost to them.

The next question was how to find a suitable Rector. Philip Mark Perry,[7] a Staffordshire man aged forty-seven, was well known to the Vicars Apostolic. After two years' study at Douai he had been sent to St Gregory's English College in Paris, and at the end of the long course

---

5. The Council of Castile (*Consejo*) was the body responsible under the King for the government of this part of Spain.
6. The need for silence is repeated in a letter from Masserin to Challoner dated 20 Oct. No doubt this, like the use of French mediation, was due to the strained relationship between England and Spain at this time.
7. See G. Anstruther, vol. 4, p. 210, and M.E. Williams, 'Philip Perry, Rector of the English College, Valladolid (1768–1774)' *Recusant History*, vol. 17, pp. 48–66.

obtained his Doctorate of Divinity in May 1754.[8] He returned to England and having acted as chaplain first at Hassop Hall, Derbyshire, and then Heythrop Park, Oxfordshire, he was now living in his native county with Bishop Hornyold at Longbirch near Wolverhampton. Challoner was in communication with him in November, promising that he would be provided with an assistant from Douai. On 7 December Challoner and his coadjutor Talbot[9] wrote to inform the Spanish Ambassador of their choice of Perry, saying that the Professor of Theology would be from Douai and would proceed immediately to Valladolid to begin teaching the two students there; at a later date they would be able to send a Professor of Humanities and some new students. Separate commendatory letters were made out by Talbot and Challoner in favour of Perry, and a joint letter was addressed to the Bishop of Valladolid. On 11 December a passport was signed by the Ambassador enabling him to proceed to Calais, and the next day a further one was issued for his journey to Madrid. He visited the English Colleges at both Douai and Paris,[10] and in company with Joseph Shepherd,[11] the Professor of Theology, set out in January for the 28-day overland journey to Spain.

We can follow Perry's progress from his travel notes. At St Jean d'Angeli he and Shepherd breakfasted on 50 oysters; they stayed two nights at Bordeaux, and by the time they got to Bayonne Perry's breeches needed mending; after a visit to the barber there they set out for Spain. Perry was greatly impressed by the oak forest at Roncevalles, and from Pamplona they went by way of Agreda, 'a large town at the foot of a snowy hill and full of convents'. On arrival at Madrid they spent eighteen days at the Fonda San Sebastián and then moved to stay with a Mr Costely, but they bought their own food so as not to be a burden on their host during the month they were guests in his house. It was during this time that there was a communication on 26 March from Don Pedro Rodríguez de Campomanes, the King's chief executive officer or *Fiscal* in Castile, to the Marqués de Zambrano and another to Don Juan Esteban de Salaverri informing them of Perry's appointment.

8. The obtaining of the doctorate was a comparatively rare occurrence for students of the English College in Paris. CRS, 63, p. 148.
9. James Robert Talbot, Bishop of Birtha and coadjutor to Challoner since 1759. He succeeded as Vicar Apostolic of the London District on Challoner's death in 1781. Anstruther, vol. 4, pp. 268–9.
10. M. Taylor, *The Scots College in Spain*, Valladolid 1971, p. 48. Also Perry's book of expenses, Press A, drawer 7.
11. See Anstruther, vol. 4, p. 242.

Perry, in conjunction with Shepherd, drafted a petition to the King concerning the College's re-establishment. They spent just over seven weeks in Madrid,[12] making certain that when they reached Valladolid they would be able to set to work immediately. For this they needed letters-patent restoring the College to the secular clergy and a testimonial to the *Intendente* of Valladolid confirming Perry in the Rectorship — both of which seem to have been readily granted. They also requested that books, vestments and furniture be sent to Valladolid from Madrid and Seville, that books be acquired for the library and, that they should receive assurances that financial assistance would be given to the professors and students. They also wanted to be sure that if on arrival they found the College empty and bare, a supply of food would be available. Their petition gives the impression that Perry and Shepherd had nothing but the clothes they stood up in, and few if any friends, and had to trust entirely in the assurances of the Vicars Apostolic and the good-will of the King.

Passports were granted to proceed to Valladolid on 12 April and after visiting the Escorial on the way, they arrived at the College on the 15th. Next day they took formal possession and were installed by Angel de Bustamente, *Intendente* of Valladolid; the College, with all its parts and furniture, was handed over to the Rector, but not the Chapel.[13] On the feast of St Anselm of Canterbury, 21 April, after solemn mass said by the Rector, the school of theology was opened and the two students, John Buller of Lancashire and Joseph Addis of Hereford, who had already been in the College for four years, resumed their course under secular masters. On 9 May, the feast of St Gregory Nazianzen, the church and its parts were handed over to the Rector, and on the 12th, the feast of the Ascension, it was solemnly reopened and the parish priest of St John the Baptist sang the Mass before a great crowd of people. On the very day of that solemn Mass, Robert Bannister[14] wrote two letters from Douai, one to Perry and another much more informal one to his former colleague,

12. Letter of Bannister to Shepherd, 12 May 1768.
13. CRS, 30, p. 193. The College was in good order, as Needham later wrote to Perry on 15 August 1768: 'The thunder of the Escurial with a *redde rationem villicationis tuae jam non poteris villicare* was too sudden to allow the good fathers even to descend into their house to gather up their cloaks.'
14. Robert Bannister, born in 1725, taught divinity at Douai for several years, and then after four years on the Mission in Lancashire was recalled to Douai to be Vice President in 1773. However, he was not a success and returned to England the next year. Anstruther, vol. 4, p. 17.

Shepherd. He gave the latest news and gossip, but the most important item was that Mr Douglas[15] was on his way to Spain as the new Professor of Humanities; he had needed much persuasion to accept the post, but he was now on his way accompanied by eight new students.

Although this was undoubtedly good news, Bannister saw possible difficulties:

You know the spirit that now prevails in Douai College is the spirit of popularity, of indulgence, of relaxation, of foppery etc. If then these youths are translated into a college of primitive rigour and discipline, unless by crossing the sea and changing their climate they change their minds too, they will I fear become turbulent and murmurous. I therefore recommend to your consideration that of our divine master; put not new wine into old bottles.

There was further advice from Bannister to Shepherd about teaching theology.

I imagine that neither the capacity nor the proficiency or advancement of your two theologians are such that you need fear them; yet you must study to acquit yourself with dignity.

The new students arrived at Valladolid with Douglas on 27 June. They had come via Bilbao where Talbot had secured a contact, Don Ignacio Fonegra,[16] who could arrange the importation of goods and personnel into Spain.

The link with Douai was particularly close in these early years. Perry was a Paris man, but Shepherd kept in touch for many years with his former Douai staff colleagues and students. The first eight students and three others who joined them in 1769 were from Douai, but later the policy was to recruit students directly from England, no doubt following the advice of Bannister in that letter of 12 May referring to old wine in new bottles. Shepherd expressed similar sentiments in a letter to Perry of 25 November 1769:

Those that come from Douai hither must be courted and caressed, and in short be induced by fair promises to give their consent, which makes them so difficult here, that they are very hard to deal with, which will not be the case if they come from England. Again Douai is in no doubt jealous of excelling as much as can be, so that we must be content with what it will please to send us; which are not

---

15. John Douglas, born in 1743, entered Douai as a student in 1757; date of ordination uncertain. Later became Vicar Apostolic, London district, and died in 1812. See Anstruther, vol. 4, p. 89.
16. Talbot to Perry, 10 June 1768.

always the best as experience has shown. Whereas in England little sharp boys may easily be procured, who as we shall have the forming of them, we may hope with God's grace will turn out well. And in case any should fall then we may hope Douai like a kind mother will lend her helping hand, and send us one or two to fill up the vacancy.[17]

However, the first problem was not with former Douai boys but with one of the two students surviving from Jesuit days. Perry and Shepherd were faced with an issue that was in fact a residue from the Jesuit rule.[18] Early in 1766 the students had been told that they must either take the missionary oath or leave the College. As a result, three decided to leave the College and went to St Omer, where they immediately entered the Society of Jesus. The two who remained, Addis and Buller, took the oath, but before doing so Buller signed a declaration to the effect that, in spite of having taken it, he would still consider himself free to enter a religious order.[19] Buller was close to the Jesuits and indeed he received a letter from the English Provincial, N. Elliot, dated 5 August but this was intercepted by the Rector on 24 August. It appeared from the contents that Buller intended to join the Society and was in fact to be received into it by Elliot. The distrust felt by the secular clergy for the Jesuit system with its alleged laxity can be perceived in a letter written by Bannister to Shepherd on 7 May:

Those two remnants you found at St Alban's should in my opinion be dismissed, if they do not give very good marks of sincere and solid piety. I suppose they go and confess in town, and God knows what kind of directors they choose or find — perhaps *toties quoties* gentlemen, who go no further than hearing the customary roll and giving a slight penance once and sending away with absolution and peace that is useless to the receiver and noxious to the giver. You may depend upon it young ecclesiastics in such hands have either no vocation, or will soon lose it.

It was clear that a new non-Jesuit spirituality from Douai was to be introduced into the College, and there was to be no place for such as Buller. Buller wrote to Perry on 27 August asking leave to go, and

---

17. This dissatisfaction with Douai was to be shared by others later in the century. See D. Milburn, *History of Ushaw College*, Ushaw 1964, pp. 12–18. Also below, p. 111.
18. CRS, 30, p. xl, and above, p. 59.
19. CRS, 30, p. xlvi. It is clear from the Archives of both Valladolid (Series III, L4) and Ushaw (UCM, III, 47) that Perry made careful transcripts from documents he discovered pertaining to the Jesuit administration of the College.

asking for a written statement of what Perry had said to him by word of mouth, namely that the oath he had taken left him free to enter a religious order where he could still serve the Mission. In reply Perry said he would release him as far as lay in his power from the obligation of staying in the College,

. . . . provided you go to England and accommodate your affair with the Bishops there, and as this seems to be all that you want on my part, more I shall not give, especially as what you add concerning your oath was grounded on a false exposition since you hid from me the circumstances of the explication given of your oath by the General of the Society, according to which explication your three other companions refused, and you and Joseph Addis took the path as I find since your departure hence. Now the concealing this, my dear sir, was neither fair nor generous acting, this therefore, my dear sir, is out of the case.

But it was not to be simply a matter of Buller leaving or changing his residence; Perry intended to make an example of him by expulsion. He considered he had no signs of a religious vocation; indeed there were signs to the contrary, and he was a bad influence on the new students, quite apart from the letter he had received from Fr Elliot and his secret dealings with the Society. But before even the Rector's word became effective, the matter had to be laid before Bustamente, the *Intendente* of the town, communicated to the Council, and the sentence confirmed by Aranda, who ordered that he leave the Kingdom within fifteen days.[20] Buller left on 7 September carrying a letter to Bishop Challoner. Whatever Perry may have thought of him, Buller wrote a letter from Bilbao containing no note of acrimony whatsoever; the writer reports his safe arrival and sends his best wishes to Shepherd, Douglas and the rest of the community.

The characters and personalities of Perry, Shepherd and Douglas

The temperaments of Perry, Shepherd and Douglas were the cause of several differences concerning the governance of the College. On 12 May 1768, when Douglas was about to join the staff, Bannister wrote to Shepherd from Douai giving as one of his reasons for being reluctant to come that 'he had I know not what notions of you, or of your passionate behaviour.' Bannister, a friend of Shepherd, had something to say about Douglas' character as well.

20. CRS, 30, p. 195.

He is young and has a great narrowness of mind and thinking, as yet: such persons stick close to their own few ideas, and to try to dissuade them directly not to cleave to their own preconceived and narrow notions, is the way to throw them entirely off their hinges and to get their ill will for one's pains.

But Bannister was concerned not only for the way that Shepherd and Douglas might react to each other, but he was aware of certain aspects of Perry's character too. He wrote on 7 August 1768: 'If you and Mr Douglas should be driven away by his moroseness and overbearing there would be an end to our new settlement, for I think none of our people would in any account be prevailed upon to live with him, after you.' But this incompatibility could have more serious effects on the administration of the College.

You tell me that rules are given you by the Court: but if the Doctor models them and gets the royal sanction, you will be, after all your caution, taken in fetters. I hope the recurrence of all three will be required by the wise Spaniards, before any regulation be passed into law, and then if you and Mr Douglas are of one mind, and appear to say and do nothing through passion or partiality but to judge and act candidly and equitably, you will gain your point. In my opinion considering what we clergy have suffered by trusting monies and books of account to one individual, the Spaniards cannot do us a greater service than ordering (as it is done at St Omer's) accounts to be kept and inspected and examined *communi concilio*: and that no act or deed be valid or of force, to which all three have not given free assent, or at least two out of three. As you do much commend the wisdom and penetration of the Spaniards (which I am very well persuaded of by innumerable examples of illustrious men of that nation) I do not doubt but they will perceive then through respect to our bishops they will support him in his station: but it is to be hoped provision will be made against the effects of mal-administration.

Perry too had his friendly correspondent, Needham,[21] then living in Paris. In a letter written on 15 August he remarked that he had heard of some differences between Perry and Shepherd. This trouble came to the ears of Challoner, who wrote in a letter to them both on 28 October 1768:

I should be exceedingly sorry that the common enemy should put a stop to a work begun upon such good foundation, disappoint all our expectations, and even blast all hopes of any future progress, by stirring up amongst superiors the

---

21. Was this the same man as the distinguished priest-scientist? Anstruther, vol. 4, p. 195.

evil spirit of contention and dissension so irreconcilable with the spirit of Jesus Christ and his favourite virtues of charity, humility and meekness and peace.

There were further misunderstandings when Perry went to Madrid on College business. Douglas did not want to spend the summer with the rest of the College at the country house at Portillo, and in 1769 and 1770 he refused to go there. In Perry's absence, Shepherd had more administrative work to do, and wanted Perry to get another man to teach divinity; Perry replied that the Vicars Apostolic in England would not allow a further member of staff. During this period regular correspondence passed between Perry in Madrid and Shepherd in Valladolid. Shepherd was concerned about Perry's health; Perry relied on Shepherd to administer the property and make purchases of land with the money that was becoming available from the sale of property in Madrid. The letters were businesslike in tone, but in November 1770 a further misunderstanding arose when Shepherd complained to Perry that he was showing preference to Douglas: 'If you don't find my presence at St Alban's agreeable let me know it.' On 28 November Perry defended himself against a charge of partiality and treated Shepherd to a spiritual talk on bearing his cross.[22] There is nothing very remarkable or unusual in the fact that there were differences between these three members of staff beginning a new venture in a strange country, since all were under considerable pressure. What makes these records of special interest are the psychological insights of Bannister and spiritual insights of Challoner and Perry.

Perry's business in Madrid, 1769–1771

On 25 March 1769 licence was granted from the Count of Aranda for Perry to go to Madrid, and he left Valladolid on 30 March.[23] He was to spend the next two years away from the College — only returning on 22 March 1771 — and the main reason for this absence was to attend to the disposal of College property in Madrid.

On his departure for the Capital the situation seemed to be as follows. The English had full possession of the College and church in Valladolid

22. For further information on these differences, see CRS, 30, pp. xlviii, xlvix, li.
23. In his book of expenses, there is further information about the journey to Madrid; he crossed the Guadarramas in deep snow with a strong wind that caused the snow to drift. In Madrid his expenses included blankets, galoshes and books.

and of the country house at Portillo. The College of St George and other property in Madrid were to be put up for sale according to the agreement with the Council concerning the merger of the three English Colleges into one establishment; the purchaser was the Duke of Alba.[24]

Property orginally belonging to the Jesuits (not to the College) in the Valladolid area which had been confiscated at the Suppression was up for sale. This and similar property became a suitable object to be purchased with the money accruing from the Madrid sale. Shepherd attended and made bids at the Valladolid property auctions, informing Perry by letter of what was available and asking what he should bid for. From this correspondence we learn something of the state of the property market at this time. Shepherd often found himself bidding against 'Indians';[25] few others seemed able to afford any purchase. The purchase best known to present students of the College was the property at Viana which was finally acquired towards the end of 1770 and which has for many years been the country house. It was originally a vineyard and Shepherd was rather reluctant to make the investment, but Perry persuaded him to buy, which he did for 104,500 reales.[26] The sum at Shepherd's disposal was considerable and from a letter he wrote to Perry on 4 August 1770 it appears that he had already spent 1,185,676 reales and still had 114,324 in hand.

The College of St Gregory and other property in Seville was less easily recoverable. The King, before receiving the reclamation of the English and still ignorant of the true ownership of the College, had allowed the Medical Society of Seville[27] to take temporary possession of it for their meetings until he decided what should be done finally with the

---

24. Fernando de Silva Alvarez de Toledo (1714–76), Duque de Huéscar, was Spanish Ambassador to Paris, 1746–9, and Director of the Spanish Academy, 1754–76. A figure of the Enlightenment and a friend of J.J. Rousseau, he reappeared on the political scene after the '*motín*' of 1766. J. Sarrailh, *L'Espagne Eclairée*, p. 315; Laura Rodríguez Díaz, *Reforma e Ilustración en la España del Siglo XVIII. Pedro Rodríguez de Campomanes*, Madrid 1975. Only many years later (1802) did the descendants of the Duke of Berwick, the natural son of James II, enter into the Alba line.

25. 'Indians' were Spaniards who had made fortunes in the American colonies (cf. 'nabobs' in 18th-century England).

26. Earlier in the year (Feb.-March 1770) Shepherd had the idea of buying a flock of sheep which would provide cheaper mutton for the College.

27. Originally founded in 1697 despite opposition from the University of Seville. The building up and encouragement of such scientific societies was part of Charles III's scheme for university reform. Antonio Hermosilla Molina, *Cien años de Medicina Sevillana*, Seville 1970.

building.[28] The long litigation for the recovery of the Seville property deserves a chapter on its own, but during these years the College, after some difficulty, managed to obtain a yearly alms from the Cathedral Chapter of Seville. Originally this was a donation to St Gregory's for the maintenance of the Catholic religion in England, but when St Gregory's became perpetuated in St Alban's, Valladolid, the money was directed to St Alban's.

Perry's concern was not merely for buildings and property but for their contents as well. He wrote on 26 July 1769: 'I am now busy at St George's. The pictures are put in three large cases: three or four more will come on Thursday to put up the altar of Nuestra Señora de Aránzazú. Next will come the books, which I shall stow in the old boxes found in the College.' Perry was a collector of books before he came to Spain;[29] his concern now was with the College rather than his personal library. Some books he had sent out from England 'all Mr Challoner's works of which many duplicates, triplicates etc. and six copies of "Ye Sinners Guide" '.[30] But there were many books in Spain that would be important acquisitions for the library. Among the works he was seeking were the one-volume life of Doña Luisa de Carvajal, the two-volume life of Doña Marina de Escobar,[31] the new French Benedictine edition of the Fathers,[32] and collections of acts of General and Spanish Church Councils as well as the *Corpus Historicum Hispanicum*. He petitioned for certain volumes from the former Jesuit houses of S. Ambrosio and S. Ignacio in Valladolid and from the houses in Medina del Campo, Villagarcía and Palencia on the ground that they had originally belonged to St Alban's, but under the Jesuit superiors had been loaned out or given to these other houses of the Society.[33] He was partly successful in his request,[34] but there

---

28. The ultimate destiny of St. Gregory's was to be a College of Nobles; the rights being granted to the Society of Medicine were a temporary measure. F. Aguilar Piñal, *La Universidad de Sevilla en el siglo XVIII*, Seville 1969, p. 183; also Series II, L4; CRS, 30, pp. xlvi–vii.
29. Talbot to Perry, 10 June 1768.
30. See below, p. 103, for Perry's reading.
31. The complete list which is headed by these two works is to be found in Series III, L2.
32. Shepherd told him that the fact that the College already had older editions of the Fathers would be a hindrance to his hopes of securing the Maurist editions which were in great demand.
33. For the contents of the Jesuit libraries see Perry-Shepherd Correspondence, 12 Aug. 1769, 16 Sept. 1769, 10 May 1770.
34. An Order-in-Council of 15 July 1769 restored some of the S. Ambrosio books.

Above: the principal street frontage of the College (after restoration).
Below: the Patio.

Above: interior view of the Chapel dome. *Below*: general view of the Chapel.

Above: the Martyr's Corridor, so named from the portraits.
Below: the Refectory.

P. Henrique Walpole ñal de Norfolk ministro de est Cole holuiendo á ãngĩatte a predicar la Fé despues de varias vezes atormentado por los hereges, fue arrastrado y ahorcado medio viuo del ahorca des entrañado y hecho quartos. a 7. de abril de 1595

EDOUARD (AMBROSIO) BARLOW de la orden de S. Benito nacio cerca de Manchester, se ordenó en este collegio, preso muchas vezes por la Fé y al fin ahorcado en Lancaster el 10 Sbre 1641

Thomas Benstead alis Hunt
Angliae, Wintoniensis Dioecesis Norfolciensis con-
discipul. admissus fuit in hoc collegium 12 May
1592 in Seminario 12 Nouembris eiusdem anni
ad collegium Anglicanum Hispalense translatus fuit
postquam emisit est in Angliam ubi glorios martyr
occubuit anno 1600 in ense Iulij. Vivent siue [...]
Varios Protomartyr hujus et Hispal. Collegii.

Portraits of (above left) St Ambrose Barlow
and (above) St Henry Walpole. Left: extract
from the College register for Thomas Benstead.

Left: Our Lady Vulnerata. *Right:* the High Altar of the Chapel.

Right: the 'Big Library'.
Below: the modern working
library. *Bottom*: the
communications studio.

Above: the Country House at Viana de Ceya. *Below*: figure of St George over the High Altar, Chapel, of the Residence at Sanlúcar de Barrameda.

Above: portrait of Monsignor Edwin Henson. *Below*: the belfry of the College Chapel.

was the expected delay in dealing with Seville.[35] Finally in 1771, after making up a list of his desiderata from the catalogue of the library at St Gregory's in Seville, Perry discovered that the best volumes had already been donated to the University of Seville. Realising that it would now be hard to recover them, he restricted his claim to works he considered absolutely necessary, and to compensate for the others to which he considered himself entitled, he laid claim to books from the former Jesuit libraries at S. Ambrosio and S. Ignacio in Valladolid.

Negotiations with the University

Thus Perry had acquired the College and its property, and could look to a certain measure of financial stability. He had a team of professors and a number of students. What was to be the relationship with the University? Whatever may have been his and Shepherd's experience at the English Colleges in Paris and Douai, the case was somewhat different at Valladolid, different even from the situation as it was when the Jesuits were in control.

Perry's arrival at Valladolid coincided with changes in the system of higher learning. The expulsion of the Jesuits, which had been the occasion of the new management at the English College, was closely connected with the reforms of Charles III in the universities. The Society was looked upon as one of the obstacles to Charles' grand schemes, since it represented undesirable privilege and power. Not only did it control much of the teaching in the arts faculties but it held several chairs in theology throughout the kingdom. Some of the ideas propagated, notably by the theologian Francis Suárez on the lawfulness of tyrannicide in certain circumstances, were not pleasing to the King. The expulsion of the Jesuits made it possible for the universities to be put under more direct government control.[36] It was now the Council (Consejo) that

35. For the general situation at Seville and the plan to set up a library and the exemption of books belonging to the English and Irish Colleges, see Aguilar Piñal, op. cit., p. 462.
36. For Charles III's scheme to reform the Spanish seminaries and the cédula of 1768, 'Erección de seminarios conciliares para la educación del clero', see F.M. Hernández, 'La Formación del Clero en los siglos XVII y XVIII' in Ricardo García Villoslada (dir.), Historia de la Iglesia in España, vol. II, Madrid 1979, esp. pp. 557–9. The Spanish seminaries as well as the English College were under the control of the King who appointed the Rector. Some were affiliated to the universities, and

provided for chairs, and the Rector had to give an account of his administration to the *Fiscal*. The mood in university circles in the 1760s was one of reorganisation and planning so as to improve standards, incorporate new subjects into the curriculum, reduce the number of universities and colleges that did not meet the new requirements, and even restrict the entrance of students into higher learning since this was affecting the country economically by drawing people away from agriculture and commerce.[37]

As a place of learning and education the English College could not escape these measures. All that Perry wanted was to reproduce the situation of the other English Colleges administered by the secular clergy in Paris and Douai on to Spanish soil — an English college in exile, with the privileges and exemptions which this entailed. But the government, glad as it was that the Jesuits no longer administered the College was anxious that it should not fall short of the higher standards now being demanded, and that any privileges granted should not encourage Spanish religious houses to demand similar rights. The tone of the Perry–Shepherd correspondence often indicates that the English thought the *Consejo* was being niggardly; it was difficult for them, preoccupied as they were with re-establishing the College, to take note of the general situation and the prevailing abuse whereby members of convents and colleges were doing courses at home and getting degrees under false pretences and without adequate external scrutiny. Once it was clear that Perry wanted the students to take the '*Acta*' in public and thus be open to inspection and examination, Campomanes the *Fiscal* was friendly — [38] remarkably so considering the strained political relations at that time between Spain and England.

At Valladolid it was the College of Santa Cruz[39] that was fighting for

academic standards were generally high. However they wanted to liberate themselves from the royal power, and in 1779 were once more allowed to nominate a Rector.

37. See A. Alvarez de Morales, *La Ilustración y la Reforma de la Universidad en la España del Siglo XVIII*, Madrid 1971.

38. The *Consejo* was eager to restore this custom which had fallen out of use and was substituted by '*pasos*' in private establishments. Mariano Peset Reig and José Luis Peset Reig, *El Reformismo de Carlos III y la Universidad de Salamanca*, Salamanca 1969.

39. The Colegio Mayor de Santa Cruz, founded by Cardinal Mendoza in 1479, was one of the institutions known as *colegios mayores* founded in the fifteenth and sixteenth centuries in the major university towns to give lodging and support to poor

its privileges. Shepherd wrote to Perry that every doctor was now obliged to have an '*Acta*' once a year and the *cathedraticus* twice a year.[40] However, the government-inspired university reform was complicated by the fact of the Rector of the University at this time being a Santa Crucian and the son of the *ministro decano* of Madrid, Don Pedro Colón; he defended the privilege of Santa Cruz for a right to sit '*in banco doctorum*'. 'He mightily disobliged all the professors by complaining of them to the Council that they were *flojos* [lazy] etc, so that on the eighteenth [May] was published a decree of His Majesty with some rule in order to reduce them to diligence.' The professors complained to the Council and on 8 July Shepherd wrote to Perry:

The Council's answer came last Monday and by its determination the poor *Colegiales* are reduced to the rank of common *licenciados*, without any preferences at all, in so much that any doctor can take any of them to defend under him, which you may be sure will be no small mortification to them that used to lord it in presiding before. It seems the university was afraid of them, no one daring to speak against them before, so that the Council expresses its wonder there should be only one doctor to resist their unjust pretensions. This is verifying what the Salamanca Irish students said that Campomanes said he would make them *menores*.

These events were followed with close interest by Shepherd and Perry because the English College too had its privileges.[41] The Rector of the parish of S. Juan had sung the inaugural Mass in the College chapel, and very soon the parish was claiming spiritual jurisdiction over the College now that the regulars were no longer in charge there. The new Bishop of Valladolid, Manuel Rubén de Celis,[42] wrote to Perry on 4 April 1769 requesting a copy of the Bull of Foundation and asking if there was any privilege exempting the College from the spiritual jurisdiction of the parish of S. Juan. After enquiries Shepherd learnt that 'S. Cruz is not at

---

students. In time these colleges had become corrupt and in the power of the second sons of wealthy landowning families, and their graduates formed an aristocracy who despised other graduates as '*manteístas*' (those who wore gowns). Campomanes had been a '*manteísta*'. The educational reform of Charles III attempted to get these colleges back to their original ideal.

40. Shepherd to Perry, 27 May 1769.
41. There is mention in Campomanes' *Dictamen*, 308, of the College of St Alban (wrongly called the Irish College) possessing certain privileges. This document predates the expulsion of the Jesuits.
42. Isidoro Cossío y Bustamante, Bishop since 1754, had resigned on 26 Nov. 1768.

all exempted from parochial jurisdiction. The custom is, that at Easter the curate [i.e. *cura*, parish priest] comes and says mass in their chapel and communicates them; and as to their buryings, you know, they are buried in the Carmen Descalzo. But then the reason is quite different as it is not often they have any priests among them, how is it possible they should pretend that privilege; and in all probability had they ever asked for it they would have obtained it. It is certain that some if not all, the colegio maiores [sic] of Salamanca have that privilege.'[43]

The English College did obtain a confirmation of its privileges and exemptions on 8 July.[44] Yet it was perhaps not surprising that this decision was ignored in practice[45] and it was not till 29 November 1772 that a more effectual rescript came from Propaganda Fide empowering the Rector to appoint a student priest as *parochus* (parish priest) of the College.[46] There were certain privileges Perry wished to obtain from the University, and he drafted a letter stating his views on 22 April 1769.[47] He wanted the courses pursued by students of his College to be recognised so that if there were any individuals whom the superiors considered likely to graduate in either arts or theology, they could do so without any further formality than performing public '*Acta*' in the university. This request was related to another concerning the teaching staff at the English College. It was his wish that any professors who had completed their courses elsewhere should be regarded as graduates of Valladolid; no more would be required of them beyond performing certain public '*Acta*' at the University. In November Perry drew up a formal petition addressed to the Rector of Valladolid University.[48]

While Perry was in Madrid during October and November, Shepherd kept him informed of the progress of the negotiations. The University, it appeared, was ready to accede to Perry's requests except that it insisted that the divinity and philosophy schools should be held in the university and not at home in St Alban's.[49] The Supreme Senate (*Consejo*) for its part ordered that the *alumni* and *graduandi* were to be matriculated, that they were to dispute at the University, and that the *licenciados* were to go to

43. Shepherd to Perry, 15 July 1769.
44. CRS, 30, pp. xlix–li, for documents and a full account of this dispute.
45. CRS, 30, pp. lii, liii.
46. Series III, L5.
47. L2.
48. L2.
49. Shepherd to Perry, 25 Oct. 1769.

the *sabatinos [lectures] de teología dogmática* that were to be held in St Alban's.[50]

Eventually Perry's letter of 1 November was presented and read in full *claustro* at the University, but with no apparent result; the matter was to be referred to the Council. Shepherd remarked: 'Nothing can be done without money! I fancy they will inform you in their answer to yours what has been their reason for its resolution.'[51] Perry replied[52] on receiving the University Rector's acknowledgement of his request:

You are mistaken, in thinking the University gives any reasons. The whole is comprised in eight lines and it saith, my letter has been read in full claustro, after which it adds *Quae sunt indulgenda et Religioni proficia, indulgebunt. Quae non sunt indulgenda utpote contraria aut inutilia, totis viribus repugnabunt. Regi tamen voluntati ut par est, obedient. Vale.*[53] This is all as you see dry enough and desires to go against the King's will, if they could; it's a wonder that in such a body of men, no one could be found zealous and compassionate enough to stand up for a poor and distressed church, such as ours is . . . .

Shepherd continued in his belief, based on the *Mostense's*[54] account of the meeting, that it was because money was not offered that the requests were refused. There was evidently a good deal of misunderstanding here. The case of St Alban's was to be treated like any other request, and the brusqueness of Perry's approach was not appreciated. Moreover, pleading poverty was likely to have the opposite effect to that intended. For economic reasons the policy was to encourage colleges for nobles or for the rich who would be able to contribute something of their own towards the upkeep.[55]

Emmanuel Díez, the Professor of Rhetoric, wrote Perry a warm and encouraging letter in Latin just before Christmas 1769.[56] He said that although 'our Academy' might not approve, this was no reason for him to despair — he ought to continue to press his case strongly. The *Consejo* could not be unaware that there was a difference of opinion among

---

50. Shepherd to Perry, 4 Nov. 1769.
51. Shepherd to Perry, 18 Nov. 1769.
52. Perry to Shepherd, 22 Nov. 1769.
53. 'Those things that should be conceded as beneficial to religion they will concede. What are not to be conceded, since they are contrary or of no advantage, they will refuse with all their might. But, as is only right, they will obey the King's wishes.'
54. The *Mostense* was apparently the professor of rhetoric, Emmanuel Díez, who was to advise Perry to offer to pay the customary fees and taxes.
55. See A. Alvarez de Morales, loc. cit.
56. 23 Dec. 1769.

doctors on this matter. He himself was not present when the request was discussed, and he said that Perry could use his name when Campomanes had to deal with the matter. He then went on to examine two points of the petition. He advised Perry not to insist on schools at home. As St Alban's was very near the University, there could be no question of time being wasted in travelling. It would be of advantage to the students to learn Spanish by mixing with Spanish people, and by attending the *studium generale* they would be better equipped to combat heresy. Secondly, he asked Perry not to insist on academic degrees being conferred completely gratis. The giving of such degrees would perhaps be infrequent if they were free; they would not be valued highly, and he would be admitted to the Academy with greater willingness and more quickly if he were to make an offering. There was no need to worry or plead poverty for the College, if they dealt with him with the same indulgence as they dealt with others in this kingdom. He concluded with a fulsome expression of good wishes, and assured Perry of the King's generosity and Campomanes' concern for all scholars.

After Christmas Perry drafted a reply[57] pointing out that he was not seeking degrees by private study alone, since there would be public '*Acta*' in the College each year, and at the end of the course a Public Act or examination would take place in the University. But lectures at home were essential to avoid waste of time and to keep the strict discipline necessary for future missionaries. The College was a delicate child that needed protection from harmful outside influences. Such a reason for not attending the University was also adduced by certain religious orders, and it was so as to preserve the cloister that they had been given exemption,[58] but the new element introduced by Perry was that of a missionary college claiming exemption. It was the maintenance of the Douai system that was at stake, the preservation of an English enclave in a foreign country. Any knowledge of the Spanish tongue that would be obtained by attending the public schools, he said, would never compensate for the perils and risks of mixing with outsiders. In the past, pupils who went to public schools '*didicerunt forte linguam hispanicam, sed nonne et simul didicerunt, non dico hispanorum sed certe quarundam sociorum mundanos et pessimos mores?*'[59] He said he had never yet met a Spanish

57. 15/16 Feb. 1770.
58. A. Alvarez de Morales, op. cit., pp. 90 and 91n.
59. '. . . . perhaps learned the Spanish tongue, but didn't they also learn the worldly and wicked habits of some of their colleagues, not necessarily Spanish ones?' This deliberate policy of isolating an English College from surrounding 'foreign'

scholastic whom he judged helpful in combatting heresy. As for academic degrees, he was only making two requests: first, for a reduction in the huge taxation; this was for the good of the Academy, since only the rich could become members and the poor however great their talents, were excluded; and secondly, for a reduction of tax in consideration of the special circumstances of his pupils.

Later the same year,[60] Shepherd spoke of a universal enmity in the town against the College:

They imagine that as we have come in these reformation times that we are to be the models of the university, this frets them. For this reason, I think it highly necessary we should conform to their method. I do not mean in teaching what they teach, nor of only having only two questions in their conclusions, these are only material points even among themselves, but as to the method of defensions. This I conceive can neither patronise ignorance nor idleness. As their method in substance comes to the same as ours, the manner of defending at Paris is different in form from that at Douai. Yet Douai has produced and daily produces very great divines; and has the vanity to look upon its method as good as that of Paris and would think it odd was anyone from Paris to offer to set up the method used in the university. As the country is established by Royal Authority, I think you have acted very wisely in not dedicating the conclusions to the Fiscal, another opportunity will not be wanting of showing our gratitude to so great a benefactor.

This letter of Shepherd implies that the *Fiscal* and *Consejo* were backing St Alban's as a reformed College, and yet allowing it privileges which exempted it from payment of fees and allowed at least some lectures (*sabatinos*) at home. To appease the University, Shepherd was suggesting that they conform to the methods in vogue there, namely the use of *método parisino* which had been in use in Spain since the sixteenth century but was not used at Douai. The chief characteristic of the 'Paris method' was that the allocated hour was divided into half an hour's exposition by the *cathedraticus* and half an hour of questions put to and discussed among the students. At Douai the whole period was taken up by the lecture of the master.[61]

An example of the delicacy of the situation in which Perry and Shepherd found themselves was the incident in 1770 when the royal

---

influences was also pursued by Dr Witham, President of Douai, 1715–38, CRS, 28, p. vi.

60. Shepherd to Perry, 12 May 1770.

61. For a general description of studies at Douai see CRS, 63, pp. 139–42.

prerogatives were attacked in a thesis proposed at the University.[62] Shepherd recounted the story to Perry,[63] since it concerned personalities like Díez who were known to him and whose views were to be taken seriously by the College. What happened was this. José Isidro de Torres, a calced Carmelite, defended a thesis, with leave of the Council, in which he asserted that ecclesiastical immunity was *ex benignitate principum* and not *de jure divino*. This regalist position was opposed by the University with the exception of Díez, the professor of Rhetoric who had written the letter of advice to Perry the previous Christmas. Some days later a young bachelor defended a thesis contrary to Torres with the approval of the University. He had hard words not only against Torres, but against the Government. Even though Díez was on his side, Torres could not get redress from the University. The President of the Council intervened; he went in person to the University, applauded Díez for his stand, reprimanded Dr Pedro Martín Ufano who had approved the conclusions, and deprived him both of his office as Dean of Canon Law and of his Chair.

The struggle to obtain permission to have lectures at home and not be forced to attend the public schools at the University continued for several years. When the new College statutes appeared in June 1770, certain concessions seem to have been made. In the third chapter of the constitutions, *'De Studiis'*, it was stated that lectures and the organisation of studies were an internal affair of St Alban's; they were to be according to the *método parisino*. The whole tenor of the section reads as if lectures were in the house, yet after Perry's return from Madrid in 1771, a further attempt was made to get the students to attend lectures at the University.[64] Perry had to write to Bishop James Talbot in London saying he must draw up a letter to the Rector and Doctors of the University to back the petition he had already made that they should conduct themselves at Valladolid as at Douai, namely with schools at home. Of course there would be public examinations and defensions of theses. There would have to be another letter to the *Fiscal*, since he too was of the opinion that they should attend the University. On 29 November 1772 a rescript was published from Clement XIV through

---

62 For this incident see also M. Pelayo, *Historia de los Heterodoxos*, 2nd edn, reprinted, Madrid 1955, bk. 6, ch. 2, 2, vol. I, pp. 196–7; J. Sarrailh, *L'Espagne Eclairée*, Paris 1964, p. 199; E. Appolis, *Les Jansenistes espagnols*, Bordeaux 1964, p. 97.

63 Shepherd to Perry, 22 Sept. 1770.

64 CRS, 30, pp. liii, liv.

Propaganda Fide granting Perry's request, and this obtained the royal *exequatur* on 25 March 1775.[65]

Scots and Irish

As well as the three English Colleges at Valladolid, Madrid and Seville there were also Scots and Irish Colleges in the Peninsula, and during Perry's rectorship there were not inconsiderable relationships between the three nations. When Perry and Shepherd first arrived, they found that there were three Irishmen resident at the College in Seville.[66] This was contrary to the College constitution, not so much because of their nationality as because they did not intend to work on the Mission in England or Wales, for which purpose the College had been established. Shepherd expressed the need to get them among their own countrymen at the College in Salamanca,[67] and on 18 February 1770 the Council made a decision concerning the expenses of the three Irish students found at St Gregory's, Seville, at the time of the Jesuits' expulsion. Another decision on 25 June 1770[68] was that St Alban's should pay for the support of the Irish student, Nicholas Boylan, originally an *alumnus* of Seville and now at the Irish College, Salamanca.

Perry was informed of this decision, as also was Bustamente the *Intendente* of Valladolid. On 1 July Perry drafted a protest at having to provide this pension of 2,990 reales per annum,[69] in consequence of which the Council modified the order on 14 July, Campomanes pointing out that the pension was to be paid only so that Boylan could complete his course

65. CRS, 30, p. lv.
66. For details, names etc. see Aguilar Piñal, op. cit., p. 494. In fact it seems to have been customary in the eighteenth century for Irish students to be accepted at St Gregory's, Seville. See Anstruther, 4, p. vii.
67. Series III, L3. However, it should be remembered that Salamanca had been taken away from the Irish. The Irish Bishops petitioned the Royal council of Castile for the return of their College on 19 June 1774. Later, in 1790, the Rectors of the English and Scots Colleges were instructed to assist the Rector of the Irish College in Salamanca to draw up new statutes on the model of the English and Scots establishments. Shepherd, then Rector of the English College, pointed out in a letter to the Marqués of Murillo the reasons why there could not be complete uniformity between the English, Scots and Irish Colleges. Series III, L11.
68. According to Aguilar Piñal, op. cit., p. 494, Nicholas Boylan was English, and there was another student, Mateo Boylan, who was Irish.
69. Series III, L3.

in theology, and that it was only to be effective from 1 April.[70] Perry and Shepherd were distrustful of the activities of the Irish at their two Colleges at Alcalá and Salamanca; in particular they were suspicious of Irish schemes to take over the now vacant Scots College in Madrid.[71] Since 1734 there had been no`students resident at this College, the revenues going to the upkeep of twelve Scots students at Douai. The skeleton staff remaining at Madrid were expelled in 1767 with the rest of the Jesuits, but the Scots Vicars Apostolic did not move swiftly enough to cope with the new situation. A certain Dr O'Ryan, an Irish priest, was delegated by his hierarchy to recover the Colleges of his nation. This he proceeded to do through a sub-committee of the council of Castile known as the 'extraordinary council'.[72] But he also received from this same extraordinary council permission to unite and incorporate the Scots College in Madrid with the Irish College in Alcalá on the grounds that since there were so few Catholics in Scotland no Scottish students could be expected, and that anyway most of the priests working in Scotland were Irish. As a result the house, furnishings, sacred vessels and vestments which had been stored in the Scots College were taken to Alcalá, along with a chest of the money collected from rents of the tenants of the property belonging to the Scots.

No Spaniard or Irishman informed anyone in Scotland of these decisions and developments, but Perry got to know about them. He was especially vigilant since on his journey out to Valladolid he had passed through Douai and Paris, and been asked by Robert Grant and John Gordon, the Principals of the Scots Colleges in those places, to look into the matter of Scottish property in Madrid. On 27 March 1768 Gordon urged that the Scottish Bishops should send out an agent at once, to be followed by a superior and students later, and in the mean time make Dr Perry their procurator in Spain. In July Perry was empowered to act in the name of the Vicars Apostolic of the Lowland and Highland Districts. The Scots sent a petition for the restoration of their College, but when it eventually arrived in Madrid it seems to have been misunderstood as a plea for the sort of action already taken by Dr O'Ryan.

The Spanish Ambassador here has signified to the Scotch that their petition is granted and that their house at Madrid is united to the Irish house at Alcalá etc.

---

70. Series III, L3.
71. Maurice Taylor, *The Scots College in Spain*, pp. 47 ff.
72. This sub-committee was especially concerned with the affairs of the now suppressed Jesuits.

In consequence of which Mr Grant at Douai has been here and has agreed with the said Ambassador to send an agent to Spain to transact their affairs. Which gentleman may probably conduct the three new subjects you petition for.[73]

Perry was getting anxious because of the delay and urged haste.[74] To both him and Shepherd the villains of the piece were not the Spaniards but the Irish. Shepherd wrote to Perry, who was in Madrid, concerning the Scots,[75] 'whom I beg for God's sake you would not neglect; if you do the Irish will eat them up.' Perry was equally dismayed and wrote back on the same day:

Mr Lane[76] goeth to Alcalá tomorrow. I am less surprised at Irish bulls, than angry with Irish consciences and religion in this invading the patrimony and spiritual maintenance of souls so distressed as the Scotch are. However, I shall do all I can to wring the prey from betwixt their teeth: I shall incurr their indignation, I make no doubt, but I shall easily swallow that if I can but rescue the sufferers.

And so began Perry's plan to secure the independence of the Scots College.

The Scots agent was due to arrive, and Perry asked Shepherd to inform him about his movements — 'that I may meet and take him up quietly and get all things ready for the Council, before the philistines get wind of the counterplot.'[77] On 14 April 1770 John Geddes the agent·arrived in Madrid and Perry took him under his wing. 'I begin now to be styled the enemy of the Irish by some, because a friend of justice. This to me seems like confessing themselves no friends of it, as indeed greater enemies to it cannot be than some of that nation here.[78] Due to Perry's influence, Geddes decided to move the Scots College from Madrid to Valladolid, but the King had to be consulted. Early in 1771 there were several

73. This passage is from a letter of H. Tichbourne Blount, secretary to Bishop Talbot, written to Perry from London, 17 Oct. 1769.
74. Letter quoted by M. Taylor, *The Scots College in Spain*, pp. 54–4, 11 Jan. 1770. The plan included dividing the revenues of the Scots College between the Irish College at Alcalá and Salamanca.
75. 31 Jan. 1770.
76. Mr Lane was Rector of the Irish College at Alcalá.
77. Perry to Shepherd, 16 Feb. 1770. The Council's recommendation of the union of the Scots and Irish colleges had been accepted by Charles III. But subsequently John Geddes managed to secure the annulment of the order. Taylor, p. 62.
78. Perry to Shepherd, 7 July 1770. Taylor (p. 14) describes the part played by Francis Lane, Rector of the Irish College at Alcalá, and Geddes' relations with him. On p. 67 he refers to the petition and the help given by Campomanes.

attempts to acquire the old Jesuit College of S. Ambrosio in Valladolid as a residence for the Scots. In the meantime, to back up Geddes claims, students were sent from Scotland, and took up temporary residence in the English College at Valladolid.[79]

Geddes shared in the anti-Irish feeling of the Englishmen. He wrote to Shepherd on 9 February 1771:

God forgive them who are the chief causes of all these inconveniences. I am sorry to see, that a curse seems to have fallen on them. Their house at Alcalá is in confusion. The students have made repeated complaints to the Council of Mr Lane, their Rector, who has turned out some of them and is so much disgusted with the rest, that he is just now in town, with an intention, as he told me yesterday, to resign his office.

Perry took his complaints further: to Stonor, the English Agent in Rome, to whom he wrote in March 1771:[80]

As to what regards our college, I must add (which I believe my last to you did not mention) that one of the greatest mortifications I have had here, has been from our good bretheren from Ireland who like universal lords of the manor look upon all waifs and strays and sometimes what is not so, as their claim. They not only on this principle swallowed the Scotch College of Madrid, which however is now got better than three parts out of their jaws, but have made several attempts to intrude themselves into St Alban's. Their first was on my arrival in Madrid, when they endeavoured, and by means of the Fiscal of Castile, to palm two young Hibernians upon us, but I resisted by pleading the foundation, and I did it successfully without displeasing their *empeño* [insistence, determination]. Since I came to Madrid this time, which is now two years within twenty days, they renewed their attack by pretending that we could not stock our College. But thanks to God, they themselves broached their design in my hearing before it was completed and so I had time to detect it, which I did, being pretty well in the good graces of the Fiscal, whom I called in a dextrous hour, and having found his pulse in a good tone, I ventured then even to remonstrate again the surreptitious union of the Scotch and Irish as unnatural in itself and of the utmost peril to Scotland; and I did it so effectively that while I went to him only to parry the strokes of the Hibernians, I not only effected that, but gave them a fair fling in the Scotch union, which is now in a manner dissolved and the consequences of it almost repaired. [. . .] I shall at my departure . . . leave a little memorial in the hands of the Fiscal, containing a compendious exposition of our reasons against the Irish inroads; of which I may,

79. This created certain disciplinary problems and quarrels between English and Scots students, cf. p. 98, below. Shepherd to Perry, 2 March 1771.
80. CRS, 30, p. liii.

when a little quiet, compose a treatise, entitled *De Ecclesiasticis irruptionibus Hibernorum in Scotos et Anglos.*[81]

Perry received a formal letter of thanks from Bishops Macdonald, Grant and Hay for the help he had given to the Scots College.[82] Perry returned from Madrid on 22 March 1771 and was accompanied by John Geddes, the Rector of the Scots College, now to be established at Valladolid.[83]

Perry summed up the results of his long stay in Madrid in a report he made to Rome before leaving for Valladolid. This tells of the union of the three Colleges into one, of how the Madrid property had been exchanged for land, and how Seville was to be sold and likewise converted into land. The situation he had inherited was that of having no students at all in Madrid, some Irish in Seville, and only two students at Valladolid. But now the united College could support twenty pupils, a rector and three masters. For the moment, however, until matters were finalised, only sixteen students could be accommodated. Shepherd was teaching theology, Douglas looked after philosophy, and Fryer was in charge of humanities. A new constitution had been drawn up, based partly on the old Valladolid rule and partly on those of Douai and other places. The King approved it, and Perry said that if Rome were to approve it too, this would give great joy. He then asked permission for the College to celebrate certain feast days with a Mass and office: Augustine of Canterbury, Melitus, Cedd, Birinus, Wilfred, Felix, Chad, Paulinus, Aidan and Cuthbert, each saint being a patron of one or other region of England.[84]

81. The friendly relationship with Campomanes the Fiscal mentioned in this letter is further evidenced by two Latin poems written by Perry and dedicated to Campomanes (Series III, L3). One of them '*Planctus Scotiae*', an elegy, was written at this time. Perry also presented on behalf of the English bishops a gift of books to Campomanes: 4 volumes of the British Church Councils and 20 volumes of Thomas Rhymer's *Foedera, Conventiones, Litterae et Cuiuscumque Generis Acta Publica.* Perry to Shepherd, 1 Dec. 1770. For further indication of Campomanes' interest in English writers, see Laura Rodríguez Díaz, op. cit., pp. 79 and 84.
82. 18 June 1771, CRS, 30, p. liv.
83. CRS, 30, p. 197.
84. One cannot help remarking the absence of any saint associated with Wales.

7

THE RULE OF THE ENGLISH SECULARS
ESTABLISHED, 1771–1796

College administration

The *Registers*[1] recall the achievements of Perry's stay in Madrid as follows.

First, he obtained, through the offices of Campomanes, new rules for the restored College. These rules were based on those of Douai, Paris and the old rule of St Alban's; they were confirmed by the Royal Council and then, on its orders translated from Latin into Spanish and printed. Secondly, a little before Christmas 1769,[2] on the advice of friends and with the agreement of Bustamente, the *Intendente* of Valladolid and the two professors of theology and philosophy, he came to an arrangement with the Duke of Alba whereby the College of St George at Madrid, with all its houses which had been acquired from the temporalities of the late Jesuit fathers, should be commuted. The reason for this was that the Madrid property was seen to be less secure than holdings in agriculture or vineyards. Thirdly, he obtained a Royal Decree for the sale of St Gregory's College, Seville and for incorporating the proceeds into St Alban's. Fourthly, despite the inclination of the Cardinal of Seville not to continue his customary alms, the Rector obtained the intercession of the Royal Council with the Cardinal, the Chapter and the City of Seville so that the alms were continued. Fifthly, he also obtained through Campomanes the application to St Alban's, the only College in the Kingdom for the English Mission, of a pension given by a benefactress, the Marquesa de Camarasa. This had been for the maintenance of two English Jesuits, destined to work on the English Mission, in the Madrid noviciate.[3] And finally, he obtained much also for the College in addition

---

1. I.e. *Diarium seu Registrum Collegii St Albani*; begun by Perry in 1768. See CRS, 30 p. 197ff.
2. Series III, L2.
3. Series III, L2. Although payment of this pension was backed by an Order-in-Council of 16 Feb. 1770, in 1789 Shepherd, who was then Rector, had to claim payment for arrears, receiving an order for payment on 21 July. Similar orders had to be obtained in 1815 and 1816. The last payment would seem to have been made in 1818. In 1824 the College agents claimed for repayment to be made by the Provin-

to the above: sacred vestments and furnishings, and books from the Jesuit fathers' libraries at Valladolid, Medina del Campo, Palencia and Villagarcía. Not all of these items had been finalised by the time of his return to Valladolid.

The privileges of the College and the original Bull of Foundation were confirmed by Propaganda Fide on 29 November 1772, which meant that its rights were vindicated in matters concerning the parish and University. However, the royal *exequatur* had to be obtained before this could be of any value, and the delay in its arrival obliged Perry to make another journey to Madrid, where death overtook him. The royal approval did not come until 25 March 1775.

Although the Madrid transaction was almost completed in Perry's lifetime,[4] the Seville business still proved difficult. The alms were only paid reluctantly and there was a protracted correspondence up till 1774 as to the due date for payment. It was the college property in Seville that caused most concern: during 1771 papers, pictures, books and so on were handed over to Perry,[5] but on 20 April that year there was an Order — in — Council declaring that St Gregory's or *'el edificio del seminario de irlandeses llamado en otra parte de ingleses,*[6] *se aplicará para seminario de Nobles general a toda Andalucía, quedando sus rentas a las misiones Británicas.*[7] However, this destiny for the College property was for the remote rather than the immediate future since it appears[8] that while still not knowing who were the true owners of the College — whether it belonged to the Society of Jesus or to the English Bishops — the Medical Society of Seville had been given permission to hold its meetings there. This permission was given a more permanent form by a resolution of the *Consejo*, on 13 July 1771, and the building was occupied on 22 August that year.[9]

---

cial of the now restored Jesuits. This was refused on the grounds that the Jesuits no longer possessed the capital of the fund.

4. For further correspondence concerning the Madrid houses, see Series III, L4.
5. Ibid.
6. This confusion of Irish and English is perpetuated by modern writers, e.g. M. Defourneaux, *Pablo de Olavide ou L'Afrancesado*, Paris 1959, p. 270.
7. 'The building of the Irish Seminary, otherwise known as English, will become a general seminary for Nobles for the whole of Andalusia, its rents being used for the British missions.' Aguilar Piñal says (p. 253) that the decision to make the Colegio de Ingleses into this seminary was taken on 23 August 1769.
8. CRS, 30, p. xlvi.
9. According to Aguilar Piñal, 30 July. By this date the last of the English or Irish students would have left. Aguilar Piñal, p. 375.

Perry began on 30 June 1774 the long process of reclaiming the College,[10] a process only terminated in 1965.

Although it is not mentioned in the Registers, Perry worked hard in Madrid to help the Scots re-establish themselves in Spain and open their house in Valladolid. When he returned from Madrid, he was accompanied by Geddes, the Scots Rector. For some months before this, Scots students had been residing in the English College, and Shepherd had occasion to relate to Perry (19 December 1770) some of his troubles:

I have given the Scotch, who brought none with them, books for the present use out of your closet. Mr Gordon also has desired they may have a *brasero* in the room where they study, after common mass until breakfast time because he says, one of them was sent hither because he was not able to bear the colds of Flanders. This I mention because as Mr Geddes in his letter to me desires they may be treated as our boys are, and this is something extraordinary you may if you think it worth while consult him about it.

Later, on 2 March 1771, there was a question of hygiene among the students.

Six of the bairns or loons have brought fiddles with them[11] and the misery is they happen to be dumb ones and I am very apprehensive the other six may turn musician also. As we had so much work with our own itchy boys, I am more sensible to this than anything else. Though I can assure you they are not agreeable guests but we must suffer something for God's sake.

However on 31 May 1771 Geddes, two masters and fifteen students left St Alban's for their new home in the former College of S. Ambrosio; they did so at 8 o'clock in the evening after both English and Scots students had recited the Litany of the Holy Name of Jesus and the Litany of Our Lady. Perry drafted a document on behalf of the two Rectors giving their reasons why the British Colleges in the Peninsula needed to remain distinct, each with its own traditions and privileges.[12]

In his efforts to save the Scots College, Perry had been involved with the Irish. He continued to take an interest in Hibernian affairs, and on 5 December 1773 wrote to a Mr Dowling[13] informing him that the

---

10. See Series III, L6.
11. 'Scotch fiddle' was another name for the 'itch'. So called from the motion of the fingers against the palm.
12. Series III, L4.
13. Several references are made to Mr Dowling and his wife in the correspondence of this period. They resided in Madrid and when Greenway went there in 1786 he

Spanish authorities took a poor view of the fact that the Irish Bishops had not appointed a new Rector to Salamanca. He followed this in April 1774 with a letter to the Archbishops of Armagh, Tuam, Dublin and Cashel outlining the procedures concerning nomination and royal approval that should be followed in appointing a new Rector. Although this letter was later to prove significant in the crisis of the 1920s concerning the appointment or removal of a Rector of a foreign college, there is no record of any reply to it from the Irish Bishops.

In these years the College does not seem to have been much affected by external events. The suppression of the Society of Jesus by the Pope in 1773 had little repercussion in Spain, except to confirm the opinion that the Spanish decision of 1767 had been the right one. The Royal *cédula* ordering that the papal decree be put into effect came on 16 September 1773. Joseph Bolton, the College agent,[14] wrote to Perry from England on 3 December 1773 mentioning the reaction to the papal brief and that some of the English laity were bitter in their invective against His Holiness. He also indicated some of the problems pertaining to 'our newly acquired brethren', those Jesuits who were now to be regarded as secular priests. As his nephew John was now teaching at St Omer, Perry received frequent news from there as to how it was faring under the direction of the secular clergy. The rather mysterious visit of Mgr Caprara, Nuncio in Cologne, to England in 1773 was reported by Bolton,[15] and when Corsini became Protector of England on the death of

---

stayed with them: 'Here we have our quarters with Mr Dowling. His kindness and that of Mrs Dowling was such upon the first visit we made this morning, that we have been forced to remove our baggage there this afternoon from the Parador de los Segovianos' (Greenway to Shepherd, 16 March 1786). J. Sarrailh, op. cit., p. 325, mentions a Mr Dowling who directed the factory at S. Ildefonso and who discovered a new method of steel-making. Press A, drawer 7, H. II, contains reference to a machine for glass polishing invented by Mr John Dowling at San Ildefonso in 1763. Dowling was in correspondence with Perry in 1773 on the matter of producing millstones for the College mills.

14. Chaplain to Bishop Challoner and Vicar General of the London District (see Anstruther vol. 4, p. 41).

15. 30 March 1773: 'How then could I do otherwise than slur over the Pope's Nuncio? However he came and was graciously received at Court. But what was his business there, is more than I can tell . . . The Duke of Gloucester you know met with many civilities at Rome for which acknowledgements were sent in form from Court to His Holiness, and His Holiness you may be assured would not be behindhand in returning complaissance for complaissance, and this or some such like I am informed was his errand.' For this mission and similar attempts to establish contact between the Papacy and England, see M. Buschkuhl, *Great Britain and the Holy See*, Dublin 1982, pp. 19–22.

Cardinal Lante, Perry followed the advice of Stonor, the Bishops' agent in Rome, and wrote to congratulate him.[16]

Domestic affairs and life in the College

Although most of the materials that have come down to us are concerned with College policy and administration, we are given occasional glimpses of what everyday domestic life was like. There were changes in the teaching staff. In 1770 William Fryer[17] arrived from Douai via London to teach humanities, but the advantage of having an additional member of staff was short-lived as Douglas returned to England in 1773 because of ill-health (he suffered from the tertian ague)[18] and he was not immediately replaced. At this time Shepherd also considered returning to England.[19] His friend Bannister advised him: 'If you fear a storm impending, which you can no way avert, why should you not fly away out of its fury. [. . .] Whensoever you come Bishop Petre will make you heartily welcome and if there be a vacant place, will put you in it. At present there is no vacancy.'

When the College was restored ten students were allowed for, but the number rose above this, and accommodation problems became acute in 1771 when the Scots were lodged in the College. In addition to the sixteen English students and their professors, there were now fifteen Scottish students and their two professors. Shepherd wrote to Perry on 2 March 1771: 'You may well wonder how we have stowed so many in San Albano. In the rooms over the library are nine with each one in his bed, in the procurator's room are three in the same manner, and in the room where Mr Douglas was first, Mr Gordon is. Mr Allan Macdonald in the closet of the procuration, and three in the room before the sacristy, two of our own lye in my room and closet.'

While his Rector was in Madrid, Shepherd had to ask his advice on several occasions concerning discipline. On 14 March 1770 he wrote: 'Four of our boys are continually teasing me to get their gowns dyed; they are of the same cloth as yours. For my part I see no necessity of it,

16. 1 April 1773, Series III, L5.
17. See CRS, 30, p. 197n, for further biographical details; also Anstruther, vol. 4, p. 107. Fryer was later President of Lisbon College, 1782–1805.
18. CRS, 30, p. 200.
19. CRS, 30 lv.

and yet they are such tickle[20] gentlemen that I am obliged to hum and ha.' Perry replied on 17 March 1770. 'As to dyeing the boys gowns, bid them stay till I return and in the meantime, tell 'em I think they are very vain, in seeking better colour than their Rector.' On 23 May Shepherd had to write again. 'The collegians are continually teasing me for new cassocks, if you in your next in a little line to them, will signify that I have communicated it to you and beg of them to see if they cannot go on till your return, I shall be much obliged to you.' Perry replied three days later: 'As for cassocks to be sure, those that are in much want must have 'em. Yet others that are not in such pressing necessity, may stay till I return. In the meantime I beg you'll take care not to buy cloth that is more costly than the last, but rather cheaper, if anything. For I fear we shall be obliged to let ourselves down a peg in that point.'

Another correspondence concerning dress was occasioned by the general order of the Council[21] for all to wear cocked hats. This was one of the measures to combat brigandage, since criminals could disguise their features by wearing slouch hats. But the measures were not taken seriously by the majority of the population: 'Here has been published today an order that all are to wear cocked hats: the city is like a comedy everyone laughing at himself and his neighbour.'[22] Some of the implications of this for clerics emerge in Perry's reply from Madrid.[23] 'Your comedy of cocked hats I suppose will not last much longer than an ordinary comedy: your expressing of all being made to wear the cock, seems too general, for here the ordinary is for all but those *in sacris*, whose underside of their hats is to be lined with tafeta. Here the change made very little wonder, as it fell only on the licenciados and some few of the inferior clericks, and in my opinion they look better in their three picos than under slouch.'

Perry was concerned about reports of students being sick. 'I am very sorry to hear of any tendency in the students towards sickness and therefore I beg you'll be patiently watchful about it; keeping them from any violent exercise during the heat, or even after the heat of the day; and don't know whether it may not be advisable to retrench some of their flesh meat, and instead of it, give 'em some fruit and sallato.'[24] On other

20. Tickle = unstable.
21. This refers to the Squillace law of 1766 or to some later decree.
22. Shepherd to Perry, 21 July 1770.
23. Perry to Shepherd, 25 July 1770.
24. Perry to Shepherd, July 1770.

aspects of diet, Shepherd on one occasion stressed the importance of maintaining the supply of chocolate from the Company of Caracas of San Sebastián,[25] and to a request concerning the breakfast menu Perry replied:[26] 'As to changing the fruit at breakfast for honey, if there be any in the house, I should have no objection, if that honey might not be more necessary when the fruit season is over. I should think that if they only eat fruit just enough to get their bread down it could not be otherwise than a necessary cooler, in this season.'

Perry had some general instructions for his Vice Rector:[27] 'And as to the tempers of youth, one must endeavour to correct them gently, and pass over several things, as if one did not see them. *Regum est multa dissimulare*: we see it often in Scripture, when the disciples put impertinent questions, Our Blessed Saviour only answered by saying nothing, leaving it to time and his grace to cure certain defects.' As to the student's recreation, they were allowed to visit the bullfight under certain conditions, and in 1774 Perry was anxious to avoid extravagance in this matter. He wrote to Shepherd:[28] 'I only permit it for the youngsters and such as have not seen them, and that if the others will see them also, it must be at their own cost; even for the others, I cannot consent to take such an extravagant balcony as was taken last time, but either they may be joined with the Scotch (for I suppose they are to see the toros) or else some second stages and less balcony may be taken for them.'

Somebody had donated to the students books and magazines, including *The Spectator* , for their light reading, and when Shepherd wrote asking advice, he received the reply:[29] 'As to this you will do as you think proper, but beg you would not leave it to the confessors, because the boys are indiscreet enough to tell one another, as I have experienced, that if their confessor give them leave, the Rector had [done so too]. [. . .] Really there are many parts in *The Spectator*, which on account of their softness I do not think in any ways proper to be read by people who are in the most slippery part of their life, or even by any without necessity.'

25. Shepherd to Perry, 6 March 1771 — it appears from correspondence in 1768 with Lynch, Killikelly and Morony, importers of Bilbao, that Dutch butter, tea and *bacalao* were sent to the College.
26. Perry to Shepherd, 16 July 1774.
27. Perry to Shepherd, 27 July 1770.
28. Perry to Shepherd, 20 July 1774.
29. Perry to Shepherd, 17 Nov. 1770.

Theology and ecclesiastical studies

Another kind of dangerous reading came to his attention. Writing to Shepherd,[30] Perry reported; 'Blaise [Morey] asks me for an *Exposition of the Christian Doctrine* by Messengui;[31] let him contrive to get that Joseph Addis has; for I find since, that his Holiness censured the book, and tis indeed censurable in two or three places, as I before observed, tho' otherwise an useful book; yet if Joseph should carry it to England and shew it to his old friends, who would probably make a handle of it, it might do us some diskindness, as to our reputation and therefore on second thought, I would have you by my orders withdraw the book out of Joseph's hands and put it in my study, alleging either my orders simply, or what other reason your prudence shall suggest, even the late Pope's censure; for there are books enough, that are clear of censure, to be read.' This incident was something of a *cause célèbre* in Spain, but evidently by Perry's arrival it had ceased to claim attention. However, when the matter was called to his attention, Perry was prudent enough to see that the College should not in any way lay itself open to suspicion of a pro-Jansenist regalism or anti-papal sentiment.[32]

Perry was a collector of books before he came to Spain. While at Hassop in 1762 he had asked Alban Butler,[33] then in London, to get him twenty-two volumes of Dom Ceillier.[34] Like Butler, he was interested in

30. Perry to Shepherd, 11 Aug. 1770.
31. François-Philippe Messengui (1677–1763) was a French priest and author of many books on the Scriptures. In 1761 Clement XIII, through a brief to the Nuncio in Spain, condemned his *Exposition de la doctrine chrétienne* (1744) on the grounds that it was against the infallibility of the Pope and also anti-Jesuit in its tone. Charles III refused to publish the brief, but the Inquisitor-General did publish the Roman condemnation and was exiled from court for his pains. He was only pardoned after submitting to the King. See M.G. Tomsich, *El Jansenismo en España*, Madrid 1972, p. 43.
32. Later Perry gave permission to Morey to read Calmet's *History of the Old Testament*, 'which I knew not was forbidden nor do I understand why, unless on account of some extracts of the sacred books' (letter to Shepherd, 18 July 1774). Calmet, together with other theologians like Berti, Ceillier and Duhamel, was included in Jovellanos' list in the plan of studies for Calatrava. Sarrailh, p. 145.
33. Alban Butler (1709–73), student and professor at Douai, eventually President at St Omer. Author of many works including *The Lives of the Saints*. Anstruther, vol. 4, pp. 52–3.
34. Rémy Ceillier, O.S.B. (1688–1761), *Histoire générale des auteurs sacrés et ecclésiastiques*. An erudite though rather confused work. Shepherd presented a copy to the Big Library at Valladolid, where it is still to be found with Shepherd's autograph.

the life of Bishop John Fisher, and he hoped that the Catherine of Aragon connection would lead him to discover biographical sources in Spain; in fact, he asked permission to visit libraries in Spain to look for Fisher MSS.[35] Perry's interest in history led him to seek volumes of the *Acta* of both British and Spanish Church Councils for the library, and today the College possesses the first twenty-eight volumes of Enrique Florez' *España Sagrada*. He asked Bolton, the College agent in England, to procure and send him Strype's *Memorials*, as well as the same author's annals of the Reformation.[36] But his freedom to read what he chose was restricted by the censorship of the Inquisition. Shortly after his arrival he obtained a licence to read prohibited books[37] — his plea contained the argument that because heterodox books were unfortunately to be found in England and, in order to combat and refute them, they had to be read by the Rector and professor of theology and, in so far as was necessary, by the students themselves.

Reading books was one thing, importing them was another. But he found help in Bilbao. Messrs Lynch, Killikelly and Morony, forwarding agents and importers of that town, instructed Perry in the procedures. The Inquisition had to examine all books, and the Inquisitor required 11 reales for affixing his seal to each chest. The permission of the Inquisitor-General in Madrid was necessary before any prohibited books could be let in. Perry had obtained his licence to read forbidden books but this did not automatically allow him to import them. However, Lynch and Co. were on good terms with John Reynolds, a Dominican friar who was *calificador* to the Inquisition and who was prepared to take the trouble to make an inventory.[38] The choice of a suitable text book for the students was discussed in correspondence between Shepherd and Perry. Shepherd wrote to his Rector on 4 November 1769: 'Collet's Compendium[39] is

35. Butler to Perry, 6 Oct. 1767. Perry's draft letter asking permission to visit libraries is in Series III, L1.

36. 22 Feb. 1773.

37. 14 April 1768. Two authors were excluded from the licence: Machiavelli, and Pedro Soave (Paolo Sarpi), *History of the Council of Trent*. A further request to read Soave on 12 Jan. 1771 was granted in two days.

38. Lynch and Co., Bilbao, to Perry, 12 Aug. 1768.

39. Pierre Collet (1693–1770), priest of the Congregation of the Mission (Lazarist), professor of theology at Paris, author of *Institutiones Theologiae Moralis . . . ad usum seminariorum*. Another work of his, *Histoires édificantes pour servir de lecture aux jeunes personnes*, was presented by Perry to the College library, and the library also contains several editions of his *Institutiones Theologiae*. Collet was also used by the Irish College in Salamanca (J. Townsend, *A Journey through Spain in the years 1786–1789*,

without doubt a good body of morality but will never make a divine able to defend. Habert[40] too is a very able divine, but are not both, think you, better calculated to instruct seminarists in their duties more than to fit them for their duties and the school too? I should be more for L'Herminier[41] were there not some odd opinions in him. In short I pitch upon no one but leave it entirely to be managed by you, and lest you should take any prejudice for L'Herminier from what I have said, I assure you I know not enough of him to either say anything for him or against him.'[42] In the end Perry decided on Collet:[43] 'I have partly determined on Collet for a divine; it's true he's short and he alone will not do for studying to defend, but however, he's a proper man to read doctrine out of as he's short, and as to disputable and great questions, the students will have books in the library which treat those points more at length.' From these and similar passages it would appear that the lectures in the College were based on a text book and did not rely on dictates. In this they were following the now accepted practice in Spain.

As far as one can judge, the theological views of Perry and Shepherd were very similar; both tended to favour a stricter moral theology than that prevailing among the Jesuits, yet they were anxious to avoid any form of regalism that extolled the King's authority at the expense of the Pope's. Shepherd wanted a copy of Orsi's refutation of Bossuet's defence of the Gallican Propositions,[44] but he also knew the case on the other side, and in fact gave the library a copy of Du Pin's *Traité de l'Autorité Ecclésiastique et de la Puissance Temporelle conforment à la Déclaration du Clergé de France in 1682 . . . à l'usage de ceux qui enseignent et qui étudient dans les universités, dans les collèges et les séminaires de l'Eglise Gallicane.*[45] Perhaps

London 1791, vol. II, p. 73), and was still being used by the Scots in 1819. M. Taylor, *The Scots College in Spain*, p. 175.

40. Louis Habert (1635–1718), Doctor of the Sorbonne, author of *Theologia dogmatica et moralis ad usum seminarii Catalaunensis* (Chalons-sur-Marne). The College library possesses Perry's copy of this.

41. Nicholas L'Herminier (1657–1735), Doctor of Theology of Paris, canon of Le Mans Cathedral, author of *Summa Theologiae ad usum scholae accommodata*.

42. Both Habert and L'Herminier were accused of Jansenist tendencies, and Collet, who was a probabiliorist, was accused of excessive severity.

43. Perry to Shepherd, 15 Nov. 1769.

44. Shepherd to Perry, 25 Nov. 1769. Giuseppe Augustino Orsi (1692–1761) from Florence, Dominican and Cardinal, opposed to Jesuit moral teaching, author of *De irreformabili Romani Pontificis in definiendis fidei controversiis judicio*.

45. Louis Ellies du Pin (1657–1719), a prolific writer and a church historian but often lacking in accuracy. Associated with the Jansenist party in France. The College

a special case can be made for considering the anti-Roman views of Du Pin since his work was known in England[46] and he was reputed to have had dealings with William Wake, Archbishop of Canterbury, on the subject of reunion. But one of the problems that faced people like Perry was the conflict between the Spanish Crown and the Inquisition. People like Messengui and Du Pin came under the condemnation of the Inquisition for their anti-papal and Jansenist views, yet Jovellanos recommended that theological students should read authors like Berti, Ceillier and others suspected of Jansenism.[47]

The last days of Perry

On 29 May 1774 Perry had to make the journey to Madrid once more. Three reasons are given for this in the Registers:[48] he needed to obtain the royal *pase* for two briefs and one apostolic rescript confirming the privileges of the College conceded by Clement XIV, he had to obtain 6,000 reales for foundation Masses for Doña María Alvarez from the temporalities confiscated from the Jesuits, and he had to attend to business relating to the College in Seville. His visit to Madrid also involved one or two commissions from colleagues at Valladolid. Geddes, the Rector of the Scots College, wrote to him asking for a copy of Boscovitch's *Newtonian Philosophy* in verse, and for two copies of Aesop's Fables in Greek, also for a copy of Collet. Later he wrote: 'Be so good as to enquire for a little book something like the *Guía de Forasteros* which is entitled *Grandeza de España*. Escritorio in the street of Atocha had it when we were there together.'[49] A set of Collet and a *Conduit de Confesseur* were also in demand from Fryer.

In July Perry drafted yet another official request for the College in Seville, but shortly afterwards he fell ill. Some months previously a certain Edmund O'Ryan had written from Madrid to Perry at Valla-

---

library possesses an English translation of his *History of the Church*, published London 1713.

46. Joseph Bolton, in a letter from London to Perry of 22 Sept. 1772, offered to send a copy of another work by Du Pin, *Méthode pour étudier la théologie*. This hardly suggests that Du Pin was entirely anathema in circles around Bishop Challoner.

47. See F.M. Hernández, 'La formación del clero en los siglos XVII y XVIII' in *Historia de la Iglesia en España*, vol. IV, pp. 540–1.

48. CRS, 30, p. 201.

49. 24 July and 10 Aug. 1774.

dolid: 'The Elector of Treves, our King's [i.e. Charles III] brother-in-law, has lately given me the confidence of his affairs in this Court', and he offered Perry any services he might require.[50] It so happened that O'Ryan was chaplain at the Hospital of S. Andrés de la Nación Flamenca at Madrid, and it was there that the sick Perry was taken. He made his will,[51] witnessed by Thomas O'Ryan and José Diego García y Silva in the presence of four others. On 4 September 1774 he died. The news was conveyed to Shepherd at Valladolid in a letter from Stephen Woulfe who was present when the will was made and who gave an account of the Rector's last illness, death and burial.

In the six short years of his Rectorship, Perry accomplished much. Arriving in Spain with no knowledge of the country or the language, (his account book mentions the item: 'To my Spanish master for a month's teaching'), he succeeded in putting into effect the amalgamation of the three English Colleges into that of Valladolid. Gaining the confidence of both the English Bishops and the Spanish authorities, he was able to recruit students and staff and establish a satisfactory arrangement with the University for their studies. He was truly the second founder of the College. But it was an exhausting task and the demands of Spanish bureaucracy involved him in much labour. By temperament he seems to have been rather withdrawn and even sullen. He was very much a scholar, and despite his administrative duties he left behind him many MSS., not only theological notes but devotional works including notes for a retreat.[52] Biography fascinated him, and among his papers still at Valladolid are many lives of Old Testament figures, British and Irish saints, and other holy persons, studies on the Reformation, a life of Cranmer, a life of Wolsey, a summary of English Church history from 1531 to 1608, and extracts from Grosseteste's *Epistles* transcribed from Brown's collection. The Scottish Catholic Archives possess ten bound MS. volumes of Perry's works, many of them gifts to St Alban's College, but bearing the bookplate of Bishop Cameron into whose possession they came, probably from John Geddes whom he succeeded as Rector of the Scots College, Valladolid. These ten volumes comprise a

---

50. 30 March 1774. This was the same O'Ryan who was negotiating over the Irish and Scots Colleges, p. 92, above.
51. Series III, L6. Anstruther, vol. 4, p. 210, refers to an earlier will dated 11 Dec. 1767.
52. He began to reorganise the College Archives and recovered papers belonging to St Alban's which were in the archive of S. Isidro in Madrid. Among his papers in Valladolid is a catalogue of books left at Longbirch (over 700 volumes), as well as MSS. and works of controversy.

life of Christ, a chronological catalogue of English, Irish and Scots saints and holy persons with a previous account of some of their biographers, lives of the saints, two volumes of a three-volume life of John Fisher, a four-volume continuation of Bede's *Civil and Ecclesiastical History* down to the Norman Conquest, and a life of Robert Grosseteste, Bishop of Lincoln. This latter includes two letters to the author about his work, one from George Bishop of Brailes[53] and the other from Richard Challoner. At Valladolid there is part of a second draft of his life of Grossteste in the introduction to which Perry defends himself against Challoner's criticisms of his recording the abuses in the papal court in Grosseteste's time.[54]

Perry shared many of the historical and biographical interests of his contemporaries both in England and on the continent. There is a marked similarity between Perry's MSS and Challoner's *Britannia Sacra*.[55] He kept up a friendship with Alban Butler, and the death of the author of *Lives of the Saints* grieved him. Charles Howard, writing to Shepherd from Paris on 30 January 1776, remarked: 'He wrote to me some months before, in a melancholy style, being struck with the death of Mr Alban Butler his great friend.'[56]

The Rectorship of Shepherd, 1774–1796

Although Challoner wrote to Shepherd on 3 October 1774 informing him that the Vicars Apostolic had sent his name forward as Rector to the *Regia Camara*, his official appointment only came a year later and was dated 17 October 1775; he took formal possession eight days later. With Shepherd's promotion on the death of Perry, continuity was assured, but there was now a vacancy on the teaching staff. Challoner wrote on 10 January 1775 that he was unable to provide any replacement, and so Fryer became the second *cathedraticus* to assume responsibility for both

53. Anstruther, vol.4, p. 35.
54. M.E. Williams, 'English Manuscripts in Scottish Archives: The Legacy of an Eighteenth Century friendship', *Innes Review*, vol. XXXIV, no. 2, pp. 93–6. Perry's life of Grossteste is cited by Charles Butler, *Historical Memoirs of the English, Irish and Scottish Catholics since the Reformation*, vol. VIII, 5.
55. *Britannia Sacra or The Lives of the most celebrated British, English, Scottish and Irish Saints who have flourished in these islands from the earliest times of Christianity down to the change of religion in the sixteenth century*, 1st edn, 1745.
56. A twelve-volume Spanish translation of Butler's *Lives of the Saints* was published in Valladolid, 1789–91.

philosophy and divinity. For humanities Shepherd had to call on the services of Blaise Moray, a deacon.

During his Rectorship there were never more than two members of staff besides the Rector to undertake the main burden of teaching. Greenway, after ordination in 1776, taught humanities, but later moved into philosophy, and after Fryer's departure in 1781 he taught theology until 1787. In 1782 John Griffith came out from England to teach philosophy, but he returned in 1788. Because of the lack of priests in England, Shepherd agreed in 1787 to release to Bishop Talbot both Greenway and Griffith, which meant that he himself had to teach theology again. Price, a deacon who was in charge of humanities, now began to teach philosophy and eventually took over theology. Thomas Taylor, who had been ordained priest in 1787, became Procurator the next year and held that office till 1794. For the last years of his life, Shepherd himself acted as Procurator with Thomas Price teaching both philosophy and theology, while a student, subdeacon or deacon taught humanities. This hardly seems a satisfactory arrangement, yet the College continued to present students for public '*Acta*' and there is no record of any difficulties with the University.

Over this period the numbers of students varied between sixteen and twenty-four. Addis, the only survivor from the Jesuit régime, had been ordained in 1771, and of the new intake under the seculars, seven were ordained in 1775 after the death of Perry. Often one of the students stayed on for a time after ordination to instruct in humanities, and sometimes, as with Greenway and Price, they moved on to teaching philosophy and even theology. But between 1768 and 1796 (the registers for 1787-96 are imperfect) it would seem that fifty-eight boys were sent out to Spain, of whom thirty-three eventually returned ordained: twenty-one left *re infecta* and the others are accounted for by one who was ordained in England, one who died, and one who went mad, leaving one of whom there is no record. The provenance of the pupils was varied, from both north and south of the country, but the majority were from London (twenty-one of whom ten were ordained) followed closely by Lancashire (sixteen of whom twelve were ordained). It would appear from correspondence[57] that Shepherd was under pressure from time to time to accept Spanish students at the College, probably for humanities and with no intention of going on for the priesthood, much less working on the English Mission. The College registers have no record of these

57. Series III, L7 and L8.

names, but on 26 May 1787 Shepherd wrote to Floridablanca[58] expressing his willingness to comply with an order from the King to admit to the College the son of Don Manuel Serrano.[59] On 29 January 1791, Campomanes recommended a Spanish student; a certain Señor D. José Carnide, *'un caballero gallego'*, wished to place his nephew Ramón Becerra in the College,[60] and there is a similar reference in a letter of 20 July 1793 which may refer either to this student or another one. On 8 November 1794 Campomanes was grateful to Shepherd for looking after his nephew Juanito and in return he offered his services in helping Shepherd to speed up the affair concerning the College in Seville.[61]

During the Rectorships of Perry and Shepherd, great hopes were pinned on the College in Spain especially after the expulsion of the Jesuits from Rome and the taking over of the College there by the Cardinal Protector and the Italian secular clergy. Blount[62] wrote to Shepherd:[63] 'I hope that your College will prove a considerable support to the English mission; and kind providence gives us this comfort at a time when the distressed and sinking state of the Roman College makes it most wanted and therefore more sensibly felt.' And in 1778 Bolton[64] remarked: 'The Bishops here I can assure you have conceived the highest opinion of S. Albano, and have the greatest expectations from thence and that they not be disappointed and as I heartily wish well of your establishment, I am sure you will excuse me without taking any further notice to others, if I remind you as often as you write for subjects always to continue as you have hitherto done . . . in general honest country lads to be preferred to Londoners.'

But hopes were fixed on Valladolid not only because Rome was in a bad way, but also because Lisbon was not at this time producing priests. 'The last missioner that was sent hither [from Lisbon] it had cost the college upwards of £10,000 to effect it and I very much question if it did not stand the college in an equal sum the missioner before. £20,000 for two missioners!!! What a vast sum! Valladolid, God be praised, has been

58. José Moñino, Conde de Floridablanca (1729–1808), was President of the Council of Castile.
59. Series III, L7.
60. Series III, L8.
61. Series III, L8.
62. Henry Tichborne Blount was President of Douai, 1770–1781. Anstruther, vol. 4, p. 39.
63. Correspondence, vol. 3, p. 34.
64. Joseph Bolton, Vicar General for the London District, was also College agent in England. Letter of 8 May 1778.

more fortunate. Rome I think in a deplorable situation, only one missioner from thence since my arrival here which is near ten years. Numbers both from this and the former bishop have been sent but have returned *re infecta*.'[65] Between 1768 and 1787 Valladolid sent fourteen priests to the Mission. Talbot, the Vicar Apostolic of the London District, was similarly enthusiastic on receiving Shepherd's report on 6 February 1787.[66] The situation was not very happy at Douai College either;[67] Talbot criticised its President for 'encouraging too much expense'. Horrabin recorded that the northern brethren complained that Mr Gibson, the President, was too indulgent towards the students, allowing them too much money.[68] Bannister wrote on 15 May 1788: 'As far as I can learn Douai College is still sinking and the pride and vain boasting of its inhabitants (called politeness) has appeared to me in one or two boys lately from thence. As far as we are able, we shall recommend all our boys either to Valladolid or to Lisbon, as long as the present spirit of pride, pomp, expensiveness etc. are to predominate in Douai college.'[69]

With the passing of the years, conditions at Douai and Paris became perilous because of the political situation in France. In 1790 Bannister wrote to Gibson: 'I wish the College [at Paris] may find ways and means to sell out and translate their moneys to England. But it may be dangerous for the college to sell out lest it provoke or stir up the enthusiasm of the *demon-cratic* assembly.'[70] In 1792 it was apparent that Lisbon had no room for any more students — this was due to the state of the building. At Rome the Cardinal Protector was not seeking any more students. Douai was still secure, but no one knew for how long. Douglas wrote to Shepherd[71] that there were no plans for the removal of Douai College; they were at a loss where to remove it, since the French army was likely to be welcomed by Austrian Flanders and Brabant. At the end of June 1793, there were only 60 students left at Douai instead of the usual 130,[72]

---

65. Horrabin to Shepherd, 6 February 1787. Thomas Horrabin, a former student at St Alban's, was agent in London for St Omer and Lisbon.
66. Shepherd Correspondence, 4, p. 4.
67. However, the records show that there were large numbers of students at Douai during Gibson's time, 1781–90. CRS, 63, pp. 289 ff.
68. 6 Feb. 1787, Horrabin to Shepherd. pp. 615–49.
69. Bannister to Shepherd, Shepherd Correspondence, 4, p. 24.
70. Shepherd Correspondence, 4, p. 58.
71. 10 Nov. 1792, Shepherd Correspondence, 4, p. 93.
72. The Prefect of Studies book gives the following figures for students at Douai (CRS, 63, p. 382): 1790, 140; 1791, 126; 1792, 103; 1793, 49.

and Douglas asked his former colleague on the staff at Valladolid to advise him what to do when it ceased to be any longer possible to maintain a college.[73] 'Shall we remove the college to some town in the Austrian Netherlands or shall we open a school in England for humanity studies and send our young men to Valladolid, Lisbon and Rome to study philosophy and divinity?' Thus by the end of Shepherds' Rectorship Rome was taking no more students, Douai was closed, and only Lisbon and Valladolid remained of the many seminaries that had once existed in Europe.

Shepherd's Rectorship involved visits to Madrid on College business and especially petitions to the King for the restoration of the Seville College, which was still occupied by the Medical Society. The Madrid visits of 1775, 1784 and 1790 produced no result save that some movable goods were transferred from Seville to Valladolid. He found Campomanes kindly and friendly.[74] On one of these visits to Madrid he received an anxious letter from Geddes of the Scots College expressing fear that the Irish College might try to transfer itself to Valladolid; this resulted in a united determination of the two Rectors to thwart this at all costs.[75]

The College being now well established, there were few of the excitements that had been a feature of life in Perry's day. In 1788 there were serious floods in Valladolid, and the *ayuntamiento* (city corporation) asked the College to provide shelter for the homeless. And the College made a gift of trees for the Campo Grande;[76] this plantation was one of the schemes for purifying the air of the town and the appeal for contributions from the public met with some resistance.[77] Despite the changes in staff, lectures continued as usual. The professors were able to indulge their taste for scientific experiment to a small extent; John Greenway of the English College and John Gordon of the Scots College both distinguished themselves, although the exact nature of their efforts is not clear. Greenway gave the following account to Shepherd when the latter was on business in Madrid:[78]

We have learnt to make gas and have discharged many shots, inflaming it with electrical fire. I propose letting fly a ball one of these days, perhaps it may be a

73. 27 June 1793, Correspondence, 4, p. 102.
74. Correspondence, 3, pp. 11, 116 etc.
75. CRS 30, pp. lvi–lvii.
76. A letter of thanks was received from the *ayuntamiento*, 5 March 1788.
77. Sarrailh, op. cit., p. 35.
78. Greenway to Shepherd, 16 May 1784. See CRS 30, lvii.

bladder, on which I make my first experiment. Perhaps Mr Gordon out of humility has not mentioned the honourable commissions given him by the Sociedad,[79] of examining a cast of such construction as by means of small cylinders to facilitate the drawing of an immense load by a single macho; as also of examining the Fabrica of Talavera del Campo Grande. One of the cylinders broke in the experiment but the inventor is not discouraged, and still expects to perfect his invention. Mr Shepherd was called upon by the Sociedad for these commissions but was found absent. I mention this for the honour of the Rectors, that it may be known that even in this Mr Gordon only acts as subdelegate.

From later correspondence[80] it would seem that Greenway's efforts were concerned with some sort of flying machine:[81]

I have made no experiment as yet on my flying bladder, as I had proposed. For it to take flight, we ought I fancy to inflame the gas either with electrical fire or some other way, and I presume in this case when filled, it would burst with a report capable of frightening half the city; we must wait until we learn to make the globes, and then begin our experiments.

But the experiments came to nothing owing to the failure to make the necessary 'globes'.

With regard to our globes, nothing has been attempted for want of the proper gum, or rather for want of knowledge to dissolve it. Could you send me a receipt to dissolve the gum compal? No one has been able to do this in Valladolid. I have attempted it with the best spirits of wine and a slow fire, but to no effect. A second attempt was made with spirits of turpentine, which seemed to penetrate the gum more than wine spirits but the bottle bursted in the boiling which was necessary to mix it with the proper oil, that the globe might remain flexible. I made yesterday another easy mixture for want of a better, and have 2

79. In the late eighteenth century Valladolid, in common with many Spanish towns, had a flourishing intellectual life. There was a *Universidad Literaria* and several patriotic societies going by the name of *Real Academia* — one of Geography and History, another of Mathematics and one of Law. The first newspaper, *Diario Pinciano*, was published on 7 Feb. 1787, and there were several theatres. But the most important of these societies was La Real Sociedad Económica founded by a Mexican priest D. José Mariano Beristain, and finally approved on 23 Sept. 1784. See Jorge Demerson, *La Real Sociedad Económica de Valladolid (1784–1808)*, Estudios y Documentos, no. 28, Departamento Historia Moderna, Universidad de Valladolid, 1969.
80. Greenway to Shepherd, May 1784. Correspondence, 3, p. 110.
81. Two years previously in 1782 Jerome Allen, professor of philosophy at Lisbon, had attempted a balloon ascent at Mafra: Croft, *Historial Account of Lisbon College*, Barnet 1902, pp. 86–7.

balls actually put to dry; which when effected, shall be set immediately to fly, if the varnish be capable to prevent the evaporation of the gases. If not I must wait for your receipt. According to Mr Faujas the goma copal is by far the best; but he gives no rules for dissolving it.[82]

Greenway's scientific interests were not confined to flying machines; his curiosity extended to medicine as well. In a letter to Shepherd he reported on an illness that was going the rounds of the College.

My turn came on Sunday, but yesterday I was in a manner perfectly rid of it. Some of the students have also complained of gripings etc. I should like to know from the philosophical medicos of Madrid the cause. Does it depend on the disposition of the air etc. How does the air, for I suppose this to be the great agent, operate the running effect in the posteriors? With what species of saline particles must it be impregnated with? I could put a 1,000 questions of this nature.[83]

As for Shepherd himself, he was in constant touch with his friends and family in England. He seems to have been a countryman at heart; he sent plants to England and received other plants back in exchange.[84] One of his friends, Tunstall, thanked him for 'the little Burgos dog you sent my wife' and he now asked Shepherd to send him some 'Jesuits' bark' i.e. quinine.[85] One of his brothers was killed in a farming accident in 1780, and Shepherd considered leaving Valladolid and settling back in England when he learnt that this would be possible for him. His other brother from Dorking in Surrey wrote suggesting that he go back and become a tenant on property he owned in Lancashire.[86] It was Bannister who persuaded him to stay on as Rector.[87]

He was also kept informed on the ecclesiastical scene in England. Talbot wrote[88] on behalf of the clergy of London asking him to obtain help from the Spaniards for the victims of the Gordon Riots. His correspondents were mostly those Catholics who were opposed to the activities of the Catholic Committee.[89] Bannister was worried about the way

82. Greenway to Shepherd, 15 June 1784, Correspondence, 3, p. 116.
83. Greenway to Shepherd, 21 Sept. 1785. Correspondence, 3, p. 122.
84. Tunstall to Shepherd, 16 Nov. 1777; Bolton to Shepherd, 2 Jan. 1778.
85. Tunstall to Shepherd, 7 Feb. 1779.
86. Thomas Shepherd to Joseph Shepherd, 6 Feb. 1787.
87. Bannister to Shepherd, 16 April 1787.
88. Copy of letter; 25 July 1782, Serie III, L7.
89. Catholic Committee. A group of Catholics who were cool towards certain forms of Catholic piety which they branded as superstitious. They also had a critical attitude towards the papacy and rule from Rome.

things were going,[90] and spoke of some former Jesuits taking refuge under the Catholic Committee's wings in London. 'A letter from London says there will soon be two sorts of Catholics there, some admitting the Pope's superiority and others rejecting it entirely.' Berrington's new book on Abelard 'showed a new character for a Catholic writer in England, unshackled in his thoughts and free in his expression.' Bannister also enclosed the draft of a denunciation of Berrington which he jestingly said should be sent as an open letter to Pius VI. Evidently Shepherd was regarded as a sympathetic ear, and one can speculate that Shepherd's experience of regalism in Spain may have had some effect in determining his attitude to the Papacy. However in 1788 Shepherd became more closely involved in this issue. When in this year a commission of English Catholics visited William Pitt the Younger to ask for greater toleration, they also sought to canvass the opinion of the Catholic universities on the continent as to the power of the Holy See over the civil obedience of Catholics. Shepherd was commissioned to seek the opinion of the Universities of Alcalá, Valladolid and Salamanca on this matter, which he did through the Spanish Secretary of State, Count Floridablanca. Hardly surprisingly, the Spanish universities were of the opinion that the Papacy had no real authority in England, or any other nation. Neither could the Pope dispense Catholics from their allegiance to their King, nor was there any article of faith which obliged Catholics to deny obedience to an heretical ruler.[91]

Douglas, his former colleague at Valladolid and now a Bishop, referred in a letter acknowledging Shepherd's congratulations to the Relief Bill in Parliament.[92] 'I waited on the Bishop of St David's this morning after the Bill passed, to return thanks to him and the bench of Bishops for their generous patronage.' But good relations with the Established Church were offset by some fellow-Catholics: 'We ought now to enjoy peace but I fear the Staffordshire clergy will create new uneasiness, they are endeavouring to draw over clergy in the other districts to join them in a petition to Mr Walmesley[93] to withdraw the

---

90. These complaints are to be found in two long letters of 16 April and 4 June 1787. Correspondence, 4, pp. 6 and 10.

91. Francisco Vera Urbano, 'La Consulta de los Católicos Ingleses a las facultades teológicas Españolas en tiempo de Pitt el Joven', *Anthologica Annua*, 19, Rome 1972, pp. 615–49. The answers of the six Catholic universities — Louvain, Douai, Paris, Alcalá, Valladolid and Salamanca — are printed in C. Butler, *Historical Memoirs*, vol. I, p. 439.

92. 15 July 1791. Correspondence, 4, p. 70.

93. Charles Walmesley, O.S.B., Vicar Apostolic of the Western District.

suspension of Mr Wilkes.[94] If they be refused at Bath, they mean to appeal to Rome. They will also attempt to limit our power — to have bishops in ordinary — with a new system of ecclesiastical government.'[95] A little later the same year Douglas wrote again: 'The Staffordshire clergy rise up against us Bishops, except Mr. Perry.[96] The Lancashire clergy have sent a congratulatory letter on our late exertions so we have Lancashire on our side.[97] Mr Crosby[98] has taken part against me in these public disputes, he is the only Valladolid priest that has done it.'[99]

In 1796 Shepherd undertook to make a survey of Portillo and its environs, part of his contribution to the new map of Spain that was being made. It was at this time that he fell ill and died on 30 October that year. His Rectorship had been much longer than Perry's but less eventful, his task being to continue and consolidate the tradition established in the early years of the restored College. Apart from Douglas, who was Vicar Apostolic in London, he was the last survivor of the superiors of those early days. He was not only well known to priests who had passed through his hands as students at Valladolid, but to many who had previously been with him at Douai. He was trusted for the soundness of his views by the Vicars Apostolic, and the College was now sending back a regular supply of priests to work on the mission. His death raised the question of who might be a suitable successor. The inability or unwillingness to spare priests from the Mission for work in the seminaries abroad meant that there was no outstanding person on the staff.

94. Revd Joseph Wilkes, O.S.B. Member of the Catholic Committee. For his quarrel with Walmesley his Bishop and the subsequent events, see B. Ward, *The Dawn of the Catholic Revival in England*, I, London 1909, pp. 257ff.

95. As fn. 92, above.

96. A nephew of Dr Perry, late Rector of Valladolid.

97. Shepherd was himself a Lancashire man.

98. Came out to Valladolid as a student with Fryer from Douai in 1770. Accompanied Fryer to Lisbon, and was for a time his Vice President until relations became strained. Anstruther, 4, p. 78.

99. 1 Nov. 1791, Correspondence, 4, p. 75.

8

YEARS OF UNCERTAINTY FOR SPAIN AND THE COLLEGE, 1797–1842

Shepherd's death marked the end of the era in which the English Colleges in Spain had been re-established as a single institution at Valladolid under the administration of the English secular clergy. There now followed a period marked by financial losses, scarcity of students and changes in the teaching staff when College affairs were directed by several Rectors, Pro-Rectors and Vice-Rectors. The political instability of Spain contributed substantially to the unhappy state of affairs at St Alban's.

We shall consider the history of these years in three periods: (1) *1796–1808*: the Rectorship of Thomas Taylor, corresponding to the latter part of the reign of Charles IV; (2) *1808–1812*: the College during the Peninsular War when the Vice-Rector Richard Cowban was in charge; and (3) *1813–1842*: the unsettled years of Ferdinand VII and the minority of Isabel II when William Irving, Thomas Sherburne, Joseph Brown and James Standen administered the College with varying degrees of authority.

The Rectorship of Thomas Taylor, 1796–1808

There is a lack of documentation on Taylor's Rectorship;[1] there are no books of receipts or expenditure extant, and there is little correspondence with England. Taylor himself is something of an enigma. After ordination in 1787 he remained on the staff at Valladolid as Procurator until 1794, when he returned to England. There are indications that when rumour began to circulate that Shepherd was about to leave Valladolid, Taylor expressed an interest in the Rectorship;[2] Shepherd did not resign, but soon died. Neither Craythorne[3] nor Greenway,[4] the only other

---

1. The scanty information in English College sources can be in some way supplemented by M. Taylor, *The Scots College in Spain*, especially chapters X, XI, XII and XIII; also Anstruther, vol. 4, p. 275.
2. Correspondence, 5, p. 4, 2 July 1796.
3. Francis Craythorne had been invited in 1794 by Shepherd to join the staff at

people in England familiar with the situation in Spain, was willing to return; and Thomas Smith (future Vicar Apostolic of the Northern District) was offered the Rectorship but declined it.[5] Taylor had his name officially presented by the Vicars Apostolic on 26 January 1797; he arrived in Valladolid on 22 July, his appointment having been confirmed by Charles IV on 10 July 1797. Before he left England, Craythorne was in correspondence with him, and offered advice as to the reform of the teaching at Valladolid. He called on him to put an end to the 'confused precarious manner of teaching that has so long prevailed at St Alban's', adding bluntly: 'Don't mince matters, call your subjects together, tell them plainly what the rules are and what formerly was the discipline of the House which you mean to put in full force etc. You will thus in a few weeks find who are content and who are not, if necessary make an example of the most refractory and get your House wellstocked with fresh boys.'[6]

Taylor was not short of advice, for in 1797 Greenway, the former Vice Rector, also wrote giving his views on the teaching of theology: 'What was the opinion of Luther or Calvin gives nobody much concern in this age of general, I may almost say, infidelity. May not Divines be desired to make the Bible especially the New Testament their almost only spiritual reading book?' and as for discipline: 'You know, my dear sir, that when the superiors seem to take a great interest in the improvement of boys and gain their affections how much may be done for the common good. Most of the evils that call for a remedy in our establishments, have originated from a want of an open, communicative and friendly disposition to one another. Superiors certainly should be above every little jealousy, and contribute as much as possible to their mutual content, happiness and improvement.'[7]

Valladolid and had made all preparations for the journey when at the last minute obstacles arose to his leaving the country. Although asked back on other occasions he always refused (CRS, 30, p. 210). But he did not lose interest in things Spanish and he wrote to Taylor in 1800 asking him to send *carabanzos (sic)*, *lentejas* and other Spanish foods for which he was pining in England. Correspondence, 5, p. 36; Anstruther, vol. 4, pp. 76–8.

4. John Greenway, a former Vice-Rector and scientific experimenter; see p. 112, above.

5. L. Gooch, 'Vicars Apostolic of the Northern District', *Northern Catholic History*, vol. 17, Spring 1983, p. 20; Anstruther, vol. 4, p. 251.

6. Craythorne to Taylor, 8 Feb. 1797. A further letter of 4 Dec. 1798 informed Taylor that he had a reputation of being too indulgent and familiar with the boys.

7. Greenway to Taylor, 1797, p. 18.

It seems to have been generally felt that with the founding fathers, Perry and Shepherd, removed from the scene, there was a need for St Alban's to adapt more to the needs of the day. But whatever may have been his ideals, Taylor was soon confronted with the grim practicalities of running a College in the last years of Charles IV's reign when the effects of the Revolution in France were beginning to unsettle the regime in Spain. From the College's point of view there was first of all the problem of staffing. Thomas Price, who had been in charge from the death of Shepherd till Taylor's arrival, left for England in May 1798. There is a reference the previous year to a French priest (presumably a refugee from the Revolution) teaching divinity at the College.[8] The College in Lisbon offered help of a more permanent kind. Richard Studdard, a former alumnus of Lisbon, arrived in 1797 to teach theology and act as Vice-Rector. In 1800 he left for the Mission in England, and the vacancy was filled temporarily by William Hurst,[9] who was recommended by the President of Lisbon College, William Fryer, himself a former professor at Valladolid. Hurst, a very young man, was not a success and returned to Lisbon, and Taylor therefore had to depend for his teaching staff on students staying on after ordination: first Thomas Sherburne, who became Vice-Rector in 1803, and then Richard Cowban, who took over in 1806 when Sherburne returned to England. Bishop Douglas wrote in 1800[10] that he could promise no help from England, and that Taylor would have to manage as best he could with what he had on the spot until the situation improved.[11]

But the most important changes during Taylor's period of office were those resulting from the upheavals in Europe. The English Colleges in Valladolid and Lisbon were now the only ones that were still open on the continent. The Revolution in France had seen the end of Douai and St Omer's, and the occupation of Rome by French troops had meant the closure of the College there; the students of these establishments had fled back to England. It was now possible, with the establishment of the colleges at Old Hall and Ushaw, for boys to be educated for the priesthood without leaving England, but there were no signs that the Bishops wanted to give up the idea of continental colleges. When Taylor wrote

8. M. Taylor, op. cit., p. 162, speaks of French refugee priests staying at the Scots College at this time.
9. See Anstruther, vol. 4, p. 150.
10. Douglas to Taylor, 25 Feb. 1800.
11. M. Taylor, op. cit., p. 158, says that English College students were receiving tuition at the Scots College in 1807.

to Douglas in 1802 saying that because of the political situation it was inadvisable to send out students that year, Douglas replied: 'Most happy shall I be, if I live to witness San Albano maintaining 30 students within her walls at one time. The prospect will then in truth brighten and compensate for losses at Rome and in France.'[12] In 1804 prospects did brighten in so far as eleven new students arrived, but the overall gloom remained.

During these years the French became increasingly popular in Spain and there was a widespread desire to introduce the principles of the Revolution into the country. The French army, in fact, passed through Valladolid in 1801 on its way to Portugal.[13] Besides the political uncertainty, the years 1800–2 saw a drought and subsequent crop failure. The country was desperately short of the money it needed to prosecute the war, and so in 1797 the Government appealed for gifts of money or jewellery as well as loans which could be redeemed without interest after ten years.[14] Certificates were issued for this war loan, and although there is no evidence that Taylor acquired these issues, in 1800 he had to petition to sell two houses because he was in need of cash. This would seem to be the beginning of the financial difficulties that were to dog the College Rectors for the next half century. Repairs were needed to the buildings and the River Cega had burst its banks and flooded College property.

The College had deposited a considerable sum in the national banks or *juros*, which should have produced a yearly interest. But the banks failed and no interest was now being paid.[15] Moreover if the money deposited were to be drawn upon, it was subject to a crippling tax amounting to 30, 40 and later 50 per cent. The College needed money to repair the cornmill it owned and its property at Laguna. Amid all this trouble, postal communication between Spain and England was bad, and letters

---

12. Douglas to Taylor, 5 Nov. 1802, of CRS, 30, pp. lviii–lix.
13. Taylor, op. cit., tells us that French troops, on their return from Portugal, were billeted on religious houses in the town, including the Scots College.
14. 31 Aug. 1799. The Bishop of Valladolid sent a circular letter to the parishes and religious houses of his diocese asking them to observe in letter and spirit the new tax laws.
15. 'During the last century the College deposited in the national banks or *juros* moneys to be producing the yearly interest of about £250; this bank was broken up about the beginning of this century, since when nothing has been received nor may be expected.' J. Guest, *A short statement regarding the College of St Alban's at Valladolid and property belonging to it* (June 1841?), Briggs, 1014a, Leeds Diocesan Archives.

had often to be sent via the English College in Lisbon. There were complaints that Taylor never answered letters.[16] Douglas became anxious about the Rector's health,[17] and in 1802 wrote: 'And now my dear sir, as the years of your Rectorship [the term was for six years] will expire next summer, Mr Gibson, Bishop and Vicar Apostolic of the Northern District, and myself write in requesting you to return to England before that period. And it is my request, in particular, that you will come and live with me in Castle Street, till a situation for you offers on the mission.'[18] Taylor did not comply with this request, and on 10 October 1803 he obtained from the King a prolongation of his term for a further six years.[19] Taylor's health, about which Douglas again expressed anxiety in 1804,[20] broke down completely in 1806. The following year the French entered Spain as allies against the Portuguese and English, and in 1808, after the enforced abdication of Charles IV and the Revolt of 2 May, Thomas Taylor died. His death thus coincided with the end of the *ancien régime* — the College losing its Rector at the same time as Spain lost her independence. The country was now in turmoil, and in the years that followed it was split into a conglomeration of autonomous cities and regions ruled by local *juntas* which organised resistence to the French and to Joseph Bonaparte who had been imposed on them as King in place of Ferdinand VII.

The College during the Peninsular War, 1808–1812

If correspondence is scanty for Taylor's regime, it is non-existent for the ensuing years. However, we do know that Richard Cowban, the Vice-Rector, held the fort for five years receiving the *poder* (legal authority) as Pro-Rector on 17 July 1810.[21] The registers record that no English secular priest could be found who was able or willing to take on the direction and administration of the College.[22] This is hardly surprising since on 12 June, just twenty-one days after the death of Taylor, French

16. Correspondence, 26, 29, 48.
17. Taylor suffered from gout. Correspondence, 5, p. 33.
18. Douglas to Taylor, 5 Nov. 1802. CRS, 30, p. lix.
19. Series III, L9.
20. Douglas to Taylor, 11 Sept. 1804: 'I hasten to send you an answer to your last . . . I pray our Father in Heaven to preserve you and them [the students] from the contagion and enable you to support the boys in food and raiment.'
21. Series III, L9.
22. CRS, 30, p. 223.

troops entered the city for the first time. From now on there were successive periods of military occupation, including that by the British for ten days in December. The French were permanently in control between December 1808 and June 1812. Valladolid was no place for English clerical students, and measures were taken to get the fourteen in residence home.[23]

The first three left on 10 August 1808, and four more followed in September. Each of them received a *viaticum* and proceeded to Gijon where they took ship for England. But there were no further funds available and because of fighting in the area of Valladolid, the others were not able to leave till the following year. In 1809 Robert Brindle and four companions set out on foot and with no money, to make their way to Portugal in the hope of getting a ship for England. Only in 1812 were the two remaining students able to leave. In March of that year John Challoner left for Peñafiel with some money and eventually reached England where he completed his studies, was ordained and eventually worked as a priest in the Midland District. The last student, Francis Tydiman, left in April on foot and penniless. He got as far as Coruña, and decided to stay there; he obtained employment, eventually married, and died there sometime after 1822. He is mentioned in later correspondence with the College authorities since he seems to have acted as agent for the College in that port.[24] Cowban stayed on alone for more than a year until a new Rector arrived, but there were to be no new students till 1820.

This period in College history is enlivened by the account that Robert Brindle wrote in later life of his adventures. The manuscript, which is in the College archives, begins with the story of his coming out from England in 1804, the eighteen-day sea voyage to Bilbao, his first impressions of Spain travelling overland from Bilbao to Valladolid, and the wonder he felt on seeing Burgos Cathedral. But the greater part of his account concerns the escape from Spain when fighting broke out in the Valladolid area, the journey to Lisbon and the voyage thence to England. Brindle tells us that the trouble began when, due to the alliance of Bonaparte and the Prince of Peace (Godoy), 'over 200,000 fighting men'

23. During these years there were at least two occasions when the College had to protest against the authorities for infringing its rights. On 28 Oct. 1811 a plot of land in its ownership was occupied and used as a burial ground for Frenchmen dying in the hospitals, and on 12 Jan. 1813 soldiers began felling trees on College property.
24. Correspondence, 5, pp. 78, 107.

entered Spain from France. This was the signal for Spanish resistance, and Brindle associated himself with the people's patriotic sentiments:[25] 'We are unable to meet our enemy in the field, but let us each one grapple with his man and we shall be victorious. For though it should be another Moorish war which desolated our beloved country for the space of 600 years, still at the end of that term, a Spaniard shall be found to sing the song of victory over the last dying Frenchman.' At Valladolid there were some 'few French troops in the city who were sacrificed in the first transports of popular frenzy. Arms were called for on every side but no arms could be procured. The multitude, however, paraded the streets and public squares with fowling pieces, pruning knives and other such weapons as they could provide.' The Captain-General (Don Gregorio de la Cuesta) 'exerted his authority to prevent the English students from being obliged to quit the house, but the mob declared they would burn the College to the ground if we did not join them. Accordingly we were obliged to go to the depot for arms, but, fortunately, the last musket was distributed when we were within 50 yards of the spot. If we had gone two minutes sooner 'tis probable we had been killed, for the body of students with whom we were associated was entirely destroyed.'

He goes on to describe the taking of Valladolid by the French, and after the battle[26] 'I went on to the field of battle the day after and tho' the French had stripped their dead, yet the bodies were easily distinguished from the Spaniards from their earrings, colour etc. Several hundreds, it was known, were thrown into the river, and indeed to such an extent that the magistrates of Valladolid prohibited the use of the river water for six weeks.' He tells us of how one night he was awakened by cannon fire and then, at about 4 a.m., heard a trumpet: 'I imagined the Spaniards were driving the French through the town. Without allowing myself a moment for reflection, I hastened to a window which faced the street, threw it open and to my great consternation, beheld a French dragoon immediately below the window, his arm lifted up towards me and the muzzle of his carbine within half a yard of my face.' Brindle retired back to bed immediately. The well-known Spanish patriot Roxo de Corcos, in flight from the French, was allowed to hide at the English College

25. The Vice-Rector of the Scots College, Cameron, was similarly pro-Spanish, and in his letters of this period was wont to sign himself '*El Fanático*' (M. Taylor, op. cit., p. 161).

26. This refers to the battle of Cabezón in June 1808, when a force of 5,000 Spaniards was routed by twice as many French.

property near Laguna. Brindle himself was involved in this, and his efforts to assist Roxo and escape detection by the French involved him in an escapade that meant swimming twice along and across the Duero. Then for a time there was a lull when the French retreated and Ferdinand was proclaimed as the rightful King in place of Joseph Bonaparte, but it was soon reported that the enemy were at Briviesca and were advancing on the Extremadura army stationed at Burgos. Valladolid was again threatened, and Brindle reported the dismay as the city prepared to meet the invader: 'The doors of the nunnerys were thrown open by the Bishop's orders, and many venerable ladies who for the space of fifty years had never trodden unhallowed ground were now obliged to leave the graves which they had prepared for themselves. [. . .] We afterwards heard that the French had been informed that the English College had been very busy in exciting the people of Valladolid to revolt. Hence we conjectured what treatment we should have experienced had we fallen into their hands.[27] We did not however give them time to put their design into execution. We had a little hut attached to a mill about 5 miles from Portillo, and to this place we decided to retreat for a short time. The College was instantly abandoned.'

On 25 June 1809 it was decided that some students would try to make their way back home to England via Portugal. There was difficulty in leaving Portillo since the roads were in the possession of the enemy, but they managed to escape by night and because they could hear the French cavalry nearby, they wandered around a lot in the mist. Thoughts of making towards Viana were ruled out when they learnt that the French were there. A Spanish friar they met agreed to help them reach Portugal, and their route was planned by a guerrilla party under '*El Empecinado*'[28] who, Brindle tells us, after the return of Ferdinand was raised to the dignity of a Grandee of the First Class and created Duke of Empecinado. The students passed through a series of friendly villages, avoiding Peñaranda which was under French control. They reached Flores de Avila where they attended Mass on the Feast of SS Peter and Paul, then they crossed the high road from Madrid to Salamanca and passed Duervelo. Thanks to Empecinado's passport, they were well received everywhere. At Ciudad Rodrigo they were suspected of being French

27. Taylor, op. cit., p. 161, reports that the Scots College was looted by the French on this occasion.
28. See G. Marañón, *El Empecinado visto por un inglés* (Frederick Hardman) in *Obras Completas*, V. pp. 9–84. A street in Valladolid today bears his name. Brindle tells us that his real name was Juan Martín and he came from Aranda de Duero.

spies, but they crossed into Portugal only to find that 'the name of an Englishman was not so popular in Portugal as in Spain.' A certain Colonel Cox promised them a letter of introduction to the Duke of Wellington, and they decided to make for Oporto rather than Lisbon. They went through Lamego (a beautiful town, Brindle says) along the Duero Valley to Valonga, where they were bitten by bugs, and so to Oporto. They discovered that there were few ships leaving Oporto for England, and the English Consul had left for home, so they took a coasting vessel from Oporto bound for Lisbon. They had to pay ten shillings for the journey (there were five of them): 'This made a considerable hole in our purse yet we were obliged to submit.' It took them five days to reach Lisbon and during the voyage they had to live off raw fish.

When they arrived they tried to find the English College, but which English College was it? There were three or four establishments known by that name. They met an Irish wine merchant named Murphy who sent his servant with them to the College. They were told that the superiors were busy and could not see anyone. After waiting twenty minutes while the porter went to search, one of the superiors eventually arrived and asked what they wanted. He could not offer any accommodation on the plea of poverty and lack of rooms. When they complained of his lack of hospitality, they were asked what regiment they belonged to. They explained that they were not soldiers but students of the English College, Valladolid, and the whole atmosphere immediately changed. They were in fact at the Irish Dominican Convent of Corpo Santo and they were sent with the porter to the English College. As they approached the College door they saw one of the superiors going up the stairs having locked the outer door against them, thinking they were robbers. Eventually a priest answered the bell, and, once they had been able to identify themselves, they were received with open arms. All the English students of the College had returned home; the President, most of the masters, and all the Portuguese pensioners were at the country house and had taken the beds with them. So mattresses had to be found and laid on the floor, and after being given a good meal they slept soundly. In the morning they were provided with second-hand clothes, and the English envoy in Lisbon, the Hon. C. Villiers, promised to send them to England at no cost by the first available transport. A passport was issued to prevent them being press-ganged at any of the ports. On Sunday 13 September they sailed from Lisbon in a convoy of eighty vessels.

Twenty-one days later they landed, not at Portsmouth as they had expected, but at Falmouth, 280 miles from London. They had no money and so they began the long journey on foot, begging from people who found it hard to believe the story of their adventures. They passed through Bodmin, Launceston, Okehampton and Exeter, and when they reached Bath, they called at St John's Catholic Church where a saucy servant shut the door in their faces. However, the landlord of a nearby public house received them well and informed them of the existence of a society in Bath for the relief of distressed travellers. But when this society found that they were Catholics they were handed over to a Catholic society with similar ends. This brought them back to St John's. The priest did not believe that they were from Valladolid, but gave them seven shillings towards their fare. Back they went to the landlord (a protestant). There another priest soon arrived, a Mr Birdsall, who believed their story and apologised for the rudeness of his colleague, Mr Ainsworth.[29] They left Bath at 6 a.m. by coach and arrived in London at 10 a.m. the next day. Brindle said good-bye to his companions in London and made for Liverpool; from there he proceeded to Preston, and then walked the last 18 miles to his home at Singleton in the Fylde. This was the end of his adventures. He eventually completed his studies at Ushaw and, as we shall see, he was to return to Spain in 1820 with seven new students.

The unsettled years of Ferdinand VII and the minority of Isabel II, 1813–1842

Wellington had entered Valladolid on 30 July 1812, but he had to withdraw his troops later that year, and it was not till 4 June 1813 that the French finally left the town. Ferdinand eventually returned to Spain in March 1814, but before that date the pattern of the future was being sketched out. For some the War of Independence had been a campaign simply to drive out the French and re-establish the old absolute Bourbon monarchy; but for many it had provided an opportunity of drawing up a fresh constitution for a new Spain. In 1808 the Council of Castile had refused public recognition of Joseph Bonaparte's title to the Spanish Crown; his claim was invalid because the nation had not been consulted. There was in this an implicit suggestion that ultimate sovereignty rested

---

29. Both Birdsall and Ainsworth are to be found in Birt, *Obit Book of the English Bene-dictines*, Edinburgh 1913, pp. 141 and 130.

with the nation, and any future form of kingship would have to take account of the popular will. When a Cortes or Assembly made up of Deputies drawn from the various provinces met at Cadiz, in 1810, it proceeded to draw up what was to become the Constitution of 1812. Certain principles of the French Revolution were thus introduced, and these would create new problems for the Church which was highly suspicious of any talk of the popular will or of democracy.

To the relief of many clerics, but to the dismay of the 'liberals', Ferdinand repudiated the 1812 Consttution. The new Rector of the English College wrote: 'The Regency together with their new fangled constitution was happily extinguished to the extreme joy of all well wishers to social order.'[30] However, the current became so strong against Ferdinand that in the end, in 1820, he had to swear adherence to the Constitution. From this day forward there was a series of governments which, as well as enacting liberalizing measures, were from time to time markedly anti-clerical in tone and especially hostile to the religious orders. This new situation faced William Irving[31] when he became Rector in 1813.

The Rectorship of William Irving, 1813–1822

Irving, who had been a student at Valladolid in 1792–1801 had to wait for some time before he could set off to assume the Rectorship.[32] Like his predecessor, he had plenty of advice offered to him during this interval. Bishop Cameron[33] had written to him:[34] 'In your connections with the natives of all ranks, situations and descriptions, you must *appear* free and easy, but much prudence and caution will *always* be necessary. [. . .] When you have students take care that none of them become familiar with the servants or with anyone without the College. Teach them to be particularly attentive to the external marks of attention or politeness among the natives, always answering their salutations in the appropriate words and taking off their hats. [. . .] Take care whom you take for

30. Irving to Craythorne, May or June 1814, Correspondence, 5, p. 65.
31. In England he was known usually as Irving, though he sometimes used the name Sherburne. In Spain he was known as Irvin.
32. Gibson to Irving, 30 Sept. 1812.
33. Formerly Rector of the Scots College, Valladolid, and now Vicar Apostolic of the Lowland District of Scotland. He had a nephew at the Scots College.
34. 23 July 1813.

professors — *turpis ejicitur quam non admittitur hospes*[35] . . . take advice. Your predessors were all too wise and knowing.'

Irving's official appointment as Rector by Bishop Poynter, Vicar Apostolic of the London District, is dated 4 August 1813 and the Royal approval was given by Ferdinand VII from Cadiz on 15 September 1813. When at last Irving arrived at Valladolid in November, he was confronted with something approaching disaster — not so much because of the political situation as because of the material condition of the College property. There had been thefts, burnings and other damage by the French troops, and the two riverside properties — *riberas* — near the city were almost entirely destroyed. Most of the land had not been cultivated for three years, and it was clear that the College had either to abandon the *fincas* and other possessions as a total ruin or sell some of them to raise money to restore the rest. He wrote to Ferdinand in December asking for Royal protection and help to prevent the property from total loss and asking permission to sell one of the mills and some of the houses owned by the College; an enclosure called La Perrera outside the city walls and the Ribera S. Ambrosio which was so decayed as to be quite unproductive.[36]

The following year Irving gave in a letter to one of his friends a full account of the situation in which he had found the College on his arrival:[37]

'The debts exceeded 300,000 reales, and there was not a farthing. Viana did not defray the expenses of culture. Laguna and S. Ambrosio were almost abandoned. Portillo ditto. The best lands about Valladolid were let out to people at a very low rent, which was not well paid; and the walls and houses threatening ruin everywhere. The expenditure since November 1813 up to the present moment amounts to the sum of 212,018 reales and the receipts are only 33,089 reales. Many old debts have been paid, the Labranza has been increased, and the vineyards have had their regular, but long disused, course of labour. Many of them, owing to the neglect of regular pruning, have been cut down; an expensive operation, but necessary even for their existence. Three years must elapse before an adequate return can be expected. A flock of twenty sheep has also been purchased. It is a lucrative branch, and, if I may be allowed to judge from the

---

35. This tag 'It is better to refuse hospitality in the first place than to eject someone you have accepted as a guest' was quoted later by Henson in the Burns affair.
36. See Correspondence, 5, p. 63. In this letter (probably Dec. 1813) Irving details the College losses, which include 2 *riberas* destroyed, 6 pairs of mules lost, 600 cargos of grain sacked — in all amounting to 1 million reales.
37. 20 Nov. 1814, Correspondence, 5, p. 81; cf. CRS, 30, p. lx.

enormous debts contracted with butchers, wholly necessary to the future temporal prosperity of the College. I have likewise placed a few wild cows in the plains of Portillo, in a herd belonging to various individuals. But much still remains to be done . . . In the meantime that system of oppression, introduced by the French, of billeting troops on the College is still continued; I believe from necessity, because the Government cannot pay them. Often times I have to the number of 20 lodged upon me. It is expensive and a real burden, in which circumstances a man can scarcely be said to be the master of his own house nor could any sort of regular discipline be maintained.

Only when this situation was a thing of the past and the mill had been sold could he again think of receiving students once again.

The problem was how to raise money in a Spain devastated by war and already beset by political and constitutional changes. Two years later, the situation had scarcely improved, and in a long letter to Bishop Gibson, Irving explained what were the impediments to the resumption of normal life at St Alban's:[38] the harvest had been bad, the fruit had failed in the two gardens, and the revenue from the vineyards scarcely covered expenses. The rents were inadequate, and it had proved impossible to sell any of the property for want of a purchaser. Claims had been laid on the Government for payment of the interest on money invested in the *juros* from which nothing had been received since 1802. Apart from the long neglect of the vineyards, the arable land was in a sorry state.

There are 800 statute acres, of which 300 lie uncultivated and produce nothing. This is owing to the total want of enclosures, and to the peculiar privileges which shepherds in this country enjoy, of entering with their flocks every man's land the moment it ceases to be ploughed . . . 300 acres are cultivated by the College, and the remaining 300 are in the hands of various tenants, who, during the tyranny of the French, when he who sowed could hardly expect to reap, took them for a term of nine years at the rate of little more than two shillings and sixpence an acre. Great advantages would undoubtedly be obtained if the College had the means of cultivating all its possessions; but for this purpose a considerable capital is required, and the debts must previously be paid, which still amount to about £2,000. The mode of agriculture in these parts is expensive, principally on account of the uncouthness of their implements of husbandry. The Spanish plough can scarcely be said to be good for anything . . . After much trouble I have succeeded in introducing two English ploughs, which, notwithstanding their unwillingness to adopt the slightest improvement not arising from themselves, are the admiration of the natives. At the suggestion of the first Minister of State, the Royal Economic Society of Madrid[39] has

38. 6 Feb. 1816, cf. CRS, 30, pp. lxi, lxii.
39. See p. 113, above, fn. 79.

directed to me an Official Dispatch requesting information on the subject of English ploughs and harrows, as well as models. And it is with pleasure that I have complied with the request. Besides the advantages which, I flatter myself, will accrue to the College from the adoption of the English plough, it may, also, be the means of obtaining more powerful protection.[40]

It was in these dire circumstances that Irving mortgaged the valuable property of the Ribera de S. Ignacio, and in order to repay it he secured a loan from the Lancashire Clergy Fund at 4½% through the good offices of Craythorne. He hoped to be able to pay the interest and refund the principle within two years.[41] In addition to this loan from the Lancashire Clergy, there were other borrowings from people in Spain and in England, the object of which was to repay debts dating from before the Peninsular War and repair the damages and costs incurred by the effects of the war and subsequent neglect of the property.

Towards the end of Irving's Rectorship, the Government did acknowledge its debts to the College in respect of the deposits placed in the *juros* before the Peninsular War. But the suggested method of repayment was not acceptable, since it involved the College taking advantage of the government's confiscation of property belonging to the religious orders as a result of the anti-clerical measures of the liberals.

The juros or moneys in the Spanish Funds belonging to us, and amounting to the sum of from 3 to £4,000, have been acknowledged as a lawful debt of the nation, and as payable out of the possessions of the suppressed monasteries. Either land may be purchased to the above amount with government paper, or said paper may be sold for real cash at a discount however of 80 and 82%. One of these two measures must be adopted, or the debt will be cancelled. The purchase of monastic possessions is considered by some (I may venture to say by many) as unlawful. Moreover, in the event of a change, of which there is a *possibility*, it is to be presumed that all purchases of the above description will be declared null. In the meantime the purchases are looked upon with an evil eye. On the other hand to be necessitated to lose 80% is painful.[42]

Thus the College was indirectly affected by the anti-clerical legislation following on the events of 1820. In 1814 Cowban, who had remained at

---

40. The letter of congratulation to Irving from the *Real Sociedad Económica*, 5 Jan. 1816 is in Series III, L9.
41. Irving to Craythorne, May or June 1814. Craythorne to Irving, 31 March 1814. Series III, L9.
42. Irving to Bishop Smith, 25 July 1821. Leeds Diocesan Archives, Smith Correspondence, 121.

his post all through the war, returned to England, and George Laytham came out to assist Irving as Procurator, but after little more than a year he returned home.[43] Correspondence passed between Irving and well-wishers at home, including Bishop Poynter who not only promised a gift of £100 for the College[44] but also unburdened some of his own troubles about Milner and the Irish Question.[45] Irving in his turn kept Poynter informed of the position of the Jesuits in Spain. The English Bishops were fearful lest the restored Society should make a claim for the College they had administered in the past.[46]

The Jesuits as yet have not been re-established in this Kingdom by any public edict, but of their ultimate re-establishment there is little or no doubt. In the first instance they will be few in number, and therefore not dangerous. They will, moreover, proceed with a cautious step, remembering what they formerly suffered. But they will aim at aggrandisement, and gradually obtain their object. This establishment, I think has nothing to fear from them, tho' all its possessions formerly belonged to the order. The Duke of Alba purchased from the Crown and we from the Duke of Alba. But had this property been a Royal gift, perhaps there might be some slight cause for apprehension.[47]

Somewhat ironically it was only after Ferdinand repudiated the 1812 Constitution, an act which Irving welcomed, that the return of the Jesuits became at all likely. The fear of a Jesuit revival receded when in 1820 the Society, along with other religious orders, was openly persecuted by the liberal governments. Although matters were to deteriorate in the succeeding years, as a foreign establishment the English College was in no immediate danger when the 1812 Constitution was established in 1820.[48] Indeed this was the year when conditions at the College had

43. Writing to Gibson on 3 Feb. 1816, Irving said of Laytham: 'He is of an unequal and turbulent temper, and . . . on the whole his conduct does not satisfy me. In the actual state of this establishment, as a procurator he is useless, and must therefore soon become hurtful. His want of discretion causes me sincerely to regret his abode in San Albano.'
44. Poynter to Irving, 31 Jan. 1814.
45. Ibid.
46. The same fear was expressed about the College in Rome. M. E. Williams, *The Venerable English College Rome*, p. 80, and for the Scots College in Valladolid, M. Taylor, p. 168.
47. Irving to Poynter, 5 Jan. 1815. Also letter of 16 Feb. 1816 to Gibson.
48. M. Taylor, op. cit., p. 176, quotes a letter of Rector Cameron to Bishop Patterson, 18 Aug. 1820: 'The late changes have not affected hitherto our establishment, but may affect it very materially by depriving us of a considerable part of our income if all tythes are done away with, as is currently reported.' On 21

sufficiently improved for it to be ready to receive students once more.[49] Seven of them sailed from Liverpool bound for Bilbao, accompanied by Robert Brindle of Peninsular War fame who was to join the teaching staff. Of this new generation of students two were from London but the rest were Lancastrians — of whom two were sponsored by Craythorne. But Irving did not live to see any further increase in numbers, since he died on 3 August 1822, at the age of forty-six. He had done much during his Rectorship to repair the damage done to College property during the war, and his knowledge of agriculture was considerable and received recognition from the Spanish authorities; but his borrowing plunged the College into even greater debt. News of Irving's death was received in London from Cameron of the Scots College who informed Poynter, who in turn passed the news on to Bishop Smith of the Northern District.[50] Cameron had written as follows:

This irreparable loss was caused, in a great degree, by the immense fatigues he underwent daily in improving the extensive property of the English College. It is incredible what he has done, and, if God had spared his life a few years more, he would have left St Alban's on a most brilliant footing [. . .] Some one must be sent out immediately, immediately, immediately without losing a moment's time; for nothing can be conceived more distressing, than the state of the house, the lads being all young, mere children, are incapable of doing anything: and Mr Brindle, the only remaining superior, has been all this while in bed, dangerously ill, so that there is not a single soul to watch over the internal discipline, or to take care of the temporal concerns of the college . . . nothing is to be apprehended from the disordered state of this country. Travellers are allowed to pass without being molested by either party.

Poynter urged Smith that another person who knew the language of the place should be sent out immediately, 'not only for the internal government of the College, but particularly for the temporal concerns and especially for the ensuing vintage. [. . .] The College has nothing to depend on but the produce of its land.' He then went on to suggest a suitable candidate for the post. 'I think of no person so proper as Mr Thomas Sherburne, Mr Irving's brother. Engage him, as you think proper, to go *immediately* at least for a time.'

July 1820 the *Ayuntamiento* asked Irving for information about the college in compliance with the *Real Orden* on Elementary Education of 23 May 1820. Irving replied by saying that the *Orden* did not apply to the College.

49. Craythorne to Irving, 13 Oct. 1820.

50. Letter of 19 Aug. 1822, Leeds Archives, Smith Correspondence, 139.

Thomas Sherburne, 1822–1825

Poynter's suggestion was acted on, and towards the end of August 1822 Irving's brother Thomas Sherburne arrived at Valladolid. He was nominated Rector by the English Bishops, but because of the difficult situation of Ferdinand VII, whose absolute rule had been challenged by the liberals in 1820, the appointment was never ratified by the Spanish authorities and he is sometimes referred to simply as Pro-Rector. He had first gone out to Valladolid as a student at the age of nine, he had served for a time as a member of staff and was familiar with the situation now since as recently as 1819 he had paid a visit to the College while his brother was Rector.[51] His appointment seems to have been to some extent provisional, but as we shall see from now to the end of his life, whether as Rector or not, he was deeply concerned in College affairs. He brought with him Thomas Pilling, a student from Ushaw then in minor orders, who was ordained priest in Spain in 1823 and then became Vice-Rector and did some teaching. With the disunion among the liberals and the increasing anti-clerical feeling, the troubles in Spain were increasing.[52] But in spite of this the Bishops still supported the College. Poynter wrote:[53]

I feel as great repugnance to the idea of abandoning that excellent establishment for which your late lamented brother had done so much. I think it our duty to hold it as long as we can. Qui tenet, teneat. At present, I think that we should keep all together as well as we can, in hopes that a better order of things will be established in that country, which may be favourable to the College. Take courage then, my dear sir, for the present. You being on the spot can form a much better judgement of the prospect of things than we can and devise measures for the benefit of the establishment. I have absolute confidence in your skill and prudence.

But the College's creditors were making their demands on the new Rector. Sherburne received a letter, somewhat arrogant in tone, from the Administrator of the Secular Clergy Fund:[54]

---

51. See CRS, 30, p. lxii, 217. For further details concerning Sherburne see CRS, 15, pp. 225–6, 'The Registers of The Willows, Kirkham', where Sherburne resided for many years.
52. According to Taylor, op. cit., pp. 176–7, revenues from ecclesiastical sources were stopped.
53. 14 Aug. 1823.
54. R. Thompson to Sherburne, 22 Dec. 1823, CRS, 30, p. lxiii.

As a considerable sum of money, £1,000 was borrowed by your late worthy brother, your predecessor, as Rector of Saint Alban's College at Valladolid from the Fund of the Secular Clergy of this Vicariate, over which it has pleased Almighty God and the venerable Bishop of this District, that I should preside as Grand Vicar; I beg to signify to you that it is the wish of our Brethren, the meritorious labourers in our Lord's Vineyard, that the sum should be repaid. I, therefore, request that you will have the goodness to pay into us the said sum, as early as you possibly can: at any sacrifice to yourself. And you will oblige me.

Your most obedient Servant and Friend
RICHARD THOMPSON
Superior of the Fund
and Vicar General to the Bishop of B[olina]

Further correspondence from Poynter the following year[55] showed the Bishop's continued care and understanding of the difficulties confronting Sherburne: 'The cultivation of those distant lands is a great charge on the Rector; it must necessarily draw him off very much from the internal direction and government of the College. I hope that the motive of discharging the debts of the College will be admitted as a sufficient reason for granting permission to sell.' But in the same letter there are indications that Sherburne's tenure of office was coming to an end as soon as the authorities in England were able to find a successor. 'I have been lately at Ushaw . . . Mr Thompson was there, and we had much conversation with Bishop Smith about you and the plan you had proposed in your letter to Mr Thompson.[56] Bishop Smith agreed that you should return to England, as he had promised you; but the question was about your successor. The Person whom he had fixed his eye upon some months ago was thought not qualified for the management of the affair of a college, 'tho he would be a good professor in school. Besides, he has a natural defect which would be an impediment to him. As I have no one at all qualified for the office, Bishop Smith said he would apply to Dr Milner for one whom Bishop Smith mentioned and who appeared to be a fit person.' It was not for another twelve months that Sherburne left Valladolid for England. Thomas Pilling the Vice-Rector was in charge of affairs from August 1825 till January 1826 when the new Rector arrived.

---

55. 18 July 1824.
56. Thompson was the administrator of the Clergy Fund from which the College had borrowed.

Several years later,[57] John Guest wrote as follows of Sherburne's term of office: 'By the sale of about 40 acres of the best land, jewellery, vestments, pictures etc. aided by the produce of three good years, [he] was enabled to pay off some more of the old debts, and nearly liquidate the sums previously advanced by himself and his brother to the establishment.'

Joseph Brown, 1825–1839

The new Rector chosed by the Vicars Apostolic was Joseph Brown. He left London in November 1825 to make his journey overland through France, but was ill on the way and did not arrive at the College till 4 January 1826.[58] His nomination was only approved by Ferdinand VII on 29 August 1830.[59] Aged thirty-one at the time of his appointment, and with no previous experience of work abroad, Brown had been trained and ordained at Ushaw.

Sherburne briefed him before he left England and remarked in a letter to Pilling:[60] 'If he takes a liking to the country and his own occupations, I anticipate prosperity to San Albano under his administration.' Throughout his Rectorship Sherburne kept him informed of clerical affairs in England, where Catholic emancipation was the main talk. But he also offered help and advice on matters concerning Valladolid,[61] and this was to cause irritation to both Brown and Pilling, who felt at times that Sherburne was behaving as if he were still Rector.

On arrival at Valladolid Brown found that things were far from 'quite correct' as Sherburne had maintained. The property was crumbling, the discipline and studies were at a low ebb, and many of the students in residence were evidently unfit.[62] Brown was also to find himself soon under pressure from the College creditors in England. Sadler, the new treasurer of the Catholic Secular Priests Society of Lancashire, asked him

57. 'A short statement regarding the College of St Albans at Valladolid and property belonging to it.' Probably dating from June 1841, Leeds Archives, Briggs Correspondence, 1016A.
58. CRS, 30, p. 225.
59. Series III, L9.
60. 13 Nov. 1825, Correspondence 6, no. 8.
61. 8 Nov. 1826, Correspondence 6, no. 15.
62. Leeds Archives, Briggs, 492A.

for the interest due on the £1,100 loan.[63] Pilling had to take a vacation in England for reasons of health, and while there he wrote to Bishop Penswick[64] acknowledging receipt of £300 from his lordship and pointing out some of the difficulties in trying to repay debts contracted before the Peninsular War and immediately after the restoration of Ferdinand. The fall in prices had meant a fall in revenue for the College from the sale of its grain and wine products. On the bright side, however, he was able to report that the College would soon be three times as large a community as it had been in Sherburne's time; in fact five new students had arrived in 1826, six in 1830, four in 1831 and three in 1833. Of the 25 boys who had come out to Spain since the restoration of the College in 1820 only two were ordained in Valladolid. However, ten were subsequently ordained elsewhere, and one became a Cistercian monk. The correspondence of this period indicates that the recruitment of students for the College was due in no small measure to the personal efforts of former members of staff like Cowban and Sherburne, who had an ability to single out suitable candidates for the College.[65] But the small numbers were not so much due to scarcity of vocations as to the inability of the College to accommodate any more. Pilling in his visit to England in 1831 did some canvassing for students, but Brown had to write severely to him about the fees that would have to be charged:[66] 'I have told their lordships I could take no more boys on at £100 after the colony that was to come out in 1830 . . . How . . . you could so far mistake your commission as to think of sending here boys on £100 I cannot possibly explain.' He goes on to speak of the bad harvest, the poor wines due to rain at vintage times, and the repairs that needed to be done to the House.

Portillo falling about our ears and having to spend in Viana (in building up what is falling down) at least £50 . . . We must always count about 11 or 12 years for a course of studies during which £100 would nearly be spent in *clothes* and *shoes*

---

63. Jan. 1828, Correspondence 6, no. 21.

64. Leeds Archives, Penswick, 125A, 6 April 1832.

65. In these days a student had to bring 6 shirts, 6 pairs of stockings, 6 pocket handkerchiefs, 2 new suits of clothes, a knife, fork and silver spoon. 'The clothes and stockings must of course be black . . . I would likewise suggest the use of an old suit for the sea as one suit is generally by this rendered unfit for further use. As the number of boys here already greatly exceeds what San Albano with the exception of once or twice has ever maintained, we are in great want of dictionaries particularly Spanish ones and therefore . . . I add this to the above requisites' (Brown to Penswick, 16 Oct. 1833, Leeds Archives, Penswick, 152).

66. Brown to Pilling, 19 Dec. 1831. CRS, 30, p. lxiv.

only. And if formerly only 7 students could be supported here when times were so much better have we not sufficiently exposed the establishment, consulted the good of the missions and made every personal and pecuniary sacrifice, without a friend on this side of the Pyrenees to assist us in our distress. The new boys on £100 might easily be supported for 4 or 5 years and if the Rector that takes them on that is obliged to expend it all, how reasonable would be the complaints of his successor who would have to support them *otro tanto* or nothing. Besides who is to teach them? Mr Standen[67] has two schools, one of them poets: with two divines (which of course take the same attention as twenty) Mr Gornall and Luke Abbot in different classes and will never be able to join the six others. I have nearly all my time occupied being able to do little out of doors and not willing that others like Rimmer, after going home should say they were obliged to leave San Albano because no attention was paid them in their studies. I have made every calculation and I am of Dr Alejandro's opinion that each student should pay little less than £30 per annum.

Towards the end of the letter his mood softened: 'If I feel a little *incomodado* on this subject, you must attribute it solely to my interest for San Albano in which I should not like to leave you at the end of my rectorate or before, without the means of supporting your collegiales with credit to yourself.' Pilling tried to get a further loan, and Sherburne was becoming more anxious since the interest had not been paid on the previous loan.[68] The reason for Sherburne's insistence on repayment may have been that he felt in some way obliged to bring his brother's borrowings to a happy conclusion for the honour of the family as well as that of the College. But his motives were not understood in that way by Pilling.

Sherburne wishes to send Guest's brother, and so clear off the remainder of his debt, fingering, as he intends to do, whatever he can get from Guest's father, if the proposition be admitted. You will determine what you think best; nor can I say that I should advise you to accept it; but he is a leech, and will stick close to his bite till he has got the money or its equivalent. We have nothing to thank him for this long time past.

Pilling and Brown felt threatened by Sherburne, as Pilling continued in the same letter:

Both the Bishop and Mr Thompson consult him in what regards S. Albano and I fear that his *parecer* has more weight with them that all that either I or you can

---

67. Brown had made a visit to England in 1829 and returned in April 1830 with James Standen, an alumnus of Ushaw and minor professor there, who was ordained at Valladolid in 1832. See below, p. 142.
68. Pilling to Brown, April 1832, cf. CRS, 30, p. lxiv.

say. And, after all, he has nothing to ground an opinion upon, but his having left the College, *corriente*, so he is pleased to call it, in the year 1825. He is a genuine Scotchman and has the same love for me as he has for you. He wished to detain me in England, but I gave him a flat 'No' and he has since turned his back upon me. I return to S. Albano with greater pleasure that I left it. I gave you my word that I would return, and am happy to say, that in perfect health I hasten to receive it back from you.

While in England, Thompson had suggested to Pilling that the Rector himself visit England to beg for funds for the College. 'It is what so many of our good priests have been under the necessity of doing, in order to establish new missions, or remodel their old ones, with incredible success.'[69] But this suggestion was not taken up till 1836. One of the features of the history of this period is the travelling between Spain and England of the superiors of the College. In contrast to the troubled days of the Peninsular War, not only were the affairs of the College known and discussed in England, especially in the North where the superiors came from, but the problems of Catholics in England were well known in the College. Often the Vicars Apostolic confided their troubles to their friends overseas. We have already mentioned Bishop Poynter informing Irving of his worries concerning Dr Milner, the Irish and Catholic Emancipation.[70] In September 1830 Gillow wrote to Brown[71] about certain relaxations in Catholic practice and discipline. There was to be the abolition of Saturday abstinence from meat during Lent and on the Ember Days; and St Martin's Day, Easter Monday and Whit Monday were now no longer holy days of obligation. These changes did not please Gillow, and he remarked: 'Such are the dispensations and mitigations in her wholesome discipline the Church is compelled to make in favour of the sluggish and heavy arsed Christians in England. How fast are we degenerating into infidelity.'

It was during Brown's Rectorship that Ferdinand VII visited Valladolid and the Rector presented a loyal address to the King on behalf of the Bishop and Catholics of England. '*Los ilustrísimos obispos, la nobleza y los demás principales Católicos de Inglaterra me hacen el humilde órgano de render el justo tributo de su amor y agradecimiento a la augusta persona de V.M. y golosos en ver los Castillos de Fernando triunfar de las águilas de Napoleón.*' For this occassion Brown was accompanied by his Vice-Rector and three

69. Thompson to Pilling, 25 March 1832, 82.
70. Cf, p. 131, above.
71. Gillow to Brown, Sept. 1830, Cor. 6, 36.

students, Charles Walker, Robert Latham and John Guest. On Saturday 27 July 1828 the King and Doña Amelia, the Queen, paid a visit to the College and toured the whole house in the company of the Rector, Vice-Rector and alumni. A few years later George Borrow visited Valladolid.[72]

From the house of the Philippine Missions [the College of the Augustinian Fathers who prepared missioners for the Philippines] my friend conducted me to the English College. This establishment seemed in every respect to be on a more magnificient scale than its Scottish sister. In the latter there were few pupils, scarcely 6 or 7, I believe, whilst in the English Seminary I was informed that between 30 and 40 were receiving their education.[73] It is a beautiful building, with a small but splendid church, and a handsome Library. The situation is light and airy: it stands by itself in an unfrequented part of the city, and, with genuine English exclusiveness, is surrounded by a high wall, which encloses a delicious garden. This is by far the most remarkable establishment of the kind in the Peninsula, and I believe the most prosperous . . . I could not however fail to be struck with the order, neatness, and system which pervaded it. There was however, an air of monastic discipline, though I am far from asserting that such actually existed. We were attended throughout by the sub rector, the principal being absent. Of all the curiosities of this College, the most remarkable is the picture gallery, which contains neither more nor less than the portraits of a variety of scholars of this house who eventually suffered martyrdom in England, in the exercise of their vocation in the angry times of the Sixth Edward and the fierce Elizabeth. Yes, in this very house were many of those pale smiling half-foreign priests educated, who, like stealthy grimalkins, traversed green England in all directions; crept into old halls beneath umbrageous rookeries, fanning the dying embers of popery, with no other hope nor perhaps wish than to perish disembowelled by the bloody hands of the executioner, amongst the yells of a rabble as bigoted as themselves: priests like Bedingfield and Garnet, and many others who have left a name in English story. Doubtless many a history, only the more wonderful for being true, could be wrought out of the archives of the English Popish Seminary at Valladolid.

When George Borrow visited the College in 1836, Brown had already left for his long-overdue visit to England and there were indications that he was unlikely to return to Spain. He settled down to act as chaplain to the discalced Carmelite nuns near Darlington, and Pilling complained in 1837 that he had only received one letter from him since he left the College.[74]

---

72. *The Bible in Spain*, ch. XXI.
73. This number is exaggerated.
74. Pilling to Brown (draft), 1837, Cor. 6, 106.

Meanwhile, the political situation in Spain had deteriorated. When Ferdinand VII died on 29 September 1833, further troubles beset Spain. The law of succession had been changed to enable a woman, his daughter Isabel II, to succeed, but as she was only a child, María Cristina his fourth wife and widow assumed the direction of affairs as Regent. This provided a further crisis since she was more and more drawn to support the liberals against those who challenged her position and recognised Carlos, Ferdinand's brother, as King. The clericals who had become disillusioned with the liberal governments were sympathetic to the Carlists who, in contrast to María Cristina, appeared as a party supporting the throne and the altar. However, their strength was mainly in the north and in the rural districts rather than in the towns. Valladolid was sufficiently far to the north to become a battleground in these Carlist wars, and by 1837 preparations were being made for its defence. Pilling wrote to Brown:[75] 'The Church plate is on its way to Madrid . . . the convent bells have shortly to be conveyed to Bilbao. They are busy taking them down, those of the Merced were taken down several days ago.' Some days later Pilling drafted another letter to Brown describing the hostilities in so far as they affected the College.[76]

On the morning of the 18th of last month, the factions entered the town after the national guards had retired towards Zamora and some 500 regular troops had thrown themselves into the Fuerte of San Benito. What capitulations had been made, I cannot exactly say; but it is certain that the factions appeared on the hill of S. Isidro between eight and nine in the morning and did not enter till eleven, nor did they molest any of the small parties of troops and private families who were leaving the town. At eleven the bells began to ring and the Carlists to descend, at twelve they were all in the town. It is needless to say that half the town had previously gone out to see them. They all wear a red cap called in their language '*goina*' [sic]. It is of cloth and flat and invented by Zumalacárregui.[77] From Charles inclusive downwards all wear it. In the rest of their dress there was no uniformity. Some 6000 men might enter and among them was a batallion of Navarros: all these wore red trousers and were decently dressed. An edict was immediately published that the least disorder would be punished with the greatest severity and that the arms of all who would not follow the faction were to be given up. [. . .] During their stay the town was illuminated every night at 7 o'clock. The cathedral bell gave the signal and no other was allowed to be rung. As we had a good view of them from our top gallery as they descended,

75. Pilling to Brown (draft), 1836, Cor. 6, 106.
76. Ibid., 107.
77. The great leader of the Carlists, by this time deceased.

we did not go out; besides it was a very hot day. Zaratiegui[78] is of the middle size, and taking away his military dress, he looks more like a chaplain then a general. During the stay of the factions I can not say that any disturbances took place.

After about a week there was a counter-attack, and the Carlists were forced to leave. Such incidents, exciting as they may have been, added to Pilling's worries. The real problem was not so much the Carlist war as the increasing anti-clerical measures during these years. In March 1836 all monastic property became *bienes nacionales*, and in July 1837 the sale of all landed endowments belonging to the secular clergy was proposed. This was accompanied by waves of anti-clerical violence — murders of monks and desecration of churches.[79] Although there are some improvement when the moderate liberals were in power, it was not till the overthrow of Espartero in 1843 that the threat to the Church was lifted. Not being a Spanish institution, the College escaped comparatively lightly, yet in February 1837 a bullet was aimed at English College students in the street.[80] In these circumstances it is not surprising that there had been talk of the advisability of sending the divines back home to complete their studies at Ushaw,[81] and Pilling was preparing for this action when he was struck down with brain fever and died on 2 August 1838.[82]

The situation created by his untimely death was serious, but fortunately for the College, Sherburne was still concerned with its affairs. He wrote to James Standen, the only superior now residing in Valladolid,[83] and told him that Brown would not be returning, nor would there be any replacement. The financial state of the College and the political situation in Spain made it advisable that the students should return to England to complete their studies there. By the end of 1839 all had returned except for John Guest.[84] He was ordained at Valladolid in 1840 and then he too went home, leaving Standen alone, just as Cowban had

---

78. The Carlist leader of the time.
79. For the state of things at Valladolid at this time, see Taylor, *The Scots College in Spain*, p. 193.
80. Taylor, p. 194.
81. Correspondence, 6, p. 106.
82. Series III, L9.
83. Sherburne to Standen, 14 March 1839, correspondence, 6, p. 109.
84. Some of these students went to complete their studies in divinity at Ushaw, where they 'represent themselves as degraded by us' and asked for early ordination. Newsham to Briggs, Leeds Archives, Briggs, 749, 752, 858, 903.

been alone at the end of the Peninsular War. Brown now all but disappears from the College history, but there is extant a letter from him to Standen[85] expressing 'grief for poor S. Albano', and remarking: 'The past overpowers me and my heart fills at the recollection of the sweet place for which I once thought I suffered something; but, should I say, that was indeed pleasure compared with what I have endured for her since, and which is shortening my days.' In the event his days were far from short since, despite his poor health, he spent the last thirty years of his life as chaplain to the same convent near Darlington, dying in 1870 at the age of seventy-six.[86]

James Standen, 1838–1845

Standen had accompanied Brown on his return from England in 1830. Still *in statu pupillari* (he was not ordained until 1832), he came to Valladolid from Ushaw to be professor of humanities. He has left us an interesting account of his travels from the time he left Manchester to his arrival in Valladolid. To widen the horizons of his new professor, Brown took him before his departure on a visit to the colleges and seminaries at Sedgley Park, Oscott and Old Hall so that he should have something with which to compare Ushaw.[87] They also visited Stratford-on-Avon, Oxford, Henley and London before travelling overland by way of Paris, Blois, Tours, Bordeaux and into Spain. As with many travellers, it was Burgos Cathedral that made a big impression on the young man. He wrote: 'You have indeed fine music at Ushaw and fine ceremonies and fine processions, but, until you have heard Catholic music, seen Catholic ceremonies and followed Catholic processions, you can form no idea of the great effect they are capable of producing.' Such sentiments were not

85. 28 Sept. 1840, CRS, p. lxvi.
86. Series III, L10, contains the sermon at Brown's funeral preached by the Very Revd Canon Bewick, D.D., Vicar General; also a MS. copy of a life of Canon J. Brown sent to E. Henson *circa* 1928 by the Carmelite convent near Darlington. In this life it is stated that Brown set out for Valladolid in September 1838, but on account of the civil war raging in Spain was assured that it would be unsafe for him to continue his journey.
87. Extracts from this journal, which is presented in the form of letters to his sister, were printed in *The Ushaw Magazine*, ed. C.G. Clifford, vol. XLVI (1936), pp. 25–47; vol. XLVI (1936), pp. 111–24; vol. XLVII (1937), pp. 55–62; and vol. XLVII (1939), pp. 205–18.

unlike those which another Ushaw man, Nicholas Wiseman, expressed on arrival in Rome twelve years before.[88] Standen's account of the College in Valladolid as he found it in 1830 contains á detailed description of the building and bears out the impression created on George Borrow.

It now fell to this comparative newcomer to guide the College after the death of Pilling and resignation of Brown. But Sherburne, as well as informing him of Brown's resignation, laid down the course of action he should take:[89]

You remember the plan arranged to send another Rector, and allow Mr Brown to remain with the nuns. Mr Brown would have done you no good had he returned and his intended successor was not Mr Walker.[90] But you seemed so disappointed that a change was made, and gave too the appalling information about the debt, that the Bishop was led to apply again to Mr Brown, the substance of whose reply is contained in the following extract: 'I cannot justify myself in again accepting so arduous a situation. I am sorry to be compelled to come to this conclusion. I would fain it were more in accordance with your Lordship's wishes: but I feel that under all the circumstances, which I need not detail I could not long outlive the appointment. Your Lordship will therefore be pleased to consider the decision as final. I have satisfied myself I can come to no other; a different one would not realise the object of Your Lordship's wishes.'[91] The idea then of Mr Brown's return is and must be abandoned. You must also give up the expectation of any other person going to San Albano from England. Courage, notwithstanding. *Infirma mundi elegit Deus etc* and if you will keep up your spirits all will end well. Henceforward you are to take the title of Vice Rector;[92] as such you will receive Dimissorials for Mr Guest, perhaps as early as you receive this letter, and we doubt [not] will get him ordained with all

88. M.E. Williams, *The Venerable English College Rome*, p. 94.
89. Sherburne to Standen, 14 March 1839.
90. Charles Walker was ordained in Valladolid and on his return to England from Bilbao in 1834 was shipwrecked off the coast of Ireland. The student who accompanied him was drowned. Walker wrote a full account of the incident in a letter to Brown, 16 Dec. 1834, 96, cf. CRS, 30, p. 231.
91. The full text of Brown's letter to Briggs is in Leeds Archives, Briggs, 492A.
92. There were perhaps special reasons for this title. When John Cameron received his nomination by the Vicars Apostolic of Scotland as Rector of the Scots College in the summer of 1836, 'He chose not to present it to the Queen Regent for her approval since by so doing he felt he would be making an admission of the Government's right to interfere in the affairs of the College as they were interfering in all religious communities of Spaniards.' Taylor, op. cit., p. 184. Not till 1867, 30 years later, did Cameron present his letter of nomination and receive the royal appointment in accordance with the College statutes.

dispatch. Then as your sufferings and privations must increase in proportion to numbers, it is thought proper that the four oldest divines should return to England, and finish at Ushaw. To aid you in this I hold £30 at your disposal, and you can tell me how it can be made available. I would willingly relieve you of every student, but in that case there would be more danger to the establishment; the plea of the removal of the four is the misery of the times.

Now comes the greatest difficulty, the load of debt. With a war contribution of 92% in addition to other burdens, how can this be met? Three expedients present themselves: First, to remit money to England; but such sums, under present circumstances, would only help to feed a war already of too long continuance, and besides the College already owes £1,200 to the Clergy Sick Fund, besides other sums and for which S. Ignacio is held on mortgage and people have no relish for further speculation. Second, for creditors to wait with patience till the amount is cleared from the property, or third to dispose of, to the creditors themselves, such portions of the College property as may suit both parties and at a reasonable price . . . should this be acted upon (i.e. the third proposal) the Bishop requires that you consult me as to each sale of any magnitude, and probably you would not object as it divides the responsibility. The plán of selling is painful, but it is preferable to debt . . . Supposing all this in progress you and Mr Guest will be left as Managers, and the two boys will continue their studies as usual. I know very well that the house will appear lonely and things dull, but even this is better than dire want. Mr Guest and you will still be company and no harm would be done if you were to admit the two divines into something like Society. It would be an advantage to them, and no sinking to you.

Things did not turn out exactly as Sherburne planned. All the students except Guest had returned to England by 1840. Guest himself was ordained priest, and his first Mass on Easter Sunday 1840 in the College church was the occasion of an extraordinary celebration.[93] This was at the time when the new government of Espartero was seeking to put into practice the anti-clerical measures of the 1830s. Although only Standen and Guest were resident there, the English and Scots Colleges were almost the only ecclesiastical establishments left unmolested in the town. They had not been affected by the decree of 11 October 1835 which had forbidden prelates to confer major orders on the grounds that there were more than sufficient clerics.[94] When the news spread that there was to be

93. *The Albanian*, vol. 1, nos. 3 and 4 (1911–12), pp. 29–32 and 29–34, contains an article transcribed from the *London and Orthodox Journal*, 13 June 1840.

94. Series III, L11, correspondence between Guest and Gartlan, 26 Feb. 1856, re Mortmain laws. A *Real Orden* obtained by the Scots on 12 Jan. 1836 exempted them from the *Orden* of 8 Oct. 1835.

a first Mass in the English College, preparations were begun to make of it a memorable display of that popular religious piety that survived despite the anti-clerical legislation. The church was cleaned and the pillars and arches were again clothed in rich silk hangings; 'a choir was formed of walnut benches, occupying two sides of the body of the church for the invited, the gentlemen to occupy the seats, the ladies, according to custom, to kneel and sit on the carpets spread for them in the middle and within the rails 50 silk-covered chairs for the ministers, canons, Scotch collegians and other ecclesiastics.' The crown of the Vulnerata was entwined with roses, and Guest refused the several ladies who wished to be his *madrina* on the day, saying that his *madrina* was the Vulnerata. Various dependants and tradesmen of the College helped to order and marshall the crowd which arrived in great numbers, summoned by the rockets that were let off the preceding night in the plaza in front of the College. The canons and chaplains of the cathedral as well as the students of the Scots College assisted at the ceremony. And the solemn Gregorian chants which many of the people had not heard for five long years of affliction and terror could not but remind them of happier days gone perhaps for ever. At the end of the Mass the chronicler refers to the 'harmonious confusion' that attended the ceremony of kissing the new priest's hands.

Guest returned to England in September and Standen was now alone. The next two years were to try him severely. If he was to carry out the sale of the property, he had to have some sort of authorisation, and on 24 July 1840 he drafted a letter to Bishop Briggs asking for someone to be put in full charge of the College. There was need for 'a man of character, business and experience aided with a decent supply of ready money'. He penned an eloquent plea to keep the College open:

A trip of half a dozen weeks into a foreign country is nowadays considered an indispensable finishing off of a liberal education. A residence of as many years abroad cannot surely be of inferior advantage. The truth is that the removing of prejudices, opening the mind, elevating the sentiments, rectifying the judgment and the forming a dignified, enlightened form and amiable character which are the most important results to be expected from a temporary removal from the scenes and society in which we have been brought up are much more effectually produced and more permanently secured by a fixed residence in any foreign country of note than by a hurried tour through many lands that leaves not time for observation much less for reflexion. Next, a knowledge of languages is one of the most admired acquirements of the age. Those who are educated here, from the very fact of being in the country, acquire and with more than ordinary perfection one language more than those who remain at home, and one perhaps not equalled, certainly not surpassed in elegance, strength and dignity by any other in Europe. Lastly, not to expatiate more than necessary, if the association of ideas attached to the objects that daily meet the eye of the student and the bright example of those who in former years have pursued the same career under the same circumstances as himself inspire a noble ambition of imitating them, excite to diligent and steady application, and above all tend to form minds of that superior order that are usually met with in descendants of a noble race — in their case these old walls must have a more than magic power. A priest educated in Catholic, ecclesiastical Spain, familiar with the apostolic principles and thought of Avila and Granada expressed in their own sublime language, who has studied the same books, contemplated the same scenes and daily knelt before the same altars whence our holy old English missioners drew all their knowlege, zeal and piety — can he, My Lord, help turn out according to Your Lordship's and God's own heart?

Although Standen was eventually given powers as Procurator by the four Vicars Apostolic in July 1841,[95] he still needed authorisation to sell the property. So he sought a power of attorney from the English Bishops. But even were he to obtain this, it was not likely that the Spanish government would recognise such a power to sell since it too had claims over the property. In November Standen fell ill, and so got Cameron of the Scots College to write to Briggs on his behalf.[96] He also made the point that if there were to be a power of attorney he would like it to be in the name of Mr Guest, who was about to return to Valladolid. Standen felt himself inadequate to deal with the situation, and Sherburne wrote a series of letters that autumn and winter to Briggs[97] in violent disagreement with Standen's policy and asking that he himself should be appointed Rector in Standen's place.[98] 'Standen is quite unmanned and mostly in bed by a vile intermittent nervous fever.' The news of Guest's return caused him to rally, but he was still not able to do College business. 'Yet to give Mr Guest, quite a young man, a carte blanche will never do. [. . .] Your shortest and I think, My Lord, your best will be to name me Rector. Is this presumption? I hope not. The College and the country are well known to me and they are not nor can they be to Your Lordship. I could give such direction to Mr Guest as could enable him to proceed; and still for Mr Standen to hold that post of honour which is his due. [. . .] It is neither for my own satisfaction nor ease that I make the

95. Leeds Archives, Briggs, 1014.
96. Briggs, 1090A.
97. Briggs, 111B.
98. 15 Nov. 1841.

proposal, but solely for prolonging the existence of the establishment.'

Five years were to elapse before Sherburne was made Rector and Guest his administrator. The hesitation of the Bishops was due to their unfamiliarity with the situation in Spain and the ways of Spanish officials.[99] Bishop Briggs was prepared to write an open letter enquiring about the College as his property, and stating that if it were in danger he as an English subject might have to get his government to act.[100] Bishop Griffith was surprised that his signature on a document had to be attested by a notary before it would be recognised legally in Spain.[101] Unable to make up their minds about the contrary advice from Sherburne and Standen, they asked Guest on his return to England to draw up a report on the conditions in Valladolid; this he did from memory in 1841,[102] and in it he pointed out that the value of the College property had declined considerably due to the low state of farming in the Valladolid district and to the immense amount of Church property that was already on the market at exceedingly low prices because money was scarce and the country was impoverished. Conditions had changed since Sherburne's day, and Standen's 'fidgets' had some justification.

The situation was saved by Guest's return, bringing with him five new students, on 25 July 1842. From this date, although only technically assistant to Standen, Guest took charge of the money and this meant opening an account with Sherburne.[103] Standen had little wish to remain in Valladolid, but his impending departure would only heighten the anomaly of a College without an official head. Guest wrote to Sherburne: 'I cannot but feel some little anxiety about the arrangement that may be made on Mr Standen's leaving Valladolid, for I have no confidence in the management of our good bishops. You are the only

---

99. Brown's resignation was due not least to his lack of support from the Bishops. To the Bishops' request that he should return 'for the sake of religion, that House and its inmates', he replied: 'Religion so far from being benefited would be scandalised in the persons of your Lordships by the contempt you would necessarily bring upon yourselves and everyone connected with you, who rather than gratefully discharge the sum of £300 or £400 kindly advanced in a moment of painful needs would let an establishment (which should be your pious care) perish together with its too generous but ill-fated inmates. [. . .] I believe in the whole history of men united in one common cause a parallel case will not be found. So much for episcopal means in support of religion in this country.'

100. Briggs to Standen, 21 Oct. 1841, Correspondence 6, 116.

101. Briggs, 1067, 20 Sept. 1841; later, in 1860, Goss was indignant about a similar matter, Correspondence 7, 198.

102. Briggs, 1014A.

103. Bundle D, bottom shelf.

person who knows anything about our position here, and must be well aware what kind of person ought to be sent out.'[104] Standen went to England on 13 June 1845, and returned to his native North-East. He died in Newcastle on 11 October 1847, aged only forty-one, a victim—like many priests of the day—of typhus brought on by his work among the poor.[105]

104. Guest to Sherburne, 25 Jan. 1845, Cor. 6, 128.
105. L9. The Ushaw Archives (U.C.M., IV, 39a) contain two letters from Standen. One to J. Walker (Walker, 12 Miscell.), dating from 1838, gives an account of his life in Valladolid preparing lectures (he used Billuart as a text). He also tells us that the students under his direction used to preach, in English, sermons they had heard delivered in Spanish by the leading preachers of the town.

9

JOHN GUEST AS ADMINISTRATOR, 1846–1878

In 1767 the administration of the College became the responsibility of the English secular clergy. But apart from the fact that the superiors were English secular priests and that more students were provided for the English Mission, there was little change in the years following the end of Jesuit rule. The Vicars Apostolic did not feel any strong obligations towards the establishment; they were unable to ensure a regular supply of professors,[1] and recently had even been reluctant to make a firm decision on the appointment of a Rector. Financially the College had always supported itself and been administered by the superiors in Valladolid, but continual disasters in Spain, natural and man-made, had meant increasingly frequent appeals to England for help. To date the greatest single item had been the loan secured by William Irving from the Lancashire Brethren. The difficulty experienced in its repayment could not be disguised from the secular clergy at home, and it was becoming clear that the College would now have to rely on the English Bishops for a large measure of its financial support. Thomas Sherburne (William Irving's brother) introduced the idea of the fees of the students being paid for from funds raised in England. When he died, his will caused great embarrassment to the College, and Guest attempted to set up the fund on a more secure basis.[2] As we shall see, most of his Rectorship was taken up with establishing a closer and more formal relationship between the College and the newly-restored English hierarchy. In this he only achieved moderate success.

John Guest and Thomas Sherburne

With the return of Standen to England, Guest was now alone in the

---

1. There was now no alternative to holding classes in the House. With the restoration of peace after the Peninsular War, the Spanish universities were becoming increasingly secular. The Concordat of 1851 was to recognise this position by excluding the teaching of theology from the universities. Malquíades Andrés Martín, *La supresión de las Facultades de Teología en las Universidades Españolas (1845–1855)*, Burgos 1976.
2. See below, p. 153.

College. He was aged thirty-three. All the students he had brought out with him in 1842 had left, and for company he invited a Dominican priest from San Gregorio to stay with him at the College. 'A prudent, pious upright man about 56 years of age, he pays three and a half reals per day for houseroom, his dinner, and supper which generally is a collation.[3]

From his residence in England, Sherburne proferred advice to Guest on the best way of discharging the College debts and administering the property, but Guest felt diffident about his own abilities, and consultation by letter was far from satisfactory. He urged Sherburne to come and visit Valladolid, and asked Bishop Briggs to try and persuade him to take time off to do so from his pastoral duties. 'In my humble opinion there are few on the mission of more experience in business and none so thoroughly acquainted with the property of the establishment and this country, and consequently so capable of giving direction and deciding so advantageously about the College affairs as Mr Sherburne. But it is necessary that he sees the state of our property etc. and that he be on the spot.'[4]

There were dangers too in Guest being virtually alone in a deserted building. He recorded in the same letter a break-in at the College: 'They did me no harm in my person but carried off some £60 in cash, my watch, cloak and a few trifles. I with the Dominican father and the servants with our hands tied were locked up in a small closet in my room. I was somewhat alarmed but have not felt any bad results in regard to my health.' Shortly afterwards Guest learned that the Vicars Apostolic of Yorkshire, London, Lancashire and the Northern District had appointed Sherburne Rector of St Alban's for a period of three years from 24 July 1846 'to act as he judges best with regard to the property belonging to the same, with full power to sell, or otherwise. In hopes that by his aid and discretion and the co-operation of the superior actually on the spot, that establishment may be freed from its incumbrances, and again be made useful to Religion.'[5]

Although this meant that Sherburne was now the administrator responsible to the Bishops, it did little to help Guest, since Sherburne intended to direct affairs from England and in reply to Guest's request that he visit the College, he pleaded that it was impossible for him to get any priest to look after his parish while he was away. Eventually in the

3. Guest to Sherburne, 25 Aug. 1845.
4. Guest to Briggs, 30 May 1846. For Sherburne's work as a parish priest in England, see F.J. Singleton, *Mowbreck Hall and The Willows: A history of the Catholic community in the Kirkham District of Lancashire*, Kirkham 1983, pp. 31–8.
5. Sherburne to Guest, 4 Aug. 1846, cf. CRS, 30, p. lxvii.

summer of 1847 Sherburne did pay a very short visit of about a month, and on the way back to England called at the English School run by the Benedictines at Douai with the intention of recruiting prospective students for Valladolid.[6] But Guest was not anxious to accept any students until he had someone to assist him in running the College who would also be able to help with the teaching. However, Sherburne told him: 'No bishop will part with a proper subject master, and you are far better alone than with an improper one, and I really believe that your anxiety to have someone from England is more a temptation than anything else. Your feelings too of solitude will be removed by the presence of the students.' On 8 June 1848 six new students arrived, and so the College Register recording their names resumes and continues unbroken to the present day. For theology classes they had the Dominican priest who had taught for many years at S. Gregorio and was now resident in the College. The other three students who were rhetoricians went for classes to the Scots College. As for Guest himself, 'I have not much time for teaching, but I manage to give a few lessons in Spanish and Greek, in history and, now and then, in rhetoric, to supply those times it is not advantageous for them to attend at the Scotch College.'[7]

Thus we have the repetition of a familiar pattern. After a period of closure, the College reopens with a few students and a makeshift arrangement for teaching. However, there was at least one big difference now from previous new beginnings. The College did not have to find all the money for the upkeep of its alumni, since Sherburne undertook to provide from sources in England £20 annually for each of the new students. An embarrassing incident occurred in 1850. Bishop Briggs wrote to Guest on 5 March that year asking him whether he wished Sherburne to continue in charge, the time having now expired for which he had been appointed Rector. 'But in speaking of this point you will please not to say anything of my making this suggestion to you.' Unfortunately Briggs sent this letter to Guest via Sherburne himself who inadvertently opened it! He sent it on to Guest with the note: 'Yesterday I received the enclosed in another from Dr Briggs, and opened it without looking at the direction, but closed it immediately on finding my

6. In 1816 the English Benedictine community of St Edmund in Paris secured the property which had formerly belonged to the community of St Gregory at Douai. These latter monks were now in residence at Downside, England. A school was established by the Benedictines at Douai, which lasted until 1903 when it was transferred to Woolhampton, Berkshire, where it still exists.
7. Guest to Briggs, 26 Feb. 1849, cf. CRS. 30, p. lxviii.

mistake. You have not a day to spare in forwarding your reply. It need not be special, but . . . as to temporals you may state that I continue to pay pensions, that claims of Government are enormous, that you employ surplus, with my approval, on necessary repairs and improvements.'[8] Sherburne was given a further term of office, and the life of the College continued without interruption. In 1851 the first of the 1848 intake of students, James Sheil, was ordained priest, and Cardinal Wiseman allowed him to stay on and teach humanities,[9] thus relieving Guest of one of his problems over the teaching staff. That same year nine new boys were sent out;[10] Sherburne was having considerable success in obtaining students for the College, helped no doubt by his contact with the school at Douai as well as his own contribution to their pension which came from a fund he had set up in England.[11]

However the health of the students as well as that of Guest himself was not good,[12] and after Rogerson, one of the pupils, had died in 1852, Sherburne wrote to Guest:[13] 'In my time it was most unusual for boys to receive money from their parents, and I think it should not be encouraged, though not absolutely prohibited. It would also be better if little ailments were dissembled in the letters they write. Brindle, the other day, mentioned a little pain or ailment, that has caused a good deal of trouble to his friends, and which a day's fast would probably have cured.' There were other kinds of ailments too that caused concern. In 1852 it was discovered that the stone lantern and clerestory over the main dome of the church was unsafe; it was taken down and replaced by a wooden construction to take the weight off the dome.[14] A thorough job was made of the repair, and in February 1853 Guest reported to Sherburne that the works in the church were drawing to a conclusion:[15] 'Today we have finished replacing the lattice in the tribunes and the paintings of the Saxon kings. The high altar has undergone a change: the salomonic columns have been removed, the cornices, basement etc. let in

8. CRS, 30, pp. lxviii–lxix.
9. Sherburne to Guest, 22 Feb. 1851. Sheil left the College in 1855 to go to the Crimea as an army chaplain.
10. Sherburne to Guest, 8 Sept. 1851.
11. An account of this is found in Guest to Gillow, 28 Feb. 1855.
12. Sherburne to Guest, 25 July 1853.
13. 18 Dec. 1852.
14. The ever-resourceful Sherburne had a sketch-plan drawn in England. Sherburne to Guest, 25 March 1852.
15. Guest to Sherburne, 11 Feb. 1853.

and the plaster behind the columns brought forward. A new altar table and credence tables are being made, the Vulnerata is being enclosed in a case with glass and without the robes, and a tabernacle, templete and steps will finish our decoration or change of the High Altar.'

In spite of these expenses, Sherburne wrote to Guest towards the end of 1853[16] announcing that the £1,100 debt to the Lancashire Brethren had been paid 'off. But Sherburne was in poor health and Guest went to England to see him and get information concerning the funds from which he was paying money to the College for the student pensions. Sherburne died shortly after Guest returned to Spain, and in the same post he learned of the death of another friend, Bishop Briggs. But Canon Carter wrote with even worse news three days later, after the burial of the Rector: 'His will is very short and all, all, all is left to Rev. Charles Gillow of Ushaw College. The Very Rev. Canon Irving has £19.19.00 left him!!! A good deal i.e. £13,000 in cash was found in the house. He seems not to have known of late that he had money about him when he had £500 in his pocket. I spoke to Mr C. Gillow about the College affairs and my immediate want of £157.17.8. He said he had a receipt from you for £250 paid you lately. Is this so? We shall examine accounts when the will is proved. . . . ' For years Sherburne had been paying the students' pensions partly from his own money and partly from a fund he had set up. For some he paid the whole pension and for others half, the rest in the latter cases being paid by parents or patrons. When he left Spain for England he took with him as security for the money he had advanced to the College various College pictures, sacristy plate, vestments and documents from the archives including Blackfan's *Annals* and *Constitutions*. Some of these were at his residence "The Willows" and some at Ushaw. His will meant not only that this College property passed to Gillow but that the whole finances of the College were in jeopardy since no provision was made by him for continuing payment of the pensions for the students at Valladolid. His previous efforts on behalf of the College had secured a steady flow of students and relieved the Rector of the anxiety of having to provide for their upkeep from the Spanish funds. But now this money had been willed to someone else who was determined to exercise his rights. Gillow, the 'sole and universal heir', had received no instructions from Sherburne concerning the College students, and 'Mr Gillow wishes it to be clearly understood that nothing more can be paid by him beyond balancing the account up to last

16. 14 Nov. 1853.

Christmas, and it will be some time before he can make any payment.'[17]

This was a matter not just between Guest and Gillow, but it also concerned the Bishops whose subjects were at the College. No Bishop was having to support his students at Valladolid, but did Sherburne's death mean that these students would have to be sent home due to lack of financial means? Guest wrote to Father Billington of Kirkham (Sherburne's nephew) asking if he, as one of the trustees of the 'Sherburne-Heatley Fund', could help in any way. Billington showed Guest's letter to his Ordinary, Bishop Goss of Liverpool, who intervened in the affair, asking the College in Valladolid for particulars of the students concerned. The hierarchy nominated Goss to investigate on their behalf. He suggested that Guest should present a bill for each student to the respective Bishop, and if any Bishop declined to make provision for his subjects, then other Bishops should be given the opportunity to accept these students as their own. Guest made his own proposals: 'As the College income is still small and it is desirable that the students be not less than between twenty-four and thirty, I propose in future that a pension be required of £15 per annum, of which £13 is for the College and £2 for pocket money for the boys and for providing extras. The expenses of journey to the College and back are also to be paid by the students.'[18] Goss was sympathetic, and it was decided that the dioceses would pay for the pensions of the students at the College and then afterwards seek reimbursement from Gillow. Goss argued that if Gillow refused to be responsible for Sherburne's promise, this was no reason why Valladolid should not be paid. As to the future payment of pensions, if the Bishops refused to pay, then Guest should send the existing students home and refuse to take any others from that diocese until he had been reimbursed.[19]

The ill-feeling that this incident aroused lasted many years, embittering the relationship between Valladolid and Ushaw. Writing in 1859,[20] Goss remarked: 'It is greatly to be regretted that the large property which he [Sherburne] derived from Mr Heatley for the benefit of religion has not been more judiciously spent. It might in part have been employed in putting St Alban's beyond the reach of monetary crisis, if he had only established a number of burses thereat . . . I greatly fear that what he could convert into money is being spent at St Cuthbert's College Ushaw, already large enough for ecclesiastical

17. Guest to Billington, 21 March 1855.
18. Guest to Santry (?), 27 Sept. 1855.
19. Goss to Guest, 5 Oct. 1855.
20. Goss to Guest, 5 April 1859.

purposes, particularly, as when the hierarchy is properly carried out every Bishop will have his own little seminary.' As we shall see,[21] claims were laid by Valladolid against Ushaw in 1914 and 1921 for the return of property taken as 'security' by Sherburne.

Guest was now determined to secure some clear financial arrangement with the Bishops. He made enquiries as to how other seminaries were supported; from Ilsley, its President, he learned that at the Lisbon College many students paid a partial pension, and that funds were held in a bank in England in the names of four people: an Agent, one of the Bishops, the President of the College, and another superior. Moreover, the College was for all thirteen dioceses, and provision for two students per diocese was allowed for on the College funds, but if a bishop wished to pay a full quota of £40 per annum he could send additional students to the College.[22] From Watson he learned about the situation at Ushaw,[23] where the pension was £50 per annum and extra was charged for items such as piano and drawing lessons and dentist's fees. The information from Lisbon concerning the responsibility of all the dioceses for the College bore out a point Guest had already made to Wiseman,[24] namely that whereas the College in Spain had formerly been considered as belonging to the whole English Mission, it had been looked upon latterly as belonging only to the London and Northern Districts. In 1819 the Vicar Apostolic of the Midland District declined to have any part in it, and the Western District had never been concerned with it at all.

Guest recognised that the requirement of royal approval for the appointment of the Rector might be considered to place a constraint on the Bishops' powers. Although in many ways this 'Nomination' was a formality, the recurring governmental crises often presented a threat to Church property and made this requirement an inconvenience. These years 1854–6 were particularly anxious ones for the Church in Spain since the Liberals were again in power. Although the Rectorship had been technically vacant since the death of Sherburne, the Bishops thought it prudent to make no application to the Spanish government on the subject since this might have provided a pretext for immediate inter-ference.[25] Guest was asked — and agreed — to consider himself *de facto*

21. See below, pp. 184 and 191. An article in *The Albanian* of June 1914 by Kelly, was approved of by Bishop Burton, correspondence, 13, 226.
22. Ilsley to Guest, 20 Nov. 1855.
23. Watson to Guest, 23 Jan. 1856.
24. Guest to Wiseman, 25 Jan. 1855.
25. Goss to Guest, 5 Oct. 1855.

Rector and hence possessed of all the rights and prerogatives of that office. He said, however, that a document should be drawn up and signed by the Bishops but not presented to the Spanish authorities unless government interference should leave him with no choice. 'Our only way at present is to keep quiet and shield ourselves under the notion of our being a foreign college and not subject to the laws regarding the establishments of the country.'[26] He also expressed the opinion that 'if we could continue to do away with the royal protection it would be very advantageous to us, but I cannot see how it can be done.'

The mortmain laws

On 1 May 1855 a law was passed by the Spanish Cortes abolishing all mortmain. Property belonging to the Church, hospitals, colleges and all corporate bodies had to be sold and the proceeds invested in government stocks at 3 per cent. There was little hope that this interest would be paid, and so for all practical purposes the property was lost. In past revolutions in Spain, the English, Scots and Irish had been for the most part unmolested by similar measures taken against Church property, but this time was different since it was explicitly stated that a special declaration of exemption from the operation of the law was required. James Gartlan, Rector of the Irish College at Salamanca, was the first to receive an official instruction,[27] and he wrote in some despondency to Guest that he would never be able to furnish the evidence that they required to prove his exemption from the law. Guest consulted Cameron, the Rector of the Scots College at Valladolid, and realising that their own futures were at stake, the two Rectors urged Gartlan to stand firm and press his case that his was a foreign establishment that had obtained its property legally and had enjoyed previous exemptions from the law such as being allowed to have students ordained priest when there was a general prohibition against this throughout the land. Guest wrote to Wiseman explaining the position.

The position of these Colleges [i.e. English, Scots and Irish] at present is an anomalous one. [. . .] We certainly as individuals are foreigners and we are in possession of the property, and no part of it that we now possess has been given by the Spanish kings or government; but on the restitution of the Colleges and

26. Guest to Goss, Jan. 1856.
27. For the correspondence between the three Rectors at this time, see Series III, L11.

property after the expulsion of the Jesuits, the King constituted himself Patron of the Colleges in the right of nomination of Rector and intervention in the inversion of the income, and in consequence the property cannot be alienated or sold without his permission. For the last 20 or 30 years the government has not interfered with us, and for long before it had done little more than nominate the Rector presented; during these last revolutions these colleges have always been regarded as foreign establishments. But should the legal existence of and the titles on which these colleges hold their property be examined into, I fear that they will be declared as national not foreign establishments and as such under the operation of the law. We propose first to endeavour to obtain directly from the Spanish government a declaration that our colleges being foreign establishments are not included in the general law: we shall try with the assistance of the British Legation to make out a case that can be presented through the British Legation claiming exemption from the law on the grounds of foreign property. Lord Howden the present Ambassador does not seem inclined to be over-officious in our regard. He will no doubt protect us personally as British Subjects, but he seems to require clear tangible proofs that our establishments are foreign before he can do anything in their defence. [. . .] Lord Clarendon when Ambassador at Madrid was of great service to the Irish Rector in a way not strictly official and Lord Howden, could he be interested in the matter, might certainly do much for us. We would request that your Eminence would obtain from the British Government and from such source as Your Eminence may consider advantageous a strong recommendation of our case to the British Legation in Madrid.[28]

On 22 November 1856 the Scots obtained a declaration from the *Ministero de Hacienda* that their property was not subject to the requirements of the mortmain law, and the Irish received a similar decree dated 9 January 1858. But it was not until the efforts of Edmund Stonor in 1868[29] that the position of the English College was finalised. However, with a more stable government under the Liberal leader O'Donnell the danger receded after 1858.

John Guest, Cardinal Wiseman and College affairs

As a mark of recognition for his work for the College and as an incentive to further effort, Wiseman obtained a rescript from His Holiness conferring the title of Doctor of Theology on Guest in 1858.[30] But for Guest this was a poor substitue for the really important title of Rector; as he

28. Guest to Wiseman, 23 April 1856.
29. Below, p. 162.
30. Wiseman to Guest, 26 Nov. 1858, Series III, L11.

wrote to Goss:[31] 'I am no rector, I have merely *accidentaliter* the government of the establishment, and in such a position I dare not act in many
things. The times too are difficult as regards the arrangement of the
property, and without the direction of Your Lordships I dare not
proceed to make such changes as I consider of the greatest importance for
the good of this house.' Writing to Wiseman,[32] Guest complained that
he had now been sixteen years in the strange position of being in charge
but without any real powers as Rector. He had continual difficulty in
obtaining a regular provision of assistants. He had been forced to take
young boys who were not suited to undertaking an eleven-year course
away from home in Spain.[33] As he had earlier remarked to Goss,[34] 'More
care should be taken in choosing subjects for a foreign college than for
those at home and for a small one than for those where all classes at once
are taught.' Were he to be given full powers, he would be able to
increase the income from the college property; hence he suggested that it
was now time to make a formal presentation to the Crown of three
persons for the office of Rector.

Within a week Wiseman replied[35] agreeing that something had to be
done, offering suggestions about the disposal of some of the college
property in Spain and giving reasons why it was difficult to provide
students.[36] A full report of the past and present state of the College dated
2 January 1862 was sent to Wiseman on 16 January, and in the ensuing
months Guest kept up a steady stream of suggestions and proposals,
some of which were printed for consideration by the Bishops at their
annual Low Week meeting, Wiseman having pointed out that he could
take no action without the approval of the other Bishops.[37]

The chief of these proposals were as follows. The College should
accept ecclesiastical students for the English Mission only, and they
should be fit to enter the classes that were being offered. This would be
regulated by the prevailing situation concerning the teaching staff. At
the moment only two classes of student could be admitted, for poetry

31. Guest to Goss, 6 Aug. 1861.
32. Guest to Wiseman, 30 Nov. 1861.
33. On this point see also Guest to Wiseman, 8 July 1859.
34. Guest to Goss, Jan. 1856.
35. Wiseman to Guest, 5 Dec. 1861.
36. 'Rome and Bruges absorb students and drain our home colleges in a most trying
    manner.'
37. Wiseman to Guest, 8 March 1862. The more important communications from
    Guest to Wiseman are of 27 March and 19 April.

and philosophy, and those coming to begin philosophy would have to know Latin already since the professor of logic and metaphysics was a Spaniard, Guest having been unable to secure a professor from England. He then made the suggestion that in the present straitened circumstances it might be advisable to put the College under the direction of a religious order such as the Oratorians. Perhaps it should become a college for older students and for recent converts? How far he expected these suggestions to be taken up we do not know, but he did think that at least three English priests should be resident in the house, and by way of an incentive to the Bishops to release men he suggested: 'It seems proper that for each English priest in the College, a student should be educated without the payment of any pension for the diocese to which the priests may belong.' In laying down requirements and qualifications for prospective students, Guest remarked that more than half of those recently sent to Spain had either 'severe bodily defects' or were deficient in elementary education. Twenty-eight students were able to be admitted on College funds, which in effect meant that the College paid part of their pension, leaving £14 to be found from other sources. The full pension was £34 per year. Each student was required to bring out certain articles of clothing.[38]

These proposals were to be discussed at the Low Week meeting of the Bishops in 1862 and a printed circular was produced for this purpose, but unfortunately for Valladolid the meeting was postponed to enable the Bishops to go to Rome for the canonisation of the Japanese martyrs and it was only in December that Guest received anything by way of a decisive reply from Wiseman.[39] This took the form of one of those flamboyant gestures that are often associated with Wiseman, especially where European interests are concerned. It had been decided that Wiseman's private secretary Mgr Searle, a man who had been involved in administering educational properties in France and who was at present wintering on the continent, should visit Spain. He would attempt to secure official recognition of the hierarchy's role in the administration of

38. The list was 6 shirts, 6 handkerchiefs, 6 pairs of stockings, 2 pairs of shoes, 2 pairs of black cloth trousers, a coat, and a cap or hat. For classes under philosophy, thirty shillings for books was needed and they had also to provide the first College uniform viz black cloth jacket, cassock and mozetta, biretta and collar — the cost about £3. For those who entered the classes of philosophy or theology the College provided the uniform, but they had to provide whatever secular dress they should need at any time.
39. Wiseman to Guest, 10 Dec. 1862.

the College and so eliminate the need for the *Cédula Real*. Searle would stay with the Conde de Torre-Díaz, senator and chamberlain to the Spanish Queen, and Wiseman hoped there could be direct negotiations with Isabel herself:

La Reina has several times sent me messages, and two lately that she will be glad to see me in Madrid, and the occasion of the marriage of the Count's daughter there in February (to which she is to be godmother) gives an additional personal reason for my being there for a few days. [. . .] It is not therefore impossible that at the beginning of February I may undertake the somewhat formidable journey to Madrid, in which case I should hope to bring our affairs to a prosperous termination. And I shall hope to have the pleasure of visiting the noble college of Valladolid.

Mgr Searle kept Guest informed of his progress towards Madrid. There were letters from the Hôtel des Deux Mondes, Paris, and the episcopal palace at Burgos, but already a note of hesitation and doubt had begun to creep in, if only as to which ministry at Madrid would be the one dealing with the case. Shortly after his arrival at Madrid, Searle learned that Wiseman was ill and would not be able to make the journey to Spain after all. Then his mission ran into a new and unexpected difficulty. In February there was a government crisis and this meant that any attempt to secure an audience of the Queen would be construed as a political device; the Nuncio would not let himself be involved in this. There was further delay, and when an audience was eventually granted it was an anti-climax. All that happened was that the Queen said '*Yo creo que el Cardinal es un santo. Quiero mucho verlo*' and promised to give the document to her minister that evening.[40] But Searle left Madrid well satisfied. The *Real Autorización y Acuerdo* modifying the *Cédula Real* of 1779 is dated 18 May 1863, and the only thing achieved was that the *terna* of names for Rector was now to be presented by the Archbishop of Westminster alone, not by all the English Bishops. How far this was an example of the Spanish authorities outwitting Wiseman, and how far it was a successful move by Wiseman to assert his authority over the rest of the bench of Bishops, is not clear. Guest was nominated Rector by Queen Isabel on 1 August,[41] and there was no further talk of abolishing the royal patronage. But Wiseman did not live long to enjoy the fruits of his victory if that is what it was. He died in 1865.

40. 'I believe that the Cardinal is a saint. I very much wish to see him.' Searle to Guest, 7 March 1863.
41. Guest to Searle, 7 June 1863.

Searle's association with Valladolid was not entirely finished. Guest has left correspondence with people on matters of historical interest,[42] and we must not forget that in 1855 he rearranged much of the material in the College archives. In June 1863 he wrote to Searle: 'Many thanks for your kindness in sending us the newspaper with the interesting account of your discovery of the hidden treasure in the old college at Douai. I fear your search for the relics has not been so successful.' Correspondence between the two continued, and it was not all on official business. Guest sent a gift of wine to the sick Cardinal,[43] and Searle regarded himself as something of a connoisseur: 'The white wine as well as the red last sent, I must suspend my judgement on. They both came when we were upset by the Cardinal's illness and death. The whole has been bottled since the death and has been removed to my cellar in the country which is not yet at the right temperature. Both these wines are much more delicate in their flavour as well as being lighter in their body.'[44] In 1861[45] the Archbishop of Burgos in a letter to Guest had referred to the immense returns for wine that would be obtained once the new railway line was opened,[46] and Searle, perhaps during his stay at Burgos, was aware of the possibilities this offered to the College: 'I should like to spend a vintage with you and should be inclined to ask you to try some experiments with your wine which has, I am satisfied, all that is required for making a thoroughly good article of commerce.'[47] It was due to Searle's encouragement if not initiative that the College now began to export wines to England. Guest wrote to Manning on 23 October 1869 with a full account of how the wine was made, asking that he should recommend it as an altar wine. 'The wines marked A and B, I consider good wines for the altar. The A more dry, less sweet than the letter B. We have named F.A. Rangel Esq., Commission Merchant, of Moorgate St. Chambers, 49 Moorgate St., our agent in London for the sale of the wine. Mgr Searle I believe is acquainted with him.' At the time of writing Guest said that the College had on hand 64,000 gallons ready for export.

42. For example the correspondence with Canon Dalton of Northampton about the works of St Teresa of Avila, Sept. and Oct. 1856; about the Walpole family and its Spanish Connection, Feb. 1863.
43. This was acknowledged by Searle, 18 Nov. 1863.
44. Searle to Guest, 10 Jan. 1866.
45. 4 Feb. 1861.
46. The railway from Valladolid to the French frontier was opened in 1864.
47. Searle to Guest, 10 Jan. 1866.

The last years of Guest's Rectorship

Although formally appointed Rector and able legally to dispose of and change property, Guest wanted to secure explicit approbation of the English Bishops but found that any talk of disposing of property was not well received.[48] 'The general feeling of the bishops was decidedly against disposing of any real property because no funds can afford a security so great as that of property itself, and wherever we have retained the real estates belonging to our college, sooner or later they have been of value, whilst the money sunk in government funds of different nations has to a great degree perished.'[49] The property deals Guest wanted to complete concerned lands and buildings at Sanlúcar de Barrameda[50] and also in Valladolid where the new railway company was keen to buy up land adjacent to the track which was in possession of the College. Moreover, the recent experience of the mortmain laws indicated that in Spain not even property was as secure as some of the English Bishops imagined. In 1868 Edmund Stonor[51] paid a visit to the Nunciature in Madrid and spoke to Cardinals Barili (the Nuncio) and Moreno (the Primate) about securing exemption of the English and Scots Colleges from the law of mortmain.[52] In September, however, the Rising and *pronunciamiento* forced Isabel into exile. In 1870 she formally abdicated and although she named her son Alfonso as her legitimate successor, Amadeo Duke of Aosta became King, and at same time the Carlists rose in favour of their candidate for the throne, Don Carlos. Their war against the Republic that was set up after Amadeo's abdication lasted into 1875.

Not surprisingly the correspondence of these years is marked by anxiety for the future of the College and of the Church. We must remember that the Revolution in Spain and the setting up of the Federal Republic coincided with the last days of temporal Papal rule in Rome, and there was the feeling that the Church was being assailed on all sides

---

48. Guest to Bishop Brown (Shrewsbury), 28 May 1864.
49. Bishop Brown to Guest, 10 April 1864.
50. See Appendix F.
51. Edmund Stonor, third son of the third Lord Camoys, spent most of his life after ordination by Cardinal Wiseman in Rome and was engaged on several diplomatic missions. This visit to Madrid was a short one since he had to hurry back for his duties as chaplain to the papal Zouaves then preparing to defend Rome against the Piedmontese. He was made titular Archbishop of Trebizond in 1889 and died in 1912.
52. Stonor to Guest, 3 April 1868.

by her enemies. In 1869 Manning applied to Lord Clarendon with the view to his obtaining the protection of the English government for the College at Valladolid.[53] But except for the fact that in 1871 it was thought inadvisable to send out any new students, the College did not suffer as badly as was expected. True, the number of students fell,[54] but eighteen new ones arrived in 1872,[55] and if Guest found difficulty in keeping a supply of superiors to assist him in the teaching, this was a familiar situation and not one to be blamed on the political situation in Spain alone. Students who had completed their course returned to England, and one of them on his arrival home sent Guest an account of their adventures:[56]

The train went all right up to Vitoria; at that place two companies of troops with their officers got in. A Carlist party had been down to the railway line at Salvatierra, and cut down the telegraph wires; it was expected they had also torn up the line; on that account the train ran very slowly; every hundred yards it kept stopping and the engineers got off to examine the line. The officers and troops were also continuously descending from the train and examining the country round about. A more miserable journey I have never had, it was raining all the day. However we met no Carlists; the people said they had marched off to the mountains. Another bad portion of the journey was from Zumarraga to San Sebastián. We travelled in an omnibus, there were eight of us in a conveyance that would not conveniently hold more than six.

The College itself saw little military activity; in January 1874 barricades were set up in the streets of Valladolid by the 'Volunteers' but the next day the regular forces arrived and the volunteers were disarmed.[57] The Rector of the Scots College, Cowie, reported that a cannonball discharged in the Campo Grande struck the front of the English church.[58]

Hardly surprisingly, Guest was beginning to feel the strain of governing the College in these circumstances. In July 1867 he visited Rome for the eighteenth centenary of the deaths of SS Peter and Paul, and the journey shook him up. In 1870 he suffered an unpleasant accident at Viana. On a visit to the vineyard on horseback, he halted to speak to the *cachicán*, and as he did so allowed the bridle to fall over the neck of the

53. Johnson (Manning's secretary) to Guest, 3 May 1869.
54. Guest to Carter, 24 May 1871, 9 June 1871.
55. Carter to Guest, 9 April 1872, 20 May 1872.
56. T. Ratcliffe writing to Guest, 9 April 1873 from Macclesfield.
57. Guest to Bishop Vaughan, 14 Jan. 1874.
58. Quoted in M. Taylor, *The Scots College in Spain*, p. 212.

animal, which had lowered its head to pick the vine leaves. As he bent to recover the bridle, he lost his balance and fell heavily to the ground.[59] The following year he wrote to Carter:[60] 'Do you advise the Archbishop and the bishops to remove me and put me on the shelf as worn out and now useless and send an active intelligent person in my place. This would be doing me a real favour. I have no longer pluck for anything.' In 1873 John Cameron, the Rector of the Scots College, retired after a Rectorship of forty years; he and Guest had been very close and recently they had both obtained permission from the Embassy to fly the Union Jack should the Colleges be in any way threatened.[61] Guest was worried by the new powers the government had obtained which authorised entry and search of houses of both foreigners and Spaniards at any time of the day or night. The political turmoil wearied him: 'I am tired of this liberty,' he wrote in 1873, and when the Bourbons were restored in 1874 he could not forbear heading his letter to Stonor '*In Collegio S. Albani Anglorum Vallisoleti in Hispaniae Regno*'.[62] He deplored the demolition of the 'fine stone gateway that gave entrance to the town and Campo Grande'[63]

References to retirement grew more frequent and on the occasion of Manning's receiving the Red Hat, he included in his letter of congratulations a formal request that he be relieved of his duties.[64] In it he gave an account of the College and the recent record of staff, students and ordinations, and expressed his desire to increase the number of students from nineteen to thirty. He did not want to take young boys, and quoted the fact that 'to the Scotch College in this town, no subjects are sent who have not been several years in a College in Scotland.' The financial situation of the College was fairly satisfactory, and a great sum was invested in wines for export. He wanted to invest more money in England and less in Spanish rents. He had made a proposal to lend out College money to Catholic churches and schools in England at 4½%. At this point in his letter he requested that after thirty years he should be

59. An account of this incident is given by Joseph Jones in *The Albanian*, vol. 1, no. 4, p. 39, but he states that it took place a few months before Guest died. Unless there were two falls this is improbable. The correspondence, especially a letter from Carter to Guest (5 Dec. 1870) referring to a fall, suggests otherwise.
60. Guest to Carter, 24 May 1871.
61. Guest to Ambassador, 23 July 1873. Ambassador to Guest 25 July 1873. Guest to Consul at Santander, 1 Aug. 1873. Guest to Carter, 20 Nov. 1873.
62. Guest to Stonor, 22 Dec. 1874.
63. Guest to Carter, 20 Nov. 1873.
64. Guest to Manning, 31 March 1875.

relieved of the Rectorship or given a year's leave. Only the Vice Rector, Charles Allen, was at present sufficiently informed to manage the College; Guest also submitted names for a successor to the recently deceased Carter as College Agent. As no reply came from Manning he wrote again,[65] and eventually heard from the Cardinal's secretary.[66] The news was disheartening. Despite all Guest's efforts for the College there was little enthusiasm among the hierarchy for its affairs; he was told that the Bishops were only interested in what was close to them, in other words the Colleges in England. Of the Colleges abroad 'it is only Douai they know well because it is not far off. They all take an interest in the College in Rome because it is at Rome. Lisbon is known because there has been a constant succession of priests from there, but Valladolid was only reopened some 25 years ago and is still for the most part unknown and the fact of its being in such an unsettled country is of itself a serious drawback.' The Cardinal had not read Guest's letter as 'it was in fine writing and on thin dark blue paper'; Johnson told Guest that if he wanted his letters to be read they should be 'short and boldly written'.[67] Eventually Guest obtained his leave of absence, and Manning informed the Bishops that Charles Allen would be in charge during his absence, and a priest was to be sent out to assist in the teaching.[68] However, Guest did not leave the College yet because of a new development in the hierarchy's interest in College affairs.[69]

Frail and weary, Guest left Valladolid on 3 April 1876 for Madrid. From his *Libro de Gastos*[70] we can construct his travels and see that there were surprising reserves of energy that kept him going for sixteen strenuous months. From Madrid he went south visiting Cordova, Seville and Puerto de Santa María where he was based for about three months at the Colegio S. Luis. From there he visited Jerez and Sanlúcar de Barrameda. He travelled to Cadiz and Gibraltar and then sailed from Cadiz to Lisbon. He stayed at the English College in Lisbon, visiting the *quintas* at Luz and Pera. Then, after three weeks in Portugal, he sailed for

65. 30 June 1875.
66. Johnson to Guest, 8 July 1875.
67. Johnson gave Allen, Guest's successor, similar advice in 1880: 'H.E. whose sight is no longer good does not like to read either documents or letters that are *long* and *closely* written . . . write as *concisely as possible* in a *rather large hand, with lines far apart and not on thin paper*.'
68. The circular of Manning to the Bishops is dated 20 Sept. 1875. The letter to Guest to the same effect, 16 Oct. 1875.
69. See p. 166, below.
70. Press A, drawer B.

Liverpool calling in at Vigo and Bordeaux on the way. He spent a year from 4 August 1876 to 10 August 1877 in England, visiting and staying with friends through the length and breadth of the country from New-castle and Darlington in the north to Taunton and Salisbury in the south. He visited his friend Mgr Searle and also the seminaries at Oscott, St Bernard's Olton, Old Hall and Ushaw, as well as the Colleges at Hammersmith and Prior Park. On 16 February he learned that he had been created a Domestic Prelate, received his robes in May, and records that he gave Benediction in them and took part in the Preston Guild Procession. Eventually he left Liverpool for Santander, where he was met by Allen. There were festivities in the College welcoming him back: a Latin address and an ode of welcome with a poetry recitation and a five-act drama, *St Louis in Chains*.[71] As a grand finale they all sang Wiseman's *God Bless our Pope*.

In 1875 the financial condition of all the English Colleges abroad came under review by the hierarchy. Herbert Vaughan was entrusted with the enquiry. He visited St Alban's in March 1876, and it was in order to receive him that Guest had postponed his visit to England. Vaughan's companion records[72] that they arrived in Valladolid on 16 March and were greeted by the Rector: 'Nice old man. One of the old school, cour-teous and a little dogmatic but evidently very good. Scrupulous or nervous, has not said Mass for two years. Done a deal for the College. Received it 20 years ago £10,000 in debt and by careful administration has paid debt and placed £3,000 to credit of College. Should be made a Monsignor. Our Bishop is first of English hierarchy who has visited College.' They only stayed until 20 March, but in those four days they managed to visit the College property, pay their respects to the Scots College and the Archbishop of Valladolid, and assist at the entrance of King Alfonso XII into Valladolid and his reception at the cathedral. The diarist records that the ceremony was slovenly and the King looked very boyish; he was evidently worried and anxious and was biting his nails.

When Vaughan's Report was published later in the year, it paid tribute to the services rendered to the English Church by the Colleges in

---

71. See playbills etc.
72. A copy of pages from the diary of this priest travelling-companion is to be found in the Salford Diocesan Archives (Bishop Herbert Vaughan — box 1). It tells of their journey through France, visiting Lourdes and Biarritz, and their impressions of the Basque country, war-scarred as a result of the Carlist conflict. After Valladolid they proceeded to Madrid and then to Cordova, Seville, Sanlúcar de Barrameda and on to Lisbon.

Lisbon and Valladolid, and said that it was desirable that they should be maintained. They might at some future date be needful for the Church as they had been in the past, and the climate could benefit delicate students. The report remarks that no one can visit St Alban's without being impressed by the College and its way of life.[73] However, the studies at the Iberian Colleges fell below what was considered a desirable standard, and it was suggested that each College should limit itself to one course in either humanities or theology. Should there be plans to close the Colleges, one would have to remember that Valladolid was under the royal patronage and that were Lisbon to close, half of the proceeds of sale would, according to the Deed of Foundation, go to the Misericordia. Special recognition was expressed for the way Lisbon had served the cause of religion in Portugal in times of persecution there. Before departing for his extended leave, Guest had been in communication with Vaughan on the subject of holding a competitive examination for prospective students. Vaughan approved: 'It will have the effect of stimulating study and will increase our interest in our foreign colleges by bringing them within a common circle.'[74]

Eleven new students arrived in the autumn of 1877, but Guest took to his bed in December with a bad catarrh. Formby, the College Agent, wrote to him on 12 January 1878: 'Take your rest; leave San Albano to the care of your worthy vice rector and leave all your cash in my care and you will find St Alban's standing erect, on its legs.' A further batch of students left England in February but Guest fell ill again in March and after an illness of fifteen days he died on 4 April 1878.[75] Apart from two years spent in England as a young priest and the year of his extended leave, his whole life since the age of thirteen, fifty-two years previously, had been spent in the College.

73. See also Vaughan's letter of thanks to Guest, 4 April 1876.
74. Vaughan to Guest, 4 April 1876. See also Correspondence, 11, p. 212.
75. An account of his illness, death and burial (in Spanish) by C. Allen is in Series III, L10. There is also a copy of his will, dated 19 June 1869; his executors were Allen and Walmesley. There is also in L10 a memo of 2 April 1876 concerning his personal property and his wishes for its disposal after his death.

10

CONSOLIDATION AND CONTINUITY, 1878–1915; ALLEN TO THOMPSON

Charles Allen, 1878–1904

The restored monarchy and the Constitution of 1876 ushered in a period of comparative stability and internal peace in Spain, which was to last until 1909 and the *Semana Trágica* in Barcelona when the anti-clerical violence of the 1830s reappeared. Under Charles Allen (1878–1904)[1] College life settled down to a rhythm it had not known since the days of Perry and Shepherd. Guest died on 4 April, and on 25 May the *Real Orden* appointing Allen was issued. He received the *Real Cédula* on 13 June.[2] The speed with which the English hierarchy acted on this occasion is explained by the fact that for some years during Guest's illness Allen had administered the College, and he was thus well known to the Bishops, especially Vaughan, the Bishop of Salford, who in his visitation to the College in 1876 had dealings with Allen. The new Rector was a strict disciplinarian and, although at heart a kindly man and known for his generosity to the poor of the town (he left money in his will for several charitable institutions), he appeared to the students stern and unsympathetic.

In the early years of his rule there were many students who left the College. Writing to the Agent, Formby, on 13 February 1879, Allen said: 'I fear the exodus is not entirely finished with yet. Probably there will not be wanting some who will say it is my own mismanagement, that I am not equal to the task of ruling the College. I cannot hope to make vocations, and if students when they grow into years find out that they have not got them, it is decidedly better they should give up beforehand than find out their mistake when it is too late to remedy it. It is a long time since we had such a clearing out, and I have for some time felt that it had to come.' Two years later Bishop Cornthwaite of Leeds had occasion to write to Allen voicing the complaints of one of his students

---

1. For Allen's Rectorship, see Joseph Jones, 'The late Mgr Allen' *The Albanian*, 10 (MSS); also *The Albanian*, vol. 2, no. 2, pp. 128–32.
2. The *terna* bore the names Allen, Formby, Williams. Vaughan to Allen, 6 May 1878.

who had returned home:[3] 'He says that since Dr Guest's death some 30 students have left, there are no spiritual conferences or helps to spiritual guidance; confessions and communions are rare. [. . .] With some exceptions, the students are anything but ecclesiastical in manner and speech; "saxon" words are used . . . ill language such as "silly loon", "bloody b—", "blasted ass". This sort of talk is not uncommon. There is an utter want of fraternal charity.' Allen replied:[4] 'The number stated to have left since the death of Dr Guest is exaggerated precisely one third more than the truth. Of those who have left, some have gone away through sickness and inability to stand our trying climate. Some have been removed at my own request, owing to their want of talent: some few, as is natural, from want of an ecclesiastical vocation and three or four whose misconduct caused me to send them away. . . . ' Cornthwaite's student was one of the latter. The Rector then refuted the charges about lack of spiritual direction and continues: 'As to the gross language said to be usual in the College, [he] knows well that it is expressly forbidden. He is also well aware that I should never tolerate such language were I conscious of its use. I have however endeavoured to find out what truth there could be in the report of the use of the expressions quoted, and find that they were heard once, and uttered by students who are no longer in the College.' From this time there are no more reports or complaints about students leaving the College in great numbers.

The settled state of Spain allowed the Rector to make many material improvements in the house. He built on the strict economies of Guest so that the external appearance of the College bore for many years the imprint of Allen. It was he who introduced gas and electricity. Up to his day the *capuchina*, an olive-oil lamp, served for both heat and light since petroleum was considered too inflammable. He had wooden boarding put down on the floor of the church, and the plaster moulding of the walls and ceiling of the refectory was repaired. A new dormitory was opened up by the addition of a storey to the north side of the house in 1889. He also had a new chapel built at the Country House.[5] He was fortunate in that there were few cases of litigation, which usually take up the energies of the superiors of the College in Valladolid. He did have to present information about the College to the Congregation of

3. Cornthwaite to Allen, 13 April 1881.
4. Allen to Cornthwaite, 19 April 1881.
5. See Joseph Jones, 'Then and Now', *The Albanian*, vol. 1, no. 3, pp. 17–19, and vol. 1, no. 4, pp. 35–42.

Propaganda Fide,[6] and from this we learn that a canon of the chapter of Valladolid was teaching theology to the students,[7] Father Kennedy taught philosophy, Father Joseph Jones looked after the juniors, and James Horton, a layman, taught rhetoric.

During his twenty-six years as Rector, Allen almost quadrupled the college income from its lands and property.[8] Spain was now experiencing a religious revival, and many of the religious orders were finding their way back into the country.[9] There was now a constitutional monarchy with a two-party system based on the '*turno pacífico*', almost in the English style. Catholicism was recognised as the religion of the state, but the private practice of other religions was tolerated. The Catholicism that had survived the days of persecution tended to be traditional and ultramontane, and although the Church enjoyed tranquillity it did not look with complete favour on the existing situation. Liberalism was always suspect.[10]

After the defeat in the war of 1898 and the loss of Cuba and the other overseas possessions to the United States, the theme of regeneration was reinforced in Spanish society, and the Catholic revival under Maura,[11] with its call for a crusade against the Moors, was to lead eventually to the anti-clerical reaction of 1909. But before this unheaval there were to be changes at the College. Allen died of a cerebral haemorrhage as he was preparing for Mass on 4 April 1904. Cardinal Vaughan, a good friend of the College, had died the previous year, and been succeeded at Westminster by Francis Bourne whose promotion from the See of Southwark to that of Westminster could be expected to augur changes in English clerical training. Bourne had been educated by the Sulpicians in France, and was very much in favour of the establishment of separate diocesan seminaries in England. By 1905 rumours were already reaching Rome

6. The request is dated 31 Oct. 1885; Allen's reply, dated 12 Nov. 1885, takes up three quarto pages. Another request from Propaganda came on 8 Nov. 1886, L12.
7. 'For professor of theology I have engaged the services of one of the canons of the cathedral, an eminent theologian, who stands high in the estimation of His Grace the Archbishop of Valladolid and is the ecclesiastical censurer of the diocese' (Allen to Bishop Chadwick of Hexham, 13 April 1880).
8. 1923 Report of Burns to Bishops.
9. Allen to Formby, 29 May 1880.
10. The College library possesses the polyglot edition of *El Liberalismo es Pecado* (Barcelona 1891).
11. Antonio Maura y Montaner, politician, Prime Minister of Spain 1903–4, 1907–9, 1918, 1919, 1921.

that changes were proposed at the Venerabile,[12] but in 1904 Bourne had not yet formulated his plans for Valladolid and on receiving the news of Allen's death he wrote to Kennedy, who was temporarily in charge: 'I shall be glad to have any information that you think would be useful to the bishops. I shall be glad especially to have the names of the most prominent of your former students and all details about them.'[13] The obvious man to succeed was Kennedy himself, who had been on the staff since 1881; but he had developed a spinal complaint in 1892 and been compelled to give up the Vice-Rectorship. When he was offered the post of Rector, he refused on account of his health.[14]

William Wookey, 1904–1906

The new Rector was a Salford priest, William Wookey. He had gone to Valladolid as a boy of twelve, but had only remained five years, eventually completing his course and being ordained at Ushaw in 1891. His first report as Rector to the Bishops was well received, but Bourne immediately began to disclose his plans for the future of the College. On behalf of the Bishops, he introduced once more the idea of having only humanities at Valladolid and then sending the students to complete their course of philosophy and theology at Lisbon.[15] Bourne's letter was reasonably enough phrased, but a similar suggestion had been made years before to Guest, and although we do not have Wookey's reply, we know that it was unfavourable. In fact it would appear that Wookey suggested having no humanities at Valladolid at all.[16] Previous Rectors had considered Valladolid an unsuitable place for young boys, and Wookey himself had not been happy there as a student. Moreover the link with Lisbon did not appeal at all, especially since Fr Rowntree of Salford had written to Wookey on 9 August saying that he wanted to remove a Salford student from Lisbon to Valladolid: '*Entre nous* Lisbon is far from satisfactory at present. A new regime is sadly wanted.' Bourne's

---

12. M.E. Williams, *The Venerable English College, Rome*, p. 146.
13. Bourne to Kennedy, Perth (Scotland), 12 April 1904.
14. 'He was asked by the English bishops to succeed to the rectorship, which on account of the state of his health he felt compelled to refuse' (Kennedy's obituary, *Western Daily Press*, Bristol).
15. Bourne to Wookey, 7 May 1905; also see *Acta* of Low Week meeting, 1905.
16. Amigo to Wookey, 24 Aug. 1905: 'I see you feel inclined to remove the humanity classes.'

proposal was unlikely to be accepted by either College; both had their distinctive traditions, and Spain and Portugal are two different countries with different histories and different legal systems.

In 1905 Bishop Amigo of Southwark visited the College, and on his return to England he wrote expressing agreement with Wookey that Valladolid was not the place for juniors; he promised to pursue the matter of getting Valladolid reserved for philosophy and theology students only.[17] Rowntree was also in correspondence with the Rector, asking him if he proposed to offer any advantage in return for the diocese of Salford having three professors at the College,[18] and expressing his congratulations on how the College was growing in the estimation of the Bishops: 'It speaks volumes for your administration.'[19] But matters were not in as good shape as they seemed to some. Wookey had already approached Bourne with the idea of resigning,[20] and in May 1906 Bourne wrote confidentially to Kennedy asking if, in the event of his being nominated to the position by the Spanish crown, he would be willing and able to accept the nomination: 'The bishops have reason to think that by devolving on a procurator such external affairs as your health precludes from discharging, you would be able to perform efficiently all the other work belonging to the Rector.'[21]

After only eighteen months in office Wookey resigned. The exact reasons are not clear, but in later correspondence there is the suggestion of a clash of personalities and even hard feelings between Wookey and Kennedy. The reference to engaging a procurator is somewhat ironic since it provides a cue for the entrance on the scene of another notable Albanian, Joseph Kelly. A Salford man, already on the staff, he was to exercise great influence on College affairs for the next ten years.

Thomas Kennedy, 1906–1911

So Kennedy was duly appointed rector on 14 August 1906, the *Real*

---

17. Amigo to Wookey, 8 Oct. 1905.
18. I.e. Wookey and Frs Kelly and Shea. Rowntree to Wookey, 15 Feb. 1906.
19. Rowntree to Wookey, 15 March 1906.
20. Bourne to Wookey, 17 Dec. 1905: 'I feel certain that resignation would be a very great mistake. Take fresh courage and go on with the work God has placed in your hands. You are able to do it very well. I shall be glad to see you at Easter and talk matters over with you.'
21. Bourne to Kennedy, 6 May 1906.

Orden arriving on 20 July and the *Cédula Real* on 25 October. Letters of congratulation from Bishops of England reached him, nearly all expressing concern for his health and expressing the hope that he would not be overtaxed by the duties of Rector. Like his predecessors, Kennedy had to put up with complaints about dismissed students, but one letter from Bishop Graham of Plymouth[22] throws light on his relationship with Wookey:

Without any solicitation from me or communication to him on my part I got a letter from Fr Wookey, which shows me that there have been rough times of late at Valladolid and that you have in him an enemy to contend with in England. Whether he confides his feelings about you to me, I know not. But I think you ought to know what he wrote to me, to guide you, both as to inside and outside the College. His letter, which was not marked 'private', sounds rather as if he cared not who saw it and was worded as follows:
    'I am very sorry to hear that Isaac Cowd has been sent away from Valladolid on the score of grumbling. May I say that he was never a grumbler whilst I was rector . . . I have good reason to think he is the victim of sneaking and personal animosity. The only two who could judge him were myself and Father Shea both of us being now absent from the College. Father Kennedy was confined to his room and could know nothing of the students save by report. . . . '

As events turned out, Kennedy does not seem to have been unduly troubled by any activity of Wookey in England, but there was a certain amount of dissent in the College between Salford students (many of them from St Bede's, Manchester) and the others. Kennedy celebrated the jubilee of his ordination in 1907, and among the festivities in his honour was a comic opera *Bunthorne's Boy*, adapted from Gilbert and Sullivan, and a concert by the College orchestra. The spirit in the house seems to have been good. For some time a house magazine, *The Albanian*, had been circulating in manuscript form and in December 1910 it began a brief life in print. Some of the editorial work was done by former students in England, and the intention was to use material from the College archives and those of Simancas, as well as to record current events and publish reminiscences of former students. It ceased publication in 1916.

Football had been introduced into Spain in 1882 in that period when English political and educational ideas were fashionable.[23] Madrid FC,

---

22. 6 Oct. 1906.
23. Britain sent Lord Napier as Special Ambassador to the King's wedding in 1879, and in 1881 King Alfonso was invested with the Order of the Garter.

the champions of the Spanish League in three consecutive seasons 1905, 1906, 1907, issued a challenge to all comers. The College team accepted the challenge and on 28 April 1907 defeated Madrid 6–2. Señor Santiago Bernabeu saw the game and fifty years later, when he was President of *Real Madrid* and they played Manchester United in the European Cup, he was introduced to Fr Linehan, a priest from Salford who had captained the victorious College team, and is reported to have remarked: 'That game changed the whole history of football in Spain by showing them how football should be played.'[24]

In 1908 Archbishop Bourne wrote to inform Kennedy[25] of the arrangement that had been made with the English College in Rome whereby the Bishops would be presented each year with a detailed report of the progress of the College and the students. Moreover, it was agreed that there would be consultation between the Rector and the Bishop before a student received orders and before any student could be dismissed. Bourne wanted a similar understanding with the other foreign Colleges. Kennedy, however, desired some clarifications; he said that the use of the word 'consult' must not imply that any individual Bishop had authority over the Rector, or that a Bishop could retain a student in the College against the Rector's expressed wish to the contrary. And although it was allowed for the Rector to expel anyone immediately for 'grave moral delinquency', this phrase should be interpreted according to College rules. But provided the rights of the Rector were upheld, Kennedy was not against this process of bringing the College closer to the Church at home that had begun when Guest was Rector. The following year, there was a further step in this direction when the College was transferred from the jurisdiction of Propaganda Fide to that of the Consistorial Congregation,[26] as indeed befitted a college providing priests for what was no longer officially a missionary country. Kennedy wrote to Cardinal de Lai[27] enclosing a copy of the Bull of Foundation, the Statutes and a modern rule book pointing out that it was of course a Spanish royal college, the Rector receiving his nomination from the King of Spain. To this there came in reply a lengthy

24. Obituary of Fr Linehan, *Manchester Evening News*.
25. 22 July 1908.
26. Consistorial Congregation to Kennedy, 4 March 1909, asking for details about the College statutes.
27. 21 March 1909. Cardinal de Lai of the Consistorial Congregation was, together with Cardinals Merry del Val and Vives y Tuto, a firm upholder of Pius X's policy against Modernism.

document from the Congregation[28] explaining its enactments concerning the foreign Colleges.[29] The questions posed by Rome were mainly to do with the oath of Urban VIII, and for Valladolid the Rector's position was clarified and preserved.

In 1910 Kennedy produced a handsomely illustrated brochure by way of his first official report to all the English Bishops. There were forty-two students in the College, twelve in third-year theology, eight in first-year theology, eight in first-year philosophy, seven poets and seven humanists. Eleven dioceses were represented, and the most numerous were the ten Salford students. 'The papal instructions as to frequent communion are loyally carried out on the students' own initiative.'[30] In contrast to the position during the previous century, the College's financial position was very satisfactory and the capital had been increased by additional investments. The report then mentioned the material improvements to the College, from which it can be appreciated how much Kennedy carried on and completed the work of his predecessors Guest and Allen. There were new bathrooms, the whole interior was repainted, and all the ancient brick floors were replaced by planks, Portland cement or compressed marble. 'A commodious and elegant professor's dining-room has been built', and the refectory artistically repainted and better lighted by the insertion of additional stained glass windows. The sanctuary of the church was redecorated, the altar rails were removed, and through the gift of Granville Ward[31] a new organ to the value of £1,000 and forty-eight carved walnut choir stalls were added.[32] This was so that there could be a surpliced choir, thus enabling the students to take a more active part in liturgical celebrations.[33]

28. 29 July 1909.
29. This is an interesting document since the foreign Colleges include, in addition to the English and Scots in Rome and Valladolid, the Canadian College in Rome, the American College in Louvain, the English College in Lisbon, the Irish College in Paris, and *alumni* from the United States, Canada and Ireland at Propaganda College, Rome, and All Hallows College, Dublin.
30. This refers to the directives of Pius X.
31. Known as 'the Squire' and a frequent visitor to the College. He was the eldest of the Ward children, an eccentric and devoted to ecclesiastical matters since childhood. M. Ward, *The Wilfrid Wards and the Transition*, London 1934, esp. pp. 158 and 164–5.
32. These were replaced in 1979 when the church was reorganised in the spirit of the Second Vatican Council.
33. Valladolid was different from other English seminaries of the day in so far as Prime and Compline were recited in the morning and evening in preference to morning and evening prayers, based on the Manual of Prayers deriving from Challoner.

Following Allen's improvements, further student accommodation was ensured by adding a new storey on one side of the quadrangle for eight new student rooms and a twelve-cubicle dormitory. There was special acknowledgement of the work of the Procurator, Father Joseph Kelly, and although this was not mentioned in the report, he had made himself responsible for developing further the exporting of wine.[34] Because the phylloxera reached Spain at this time, stocks became exhausted and for a time all exports ceased, but they seemed to have resumed about 1913. Another matter with which Kelly concerned himself was the lawsuit over the Seville property.[35] It began with enquiries about the property at Sanlúcar de Barrameda in June 1908, and before long the College lawyer Señor Blanco had made a formal claim on behalf of the College at Valladolid for the return of the property of St Gregory's College, Seville. Although the relevant documents were signed by Kennedy, it was Kelly who conducted the negotiations.

The report also recorded Kennedy's plan to get the students to attend the Pontifical University instead of having lectures in the house. As we have seen, there had been continual difficulty in more recent years in obtaining suitable professors from England to teach in the College. At the time of Perry and Shepherd the students had attended lectures in the town, at the University, but the civil upsets at the time of the Peninsular War had meant the closing of the University, and when independence was restored the successive liberal governments passed a series of laws that adversely affected Catholic education.[36] Things began to improve towards the end of the century, and following the decree of the Sacred Congregation of Studies of 30 June 1897, a Pontifical Unversity was established at Valladolid in October that year with faculties of theology, philosophy and canon law. Antonio María Cascajones y Azara, Cardinal Archbishop of Valladolid, granted an ample building to be used as a major and minor seminary. When James Humble became Rector of the Scots College in 1909, one of the first things he did was to comply with the desires of the Scots Bishops and begin negotiations to send students

34. See Letter Book, 1907–12.
35. See Appendix E.
36. The universities became more and more secular, the Profession of Faith was no longer imposed on members, and the episcopal control over the theological and philosophical textbooks ceased. The theological faculties at the Spanish universities were suppressed in 1824, and the Concordat of 1851 recognised the end of the theology faculties. Only in the seminaries and religious houses was it possible to follow this study, which now became more abstract and less related to the problems of contemporary society.

to the new university-seminary.[37] Kennedy was of similar mind and pointed out to the English Bishops that the University was only five minutes walk from the College and the students would be able to gain degrees if they were to attend; he had already approached Archbishop de Cos y Macho of Valladolid and the Rector of the University, and there would be no difficulty on their part. The College would continue to take younger students, but only those studying theology or philosophy would attend the University. He added that up to the present the College had not taken advantage of its position in Spain; its inmates were isolated from everything Spanish as if they were in England. They needed to obtain a perfect knowledge of Latin and Spanish and become fluent speakers of these languages so as to imbibe the Catholic spirit. The Bishops received these proposals favourably.

Bourne suggested as a way of improving the standard of humanities in the College that a priest be appointed to the staff who had studied at St Edmund's House, Cambridge.[38] Things began to move fairly quickly as Kennedy received a letter from Joseph Butt of the Beda College, Rome, informing him that the petition had been handed to the Congregation of Studies on 31 March.[39] The negotiations concerning admission and matriculation continued through the summer, and in the autumn the first students from St Alban's entered into the classes of first-year theology and first-year philosophy. However, by the following May it was clear that some of them at least were dissatisfied with the arrangement.[40] Bourne took the matter up, and in a letter of 12 October 1911 he wrote:

Very serious complaints are reaching England regarding the new arrangements now made for the philosophical and theological studies at Valladolid. It is stated that the professors are unpunctual and in several cases incompetent, that the Spanish students are disedifying even to the extent of being guilty of indecent language and gesture, that the lecture rooms are so ill-provided with furniture that there are no conveniences for writing or taking notes. Please let me know how far these criticisms are well founded, and give me your own candid opinion on the whole situation, which (it is alleged) is causing great dissatisfaction in the English College.

Kennedy was in England at the time, and when the letter was forwarded

37. M. Taylor, *The Scots College in Spain*, p. 250.
38. Bourne to Kennedy, 10 April 1910.
39. Butt to Kennedy, 31 March 1910, L13.
40. Bishop Amigo to Kennedy, 30 May and 7 Dec. 1911; Bishop Singleton to Kennedy, 23 June 1911; Bishop Ilsley to Kennedy, 22 Jan. 1912.

to him, he returned it to Valladolid asking Kelly to investigate.[41] 'I enclose a letter from the Archbishop forwarded by Jones this morning. I think you ought to show it to the Rector of the seminary so as to prepare him for the worst, and to hear what he may have to say. Then send as soon as possible a rough draft of an answer to the Archbishop.' A further letter followed a month later.[42] Kennedy said that before he wrote to the Archbishop of Westminster with the decision to withdraw the students, Archbishop de Cos y Macho of Valladolid who was to be given the Red Hat on 28 November 1911 had to be approached and pacified. He also told Kelly to secure the services of two Jesuits as professors, assuring him that their salaries would be paid. The outcome of this incident was mild. Later Bourne made a request to the new Cardinal Archbishop of Valladolid that students who did not intend to take degrees should not attend lectures in the secondary subjects,[43] and this request was granted.[44]

One of the reasons why there was no crisis and students continued to attend the University was the fate of Kennedy himself. In October 1911, much to the surprise of his friends,[45] he decided to go to England; he had by now largely recovered the use of his legs which had been paralysed. But he caught a chill while at his home in Clifton and died on 6 December 1912.[46] Despite his physical disability Kennedy had a distinguished Rectorship; he improved the material state of the College and by founding *The Albanian* and sending the students to lectures at the University, widened the horizons of its members. So closely did he follow the path set by Guest and Allen that the unfortunate Wookey episode was soon forgotten.

During the interregnum Kelly the Procurator conducted College business, and some former alumni in England expected him to be Kennedy's successor.[47] Bishop Amigo complained to him that the last appointment had been made by Bourne without reference to the

41. Kennedy to Kelly, 18 Oct. 1911.
42. Kennedy to Kelly, 15 Nov. 1911.
43. 30 Jan. 1912.
44. 16 Feb. 1912.
45. Baigent to Jones, 8 Oct. 1911.
46. For obituaries see *Diario Regional*, 7 Dec.; *El Porvenir*, 8 Dec.; *Western Daily Press* (Bristol); *The Albanian*, vol. 1, no. 4, pp. 7–11. It is good to record that Wookey had a requiem Mass sung at St Augustine's, Manchester, on 16 Jan. 1912 at which 35 priests were present and after Mass there was a special luncheon provided by Wookey.
47. Rowntree to Kelly, 5 Feb. and 4 April 1912; Burns to Kelly, 27 Dec. 1911.

Bishops,[48] and Whiteside informed Fr Jones, a member of the College staff, that the delay was due to consultations with the Foreign Office.[49]

James Thompson, 1912–1915

In early April the name of the new Rector became known :[50] it was James Thompson, a priest from the Hexham and Newcastle diocese. The exact reasons why certain people are appointed to church office are always somewhat mysterious; Wookey averred[51] that this was the second time that the post had been offered to Thompson, but did not state whether he had previously been offered it on the death of Allen or after his own resignation. Thompson had been a frequent visitor to the Peninsula and was an ardent hispanophile. For twenty-five years he had been spending his annual vacation in Spain, and as man and boy had seen the College under four Rectors; he had experience of missionary work in four parishes in the north of England and seemed ideally suited to the job.

Almost immediately Thompson began to contribute articles to *The Albanian* magazine which provide an interesting insight into the situation of the Church in Spain and the way an English cleric viewed the political situation there after the serious upsets of 1909 and the resurgence of anti-clerical liberalism. Thompson's interest fitted in well with the policy that was put forward by priest-editors in England. In 1910 they had commemorated the first centenary of the birth of Jaime Balmes, the Catholic apologist, by the first of a projected series of articles on 'Spanish divines'. This was followed by a four-part article on another Catholic writer, Donoso Cortés. One of their stated objectives for the magazine was 'to disseminate the truth about Spain and her people, her relations with the church, the work of the religious orders . . . which are misrepresented in secular journals by the enemies of Catholicity who, as in the time of Ferrer, never tire of serving up calumnies to the detriment of the church in the Iberian Peninsula.'[52] The editors wrote a year later: 'Some think it too ambitious, and have unfairly stated that its editors

48. Amigo to Kelly, 13 Dec. 1911.
49. Whiteside to Jones, 20 Feb. 1912.
50. *Real Orden del Ministerio de Gracia y Justicia*, 30 March 1912; *Real Cédula*, 19 April 1912.
51. Appreciation of J. Thompson by Dean Wookey, *The Albanian*, vol. 1, no. 4, June 1912.
52. *The Albanian*, vol. 1, no. 3, Dec. 1911.

desire to make it an apologist for Catholic Spain',[53] and then went on to remark: 'Common gratitude dictates that whenever possible we should repel the scurrilous calumnies that are contained in the Ananias-made histories and secular magazine articles against a nation and people to whom every son of St Alban's owes a whole-hearted respect and esteem.'

Thompson's articles supported this policy. When Canelejas was Prime Minister, the magazine criticised him for his attitude to the religious orders,[54] and said that there was no need for him to be alarmed at their growth, since there were fewer religions in Spain in proportion to the whole population than in any other country in Europe.[55] But one of the first contributions of Thompson as Rector [56] was prompted by the murder of Canelejas on 13 November 1912; in it he pointed out that his obsequies had included no Masonic ritual or oration, but that Masses had been said for the repose of his soul. He had fulfilled his Easter duties, and had recently had his own son baptised a Catholic by his household chaplain. The article was optimistic about both the present and the future of the faith in Spain. He remarked on the piety of the people at the cemetery of Valladolid on All Souls Day, and in a later contribution[57] wrote of a new spirit abroad: 'If France on the one side, and Portugal on the other, have had their faith filched away and robbed by the masonic government, Spaniards will have none of that.' He wrote on the situation of education in Spain, and also made a plea for a strong and fearless foreign policy that would support an expedition to Morocco.[58] These and similar attitudes were characteristic of churchmen in Spain at this time, and throw additional light on the celebrations accompanying the Eucharistic Congress in Madrid in 1911. These celebrations were attended by some of the students, and Wookey came out for them and wrote a report.[59] The magazine remarked:[60] 'Catholic Spain is arousing herself from her Rip Van Winkle attitude — and none too soon if she hopes to stem the flood of slanderous charges which are continuously issuing from the liberal and republican "trust papers". A telegraphic news agency of national and foreign news is now in full working order,

53. Vol. 2, no. 1, Dec. 1912.
54. Vol. 1, no. 2, pp. 18–19, 37, 44.
55. Vol. 1, no. 2, p. 37.
56. 'The Outlook in Spain', vol. 2, no. 1, Dec. 1912.
57. 'Beyond the Pyrenees', vol. 2, no. 2, June 1913.
58. Vol. 2, no. 3, Dec. 1913, pp. 219–22.
59. Vol. 1, no. 3.
60. Vol. 1, no. 2.

which supplies reliable news on Catholic matters to 33 Catholic news-papers.' But although Thompson's optimism regarding the Church in Spain was to some extent justified, since the liberals had to contend with a more organised and vital Catholicism, there were clouds on the horizon. Prices and taxation were rising and the rest of Europe, inclu-ding England, was moving towards an armed conflict.

The arrangement with the University meant that certain fees had to be paid for matriculation and examination, and two Bishops declined to enter students for degrees on the grounds of expense.[61] In January 1913 Thompson decided to raise the episcopal contribution for students from £14 to £20 per annum. He said that the cost of living in Spain was now higher than in England, that phylloxera had damaged the vines and so weakened a source of income, and that taxation had increased. Most of the Bishops appreciated the Rector's difficulties and accepted the new measures.[62] The outbreak of the European war in 1914 brought a letter from Baigent of Nottingham saying that it would be impossible for any new students to arrive because 'the steamers are stopped and the railways disorganised.' Nor would those students at present on holiday in England be able to return;[63] the Archbishop of Birmingham wrote to say that the two Birmingham students on holiday would be transferred to Oscott.[64]

The war brought two distinguished visitors to the College who had come on a mission to neutral Spain to plead the cause of the Allies. Mgr Redwood, Archbishop of Wellington, New Zealand, was on a tour of Europe when war broke out, and in correspondence with the procu-rator, Kelly. He visited Valladolid before going on to Rome where he met Gasquet 'who is doing his best to counteract the baneful German influence in Rome'; he reported that a permanent United Kingdom plenipotentiary with the Holy See, Sir Henry Howard, had just been appointed. 'As in Spain, the bulk of the clergy and most of the Curia are sadly pro-German and anti-allies.'[65] Later Bishop Amigo was also in

---

61. Bishop Keating of Northampton to Thompson, 16 Aug. 1912; King (secretary to Bishop of Portsmouth) to Thompson, 3 Sept. 1912.
62. Keating again objected but others wrote to Thompson accepting: Whiteside, 16 Jan. 1913; Amigo of Southwark, 17 Jan.; Lacy of Middlesbrough, 19 Jan.; Burton of Clifton, 21 Jan.; Ilsley of Birmingham, 23 Jan.; Keily of Plymouth, 2 Feb.; and Bishop Healy, 12 Feb. 1913.
63. 5 Aug. 1914.
64. 24 Sept. 1914.
65. Redwood to Kelly from S. Stefano Rotondo, Rome, 20 Dec. 1914.

correspondence with Kelly;[66] he was planning to visit Spain and see the King, and he asked Kelly to assist him in the itinerary: 'My intention is to visit the religious men and women who have influence, and especially those whom you have found the hardest to convince.' In May 1916 Mgr Baudrillart [67] was in Valladolid and he stayed at the English College; his visit too was to promote the cause of the Allies.[68]

The Albanian had to suspend publication in 1914 and although it resumed in December 1915, only one further issue was published thereafter, in June 1916. Thus not only is there no record of College activities during this time, but we have no account of Thompson's difficulties as Rector; it appears from a letter of Burton of St Edmund's, Ware,[69] that Thompson was considering resignation since he felt that he was not getting the support that was his due from the bishops. We do have Thompson's own thoughts on the subject in a draft letter to Bourne:[70]

Having heard finally from the Bishop, I herewith tender my resignation of the post of Rector . . . of which intention I gave Your Grace intimation on April 21st. The step was foreshadowed, too, in a letter of mine of 28th June of last year . . . The decision arrived at was the outcome of the reluctance of the bishops to offer a sort of guarantee or assurance against the summary withdrawal of subjects here without previous reference to the Rector, and so embarrassing him in his action, as well as making a temporary convenience of the College. It is for the safe-guarding of this cherished principle, viz. the dignity, honour and interest of the old place, that I am now acting.

He then gave a few instances of the way in which individual Bishops withdrew students,[71] concluding:

I was assured by Your Grace on my coming out here, the bishops were emphatic on the attendance of their subjects at the pontifical university here, the students of Portsmouth when recalled informed me their bishop was opposed to it. I mention these matters quite dispassionately, and more 'in sorrow than in anger' and I ask Your Eminence kindly to regard me as ever Your most obedient servant . . .

---

66. Amigo to Kelly, 14 Sept. 1915.
67. Rector of the Institut Catholique, Paris, and author of a classic history of Bourbon Spain, *Philippe V et la Cour de France*.
68. *The Albanian*, 1916, vol. 3, no. 2, pp. 140–1, 166.
69. Burton to Thompson, 19 May 1915.
70. Thompson to Bourne, 27 June 1915.
71. These cases involved the dioceses of Clifton, Portsmouth, Nottingham, Birmingham and Salford.

Thompson left for England on 16 August 1915.[72]

Thus after just under three years the Rectorship was again vacant. In the comparatively short space of nine years two incumbents had resigned and one had died in office. When recalling the difficulties faced by previous Rectors and the way they persevered in office, one is tempted to criticise Wookey and Thompson for faint-heartedness. But circumstances had changed. The closer relationship between the College and the Bishops at home, begun in the time of Guest and now actively promoted by Cardinal Bourne, had led the Rectors to expect more help and support than the Bishops were willing to give. If the College were to survive, there were certain battles to be fought by the superiors alone.

72. *The Albanian*, vol. 3, no. 1. A private notebook of Thompson's has recently come to light from which it appears that from the beginning of his Rectorship he felt he did not have the full support of his staff. He made matters worse for his sensitive and suspicious nature by eavesdropping on conversations and even opening letters, by which he made the unpleasant discovery of what the students thought of him.

11

ENGLISH BISHOPS, A ROMAN CONGREGATION AND THE SPANISH CROWN

The Rectorship of Michael John Burns, 1915–1924

Since the time of Kennedy, Joseph Kelly the Procurator had been administering the College property. He had resurrected the Seville lawsuit in 1908, and it had now apparently reached a satisfactory state.[1] He had also undertaken to raise money for the College from the sale of a painting attributed to El Greco.[2] He was managing the export of wine to England, and had recently persuaded Thompson to renew the College's claim for goods taken by Sherburne and now in the possession of Ushaw.[3] The President of Ushaw had given a cautious reply:[4] 'I have carefully read your letter but I feel that I cannot do anything in a matter of this kind without instructions from the bishops. I will bring the case before them in the next meeting after the vacation and let you know the result.'[5] Kelly had dealt with much of the correspondence between the

1. Archbishop Whiteside wrote him a letter of congratulation on 29 Nov. 1915: 'I hope one effect of that may be to put the salaries of the superiors of the College on a satisfactory basis; so that those of you who are making sacrifices by being away from the English mission may have a comfortable Maintenance.' Similarly Baigent to Kelly, 15 Dec. 1915. These congratulations were somewhat premature.
2. Concerning the El Greco sale see Kennedy to Kelly, 15 Nov. 1911; Kelly to Burns, 17 Jan. 1917; Kelly to Burns 16 June 1920. The picture was eventually sold for £3,000. In 1937 there was an enquiry from Langton Douglas about this painting, which was now his and which was said to have been given to the College by Sir Francis Englefield.
3. Kelly sent a long document to Mgr Brown of Ushaw on 10 May 1914 in which he identified as belonging to St Alban's property now in the possession of Ushaw: the *Annales Domestici* (corrected and continued by Fr Blackfan), the original copy of the constitutions of the College, a large painting of Pope St Gregory brought from the College of St Gregory in Seville (the artist was Roelas), and also various chasubles and dresses for the Vulnerata. The College was also missing six paintings, and these were believed to be in the church at The Willows near Kirkham, Lancs. These last pictures were eventually discovered at Upholland and returned to Valladolid. Burns to Archbishop of Liverpool, 24 Aug. 1921.
4. 14 May 1914.
5. In the June issue of *The Albanian*, Kelly had written an article on the Sherburne case which had won the approval of Bishop Burton of Clifton in a letter of 25 May 1915.

Bishops and the College. Furthermore, successive Rectors had relied heavily on his experience. However, it later transpired that one of the reasons for Thompson's resignation was the role Kelly had assumed. Shortly after his successor was appointed, Thompson wrote to him:[6]

He [Kelly] resented my going out at all, especially as he had run the show some nine or ten years, and as life is too short to be made miserable, we chose to retire to the mission again, because it is an invidious thing to dispense with one who has been out there so long and is well acquainted with the various rents, lettings and properties.

There was to be no long interregnum, Canon Michael Burns of Plymouth being appointed in the very month that Thompson left (the *Cédula Real* was dated 15 September 1915). The appointment of Burns as Rector meant that Kelly had been passed over for the second time. He very soon decided that he ought to return to England, but Bishop Amigo was against this: 'I shall be very sorry if you leave at this juncture. You can be so useful, not only at the College, but also to counteract the evil of German propaganda. Kindly distribute these six copies of *Alemania en Bélgica* among pro-Germans and I can obtain more for you, if wanted.'[7] But Burns had been warned about Kelly and his undue influence, not only by his predecessor Thompson, but also by a friend J. O'Connor, now at Burnley; the Procurator was reported to be harsh in dealing with the students, sometimes taking it on himself to dismiss them — which was in fact the prerogative of the Rector. However, Burns could not do without him in the early days even though, ironically, the very first dealings the new Rector had with Cardinal Bourne ran into difficulties largely through the promptings of Joseph Kelly.

The occasion was the seeking of permission to develop College lands.[8] Before 1910–11 the bulk of the income for the support of the College had come from the vines, and when disease had killed them off it had been necessary to irrigate the land and put it to another use. This meant a re-adjustment of certain plots and a certain amount of buying and selling. The necessary purchases could not be carried through by the Rector because an anti-clerical registrar would not recognise his right to buy and sell in the name of the College. He first objected that the authority of the King of Spain was necessary, and when this was refuted he insisted that a

6. 4 Sept. 1915.
7. 25 Dec. 1915, Amigo to Kelly. *Alemania en Bélgica* was a British-inspired pamphlet in Spanish. See later for similar pro-Allied activity during the Second World War.
8. The account which follows is substantially that given by Henson in a letter to Cardinal Gasquet, 16 Oct. 1924.

document should be obtained from those who had a right to present to the Spanish Crown the *terna* for the Rectorship, namely the Bishops of England. Cardinal Bourne was appealed to and Mgr Bidwell answered in his name that the effect of such a document would be so far-reaching that it was necessary for him to submit the matter to the Bishops at the Low Week meeting. This was done in April 1915 and the Bishops agreed that the document should be issued, with the proviso that the consent of the Archbishop of Westminster should be obtained before any sale could be carried out. The Cardinal told Kelly, the Procurator, that the matter was settled, but he then refused to give the document on the ground that it would be better to issue it to the new Rector after the departure of Thompson who was about to resign (he did so with effect from 27 June 1915).

Thus almost immediately after his arrival in Valladolid on 9 October 1915, Burns wrote for a 'faculty' enabling him to act in the name of the English hierarchy. Bourne was cautious and said that he did not wish to assume any responsibility that was not his; there was good reason for this caution. Burns may have thought that the matter in question was simply one of obtaining authorisation to dispose of College property, but behind it all lay the assumption that the College was independent of the Crown and that it was the English Bishops who had rights in the matter, not the King of Spain. For years Kelly had been fighting, in the Seville affair, for the independence of the College from the Crown, and he had convinced Burns that the Crown had no rights in the matter. Burns, by writing to the Nuncio in Madrid and also to Ilsley the Archbishop of Birmingham, exerted pressure to get Bourne to yield, but the Cardinal decided to investigate further.

On 19 January 1916 he wrote to Burns that he was sending Mgr Bidwell, who spoke Spanish and who was at present staying with his mother at St Jean de Luz, to make a canonical visitation to the College in Valladolid — a move embarrassing to both Kelly and Burns since it looked as if they had escaped from the Scylla of the Spanish Crown only to run foul of the Charybdis of the English hierarchy. Burns immediately wrote to his own bishop, Kiely of Plymouth, protesting that 'the English bishops either collectively or singly have no jurisdiction out here. [. . .] This is the first attempt ever made by the English bishops to hold a canonical visitation.' Vaughan's visit to all the foreign seminaries in 1876 was in no way comparable to the sending of Mgr Bidwell. Burns also wrote to the Archbishops of Birmingham and Liverpool complaining of Bourne's action, knowing that not all the hierarchy always saw eye to eye with the Archbishop of Westminster. Whiteside of Liverpool advised against opposition to the visitation, and said that any appeal to the Spanish tribunal would be of no benefit the College in the long run; an appeal should be made later, and then only if the effects of the visitation proved injurious to the College. However, Burns in his letter to Kiely recognised that Bidwell might be able to help him, and he looked forward to discussing such matters as the attendance of students at classes at the seminary in Valladolid, the gradual transfer of college funds to England, and a scheme for obtaining students from Ireland should conscription into the armed services prevent English boys from arriving. The rapprochement of the College to the English hierarchy that had been developing over the years was not yet put into reverse.

Bidwell arrived and departed within twenty-four hours. He had no letter of commendation, there was no message from Rome addressed to the Rector, and he had not even seen the document drawn up by Vaughan in his 1876 visits to the Colleges abroad. But the visit had some results. A short time afterwards there arrived a statement of the Rector's *personalidad*, and although it was very late in the day, the Rector was able to start negotiations about the transfer of lands. Bidwell wrote to Kelly that he had now read Vaughan's report, remarking that in it was a clear statement there that a royal sanction was necessary for the buying and selling of property. Did this mean that the Bishops had been misinformed, and that their powers were much less than they had been led to believe? He felt it would be better if a Spanish lawyer looked into the situation and reported on his views of it. Kelly seems to have been somewhat worried by this turn of events since he was claiming exemption from the Spanish crown in his claims on the Seville property, and wanted no other Spanish lawyer interfering with his case. He wrote back to Bidwell giving his opinion that the crown had no legal authority over the property, any more than it had over than of other foreigners in Spain; but neither had the English Bishops any legal standing. The only occasion when the hierarchy had intervened in College affairs was when Dr Challoner petitioned Charles III to respect the English foundations in Spain. In fact the legal authority over the College was vested in the duly appointed Rector; it was in fact the Rector who was challenging the crown in the long legal lawsuit over the Seville property. All the *títulos civiles* were expressly drawn up in the Rector's name without reference to the ecclesiastical authorities in England.

At this point in the story (March 1916), Kelly made his departure from Valladolid to take up an appointment in England, first at St Bede's

College, Manchester, and then at St Augustine's, Chorlton-cum-Hardy. The next year, at the special request of the Albanian Society, he was made a Domestic Prelate for his services to the College in Valladolid. So Burns was now left on his own to deal with the situation, and he handed the affair over to Don Federico Blanco, the College lawyer. Bidwell for his part was using the services of another Spanish lawyer. At the Low Week meeting in April 1916, Bourne reported on the Valladolid situation, and said that he had placed the whole matter in the hands of the recently constituted Congregation of Seminaries and Studies in Rome and that the Bishops after meeting had expressed their wish to exercise some ecclesiastical control over the College.

For two years the matter rested there, and then in April 1918 Bourne wrote to Burns telling him that a decision had been made by the Congregation of Seminaries and Studies: Valladolid had to cease taking students for the humanities and concentrate on philosophy and theology. This was news to Burns, who had received no communication from Rome; when he did get hold of a copy of the new decree, he found that the College had been placed under the control of the English hierarchy, who were to appoint five prelates as moderators of its affairs. The Rector was to be appointed for a fixed term of six years. In fact by the time Burns got to know of the new arrangements, the Bishops had decided at their meeting that the Cardinal, together with the Bishops of Menevia, Southwark, Plymouth and Brentwood, were to manage College affairs. The *Acta* of this meeting contains the rather enigmatic line: 'With respect to the question *sub secreto Pontifici*, the bishops considered that the matter was not sufficiently clear as to justify attention.'

When these new regulations became generally known there were reactions from several quarters. Walmsley, the College agent, wrote from Upholland in 1918, expressing the view that the Spanish government would have something to say about the matter; he said it was not likely to tolerate any change in the appointment of the Rector, and might even try and lay hands on the property. As for the Rector's six-year term of appointment, exceptions should be allowed. If the Rector were giving satisfaction, it would be foolish to retire him; there were so few priests in England capable of taking up such an office, or willing to do so. Bishop Amigo of Southwark advised Burns not to appeal to the Spanish crown, since the right of patronage established by Charles III had lain dormant for years, and authorisation to dispose of property could be obtained without the King's intervention. Although Kelly was now a parish priest in England, he was still interested in Valladolid affairs, and he wrote his word of advice to Burns: 'Politely ignore the whole matter of the Congregation of Seminaries.' Nothing more should be done, he said, until an attempt was made to translate into action the new constitution, which in fact transgressed the College's *legal* constitution. The Congregation had the right in ecclesiastical matters, but no authority to abrogate indirectly and without reference to the Papal Bull of Institution of 1589 or the Royal Charter of Charles III 1779. 'To directly challenge the new resolutions of the Congregation, however, would be doing exactly what is wanted by the personage interested in obtaining the said resolution, viz. it would be taking up the onus, worry, expense and litigation in fighting an illegal *assumption* of authority. Time enough to act when it is attempted to translate that assumption into action. Let them do the worrying.' From subsequent events it is clear that Burns heeded Kelly's advice; he wrote to Bourne expressing surprise that he had still received no official notification of the new statutes, and stating that he also thought it curious that they had not appeared in the *Acta Apostolicae Sedis*. As they involved a big change, he presumed that notification would be sent to the ecclesiastical and civil authorities in Spain.

Kelly's suspicions regarding Bourne's intentions seemed to be justified by what took place at the Low Week meeting on 29 April 1919. As the *Acta* record, 'it was decided by 9 votes to 3 that it was advisable to sell the college at Valladolid subject to the following conditions:

1. That a suitable price can be secured.
2. That the allocation of the resulting funds be not settled without the consultation of the bishops.
3. That their rights to free or partially free burses be retained wherever the money is spent.

With respect to Lisbon it was decided by 8 votes to 3 that it was not advisable to part with the College.' There for a time the matter seemed to rest.

More than two years later, on 19 October 1921, Bourne wrote to Burns: 'When I know from you that you have definitely accepted the regulation laid down for the English College at Valladolid by the Holy See I shall be glad to help you to the full extent of my power.' Kelly was again consulted, and as always, he was ready with advice. He reminded Burns that he had received no official notice from Rome, and that a communication from the Archbishop of Westminster, whether one agreed with it or not, could not alter the constitution of a papal and royal college. The wisest course would be to get a cardinal protector, such as other papal colleges had, and as Valladolid had formerly: 'Any cardinal who had once been Nuncio in Madrid would I think be a good protector.' At the Low Week meeting of 1922, as the *Acta* for 25 April record, 'The Cardinal reported that he had received no information about the English College, Valladolid, and the bishops decided they could not accept responsibility for undertakings at the College until proper information was submitted.' An indication of the nature of this lack of information of which the Bishops complained is given in a letter that reached Burns in March 1923 via the Archbishop of Valladolid from the Congregation of Seminaries and Studies. This informed the Rector that he had to submit a yearly report to the English Bishops, and appears to have been the first communication Burns had ever received personally from Rome and it was now too late to do anything in time for the current year's hierarchy meeting.[9] However, Burns did draw up a very full report of the state of the College at the end of 1922, but this too was too late for the Bishops' meeting, and the five moderators decided on a special meeting to be held at once to consider the present state of the College.

During all these manoeuvrings, College life seems to have carried on fairly peacefully. Burns was a good host, and welcomed former students as visitors to the College after the end of the Great War; his letters were remarkably cordial, and he was known to the students as 'Daddy Burns'. But he found it difficult to keep staff, and was particularly unfortunate in his Vice-Rectors, till 1922 when he managed to secure the services of Denis O'Connor, an Irish priest working in Burns' own diocese of Plymouth. But after only a year, O'Connor returned to England and began to spread reports of an unhappy state of affairs in Valladolid. When one student, Muldoon, had had to leave Spain because of ill-health and died shortly after reaching home, it was claimed that this indicated negligence on the part of the College. The food was said to be inadequate and the students were generally neglected. In view of these reports the Bishop of Plymouth decided to withdraw his students. Burns wrote a long letter defending his conduct, asserting that the food shortages were the result of the war and that Muldoon's tragic death had not been due to negligence by the College. Indeed, Burns' warm-hearted correspondence with the parents of a student who had been withdrawn by his Bishop to continue his studies elsewhere excites sympathy for the Rector.

9. But of course an arrangement similar to this had been made with Kennedy. See above, p. 174.

In 1921 there was a satisfactory conclusion to the College's claim for its copy of the *Annales Domestici* and the constitutions which were at Ushaw as a result of the Sherburne bequest. Both were returned. As to the picture of St Gregory, the Bishop of Salford wrote to Burns that the Bishops had agreed it would be returned if Valladolid were prepared to undertake the cost of removal and any other expenses Ushaw might have incurred in connection with it.[10]

In the autumn of 1923 Burns secured a replacement for O'Connor. This was Andrew O'Loughlin who had been a student both at Lisbon and at the Venerabile in Rome. He had been for many years chaplain at Portland Prison, and was now receiving a pension. He had been on the sick list for some time, but he was exceedingly able and, fortunately for Burns but less so for the College, he shared Burns' views on the Bishops and their relations with the Colleges abroad. The year 1924 began with a letter from the Congregation of Studies announcing the arrival of Mgr Bidwell, now Titular Bishop of Miletopolis, to look over the administration of the College. Burns wrote to Bisletti, the secretary of the Congregation, that unfortunately the visit would have to be postponed since he himself had to leave Spain to attend the funeral of his brother and settle family affairs. He promised to see Bidwell in England. Bidwell sent in his report to the Bishops, as did Burns, who also informed their lordships that he had appointed Mgr Kelly as College agent in England in succession to Walmsley who had retired. At the Low Week meeting the Valladolid affair reached a climax:

The Cardinal submitted the report of Mgr Bidwell on the English College, Valladolid, and it was resolved that Mgr Bidwell should be invited to come to the meeting to amplify it. After discussion with Bishop Bidwell, the bishops decided that Canon Burns should be informed that his term of office as rector of the College having expired, they did not propose to reappoint him. Later, after thanking Mgr Bidwell for his extremely valuable services as visitor of the College, the bishops, at the suggestion of the Cardinal appointed Mgr Bidwell as Visitor and legal agent to the College, *usque ad revocationem*, his expenses to be a charge on the College. The bishops resolved to offer the rectorship of the College to Mgr Morrissy of Plymouth.

Bourne wrote to Burns on 27 May 1924 that the Bishops at their annual meeting had given full consideration to his report 'taking all the circumstances into account, and having now the responsibility of nominating a Rector on the conclusion of your own term of office, they

10. *Ushaw Magazine*, vol. LXXV, no. 224, July 1965, pp. 72–4.

feel it would be best not to ask you to bear the burden of government for another period.' However, their nominee Morrissy refused the Rectorship, and so Bourne approached Edwin Henson, inviting him to come and see him on 22 or 23 May. However, Burns had no intention of leaving Valladolid just yet, and thus began the régime of the two Rectors.

The years of the two Rectors, 1924–1925

Henson was a curate at the Cathedral, Nottingham, when he received a letter from his Bishop enlightening him as to the reason for the summons to see the Cardinal. The Bishop of Nottingham thought that he would be a suitable Rector, and told him: 'One thing which made me hesitate about you was that you would be associated to some extent with Bidwell and would not therefore have a free hand. I foresaw the possibility of a beautiful row! However now that you have been sent for, I take it that the rectorate may, very possibly, be offered to you. If it is, I hope you will take it and put up with Bidwell. You ought not to have much difficulty in getting rid of him in the near future.'

Henson accepted the appointment and straightway began preparing himself. In July he wrote to John Petit asking him to be his Vice-Rector, and it is clear that he was aware of some of the difficulties that confronted him. On 19 July 1924 he wrote: 'The Rector has been severely handicapped by — to put it mildly — the indifferent type of priest he has had to put up with as his assistants in his responsible task of training those upon whom, in due course, the future of the Church in this country will depend.' He had already offered to go out and work in the College archives some years before, and now that he was Rector he stated: 'It is my intention to publish the ancient records of the College.' He received a letter from Burns about making arrangements for the transfer of responsibility, and in his turn he inquired of the outgoing Rector how long it would be before the formal document of appointment would arrive. He could not have known that Burns in no way acquiesced with the decision of the hierarchy, and that his letter to Bourne contained the line 'Their lordships are not the only superiors. St Alban's is a Pontifical and Royal College and a rector has obligations towards all his patrons.'[11]

11. O'Loughlin drew up on behalf of Burns a long document in Latin addressed to Bisletti at the Congregation of Seminaries and Studies, giving an account of the procedure in appointing a Rector by submission of a *terna* to the King. Also an *apologia* for Burns' Rectorship.

The delicacy of the situation became apparent to Henson with the second letter he received from Burns, dated 31 July 1924. After giving details of the plans for the students' retreat and assuring him 'The minute you come of course you act as Rector', he went on to say that he had not yet told the students he was leaving, although they had probably discovered the news from the newspapers or their friends at home. The housekeeper, Miss Cull, had left for England and would not return, so he, Burns, would be able to move into her apartments and leave the *Rectoral* for Henson to occupy. The letter closed on an ominous note:

You mention about the documents from Madrid; well that is just the problem. You see, you are named by the Cardinal according to the new statutes, not as the old statutes required, where the English bishops sent three names to Madrid and the King selected one, and that was the official nomination. In Madrid they know nothing of the new statutes — and so I suppose that there the old ones are still in force. Well, there is no vacancy for Rector there for three years more, as I have not resigned nor been asked to resign. It seems you are coming as the first rector of the new regime, which is so contrary to the whole tenor of the old College statutes. However, it is not my place to step in between the English bishops and the Spanish law — for the old statutes are still founded on that law by special charter of 1769 — and the property of the College being fully Spanish property[12] entrusted by the King to the Rector for the upkeep of the seminary, he is as far as administrator [*sic*], an official of the Spanish government. Accept my best regards and I shall be awaiting your next with dutiful interest.

Henson replied: 'You have not resigned, you say, nor have you been asked to do so. The only thing that concerns me is whether or not you intend to do so. I can quite understand your unwillingness to establish a precedent in the matter.' That same day he also wrote to Cardinal Gasquet putting the case before him. Gasquet was resident in Rome, and as Protector of the English College there was aware of the activities of the Congregation of Seminaries and Studies. He promised to look into the Valladolid situation.

During the summer of 1924 letters continued to be exchanged between Spain and England. Burns received messages of sympathy and support from friends like Kelly and Thompson, the former Rector,[13] and Henson made arrangements for his departure to Spain and accepted

12. Kelly in a letter to Bidwell, 24 Feb. 1916, had denied it was Spanish property! Cf.p. 186, above, and p. 202, below.
13. 'If they did odd things to me and Mgrs Allen and Kennedy, one must not be surprised if they act strangely and autocratically with you.' Thompson to Burns, 20 July 1924.

new students to begin their course at the College. Bourne gave him a document of appointment, and he visited Bidwell in London before leaving for Spain in September. Soon after his arrival, he was finding that his position was almost impossible. He wrote to Bourne at the beginning of October: 'I arrived September 10th. Burns made no difficulty about handing over to me the government of the College, but my position is becoming increasingly more difficult on every side from the fact that I have not yet received my appointment from the Spanish authorities.' He wrote in much the same vein to Gasquet,[14] and to his own Bishop at Nottingham: 'It is very awkard . . . to have no bank account and to be in charge of a college with the roof letting in the rain, and practically destitute of all domestic appliances.' Perhaps due to the influence of Gasquet, the Congregation of Studies now intervened, but to a letter from Bisletti, the Congregation's Secretary, which requested him to hand over the College completely to Henson, Burns replied that he was unable to do so because of Spanish law. Henson again appealed to Gasquet, remarking: 'Between the six of them, the Holy See, Cardinal Bourne, the English Bishops as a body, Bishop Bidwell, the Spanish Government and Canon Burns, it looks as though I am going to run great risk of burning my fingers.'

Desperate for money, Henson wrote to Kelly, now the College agent, asking him to pay over to the College account the whole of the agency money except for £25. Kelly refused to do this until he saw Henson's official letter of appointment from the Spanish government. At this Henson said he would dispense with Kelly's services as agent; but Kelly said that the most he could do would be to resign his office into the hands of Burns, the lawful Rector. Moreover, he accused Henson of being overbearing and reminded him that he would not be Rector until he had a royal document. 'Civilly and legally you cannot command the College funds until you are validly appointed.' Little satisfaction was to be had from Cardinal Bourne, who could only promise that some official document would arrive soon. Henson therefore decided to return to England in early 1925 to see the Cardinal and some of the other Bishops. During this absence from Spain, Henson, first from England and later from Rome, was in regular correspondence with Petit, the Vice-Rector in Valladolid, and their exchanges have certain similarities to that other collection of letters between Rector Perry and Vice-Rector Shepherd in the eighteenth century.

14. To Gasquet he gave a full account of events in the College since 1910.

Edwin Henson's travels

On arrival in England, Henson asked for interviews with Bourne, and the Bishops of Liverpool, Nottingham and Brentwood — that is, the two senior members of the hierarchy and his own and Petit's ordinary. He learnt that the Spanish ambassador in London had been informed of his appointment as Rector, and that it was the Holy See that had reminded Bourne that Burns' time had expired, hence the decision of the English Bishops not to reappoint him for a further term. He wrote to Petit: 'Burns will be in a frightful mess if he is not careful. You see he is opposing (at least indirectly by remaining in the College, if not by letting the row come before the people in Madrid) an enactment of the Holy See. He is appealing from the Holy See ill-informed to the Holy See well-informed.'

As Petit had suspected, the College was in danger of being drawn into the pro-and anti-Bourne factions in the English hierarchy. After visiting Archbishop Keating at Liverpool, Henson wrote: 'What a rage he is in against *Eminenza* (who by the way, torpedoed Liverpool again, last Thursday, by turning up for Salford's funeral). So he was in no humour to favour another scheme of Westminster's. He told me that, at one time, Eminenza had it in mind to nominate Bidwell Rector and to send out a Vice to run the College. Liverpool himself was chiefly instrumental in scotching that.' Henson had so far picked up some interesting information, but the problem was no nearer to a solution, and he thus resolved to go to Rome. He wrote to Burns recommending that he send in his resignation, quoting canon 2333 on the censure against those who appeal to a civil authority against the Church, and concluded with the remark: 'I hear there is an outbreak of what looks like influenza at Valladolid. Take care not to catch it.'

Henson arrived in Rome on 30 January 1925 and went to stay at the Beda College. His first target was Gasquet who advised him to see Rogonesi, the former Nuncio in Madrid. He also called on Hinsley, the Rector of the *Venerabile*, who took a very gloomy view; he gave Henson an introduction to someone in the Congregation of Studies which would open up the way for him to meet Bisletti himself. He also advised him to see Gaspari, the Secretary of State at the Vatican; he feared that the matter might take on a diplomatic aspect. He happened to meet an official of the Consistorial Congregation, who told him that the appointment of anyone in Burns' place might possibly be declared irregular. Henson also explored the possibility of obtaining a Cardinal Protector for the College; this met with Hinsley's favour, but Cardinal Ehrle thought it better to try and settle things without one. Cardinal Merry del Val was approached to accept such an office, but he declined on the grounds that it would be a tactical error to get a Protector before the exact position of the Holy See in the matter was established; moreover he did not consider himself, as a Spaniard, to be a suitable candidate. There was much to-ing and fro-ing during the months Henson was in Rome, but no decisions were made and Henson found the Romans even slower and more dilatory in their affairs than the Spaniards. Documents had to be drawn up, brief histories of the College written, bulls and briefs presented;[15] the parties communicated in four languages — Latin, English, Spanish and Italian.

Very soon Henson became aware that many of the difficulties were due to Cardinal Bourne.[16] He learned, for example, that the new constitutions of the Beda College which they received a few years previously were thrust upon them without anyone being consulted who knew anything about the actual working of the place. After an interview with Bisletti, Henson wrote to Petit: 'The new statutes were not the original idea of the Congregation. They are, as Blanco[17] shrewdly suspected, an emanation from Westminster. The thing I cannot understand is how the Congregation could have sent them out under its name without having made full enquiries as to the old statutes and the status of the College. Nor can I understand, how they of the Congregation have allowed themselves to be deceived (as they have been) by Bidwell.' The result was that Burns was in fact in a much more impregnable position than he had previously believed! Bisletti had no idea what to do; he did not want to burn his fingers again by forcing Burns out, since this might cause a row with the Spanish government. When asked whether, in the event of Burns' going, the new statutes would be reconsidered, he replied: 'Of course, and if necessary we shall retrace our steps.' There was talk now of the Nuncio in Madrid visiting the College to hold an official enquiry.

15. It is likely that the Bull of Foundation of the College had to be produced — which would explain the discovery of this document in the archives of the English College, Rome. It was returned to Valladolid in 1950.

16. Although he was Bourne's nominee, Henson was now coming close to Burns' and Kelly's assessment of the Cardinal. He wrote to Petit: 'I am more firmly convinced than ever that there was (even though there may not be now) a plot to seize the College or at least its funds. And (let me whisper in your ear) if the people at the Beda could pull a string or two to get Valladolid transferred to the Beda, they would do it! But I must say no more. I am their (paying) guest.'

17. The College lawyer.

Apart from a short note accusing him of wanting 'to oust the King yet farther, and with menaces, from his acknowledged rights in his own house', Henson had heard nothing from Burns himself for over a month. Then on 5 March a telegram from Petit arrived in Rome informing Henson that Burns had received a cable from the King inviting him to an audience. At almost the same time, Henson heard that Bidwell had been seen in Rome. There was mystification and confusion all round. The summons to see the King had come as a complete surprise to Burns, who thought that it was Henson's doing — whereas Henson believed it was the result of some communication from Bourne. But Burns knew how to play his game. After his audience he wrote to Petit that he was going to take a few days' holiday and visit some friends in Spain before returning to Valladolid. When he returned a week later, he informed them at the College that the King held that he, Burns, was still Rector, and the Cardinal had no right other than to send in three names; he had no right to nominate as he had done, and Madrid did not recognise the new statutes in any way whatsoever. The Cardinal had been informed the previous September that the new statutes were not recognised, and although Bidwell had been round the offices in Madrid, he had not — as far as Burns knew — had an audience of the King. To Petit in Valladolid it looked as though the case was lost: 'Either the Cardinal eats humble pie and says he is wrong, and asks Burns to resign and takes the chance of him refusing, or we shall have to clear out.'

Easter was now approaching, and Henson had to draw up his annual report for the English Bishops. He did this while in Rome, and appending to it a brief history of the College in which he particularly stressed the legal position and authority of the Rector according to Spanish law. He had hard things to say about the material condition of the College, the permeability of the roof, the dirtiness of the kitchens and the poor state of the linen and bedding. Also, 'I found on my arrival that no confessor came to the College and all the students were in the habit of wandering round the town where they would to confession.' He had now made sure that the Vice-Rector of the Scots College and a Jesuit father came to the College to hear confessions. There were thirty-one students in the College at this time, but the establishment could take a maximum of fifty. He also observed that he did not think it wise for the college to have so much of its wealth invested in land. Henson also wrote to the Archbishop of Liverpool to make sure that the true state of affairs would be made known to the Bishops at the annual meeting:

It seems to me that the new statutes were slipped across Rome. The College fell between the stools when it was removed first from the jurisdiction of Propaganda to the Congregation of the Council and afterwards to the Congregation of Studies. One thing is certain, and that is that the Spanish Government will brook no interference with the statutory powers of the Rector of the College either from His Eminence or anyone else. Mgr Bidwell has been told this quite plainly over and over again when he has been in Madrid. . . . There is no doubt that a change of rector was advisable and under such circumstances the electors (i.e. the bishops of England) have, under the old statutes recognised by the Spanish Government, powers to depose the Rector (*etiam invito*). If this had been done all would have been well. But the mistake was made by assuming that Canon Burns was at the end of one of the periods of six years when he may be removed by the bishops at their mere will. The Low Week meeting may bring to the notice of your lordships information of which I have no knowledge, but at the moment it seems to me the only solution is for His Eminence to eat humble pie, admit that he has overreached himself and ask Canon Burns to resign for the good name of the Church and Church discipline. The way will then be clear for my appointment. A drastic remedy, and perhaps too much to expect.

Another letter was sent at this time to Henson's own Bishop at Nottingham, and from Valladolid Petit wrote to his Bishop at Brentwood: 'I personally do not want to resign, but it appears to me that unless the trouble is ended shortly, there will be no other way of preserving one's self-respect.' But the Low Week meeting produced nothing, and Henson returned to Valladolid. A correspondence now developed between Henson and the Bishop of Nottingham in which very frank things were said about Bourne. Madrid was now actively involved in the case. In May Henson wrote to his Bishop:

The inexplicable mystery to him (the Nuncio in Madrid) is how the new statutes were ever issued without previous consultation in Madrid. The King is very angry about the whole business and threatened to sell up the College. A special enquiry agent was sent to Valladolid and he returned with a very good account of Burns.[18] But the King has no special predilection for Burns. What he cherishes as the apply of his eye is the Royal Patronage. If the bishops of England observed that part of the contract he will, on his side, carry out the bishops' wishes in those things that concern them.

The report of the Royal Commissioner confirmed Burns' position, but stated that it was ready to receive Burns' resignation albeit with regret. It ordered him to keep control of the administration of the

18. The visitor was Canon Juan Zaragueta, *Vicario* of the Royal Palace. When he came to investigate affairs at Valladolid, he interviewed Burns and not Henson.

College. In the event of his resigning, a substitute would be appointed —
in other words, the King would nominate an administrator for the interregnum. Writing to Nottingham on this further development, Henson
added: 'No mention of me personally is made in the document, but
Canon Burns tells me that the King was ready to order the civil authorities to eject me, but for the intercession of the Archbishop of Valladolid,
who by the way is only waiting for an opportunity for getting some
control over the College.' Bourne was kept informed of the developments, but there was no reply. As Nottingham said (26 May 1925),
'There is no use hoping that the sphinx will speak. If I know him he
won't. He will just let things work themselves out.'

It now became clear to Nottingham and Henson that the only chance
of Burns resigning and Henson succeeding would be if Burns were left in
sole charge and *de jure* Rectorship allowed to be also *de facto*. Petit left for
his summer holiday in England at the end of May; Henson went to
Country House and as soon as the students had settled down to their
summer vacation, he too left for England. But before going he wrote a
series of letters explaining his action: that in the light of what he knew to
be the situation in Rome and Madrid, he would have to absent himself
from the College for a period. Letters to this effect were drafted to
Bourne, Keating of Liverpool and the Bishops of Southwark, Cardiff,
Hexham, Northampton and Nottingham. Thus Bourne's nominee as
Rector was back in his own diocese of Nottingham, and his Vice-Rector
was on vacation in his diocese of Brentwood. Burns interpreted this as
Victory and wrote to Petit on 12 June: 'Now that Father Henson has
left the College and returned to his diocese, you will see that your services will not be required any longer, for the immediate future at any
rate, at San Albano's.' An item appeared in the *Catholic News* on 25
July to the effect that Rome had decided in favour of Burns, and the
new Rector and his Vice had been sent back to England, adding a
phrase praising 'the sense of justice and equity which prevails in the
Roman Courts'.

The Bishop offered Henson a more permanent job in Nottingham
diocese when the parish of St Joseph's, Derby, fell vacant, and Henson
asked Bourne whether he should accept the post of *Vicarius Economus*
(parish administrator). Bourne was unable to answer the question, so
Henson decided to go to Derby but to hold himself in readiness should he
be required to return to Spain at short notice. Petit also received
temporary work in his own diocese. Then quite suddenly, 'for motives
of conscience', Burns handed in his resignation.

Henson Rector de facto, but not yet de jure, 1925–1930

As soon as news came of Burns' resignation, Zaragueta, the Royal Visitator, wrote to Mgr Maurice Carton de Wiart, the Treasurer to the Archdiocese of Westminster, expressing the hope that someone who was *persona grata* to the King would be included in the *terna* proposed by the English Bishops. But Bourne was dealing with the Spanish Ambassador in London, Merry del Val, who was annoyed at Zaragueta's intervention. Bourne wrote to Henson that the Spanish government was insisting on a *terna*, and there was the possibility that his name might not be chosen. 'How do you feel about staying in Derby?' Henson replied: 'Were I not reinstated in Valladolid it would be the greatest disappointment in my life.' And he went on to inquire whether there was any precedent for the Spanish government choosing other than the first name of the *terna*. Would it be possible for Bishop Amigo, who was at present in Lourdes, to cross into Spain and see the King at San Sebastian to put in a word in his favour? However, Bourne was only prepared to act through Merry del Val.

On 5 September Henson received at Derby a telegram from Bourne saying that he had just received the document nominating the new rector, and wrote to the Spanish Ambassador officially notifying him he had received the letter. The Ambassador replied that within a week of his arrival at Valladolid he must notify Madrid that he had taken possession. However, when he arrived in Valladolid, Henson found that things were not at all as clear as either the Ambassador or Bourne had led him to believe. From a series of communications from the Ministry of Grace and Justice, it appeared that the *Real Orden* itself had never arrived in London, but only a transcription of it. When Henson dutifully notified Madrid of his arrival and, having already taken possession, he received a request for further documentation including copies of certain papers in the archives. He was told that it would be necessary for him to go to Madrid to receive the *título*; then on 30 September, a telegram arrived saying that because his name had not been proposed in a *terna*, the *Real Orden* of 17 August was of no effect. It appeared that a minor official, who was in charge while the regular staff were on vacation, had acted out of turn. Henson recalled that O'Loughlin, who was in charge at this time (Burns having returned to England), had warned him that there was a 'rod in pickle' for someone, and that he might expect some such communication as that he had now received in the telegram.

On the recommendation of Ambassador Merry del Val, Henson

approached the King's Private Secretary, and eventually secured an audience of the King on 25 October 1925. Although bearing no personal animosity against him, King Alfonso was determined that he would not appoint Henson; this incident, he said, was only one of a long series of cases in which Spanish interests had been flouted in several parts of the world, such as Palestine and Morocco.[19] He had often been asked to overlook certain matters, but he was now resolved that he had to stand on his rights. This seemed to be the end of Henson as Rector, but he did manage to discover through the King's Secretary that there would be no objection to him remaining in an inferior position were such an office to be offered him by the new Rector — the office he was thinking of was that of archivist. Such an offer was never made, but he had ample opportunity of looking into College history when the Archbishop of Valladolid came to the College with a letter from the Nunciature at Madrid entrusting him with an order from the Holy See to inspect the archives and send the Nuncio copies of all the documents referring to the appointment of the Rector. It was at this time that Henson began transcribing many hundreds of pages from the archives with the intention of getting them published.

During the next few months it was not only Henson's position that was precarious. In a letter to the Bishop of Brentwood, Petit referred to 'a plot discovered to get rid of the King or the Directory involving several highly placed army people . . . the peseta is steadily dropping.' The result of all this, not unnaturally, was that the College affair tended to get shelved. It was at this time, in fact, that Henson was able to remark that life in the College was very peaceful and orderly. The College accounts had to be tidied up, and this involved correspondence with both Kelly and Burns. The annual report to the bishops this year was able to report improvements in the College property; it appeared that since Burns had resigned and O'Loughlin had left Valladolid, Henson now had access to the finances, despite his irregular position *vis-à-vis* the Crown. He sent a copy of his report to Hinsley in Rome and visited John Cullen, President of the College in Lisbon.

It was late in March 1926 that Henson discovered an important letter in the archives that threw considerable light on the tangled situation of

---

19. Alfonso's position at home was weakened by the military coup of 1923. This led in 1925 to a civilian government under General Miguel Primo de Rivera. In that year too there was an uprising of the Riff tribes in Morocco, and anti-European feeling was growing throughout the Arab world.

the College's relationship to the Crown. The letter, dated 25 December 1914, was from the Marqués de Borja, who was in charge of the royal patronage, to Don Carlos de la Torre, the registrar of property in Valladolid, and the man who had caused the trouble by his opposition to the claim that the College was an English institution. It stated that the only patronages that belonged to the Crown at the time of writing were those assigned to it in the statutes of the realm dated 12 May 1865 and 26 June 1876, among which there was no mention of the College of St Alban. The title 'royal', which the College bore in common with many others, did not imply that it was any longer included in the royal patronage of His Majesty. What made the discovery even more momentous was the fact that the letter had been copied in Kelly's own hand. As Petit remarked to the Bishop of Brentwood: 'Since he is to a very large extent responsible for this impasse it is most curious that he has never referred to the existence of this letter, although he could not very well have forgotten that he made a copy of it.'

Relationships at this time between Henson and the Bishops were good; Bourne was most grateful for the information about the newly-discovered letter, and wrote to express the thanks of the Bishops as a body for the 'quiet holding of your position'. Henson's own Bishop made him an honorary canon. By the end of 1926 he was able to report that he could now get a notary to draw up necessary legal documents, and was able to draw interest on investments. In 1927 the College lawyer died as a result of a car accident, and Henson visited Madrid to rescue important College documents that had been in his possession. He did not succeed in finding the Seville papers, and would have to wait for these to be handed back to the College when the executors found them. Still no news came through as to his legal position as Rector. It was not even clear whether Bourne had yet decided on the names for the *terna* to be presented to the King, or indeed whether he would now bother about this at all in the light of the 1914 letter. Henson, who was now clear in his own mind of how the situation had arisen, wrote to Bidwell on 12 December 1927. He referred to:

. . . . the shifty policy of my predecessors with regard to the Seville lawsuit; at one period they took the line that the property was British, at another Spanish and under the protection of the Spanish Crown. It was at about the same time that the last *'desamortización'* of Church property took place, and on that occasion the College escaped the confiscation of a percentage of its property on the ground that it was a Spanish institution. But the question as to who could deal with the College property began to settle itself in December 1914 when the

Intendente de la Real Casa y Patrimonio wrote to the Registrar of property in Valladolid pointing out that the 'Patronato' was limited by the laws of the 12th May 1865, and the 28th [*sic*] June 1876, in which no mention is made of the College. This opened up the way for my immediate predecessor to act without any formal permission from the Spanish Crown. Had he wished to have done so, he then had the opportunity of bringing into the title deeds the name of the representative of the English Hierarchy, but of set purpose he omitted to do this. Another factor that must be taken into account in this complicated business is that the superiors of this College during the period of litigation were Irish and, to say the least, out of sympathy with the claims of superiors in England. The practical result has been that since the beginning of 1915 he bought and exchanged land at his own sweet will, without the formal consent of anybody. . . . So you see that in practice the approval or consent of anyone in England is unnecessary. In future transactions of this nature it is of prime importance that such interventions from England should be recognised as, at least, a *sine qua non*.

By 1928 Henson was in his stride as Rector of a flourishing College. There were now forty-two students, the largest number in theology and philosophy since the College had been under the control of the secular clergy. G. Catterall took his Doctorate of Divinity, the first student of the College to do so since lectures had been attended at the Pontifical University. John Healy of Southwark was staying on for a fifth year of theology to do the same.[20] A new burse had been established for the Hexham diocese. In his Low Week report, Henson pointed out that the College clothed and fed its students all the year round, not just in term time as in English seminaries. At present it was contributing to half of all the students fees, but he wished to revert to the custom whereby only thirty students were on these 'half burses'. For equitable distribution each diocese was entitled to send two students on a half burse. There was another custom operating whereby the College gave a free burse to the diocese of the Rector and Vice-Rector as some sort of compensation for the loss of the services of a priest. The Rector paid visits to College property in other parts of Spain, and he went incognito to inspect the College in Seville, found the church locked up and only part of the College still occupied by the Medical Academy. He went to Madrid and from the executors of Señor Blanco brought back many documents relating to Seville. He also visited Sanlúcar. There was a priest living in the house next to the church but he had no official position. After the visit he wrote to Henson asking for official recognition. But there was a

20. Healy later became Bishop of Gibraltar.

slight problem here since Mgr Kelly was still officially President of the College and Church.[21]

Towards the end of 1928 Henson learnt that the Archbishop of Glasgow had had an interview with the King at Salamanca, at which the King had referred to the unpleasantness about the English College, adding: 'Half a word from the Cardinal would settle the matter.' This led Henson to write to Bidwell in strong terms: 'Will you be so good as to tell me quite frankly where the truth lies and how things actually stand. I am more than half way through my fifth year here, and these long delays are injuring the good name of the College and my own good name in such a small and gossipy town as Valladolid.' He also wrote once more to his own Bishop at Nottingham, complaining 'The Rector of the Beda, a College which came into existence a quarter of a millenium after this was founded, has taken his place in the ranks of all the other foreign Colleges in the company of Domestic Prelates. . . .' Petit, the Vice-Rector, was also becoming restless. He drafted a formal letter to his Rector at the beginning of 1929, calling attention to the dilatoriness of their superiors in England: 'The conclusion to which one is irresistibly drawn is that the bishops wish the matter to be settled in their own way and not to compromise with any authority on this side. In other words it would seem they are hoping that the solution may go by default and that the Spanish authorities may through the passing of time forget that this vital point was ever brought into question.' He went on to suggest that they should give until June, six months from now, for their English superiors to say this 'half word' or else resign. It would be better to retire with honour than be sacrificed to the conventional dignity of either England or Spain. Henson did not agree with this proposal, and so the year progressed with nothing being done.[22]

When the King visited England in January, Bourne was received together with the Spanish Ambassador, but nothing came of this where the College was concerned. In September Henson wrote to Bourne telling him bluntly to send up a *terna* and to put the three names of Grimley,[23] Petit and Henson on it. But Bourne was unwilling to do anything that might 'be taken as an assumption of authority'. It looked

---

21. For Sanlúcar see Appendix G.
22. Petit did eventually resign at the end of the academic year.
23. Henson and Petit had for several years had their eyes on Bernard Grimley of the Nottingham diocese, a former student at Valladolid and of the *Venerabile* in Rome, as a suitable additional member of staff.

very much as if the Cardinal was afraid of approaching the Spanish authorities in any way. It was not till February 1930 that Henson was able to seize on a suggestion of Bourne's that the Duke of Alba might be able to help. — 'I blessed his marriage which took place at the Spanish Embassy here.' He had an interview with Alba, whose reaction was that if Bourne were to send in a *terna* all would be well. This was put to the Low Week meeting of the Bishops, and a *terna* was eventually sent to the Spanish Ambassador on 29 April 1930, four years and nine months after the resignation of Burns. By June Henson became aware that a document nominating him was on its way, but he had to wait till 16 August before the appointment received the royal warrant. There were congratulations all round. Bourne was invited out to Valladolid, the Bishop of Southwark had a new student for the College named David Greenstock, and Henson received a Domestic Prelacy dated 19 August.

12

SPANISH POLITICS AND BRITISH DIPLOMACY, 1930–1945

The College during the Second Republic

To mark the satisfactory conclusion to the long process of Henson being officially appointed as Rector, it had been suggested that Cardinal Bourne should come out to Valladolid and hold an ordination at the College, but meanwhile a period of political instability had once more come about in Spain. In 1930 there had been an attempt to burn down the College, and there were many false alarms over the burning of religious houses, which caused anxiety if not outright panic in the town. When, in April 1931, the King abandoned Spain and the Republic was proclaimed, Bourne considered that he would have to cancel his visit, but Henson reported that the country was tranquil and orderly[1] and that from a diplomatic point of view a visit from the English Cardinal would strengthen the security of the College and its property.[2] If there should be any trouble, he would always be able to fly the Union Jack. The Cardinal paid his visit and was well pleased with it. Henson, now that his position as Rector was established, felt himself very secure, and was full of self-confidence in his dealings with the authorities, civil as well as clerical. He was spoken of in England as a possible successor to Bishop Dunn of Nottingham, who had recently died, but his character showed a

---

1. M. Taylor, *The Scots College in Spain*, p. 264, reports that the city remained quiet and the Scots College was unmolested. However, it was thought prudent to remove the Spanish royal arms from over the front door of the English College. The situation in the rest of the country was far from tranquil. In May 1931 there was an outbreak of incendiarism in which eleven convents were burnt and destroyed in Madrid, as were many ecclesiastical buildings in Málaga, Valencia and Alicante. Libraries were pillaged and 90,000 volumes, including rare books, were burnt. At this time the *Archivo de Protocolos* at Sanlúcar de Barrameda was burnt down by the mob, a fact later discovered by Henson when he was in search of archive material relating to the Seville College. Cardinal Segura, the Primate, who was pro-monarchist, was forced to leave the country and the new Republican Constitution contained many anti-clerical clauses. See U. Massimo Miozzi, *Storia della Chiesa Spagnola (1931–1966)*, Rome 1967.
2. Letter of Henson to Bourne, April 1931. The correspondence of this period of College history is not catalogued or classified, but is to be found in various box-files and folders.

forthrightness that is not always considered desirable in the episcopate. He took a strong line with the English Bishops regarding the quality of students they offered the College; he also refused to admit men directly into theology, saying that experience had told him that those who had done philosophy elsewhere required special tuition before they could take theology at Valladolid. In more forceful language he opened his mind to John Cullen, President of Lisbon College, with whom he had struck up a close friendship and whom he began to visit each year after Christmas;[3] he remarked to Cullen that the College at Valladolid was not a place for waifs and strays, and he quoted the Psalm '*Benedictus Deus qui docet manus meas ad proelium*' to indicate his zest to take on all comers. As it happened, the battles he was about to engage in were with the British authorities.

Although the island site of the College was patrolled by civil guards and not molested,[4] the new church of St John at the back of the College had been daubed with the slogans '*Viva Rusia*' and '*Abajo el clero*' and its windows smashed before it had been ready for opening. He did not want this to happen to the College, nor did he want the plate and treasures to be taken away and put into a museum as was happening with other churches and colleges.[5] However, he decided to dispose of some of the land acquired by his predecessor Burns, and thus comply with the wishes of the Government that foreigners should not possess lands. In the meantime he wished to defend the site occupied by the College, and so he approached the British Embassy in Madrid for protection. Its reply of 29 July 1932 was not helpful; a legal opinion was requested stating who was the owner of the College, and whether it was a Spanish legal entity or a corporate body constituted under English law. On 23 January 1933, they gave their opinion that the College was Spanish with no legal personality under English law and thus could not expect special treatment. Henson replied to the British Embassy on 26 January as follows:

Dear Sir,

I thank you for your letter of January 23rd. It is very satisfactory in as much as it

3. These visits to Lisbon continued into the 1950s, when eventually ill-health prevented him from travelling any more.
4. In his report to the Bishops in Lent 1933, he reported that the windows of the College had been smashed and that it was necessary to cover those on the street with wire mesh.
5. Article 45 of the Constitution placed artistic and historical items under the protection of the state.

states quite clearly the opinion of our English Authorities with regard to the national status of this College according to the letter of the law.

Henceforth we must consider the matter from the point of view of equity. My chief fears have arisen from the proximate possibility of our being lumped together with the Catholic Church in Spain, with the consequent liability of arbitrary confiscation of all our property. That this is no vain fear has been shown by the attitude of the local Registrar of property in refusing to register the sale of two small parcels of lands to the tenants, unless permission be obtained from the Spanish Government for the alienation of what he considers to be church property. Under the circumstances I shall apply for the required licence to complete these sales. To hold up the matter much longer would injure in this district the good name of the College and, indeed, of England. Valladolid is a little place where everybody knows everybody's business and where what are really small fry are looked upon as very big fish. So it comes about that local opinion is firmly convinced that '*esta gente*' will not dare to interfere with 'los ingleses'. I am complying with the requirements of the Agrarian Law and am now declaring our lands with the reservations allowed by that law. My fears are further enhanced by the proposed law of Associations and Religious Congregations, in which no provision seems to be made for foreign establishments in Spain that make no claim to 'exercise jurisdiction over Spanish citizens' (see paragraph 5 — unnumbered — of the preamble to the proposed law). The whole weight of this law falls upon the Catholic church and the Catholic Associations. Though this College is exempt from the jurisdiction of the Catholic Hierarchy in Spain, it is a Catholic College. Will it, then, be affected by the proposed law, especially as regards Titulo III art 11 and art 20? This question applies not only to this College but also to the Scots College in Valladolid and the Irish College in Salamanca. If Titulo III art 20 becomes law, will, for example, the Scots College have to sell the Hotel Metropolitano in Madrid and invest the proceeds in Spanish State paper? (This is a rhetorical question — I do not expect an answer). These British Colleges in Spain have acquired rights that they have held in peaceful possession for centuries. In all previous attacks on Church property in this country they have been left unmolested. Are we going to suffer the fate of the Anglo-Persian Oil Company?

Please tell his Excellency[6] I am most grateful to him for all the trouble he has taken in this matter. I am not competent to suggest any definite line of action, beyond, perhaps, that of getting from the Spanish Government an assurance that the proposed law affects only those 'who claim to exercise jurisdiction over Spanish citizens'. As regards the particular cases of the individual colleges it would perhaps be better to await any attempt to take an inventory of moveable property, or any other attempt of aggression.

6. The Ambassador at this time was Sir George Grahame.

Soon afterwards, on 3 February 1933, Henson wrote another letter:

With further reference to your letter of January 23rd and to my reply of January 26th, I beg of you to bring to the notice of His Excellency the Ambassador that in yesterday's *ABC* is a statement suggesting that the Medical Society occupying the buildings of the English College in Seville is agitating for changes that seem to indicate that it proposes to take advantage of the present political situation to establish itself more firmly in possession of a property that belongs to the College. [Here he quotes the newspaper article]. I would take this opportunity of calling His Excellency's attention, too, to my letter and enclosures of January 14th *1932*. Foreseeing what was likely to happen in Spain, I wished to bring before him an account of the manner in which a situation similar to that expected was dealt with in Portugal by the British Government, and I enclose copies of the official correspondence between the Chargé d'Affaires in Lisbon with His Majesty's Principal Secretary for Foreign Affairs, Sir Edward Grey, concerning the position of the British Catholic Communities in Portugal. From the correspondence it is seen that the affair was rapidly and energetically dealt with officially by the British Government.

The result was the recognition by the Portuguese Government that the law of separation in *no way* altered the *status quo ante* of the foreign churches already existing in Portugal. In the correspondence it is of interest to note that by 'foreign churches' was meant not Protestant or Jewish churches exclusively, for the point raised referred in particular to two Irish communities of 200 years standing. No difficulty was made about the 'corporate' status of these communities, a corporate state they possessed and which was always and still is regarded by the Portuguese Government, though not by the British Government.

What I cannot understand is why British Catholic Institutions founded over three centuries ago in Spain are not to receive the same official consideration under circumstances almost identical. The technical status of 'corporation' of the Portuguese communities did not enter into consideration.

To approach the present Spanish Government unofficially on our behalf is perfectly useless, and if our rights are not boldly and strongly defended, I fear for the results — I mean as to our very existence under the proposed law of Congregations.

There was no reply to this letter as Henson followed it to Madrid and spoke directly to the people at the Embassy. As events turned out,[7] the College did not need special protection from the Ambassador, but Henson had showed he would not be trifled with, and six years later, when Britain became involved in war, the Embassy was most anxious to secure his services for themselves.

7. The elections of November 1933 brought a right-wing government to power.

The political situation deteriorated and on 20 March 1934 there were riots in the streets of Valladolid, with crowds waving the red flag and looting many shops.[8] In his letters back to the Bishops in England Henson looked on the bright side, and in his annual report in Lent 1935 wrote: 'The Agrarian Reform Law is still in progress of reformation, as also the land Rent Act. There is every hope that both these reforms will be more firmly based on Christian principles than the laws they will supersede.' But although Valladolid was comparatively quiet, reports reached the College of atrocities in Asturias;[9] members of the order of Christian Brothers being crucified and priests being killed and hung up on hooks in butchers' shops bearing the sign '*Aqui se vende carne de cura*'. All this led Henson to remark: 'The only solution will be a military dictatorship.' Writing to Petit (now Master of St Edmund's House, Cambridge) on 26 March 1935, he said that he expected things to flare up in April or May: 'The cause of all the trouble at the moment is the death sentence passed upon the two chief ring-leaders of the Asturias revolt. The old gang is opposing the execution tooth and nail, but until a dozen or so have been strung up there will be no peace here.'[10] In May he announced: 'Politics are moving well to the right. Gil Robles is minister of war, that means the army is in the hands of the rights [*sic*, = rightists].'[11] In January 1936 torrential rains added to the general political troubles. The Esgueva broke its banks and the College was completely surrounded by water, its cellars were flooded, and part of the sanctuary of the church subsided. The year 1936 saw elections, and although Valladolid was plastered with right-wing election posters, with not a single one supporting the left, the outcome over the country as a whole was otherwise and so when he made his annual report to the

8. This was connected with Falangist manifestations in the town. Miozzi, *Storia della Chiesa Spagnola*, op. cit., p. 170.
9. The revolt of the miners in Asturias was accompanied by an attack on the church in which 58 religious buildings were destroyed and 34 ecclesiastics killed. U. Massimo Miozzi, pp. 80–1. Angel Garralda, *La persecución religiosa del clero en Asturias, 1934 and 1936–7*, Aviles 1977–8, 2 vols. The revolt was put down by the military.
10. The military suppression of the revolt was under the orders of the centre-right government; the 'old gang' refers to the left-wingers defeated in the 1933 elections. That the head of a seminary should express such sentiments is made more understandable (although it is not excused) by the fact that many seminarians were included in the butchery in Asturias.
11. Gil Robles was leader of the CEDA (*Confederación Española de las Derechas Autónomas*), an agrarian syndicalist movement eventually ousted from power in the Feb. 1936 elections.

Bishops in the spring of that year, he said: 'The swing to the left in the recent election of deputies to the Cortes dashed the hope I expressed in my last report that the various reforms of the law would soon be more firmly based upon Christian principles.' Fear now gripped the Church, there was more destruction of Church property, and some of the convents in the town entrusted their valuables to Henson for safe keeping in the English College.[12] There was no Corpus Christi procession at Viana or Puente Duero because the *alcalde* of the latter municipality was a Communist and forbade such ceremonies. The prospects looked so bleak that on 5 May Henson remarked to Petit: 'Things here are in a hopeless state. . . . churches burnt in Madrid. [. . .] I am sick unto death of this rotten country.'

But by 16 August all these troubles had vanished, and life had returned to normal for the Church and the College. For the world at large there is a series of events clearly defined within the limits of two dates, 18 July 1936 and 1 April 1939, and known as the Spanish Civil War. But for the College there was a different time-scale; it was events before July 1936 that caused the most anxiety as the Republic declined into anarchy and hostility to the Church.[13] For Valladolid the war was over in a matter of days, and thereafter all the effort was directed towards helping the rest of Spain to reach a similar solution. The College had a special role in that it assisted in convincing Catholics in England that its view of the conflict — from the vantage-point of Valladolid — was indeed the correct one.

The Civil War

One of the channels of communication with England was the Albanian Society, the association for former students who were now priests in

---

12. The Bernardos Recoletos of San Joaquín y Santa Ana and the Cistercians of Santa María de las Huelgas Reales wrote to Henson for help in this matter in March 1936.
13. Apart from the initial incendiarism of 1931 recorded on p. 206 above, and the attacks on the Church during the Asturian revolt in 1934 (p. 210) there was a further outbreak of anti-clerical violence after the victory of the Popular Front in the elections of 1936. Once the war broke out however, it depended on which part of Spain one was in. The areas (including Valladolid) under control of the 'Nationalists' experienced no persecution. The parts controlled by the Government were subjected to a savage violence in which ten bishops were murdered between 27 July and 28 August. Miozzi, p. 126.

parishes at home. At their meeting on 22 June 1937 James Turner, the Vice-Rector, told them of his experiences of the previous July when Valladolid was the 'first town in the whole of Spain to throw off the marxist yoke'. At the time the students were at the Country House at Viana, and their first intimation of anything untoward was the non-arrival of the dinner wagon — it was customary for the food to be taken each day from the College in town to the Country House. The Vice-Rector decided he could wait no longer, went to the local store and bought up a stock of sardines; he then rode into Valladolid on a borrowed bicycle to see what had happened. There was fighting in the streets, the *Casa del Pueblo* was in the hands of the 'reds', and the College was bolted and barred and no one would open to him. He rode back to Viana but by the next day a message had reached him that all was well at the College.

There are other accounts which help us to fill out the course of events, as they affected the College, in the summer of 1936. On 26 July Henson wrote to Cullen at Lisbon about the 'exacting times in Spain' and how Valladolid had the honour of taking up the movement begun in Morocco. Five days later he wrote to Archbishop Hinsley at Westminster reassuring him that all was well; the fighting in Valladolid had 'scarcely lasted two days'. Henson at this time was in the College, and Turner, who was with the students at Viana, wrote a number of notes and letters to the Rector about the situation at the Country House. On 27 July he recorded: 'One large bus of monarchists passed here this morning about 7.30 and the sound of firing was heard from the west not long afterwards. About two hours ago the bodies of six communists were found piled in a heap on the Villanueva road, and it is conjectured that they had been "taken for a ride" by the said monarchists. Three of the students were fishing in the Duero near Confluence this morning and a corpse floated past them. It is understood to be that of a communist who was thrown into the Duero at Boecillo yesterday. Apart from these incidents and the five columns that are still marching upon us from Madrid, *hay tranquilidad absoluta aquí*.'[14] Turner also recorded: 'What a moment of tremendous emotion it was last night when Queipo de Llano

14. 'There is complete calm here.' The reader who may be scandalised by the apparently callous attitude towards casualties on the Republican side should perhaps recall the losses suffered by the Church at the hands of the anti-clericals: seculars (including seminarists) 4,184 killed; religious 2,365 killed; nuns 263 killed; total killed 6,832. Those imprisoned exceeded 19,000. A. Montero, *Historia de la Persecución religiosa en España*, Madrid 1961, gives names of the victims, their position in the Church, and the day and place of death.

announced the fall of Toledo. The village [Viana] went mad and hundreds of people came marching past here singing the fascist hymn. Previous to that, Constancio[15] says, the whole village thronged into the church and sang hymns for a whole hour on end.' `

Henson was anxious that external events should not disturb the College routine, and he wrote to the English Bishops and the students on holiday that the term would begin on the usual date although the seminary would not open till October. Those students who were in Spain were told that they could return to England if they so desired — there would be no difficulty about this since there were trains to France via Canfranc and also to the ports of La Coruña, Vigo and Lisbon. But by the end of 1936, the Rector began to realise that there would be no quick end to the conflict, and it would not be easy for the nationalists to take Madrid.

However, Henson was convinced from the beginning that the nationalist cause had justice on its side, and made his view known to those at home. He wrote to Petit in August: 'This movement is going to succeed. It is definitely a religious war. All the military and armed civilians wear religious emblems, crucifixes, medals, badges, scapulars etc.', and he wired to the Archbishop of Westminster: '*Diga lo que quiera el Arzobispo de Canterbury está claro que la lucha aquí es entre Dios y el Diablo representado por la Trinidad internacional de financieros, masones y judíos et hi tres unum sunt en Rusia anti-cristo.*'[16] And during the years that followed, the views of Henson and others at the College became more and more influential among English Catholics. Not only did the hierarchy rely on their College in Spain for first-hand accounts of what was happening, but the majority of former students in various parishes throughout the country were of a similar viewpoint. In particular, there was Bernard Grimley, the priest-editor of *The Catholic Times*,[17] who had been for a short time a student in Spain before going on to Rome, and was a fellow-diocesan of Henson's. Then there was John Petit, a former Vice-Rector, also close to Henson, and now Master of St Edmund's House, Cambridge; he encouraged people like Arnold Lunn, Allison Peers and

---

15. The parish priest at Viana.
16. 'Whatever the Archbishop of Canterbury may say, it is clear that the conflict here is between God and the Devil. It is against the international trinity of financiers, Masons and Jews, and these three are one in Russia the Anti-Christ.'
17. Turner reported (17 June 1938) that Jacques Maritain, the distinguished French Catholic philosopher, was going to sue *The Catholic Times* for calling him a heretic and communist.

Alfonso de Zulueta to address his students at Cambridge on the situation in Spain. Petit also informed Pablo Merry del Val[18] of the anti-nationalist and 'Red' views of J.B. Trend, the Professor of Spanish at Cambridge. On many occasions people in England referred to the College for confirmation or denial of recent press reports. Were Protestants persecuted in nationalist Spain? Why did Franco bomb Guernica? The philatelic correspondent of *The Universe* asked the College for information about interesting postage stamps and frankings.

To the Bishops' Committee for the Relief of Spanish Distress Henson pointed out that there was no lack of food in those parts under the Nationalist government at Burgos. To other inquirers he answered that there was already in existence a sort of Save the Children Fund: 'Under the national government there is no such thing as right and left, red and white — all are looked upon as Spaniards and relief is given where necessary and without discrimination.' He had no time for the Basque separatists and was critical of Archbishop Hinsley's implicit support of them by accepting as refugees children of militiamen from Bilbao. He deplored the attitude of Mgr Múgica, the Bishop of Vitoria, who together with Cardinal Vidal i Barraquer of Tarragona did not put his name to the joint pastoral of the Bishops of 1 July 1937 written by Cardinal Gomá of Toledo. He was scathing about busybodies who came to Spain full of good intentions but with no knowledge of the language and without sufficient means, so that they had to accept free hospitality. In his letter to the Albanian Society for their meeting in 1937 he wrote: 'I have never known the town to be more peaceable and prosperous or clean.' This was in some measure due to the prisoners-of-war who volunteered to do outdoor work. The meeting was so moved that it sent a telegram to Franco: '*El Generalísimo Franco, Salamanca. 50 sacerdotes ingleses, antiguos alumnos de Valladolid reunidos en Londres, le saludan. Arriba España.*' The reply was as follows:

Muy señores míos,

En nombre de S.E. el Jefe del Estado, Generalísimo de los Ejércitos Nacionales, tengo la profunda satisfacción de acusar recibo a la entusiástica felicitación que le han dirigido con motivo del brillantísimo acontecimiento que ha constituido para nuestra causa la toma de Bilbao. Al significarles que el General Franco me ha

18.   Chief of the Nationalist Press Service. His father had been Spanish Ambassador in London in the early 1930s (see p. 200, above), and he was a relative of the late Cardinal Merry del Val.

*encargado exprese a Vds su mas viva gratitud, approvecho la oportunidad para
saludarles cordialmente, y reiterarme*

*Suyo attmo amigo
q.e.s.m.*
FEDERICO OLIVÁN[19]

But the war was not yet over, and in 1938 the military authorities took
up the offer, made in 1936 and acknowledged by General Mola, of using
Country House as a hospital; it became the Hospital Generalísimo
Franco and accommodated 100 beds, and in view of this it was decided
that the students should spend their summer vacation in England.
During this time there were a few air raids on the city and the cellars
were cleaned out for use as shelters. Some students left to join the Spanish
Foreign Legion and fight for the nationalists. Four joined the colours,
and there are some rather sad and moving letters from the front to
Henson and friends at the College, which tell of their initial training, the
harsh weather and a soldier's impressions of the fighting. Each of them
felt isolated and eager for news of the College. Paddy Dalton was the first
to join up, and he kept in regular correspondence with Jim Saunders at
the College till his death in action at the Castellón front.[20] The others
joined up later and had to face the boredom of waiting for
demobilisation, complaining that the Legion in peace time was worse
than the dole.[21] They did not return to the College and soon found
themselves conscripted for another war.

The Second World War; The College and the Allied cause

For those at Valladolid, staff as well as students, one war merged with

19. 'Gentlemen, in the name of His Excellency the Head of State and Generalissimo of
the National Armies I am very pleased to acknowledge receipt of the enthusiastic
congratulations you have sent on the occasion of the magnificent event which the
capture of Bilbao has been for our cause. In informing you that General Franco has
charged me with conveying to you his deepest gratitude, may I take this
opportunity to send you cordial greetings. I remain yours etc.'
20. '*Patricio José Dalton Seminarista del Colegio de Ingleses Valladolid y legionario de la 7a
Bandera del Tercio. Murió gloriosamente por Dios y por España en la Sierra de Espadán
(Frente de Castellón) el día 17 de Julio de 1938 a los 23 años de edad*' ('Patrick Joseph
Dalton, seminarist of the English College, Valladolid, and legionary of the 7th
Colour Regiment, died gloriously for God and for Spain in the Sierra de Espadán
[Castellón front], 17 July 1938, aged 23'). Notice in *El Norte de Castilla*.
21. Paul Garvin, 30 May 1939.

another, and their enthusiasm for the new Spain had not destroyed their patriotism as Britons. At the time of the Munich crisis, while he was on holiday in England, Henson wrote to Bishop Dey, Bishop of the Forces, offering his services in the event of war: 'In the eventuality of this country going to war, I presume that my work here would come to a standstill at once. I presume also, although I have not consulted my bishop on the matter, that there would not be any work for me in the diocese. If therefore I should be of any use as a chaplain I offer my services as far as I can to Your Lordship.' In the last days of the Spanish conflict Henson also took up the job of English announcer at Radio Valladolid F.E.T.[22] no. 1, transmitting every evening, except Sunday, at 6.30. It was a voluntary job but he enjoyed it, and the interest in broadcasting that developed then was to find further expression during the Second World War. In the 1939 report to the Bishops, he declared that there were twenty-two students in the College and it would be possible to take another fifteen, but he wondered how much conscription in England would affect entrants to ecclesiastical studies. The previous year the students had spent their annual summer holiday in England, except for three who toured 'liberated' Spain,[23] because Viana was still in use as a hospital; however, the Country House was now free and there would be no vacation in England this year. The seminary had reopened, so lectures would once more be outside the house. Henson tried to induce the Bishops to send students to Spain by enticing them with promises of plentiful food, no blackout and no fear of bombing.

On the outbreak of Britain's war with Germany, Henson found himself the object of attention. Rosalind Toynbee of the Royal Institute of International Affairs (Section for the Holy See and the Catholic World) wrote asking for his help, but he replied rather icily: 'My insignificant position as a guest in this country makes it impossible for me, much as I would wish to do so, to extend those sources of information that you already have.' The Press Section of the British Embassy in Madrid wrote to him on the matter of publicity for suitable British material in Spanish newspapers, and asked for help in approaching *El Norte de Castilla* and *Diario Regional*. It also asked him for his views on the feelings of Spaniards in regard to the war and the Soviet-

---

22. *Falange Español Tradicionalista*. This transmitter was later to be an organ of Nazi propaganda during the Second World War. See S. Hoare (Viscount Templewood), *Ambassador on Special Mission* (London 1946), p. 286.

23. James Saunders, 'From Valladolid to Compostela: A journey in Nationalist Spain', *Ushaw Magazine*, vol. 69 (March 1939), pp. 8–19.

German alliance. There was also a communication from Lord Perth (a Catholic peer) in the Ministry of Information in London: 'It is clear that if friendship and understanding are to be established between England and Spain it must be largely through the Catholic Church. [. . .] In this question of the approach to the Spanish episcopate Cardinal Hinsley feels that there is no one else who possesses your special opportunities and qualifications.'

One of his first practical suggestions was the move to get the letter of Pius XI against Nazism, *Mit Brennender Sorge*, distributed in a good Spanish translation; it was practically unknown in Spain. In further communication with the Press Attaché in Madrid, Henson's advice led to an important appointment. The German government supported two priests in Madrid, and the French and Italians each had a chaplain. But there was no English church or English-speaking priest for the English-speaking Catholics there, although priests from Valladolid visited the capital from time to time. Joseph Mulrean of the diocese of Gibraltar, who had studied and been ordained in Madrid, was *persona grata* with the very influential Mgr Eijo y Garay, Patriarch of the Western Indies and Bishop of Madrid-Alcalá, and had been chaplain to the *Requetés* (the Carlist militia) from Navarre during the civil war; he was at the moment in Madrid and would make a suitable chaplain. One of Mulrean's first jobs when appointed to this post was to assist A.V. Philips, a former Vice-Rector of the College who had left the priesthood, and who had lately been in Spain as war correspondent for the *News Chronicle*. He was now in prison awaiting sentence for his 'Red' and anti-nationalist activities, although finally he was deported back to England. On 19 January 1940 he published an article in the *News Chronicle* about his 130 days in jail, which was very much of an embarrassment to the Embassy.[24]

Henson's links with the Embassy grew closer, especially with the discovery of a kindred spirit there. This was Bernard Malley, an English Catholic who had lived in Spain for some twenty years, including a period as a lecturer in the Ecclesiastical University of the Escorial. He had been in the country through the Civil War, and had now entered H.M. Foreign Service as Assistant Press Attaché (he became First Secretary in 1942 and Counsellor in 1950).[25] Correspondence between Henson and

24. Malley sent Henson a copy of the Philips article in the *News Chronicle*, and there was also correspondence with Pablo Merry del Val about a pamphlet *Spain under Franco* written by Philips on his return to England.
25. Malley is referred to in Hoare, loc. cit., pp. 133–4.

Malley began in December 1939 when Henson adversely criticised the bulletins put out at regular intervals by the Embassy: 'Until England breaks definitely with the USSR and until England definitely states what her war aims are, I am afraid the 'boletines' will not do much good.'[26] He sent Malley the letter he had received from Rosalind Toynbee several weeks before with the comment: 'It would be well that certain people in England should be prohibited from any active interest in propaganda in Spain. [. . .] When H.M. Government assists or absorbs any such institution as the Royal Institute of Foreign Affairs [sic], it should be a *sine qua non* that the officers should not only be technically qualified for their work but free from political bias; the public record of the Institute does not suggest that these conditions are fulfilled.' He goes on to illustrate this by pointing out that their volume on Spain is largely drawn from 'republican' reports, that the article on 'The Arab World and North Africa' was by a Jew, and that one on 'The Roman Catholic World' was by a Congregationalist minister. This was a point of view to which Malley was sympathetic. In 1940 there was a new Ambassador (a former Foreign Secretary), Sir Samuel Hoare,[27] who was sensitive to the position of the Church. Henson received an invitation to a private dinner party with Sir Samuel and Lady Hoare in Madrid,[28] one of the results of which was a visit by the Ambassador to Valladolid on 21

26. The bulletins were later produced twice daily, based on BBC news broadcasts, and circulated widely in Madrid and the provincial cities. See Hoare, loc. cit., pp. 134–5.
27. Mulrean had complained earlier that he was fed up with the way the Embassy seemed to make use of Catholics simply when it was convenient or useful. The Japanese, by contrast, had taken care to send a Catholic as their Ambassador to Spain. Hoare tells us (p. 127) that Madrid was the European centre of the Japanese secret service before Pearl Harbor. Shortly after the outbreak of the Civil War on 1 August 1936, the Ambassador and his staff moved from San Sebastián, where they were spending the summer, to Hendaye. Sir Henry Getty Chilton retired in October 1938 and Owen St Clair O'Malley became Chargé d'Affaires.
28. Hoare, in his *Ambassador on Special Mission* (pp. 148–56), has an appreciation of the English College: 'The College Rector, Mgr Henson, is a patriotic Englishman to the core. Whilst long years of foreign residence denationalises many of our fellow countrymen, in other cases they bring out all that is most national and British in their character. Mgr Henson had become more English every day of his long life in Spain . . . [his] English habits and vigorous patriotism pervaded the whole college. The 20 young Englishmen whom he was training for the priesthood had nothing in common with the furtive and academic seminarists whom the ignorant would have recognised to be its inmates. When I spoke to them of the course of the war, their flood of questions showed not only their interest in the world outside, but their unshakable confidence in an allied victory.'

October 1940 when he handed over to the *Santuario Nacional* the Church plate and other treasures that were in the possession of the Duke of Wellington, having been either given to the first Duke as a token of thanks by Ferdinand VII or, as some Spaniards maintained, stolen during the Peninsular War.

In the ensuing months Henson became more and more engaged in activities on behalf of the Embassy. He was asked for information about certain named individuals residing in Valladolid — whether they were German sympathisers or whether they would be able to help the British war effort. He informed the Embassy about a shopkeeper in Valladolid who was prepared to buy wireless receivers from England if he could get an import licence. It was important that more Spaniards should know what the BBC was saying in its broadcasts to Spain.[29] This sort of clandestine activity appealed to Henson, but when he was approached directly in a letter from Tom Burns of the Embassy on behalf of Lord Phillimore's pressure group, the 'Friends of Spain', as follows — 'The English College at Valladolid is able to help us by providing the names of correspondents who would receive such letters in a friendly spirit' — he replied: 'While I am fully in sympathy with the intentions of the Friends of Spain I am not at all sure that direct communication by correspondents from England would be welcomed by our friends here . . . It would make them marked men. The Friends of Spain might very well devote their efforts to changing the attitude towards the new Spain of certain sections of our English Press.' He cited support in certain British newspapers for 'Asturian dynamiters' and 'Basque and Catalan separatists'.

But during all this diplomatic activity, the continued residence of English Catholic clerics in Spain was being put in jeopardy. Not only was German propaganda influencing Spanish public opinion against Britain but it was having its effect on internal Spanish Church politics. In May 1941 Mulrean informed Henson of a proclamation of the Falange repudiating any attempts of the traditionalist militants — the *Requetés* — to restore the monarchy. Spain seemed to be falling into a one-party state and those who had supported the nationalist 'Crusade' began to feel disillusionment. In his report to the Bishops in Lent 1941, the Rector had to admit that the reconstruction of Spain was being

29. In 1941 there was a communication from the Embassy concerning R.A.F. personnel detained in Valladolid and the annoying restrictions placed on their movements by 'neutral' Spain. 'They find it most unfair that they are not allowed to visit the College or receive your students at their hotel. I am sending a letter of protest to the chief of air staff.'

hampered by the European war. There was now food rationing, and in a letter to Petit in the early summer he admitted: 'The country is on the verge of starvation.' The Scots College at Valladolid and the Irish College at Salamanca were both closed, and thus the English were the only students from the British Isles in Spain, and it became uncertain how long their presence could continue. In 1940 the possibility of a transfer to Lisbon had been considered,[30] and in 1941 Henson was in correspondence with Joseph Crowley, the Procurator there, about Lisbon receiving students there from Spain. The entire Atlantic coast of France being now under German occupation, the only way to England was through Portugal and it was from Lisbon that students returned home for ordination. At this time Lisbon was crowded with refugees trying to obtain passages to England. Reaching Lisbon was only part of the trouble; the onward journey from there could be very devious, since it might involve going to Tangier to pick up a convoy. Air travel was not usually available.

Early in 1942 a decision was made that the few remaining students should leave Valladolid. The Bishop of Northampton wished to recall Hardwicke the Vice-Rector, and after the latest departure of ordinands for England via Lisbon, only seven students remained, too few to support real College life. These students therefore accompanied Thomas Holland, the remaining professor, to Lisbon on 2 July 1942.[31] Henson was now left alone in the College, a situation by no means new for a Rector of St Alban's. When the party arrived in Lisbon, they found the College mourning the death of John Cullen, its President and friend of Henson.

During the five years 1942–7 when there were no students at the College, Henson completed his cataloguing of books in the library and so organised the archives, making several volumes of typed transcriptions of the Rectors' correspondence since the restoration of the College in 1767. He also intensified his activities on behalf of the Allied cause. However, the documentation of this period, although copious, is not always easy to follow: in addition to the customary difficulty of only possessing one side

30. 'I think your idea of Lisbon in the case of evacuation is probably better than coming here.' Petit to Henson, 23 Oct. 1940. This was the time when the British authorities feared that United Kingdom subjects would be expelled from Spain. Hoare, p. 79.
31. The students eventually left Valladolid for Lisbon on 2 July 1942. They were Paul Chidgey, James Beel, Benjamin Choyce, Gerald Collins, Vincent Dower, Henry Dodd, Louis Farrow.

of a correspondence, there is often the need to contend with deliberately elliptical sayings and other devices to guard secrecy. Journeys of Mulrean to Vizcaya and Andalusia, and of Henson to Gibraltar and Tangier,[32] are surely undertaken for better reasons than those of health or relief of boredom. Although seven students went to Lisbon to complete their studies, there was an eighth student at the College, Gerald Chidgey of the Cardiff diocese, and it was arranged early in 1942 that he should go to Comillas for a course in canon law with the Jesuits. From the start Henson seems to have had an ulterior motive over this; at any rate, Chidgey left Valladolid in June and in his second letter to Henson on 2 July wrote as follows:[33]

The pastoral[34] and leaflet arrived yesterday and the latter has aroused considerable interest among the students, who, so far, have had the opportunity of reading it. Information was received in the College some time ago with regard to its contents, and the arrival of the document has confirmed the fact. All the students are acquainted with the contents of the pastoral as shortly after its publication it was read in the refectory, and there are scores of copies circulating among the theologians and canonists. Unfortunately, the majority of the students have left and within ten days the seminary will be almost deserted, and hence I shall have to wait a few months before I am able to make others cognizant of the contents of the leaflet. Some have taken notes on the subject, while a few priests from Barcelona are most anxious to possess the original copy. I have promised to send it on to one influential member of that diocese in a fortnight and if you are unable to send me another copy I shall ask him to return it before the next term commences: I think that it will be of more service in Barcelona than here during the summer holidays and the next 15 days will give me the opportunity of showing it to the last remnants. I have not yet become acquainted with anyone imbued with racial sympathies,[35] in fact the majority are inclined towards the allies, and a few more documents will help to confirm their tendencies and views . . . Last Sunday a group of students claimed

32. Since 1940 Tangier had been occupied by Spain, and was no longer an International Zone.
33. In the archives there is a special file '*Comillas*' containing letters from Chidgey and others.
34. This was the pastoral against the Axis powers of the Bishop of Calahorra, Mgr Fidel García Martínez. Hoare records (p. 290) that 'his words were acclaimed from one end of Spain to the other.' Malley wrote on 27 April 1942: 'The Archbishop of Zaragoza has reprinted the Calahorra pastoral in his "Boletin oficial" and so a priest of the former diocese told me yesterday, the police have seized all the copies, preventing the carrying out of the Archbishop's instruction.'
35. This refers to pro-Spanish or pro-German sentiment. If it has any 'anti' component, this would appear from the context to be directed against the Allies.

to have seen submarines. Incidentally, an aeroplane was flying low over the sea at the time, and continued to hover about for hours.

Chidgey wrote again to Henson on 15 July, thanking him for a letter in reply to that just quoted, more leaflets and newspapers, and continued:

Two students, one from Málaga and the other from Galicia, have taken leaflets, although before arriving at their provinces they are to spend a month at Vitoria at the Catholic Action Congress. Several of the Fathers here have complained that the bulletins are not arriving, although a few days ago I am told a few English copies arrived. [. . .] A few days ago I had occasion to enter the reading-room of the Fathers in order to see the new statue of the Sacred Heart which is to be solemnly blessed during the forthcoming celebrations, and on viewing the statue from various angles, I noticed a few copies of seditious propaganda on the table. The last bulletin to arrive from the Axis H.Q. is dated 29 June. *The Tablet* and a six months old copy of *The Month* were also conspicious. If you have the Spanish translation of the papal encyclical to the German people perhaps you would send it on sometime next term. One or two students have expressed the desire to read it.

Later that summer he reported that Mgr Fidel García Martínez, Bishop of Calahorra — a sympathiser with the Allies — had preached, but he did not refer to his pastoral or its contents. He also informed Henson of some article in *Ecclesia*[36] which needed an official denial. The Embassy in Madrid wrote to Henson shortly after this: 'Many thanks for yours of 23rd. Your attack on *Ecclesia* evidently went home and has done a lot of good. Both the editor and the author have crawled to us and promised a correction.'[37] When the new academic year began in the autumn, Chidgey continued to pass round pro-Allied leaflets and asked for more copies. The Embassy recognised the importance of this contact,[38] and Malley wrote to Henson on 31 October: 'The matter of Comillas seems to me important so I have arranged for the messenger to leave here every Monday morning for Valladolid. If you prefer he could leave on Sunday. He is going on to Santander after dropping his load with you.' On 7 November Malley wrote again: 'Comillas is very encouraging indeed,

36. *Ecclesia* was the organ of *Acción Católica* under the patronage of the Cardinal Archbishop of Toledo, and particularly influential in the post-Civil War Catholic Church.
37. 28 Aug. 1942.
38. It was at this time that the Embassy launched a campaign to gain Spanish goodwill as a preparation for the Allied landings in Tunisia, then still under French rule; which took place on 8 November. Hoare, loc. cit., p. 143.

and H.E. will be very pleased.' Chidgey reported tension between the Army and the Falange,[39] and the effect of his own activity among the students:

I am now receiving applications from students who wish to work in English dioceses after ordination and the most amusing part of the situation is that they are quite serious. They promise to study English immediately. I was also asked yesterday by one of the Southern fellows if I would become incardinated in one of the dioceses of the south as they are rather short of priests down there. Matters are becoming serious and I am now waiting for the bait from the J. quarter.

The following year, 1943, saw a minor setback to this propaganda activity on behalf of the Allies. Chidgey wrote to Henson on 5 April:

One of the students here used to send our propaganda after we had finished with it to a millionaire in Santander who is very pro-English. He never trusted the postal service but always sent it by hand. About a fortnight ago the rector told this student that word had been received by anonymous letter from Santander, that he had been denounced for distributing English propaganda. No further word has been received, and the only consequence has been that I was not allowed the last fortnight's supply. However the matter has been arranged satisfactorily and the Dutchman [presumably another foreign student] and I are to be allowed to receive it but it must not be handed on to either priests (the philosophy professor was always anxious to read it) or students, and after use it must be returned to the prefect. I should not be surprised if the Santander story of the anonymous letter is an excuse, and one of the Germanofils has complained. I must try to get to the bottom of the story.

Later he became convinced that it was indeed an invention to stop the spread of British propaganda.

This 'planting' of a British agent at Comillas has to be seen in the context of the Embassy's desire to exploit the growing dissatisfaction of parts of the Spanish Church with the course of Spanish politics at this time, not only in foreign affairs but also in internal matters. After these early months, the correspondence between Chidgey and Henson becomes rather routine and there was not as much mention of leaflets and bulletins as in the early letters. However, throughout 1943 there are several letters from Malley at the Embassy to Henson concerning Church politics. He wrote on 20 February: 'There is a terrific anti-masonic and

---

39. This was connected with the attempt on the life of General Varela in Bilbao on 15 Aug. 1942 which led to the removal of Serrano Suñer from the Spanish Foreign Ministry. See letter of Chidgey, 5 Sept. 1942.

anti-communist campaign going on at the moment, yet I am told by people "high-up" that the CNT and Communists are organised — I suppose what is meant is that they are organised in the Falange and the *Policía Armada!*' And again one week later: 'The political situation is very interesting here just now. I wish we were nearer *para cambiar impresiones*. Luis is taking a small parcel which I would ask you to keep.[40] A priest named Cándido Noguera *may* call for it. He has been doing some work for us, but had the misfortune to fall foul of the police. However he is an Aragonese and as stubborn as they make them.'

On 30 March Malley asked: 'Have you heard of the oath the new bishops are requested to take? Is the Spanish Church going protestant? It sounds like the Oath of Uniformity which most anglican bishops assent to in the presence of the Home Secretary.' The Spanish Bishops figured in this correspondence on several occasions.[41] On 12 June he wrote: 'We have a first-rate friend in the new bishop of Guadix [D. Rafael Alvarez de Lara]. He is as anti-German as you and I. The new bishop of Almería[42] is another good character. The fact that the A.A. [Apostolic Administrator] of Vitoria[43] did not succeed there, is a signal defeat for Falange. The 'plum' [Vitoria] has gone to Ballester,[44] another blow for Falange.' But a more important person than any of these was 'Antonio', who ordered the *oratio imperata*, *'Petitio lachrymarum'*, at Mass[45] which caused Malley to exclaim: 'Aren't there enough tears already in this poor country!' But on 22 May we learn: 'Regarding Antonio, I have had some news from a very sure source — he has been warned and threatened. Not that such things will affect him much, as he is the sort that will stand his ground. Nevertheless I have told H.E. he must not see him when he goes to Valladolid and he agrees we should never compromise him. Your policy of not going near the Palace proves to be a very wise one.' And on 18 June: 'I hinted we did not want to compromise him by visiting him, but he did not accept the hint saying that he was not going to be brow-beaten by the local Gestapo. H.E. thinks I had better see him first and let him know we think of going to

40. Luis was the Embassy messenger, and the parcels mentioned usually contained tobacco or cigarettes.
41. For the Ambassador's view of this, see Hoare, loc. cit., pp. 290–1.
42. Enrique Delgado Gómez.
43. Javier Lauzurica Torralba – who in fact became Bishop of Palencia in June 1943.
44. Carmelo Ballester Nieto.
45. This was Antonio García y García, Archbishop of Valladolid. In the pre-Vatican II Roman Missal there was this prayer 'for the gift of tears'.

Dueñas. If the plain clothes turn up I intend telling them their services are not needed this time.' On 25 September Malley acknowledged a letter from Henson: 'Thank you for the enclosure from *ABC*. I felt exactly the same as you when I saw that picture in the *ABC*. There are very dark days ahead for the church in Spain. Between ourselves, the Nuncio[46] looks terribly anxious, and the bishops are "all of a dither". The notorious Canon Manes of Seville has preached a violent sermon in the cathedral there on the occasion of the Milenario de Castilla and used outrageous language about G.B. and U.S.A. He had his faculties suspended not long ago for the same offence, and when the Cardinal[47] returns he will probably get another dose. Don Pedro seems to be the only brave man on the bench of bishops.'

For the sake of completeness we should record that in 1945 Malley had occasion to visit the staunchly monarchist and by then anti-Francoist Cardinal Segura in Seville in the company of Douglas Woodruff, editor of *The Tablet* and a leading English Catholic journalist. He wrote to Henson on 4 April 1945:

I saw the Cardinal alone first, in order to explain who the visitor was. Between ourselves, he got out his big guns and said that the whole church policy in Spain had been lamentable, the episcopal oath was nothing but flagrant gallicanism and a disgraceful humiliation for the church. He was pessimistic about the future: the Spanish church had allowed herself to be exploited and there might be difficult times ahead. He is certainly the only bishop who has stood his ground. He kept us altogether for nearly two hours and Woodruff was impressed. It was gratifying to me when the Cardinal told Woodruff that he had always trusted me completely and that I was *'muy grande en esta casa'*. As a Catholic, this is the only acknowledgement I desire, of duty done under difficult circumstances.

To return to 1943. It will be recalled that Henson began broadcasting to England from the local station, F.E.T. Valladolid, towards the end of

---

46. Mgr Gaetano Cicognani, brother of the then Cardinal Secretary of State.
47. Cardinal Pedro Segura. Hoare has words of praise for Segura (loc. cit., p. 155). Further evidence of British involvement with Cardinal Segura is provided by correspondence in July 1941 between Malley and Henson, from which it appears that the Embassy wrote to the Cardinal offering him medical supplies that had recently arrived from England. It asked him to designate some parish or charity in his diocese that would be able to make use of these medicines that were otherwise unobtainable in Spain. There was to be no publicity; nothing was asked in return except the prayers of those who might in any way benefit from the gift. The Ambassador thought that it would be appropriate for the College to have a part in his idea of helping Catholic institutions.

the Civil War, and he now continued his involvement in radio but in a different way. First of all, he encouraged and helped Spaniards to listen to BBC broadcasts. He also fed information to the BBC, and offered criticism of such things as the tone of their reports, and inaccuracies in the pronunciation of Spanish names and phrases; he also advised on the best wavelengths to use and how to avoid 'jamming' by the enemy. For this he received several notes of appreciation and thanks from London. In 1943 Malley let him know how much his activities were appreciated and quoted what he himself had written in his confidential report to the Foreign Office:

Valladolid has its own 'resident' visitor. Mgr Henson, Rector of the English College there, undertakes all distribution, not only of religious propaganda but of all the other Embassy bulletins, newspapers, reviews etc. A weekly messenger carries the material to him. The various Embassy departments, consulate, prisoners of war etc make full use of the Rector's activities and knowledge, and the hospitality of the College is extended to every member of the Embassy who cares to avail himself of it.

There were other correspondents too. He was occasionally asked to forward to the British Authorities some impractical invention that was supposed to shorten the war in the Allies' favour. Gregory Dix, the Anglican liturgist, asked for information about the Spanish Cistercians, and Mgr Ronald Knox had a bizarre inquiry about angels: 'My question is whether this precise speculation about the point of a pin is a genuine extract from one of these, or whether (as I rather suspect) it is just Sterne's parody of their methods. You will always hear it quoted as genuine, but I could never trace its origin and Canon Smith and Canon Mahoney[48] who took the thing up have had no success.'

He kept in touch with former students and learnt of the dissatisfaction of those now at Lisbon with the new régime there that had followed that of the late Mgr Cullen. Every year he continued to send an annual report to the bishops, although there were now no students at Valladolid.[49] In 1942 he reviewed the previous eleven years in which ninety-one priests had gone to work in England from the College, an average of five per

48. Canon George Smith and Canon E.J. Mahoney were members of the teaching staff at the Westminster Diocesan Seminary at St Edmunds College, Ware.
49. The Bishops, in appreciation of his services, secured for him nomination as a Protonotary Apostolic. Due to a misunderstanding he was also presented with a bill for 4,155 lire which he promptly returned to Rome via the Madrid Nunciature, saying that this bill was to the charge of those in England who had petitioned the Holy See for the favour.

year. In subsequent years he recorded ordinations of former students who were completing their courses at Lisbon, and the academic progress at Comillas of Chidgey, who had a companion in 1944 when Beel moved from Lisbon to do the canon law course there. Henson was not completely alone in the College since, in addition to a small domestic staff, Don Justo, who had taught Spanish, resided there till 1944. It was only in 1946 that he had no students to report about, but by that date he was planning the reopening of the College, and David Greenstock, the prospective new Vice-Rector, was at Salamanca.

13

THE FOURTH CENTENARY

In its own way the College at Valladolid played a not insignificant role in Britain's war effort. Several of its former students served as Chaplains to the Forces: Fr Thomas Holland, a former theology tutor (later Bishop of Salford), gained a naval gallantry award, the Distinguished Service Cross, and David Samuel Lord, a student for a short time in the 1930s, won the Victoria Cross at Arnhem in 1944. When hostilities ended between the Allies and the Axis powers, the Rector had further duties to perform on behalf of the British Embassy in Madrid, inquiring about enemy property in the Valladolid area which was now claimed by the British Government. He was also asked for information about German nationals resident in the Provinces of Valladolid, Salamanca, Zamora and Avila; many of these were men and women religious, dispersed through the convents and monasteries of the area. Although congratulations on the Allied victory were received from a former Captain-General of Valladolid, the pro-German feeling of many Spaniards, especially those in Church circles, persisted. The official attitude of the United Kingdom and United States Governments was cool and non-cooperative towards the Franco Government since there was no longer felt to be any need to curry favour with Spain. This meant that in the matter of reopening the College and admitting new students, no positive encouragement could be expected from the British or Spanish Governments. The Spanish Church had no particular interest, so in the end it depended on the Catholic Church in Britain.

Even before the end of the war, in 1944, Henson made it known that he planned to reopen the College in 1946; at the time, this date seemed unduly pessimistic. John Petit wrote from Cambridge on 5 September 1944: 'I will see what I can do about students on the assumption that you start up again in 1946. [. . .] Had I my way, I would open up Valladolid this coming year for propaganda effect alone. The same is felt about the Roman College and I think there is a distinct possibility that it may open shortly, i.e. six months.' In the event, Henson's prognostication of 1946 was twelve months ahead of the reality. The long delay was partly due to the unsettled affairs in Europe, such as scarcity of food and the difficulty of civilian transport, but the hierarchy of England and Wales was hesitant. The war had resulted in an intensification of British insularity, and like most of the population they were too preoccupied with problems at home to care much about commitments abroad. There was an acute food shortage, rationing was more severe than at any time during the war, and the new Welfare State created by the Attlee government was undergoing its birth-pangs. The possible merits of a foreign education did not rank high in their priorities. Petit described it thus:[1] 'I think the mental trend here in this country is to keep the students at home rather more than they would have done before the war. The feeling of insecurity which has developed in people's minds about the safety of the continent has extended itself to the Bishops.' This 'mental trend' has continued for most of the period under consideration in this chapter, and has provided the most serious challenge to the continued existence of the Colleges abroad.

In such circumstances there was need for the Rector to make his own and the College's presence felt in England. First the Civil War in Spain and then the World War had removed Valladolid from the hierarchy's agenda; any decisions were left to the Rector, and he was out of sight. Petit urged Henson to visit England and place before the Bishops a full programme for the reopening and restoration of the College. Archbishop Griffin of Westminster had visited Rome while it was still under Allied occupation, and was anxious to re-open the Venerabile and the Beda Colleges; but Valladolid would have to argue its own case. Petit was himself pessimistic about the future of all the foreign Colleges except for those in Rome, a view no doubt stengthened by the current difficulties being experienced by the College in Lisbon.[2]

Early in 1947 there came a turning point for the future of Valladolid. John Petit, who had left St Edmund's in Cambridge to take charge of a new junior seminary at Tollerton in the diocese of Nottingham, was appointed instead Bishop of Menevia. This not only brought Henson to England for his consecration and enthronement, but the appointment was providential for the College; it meant that St Alban's now had a strong advocate on the bench of Bishops, and one who could report back to the Rector on episcopal opinion.[3] It was not long before Petit told Henson that the Bishops thought that he was out of touch, but he insisted that he was not to think of closing the College. In fact it was

---

1. To Henson, 20 Jan. 1945.
2. See correspondence between Peter Whitty at Lisbon and Henson in Valladolid.
3. Petit succeeded Daniel Hannon, who himself had been a student at Valladolid. Clearly Petit was more knowledgeable than Hannon of the College's recent history.

largely due to Petit's influence with the Bishops that sufficient students were recruited to enable the College to reopen in the autumn of 1947. Due to Henson's own foresight there was no difficulty in recruiting staff — David Greenstock and James Beel had been preparing themselves by further studies at Salamanca.

However, some of the difficulties were associated with the person of the Rector himself. Henson was fifty-nine, not old by absolute standards, but in effect he was beginning a new Rectorship since he was embarking on the task of building up the College from scratch. He had already been in charge for more than twenty years, but to what extent would this experience be of assistance in his dealing with a post-war generation? Concerning his first ten new students, he remarked to Petit: 'They are a queer lot but falling into line fairly well.'[4] He was appalled by their lack of knowledge of Latin. He set a test and discovered that they were quite unable to translate the *O Salutaris* or *Tantum Ergo*, and this caused him to worry whether as priests they would understand the Breviary and Missal. Within twenty years Rectors of seminaries would be relieved of such anxieties, but in Henson's day the manner in which this relief was to come about was quite unimaginable.

It was not long before he had to engage in a fight to retain the services of James Beel, whom the Bishop of Nottingham wanted back in his own diocese. Despite an appeal to the Apostolic Delegate, Archbishop Godfrey, who was well disposed to the College, Henson lost. Nevertheless, the Bishops continued to send him students although he had reason to think that they were not sufficiently discriminating in their choice of suitable candidates for study in Spain. He had always been a keen judge of character,[5] and he never hesitated to send home those whom he considered lacking in the necessary qualifications. Some students left because they found the discipline too harsh, and indeed Henson did not always appreciate the changed post-war conditions or pay sufficient attention to the effect of the severe food rationing in Spain on the health of some of the students. On the other hand, the administration of the College in these years could not easily be faulted. In 1949–50 the gross income from the Country House was double that of the previous year, and Petit informed Henson that his seminary was the only one to have a credit balance.

4. To Petit, 30 Sept. 1947.
5. See some of his reports on students that he sent to the Bishops. On one occasion he won praise from the psychiatrist E.B. Strauss for his report on sick students.

Rather than be constantly visiting England, Henson preferred to make the College known by inviting visitors from there to see things for themselves. The Apostolic Delegate was the first to pay a visit in the course of a journey he was making to Gibraltar in 1948, and was impressed. As a former Rector of the College in Rome, he appreciated the value and calibre of Henson's work. Long before the influx of British tourists into Spain began, there was a regular stream of visitors to Valladolid. Distinguished former students such as Victor White, O.P., and Alfred Wilson, C.P., conducted retreats for the students, and secular priests as well as lay scholars visited the College either for a holiday or to consult the Archives. In 1950 John Macmillan, Rector of the *Venerabile*, returned to St Alban's the original Bull of Foundation which had long been lodged in Rome — no doubt as a result of one of the many lawsuits in which the College had been engaged. A feeling that the College was once again fulfilling its purpose as laid down in the Bull of Foundation was strengthened by the ordination of the first post-war students in May 1950.

Outside the College the future was much more uncertain. The Irish Bishops petitioned Rome for the closure of their College in Salamanca, and there were Spaniards who were only too keen to get hold of the property. The Scottish Bishops acted differently: hearing rumours that the *Santuario Nacional* wanted to annex their College at Valladolid, they decided to reopen the College and sent out students in 1950. Apart from the superiors, the College had been empty since the Civil War, the last students leaving in 1937.[6] When Lisbon College made an appeal for funds in 1950, Henson encouraged former students of St Alban's to support it; he saw the need for the two Iberian Colleges to stand together. This instinct was well grounded. In 1951 the English Bishops sent out two of their number to visit and report on the Colleges at Lisbon and Valladolid. Perhaps because Petit was one of the delegates, little was suggested concerning Valladolid;[7] however, a visit from Archbishop Masterson of Birmingham the following year had a far greater effect on the College. Masterson had accepted an invitation from Henson to conduct the students' annual retreat. Petit was aware of the potential importance of this visit since the Archbishop was a very close friend of Cardinal Griffin: 'He is the Cardinal's great friend and a power, for all

---

6. M. Taylor, *The Scots College in Spain*, pp. 268 ff.
7. Suggestions were made that Lisbon should dispose of the House in town and modernise one of the country residences. This was flatly refused by the President.

his slow movements. He is keenly observant and at times caustically critical. If he is impressed he will not fail to tell us at the October meeting.' The visit did indeed prove significant. The Archbishop heeded the complaints of some of the students about the bad food and the quality of lectures at the Pontifical Seminary.[8] Objections on these grounds were no new thing in the College, but the real clash seems to have been one of personality: Masterson was temperamentally poles apart from Henson and during the visit both men were far from well. The Archbishop was already suffering from the cancer that was to bring about his death the following year, and this normally kindly man was becoming short-tempered. Within a few weeks of his departure, the Rector himself took to bed with rheumatic fever, from which he never fully recovered.

There now followed a lean period when the English Bishops sent few students to St Alban's: there were four in 1953, six in 1954 and three in 1955. That these low numbers were not due to a general scarcity of vocations or even lack of confidence in the foreign seminaries can be ascertained from the numbers in Rome at this time and the growing numbers at Lisbon. When Archbishop Masterson visited Lisbon, James Sullivan, the President of the College, had created a favourable impression so that the College received support from the hierarchy at the expense of Valladolid. Petit was worried at this turn of events and encouraged David Greenstock the Vice-Rector to keep him informed about the Rector's health. Bishop Grimshaw succeeded Masterson to the see of Birmingham and renewed an acquaintance with the College begun in 1951 when he gave the annual retreat. Greenstock began to make regular visits to England, and the recruitment of students picked up. Henson's health grew worse, and although many thought he should resign, the new Archbishop of Westminster, William Godfrey, was not prepared to take action. On 1 April 1959 the government awarded Henson the decoration of *Encomienda de la Orden de Isabel la Católica*, in belated recognition of his services. He died on 1 February 1961.

Among the tributes received at the College was the following from a former parishoner of his with whom he had kept up an intermittant correspondence:

Should anyone ever try to write his biography, it would be difficult to convey

---

8. In 1933, as a result of the decree *Deus Scientiarum Dominus*, the Seminary lost its status as a Pontifical University. During the Civil War students of St Alban's had their lectures in the College. After the Second World War they resumed studies at the now down-graded diocesan seminary.

his original and strong personality on paper. He was so much alive, so quick in humour and his knowledge of literature and music were a great bond . . . he first visited a catholic church because he had heard so much abuse of it (characteristic) and a few weeks later found a second hand paper copy of Fr de Bruno's *Catholic Belief* in a bookstall for 3*d*. When he had read it he went and rang the bell at St Mary's Rectory and when the door was opened to him by a 'vinegar faced virgin' (his words!) he said 'I want to become a catholic' and so he began his instructions under Mother Agnes of the Convent of Mercy in Bridge Street, Derby. His father turned him out of home . . . I remember his last sermon at St Mary's was on the opening of the 8th Chapter of St Paul's Epistle to the Romans 'There is now no condemnation to them that are in Christ Jesus' . . . He had more *moral* courage than any man I have ever met — a scarce virtue dare I say it among men.

With Henson's death a detailed account of St Alban's must end. The challenges faced by his successors — David Greenstock up to 1975, John Ryan up to 1984 and the present Rector Ronald Hishon — have been considerable. The College properties at Valladolid and Viana have been improved and modernised, with help from the final settlement of the claim to the College at Seville. A lawsuit begun originally in 1768 was settled when a cheque for 7,999,995 pesetas was handed to Dr Greenstock, the Rector, in Madrid on 20 February 1965 (5 pesetas were deducted from the total for stamp duty!). From this compensation a new wing was built.

A college is more than bricks and mortar, and much serious rethinking about the training of priests took place during the quarter of a century following the Second Vatican Council. Valladolid like all seminaries and colleges was in need of *aggiornamento*, as was already apparent in the immediate post-war years. The virtues that enabled Henson to survive and preserve the College during the Civil War and the Second World War were no longer in demand. One of the reasons why Henson refused to resign, although in failing health, was that if he had done so, the continuance of Valladolid might have been put in doubt. No such doubt had previously been raised. Even during the Burns dispute it was simply a matter of who should be Rector, not whether there should be a Rector or a College at all. But Valladolid has survived, and when the College in Lisbon closed in 1974 it became the sole remaining English seminary in the Iberian Peninsula. The Irish have gone home too, but happily the Royal Scots College remains in Valladolid on the site secured for it by Philip Perry in 1771.

It is not the historian's task to attempt to foretell the future or even to suggest a strategy for the present. But after four centuries it is permissible to look back and be grateful for the services rendered to English Catholicism by St Alban's College. Its history embodies many links, personal and institutional, binding together the Catholics of England and Spain in their common faith.

APPENDIXES

A
EVERYDAY LIFE IN THE COLLEGE
I

Fray Diego de Yepes (*Historia Particular de la Persecución de Inglaterra*, Madrid, 1599, p. 753), in his account of a visit to the English College in Valladolid by Philip II on 3 August 1592, says that the King was much impressed by the notice of the distribution of time that he saw posted up on a board. Yepes gives a copy of this which is of earlier date than anything in the Archives today. An English translation follows.

Rule of Life and Time Table of the students at the English Colleges concerning the things that are done every day

MORNING

1. All rise in summer at 4.30 a.m.: in winter at 5.30 a.m.

2. During half an hour they wash and dress, make their beds and prepare for morning prayers.

3. They then spend half an hour in mental prayer all together in their chambers, each in his appointed place.

4. Afterwards they all assist at Mass.

5. All the rest of the morning until dinner time they spend at their lessons and in private study in their chambers.

6. They dine in summer at 10.30 a.m.: in winter at 11 a.m. There is reading during the time of the first table, and during that of the second, one of the College professors expounds that part of the Holy Scripture that was read during the time of the first table, and at this exposition all attend, both those who are eating at the second table and those who ate at the first.

AFTERNOON

7. Afterwards there is recreation for half an hour, during which all meet together in some appointed place where they spend the time in talking, sometimes of the reading of Holy Scripture they have heard, at

other times of good, pious or indifferent things concerning their state of life; they then spend another half hour learning Castilian or at choir practice.

8. After this, all go to the church where they say the Litany of Our Lady for the needs of England.

9. They then go to their chambers where each in his place spends half an hour in spiritual reading.

10. They then spend an hour in conferences on and repetitions of their ordinary lessons, presided over by their own prefects.

11. Afterwards they recite Our Lady's rosary.

12. Then for the space of half an hour the philosophers have a lesson and exercise in Greek and the theologians in Hebrew.

13. All the rest of the afternoon until supper time they attend classes and study privately in their chambers.

14. Supper is at 7 p.m. in summer and at 8 p.m. in winter: and during the time of the second table at supper the Professor of Scripture finishes the exposition of the sacred Scripture appointed for the day that he began at dinner time: thus in the space of two years the whole of Sacred Scripture is expounded.

15. A quarter of an hour before retiring to bed, all gather in the Church where they say the Litany of the Saints for all the needs of the Church, and afterwards they make an examination of conscience for that day.

16. They go to bed at 9 p.m. in summer and at 10 p.m. in winter but before that the prefect of each chamber reads to all the points of meditation for the following morning.

17. Those in sacred orders have their own appointed times in the morning and afternoon in which to say the divine office, and each says Mass daily.

Concerning other things that are to be done on certain days of the week, month and year

1. On Saturday afternoon all usually go to confession, and on Sunday morning, immediately after morning prayers, they hear Mass and receive the Most Holy Sacrament and the same happens on all the principal feasts of the year.

2. On these days they give more time to prayer and spiritual reading: they hear a sermon, and one of them, appointed by the superior, preaches

in the refectory at night during the first table at supper time.

3. Every other Friday, in the early afternoon, all hear a spiritual talk lasting three quarters of an hour on matters concerning their state of life and the end they have in view.

4. Every month each one of them is given by lot a saint whose feast falls within that month, to whom he pays special devotion every day.

5. Once a week, on days when they have no class, all meet and hold disputations for two hours on controversies against heretics, especially those that are found in England: they do the same on Sunday for an hour and a half, so that every year they revise all these controversies.

6. On Saturday and Sunday afternoons they hold a disputation on all the ordinary classes of the week, and every month in defence of some question of theology or philosophy which go on during the whole day.

7. During the vacations that are given each year they revise all the lectures they have heard during the year, and those whose health permits make a retreat: they give more time to the study of languages and mathematics, and other literary exercises, and those who have finished the courses hold public disputations on philosophy and theology.

II

At the beginning of the *Liber Primi Examinis*, there is an account of how students made their first probation. (The Latin original is printed in CRS, 30.)

Concerning the method of examining and admitting those come hither from England or elsewhere to be ascribed as students of this Saint Alban's College

First, because reasons of charity and edification seem to require, in these most difficult days in England, when Catholics of that nation are afflicted with so many hardships, that as many as come over here and bring evidence that they are Catholics should be given hospitality in this College for two or three days according to each one's need; in the same way also may be received those who come in order to study, and that without great difficulty whether the Rector be at home or not; but it should be done in such a way that during these two or three days they should be permitted no communication with the students either by speech or writing, but they should remain in a room in the hospice near the door under the care of the one in charge of the hospice, who ought to be a man trustworthy, taciturn, discreet, and given to works of charity.

During these three days, first of all let them be interrogated by some English Father of the Society deputed for the purpose at the Rector's judgment, and let them be asked their name, age, parentage: in what county were they born, their condition of life, what study and progress they have made in letters, where and how they formerly lived. On what grounds were they made Catholics and what priest reconciled them to the Church? What outstanding priests and other Catholic gentlemen do they know in England? From whom have they brought letters of recommendation, if any? Do they know anyone living in this College? Who persuaded them or what reasons led them to leave England and come hither? Which way did they come and did anything special happen when they came away or on the journey? — and similar questions.

In the first place these things can be enquired into briefly, kept in the memory and passed on to the Rector, and if there is a doubt about anything, students who were born in the same county can be questioned about him and his repute, as for instance, whether they know or have heard of anyone of his name or his parents. If, all things considered, it is decided that someone is not to be admitted as a student it is better that he should be told so straight away, that he may prepare for his departure with an unruffled mind, but he should be helped in word and deed and other works of charity according to his needs and the means at the disposal of the College.

If, however, it is decided to admit him, he must not be told so at once (unless it happen that at the invitation of this College he has been sent from the College at Rheims or Rome), but difficulties must be alleged so that his constancy and propensity of mind may be proved, and also in order that he should receive this notable benefit with greater longing, humility and gratitude; nay rather it is fitting that during the whole of this time of first probation he should be told (which is indeed true) that the question of his admission or not is being gone into seriously, and urged to commend the matter to God in earnest prayer; nor should he nor the one who looks after him and is in charge of the hospice get an inkling of the inclination of the superiors' mind as to his admission or dismissal.

If however, he is considered suitable to be admitted to the College, he must be kept at least eight days in the hospice, and after three or four days interrogated again and more strictly by the same English Father who questioned him before, and all is to be written in the special book for the purpose and signed by him and the Father. They should be alone lest bashfulness in the presence of others prevent him from telling certain things, and the Father should take note whether or not what he now alleges agrees with what he formerly said.

He should now be taken in hand by the confessor of the College, or some other spiritual man whom the Rector judges more fit for the purpose, who shall give him some general or special instructions according to the need and the capacity of the man to prepare him for making a general confession; but it does not seem expedient that he should be obliged immediately to make the spiritual exercises unless he himself not only freely but also urgently desires to do so; but he can be told about such exercises, to dispose oneself more perfectly for the service of God, that will be made in due course and at least within a year from anyone's admission, and if possible before the end of the six months when they have to take the oath (unless the Rector for special reasons thinks otherwise). Each one must be obliged to make the spiritual exercises in that form which is specially adapted for the use of this College, and they will last for ten or twelve or more or less days according to the judgment of the one who gives the exercises.

After eight or more days according to the judgment of the Rector, and after having made a general confession and received the most holy Body of Christ, and after having seriously considered the rules, statutes and regulations of the College (which during this time should be put before him and explained) together with the form of the oath he must take after six months, if he shows himself ready and prepared for all these things he may leave the hospice and be admitted to live with the other students but in lay dress for so many days, unless the Rector for special reasons think otherwise. All these days when he wears lay dress, or even more if the Father confessor thinks it expedient, he will spend in learning the rules and regulations for praying well and meditating, and in this he will be occupied for certain fixed hours of the day to be fixed by the same confessor: and finally, when he is about to receive the College dress and before he is actually clothed with it, the Rector will interrogate him again as regards the end of the College, and as to his readiness to be obedient in all things, that is both his course of studies and other things, and all the College rules which he will simply and humbly and sincerely observe to the best of his ability, and having accepted this promise the Rector can admit him and order the keeper of the wardrobe to clothe him with the College dress. He should be warned, however, that he is on six months' probation, so that the superiors of the College in the mean time may decide whether or not he is to continue in the College.

When these things have been done the Rector will inscribe in the book his name and the date of admission, and six months later he should be warned to petition the Rector to be allowed to take the oath for the end and object of this College, at which time it is fitting that, if possible, he should make the spiritual exercises before he takes the oath, so that with greater light and fervour of mind he will make his oblation to the Lord for His glory, and this ought to be noted in the Rector's book.

III

The earliest timetable and rules that are to be found in the College archives are contained in *Diario de Costumbres, 1600–1731* (Serie II, L16). This is a collection of documents with additions in various hands which together give a very vivid picture of life in the College in its early days. The more important of these accounts are given here in Mgr Henson's translation from the original Spanish. The basic document is entitled 'General observations concerning the Government of the English Seminary drawn up after consultation with Father Creswell and Father Tichburn when they came to make a visitation of the College by order of His Holiness and of our Father General in the year 1600, and approved by Father Juan de Montemayor, Provincial'. Among the documents are the following:

1. *What is observed in devotion to and veneration of the statue of Our Lady, Saint Mary Vulnerata*

On all Saturdays of the year there will be sung a votive Mass of Our Lady; in summer at 10 a.m. and in winter at 11 a.m.

A Mass of Our Lady will be said all through the year at 10 a.m. and 11 a.m. of which notice will be given by ringing the bell at full swing, and at this Mass, the statue of Our Lady will be exposed to view.

The Mass at 10 a.m. will be said from Easter to St Michael's, and that at 11 a.m. from St Michael's to Easter, and on all Saturdays the statue will be exposed to view after the Mass.

Every Saturday the Salve will be sung, in winter at four o'clock in the afternoon, in summer at six, and the statue will be unveiled.

On Christmas Day, Easter and Whit Sundays, the nine feasts of Our Lady, the feasts of the Apostles and Evangelists and on others marked on the College list as feasts with Mass, vespers and antiphon, on the eve, at winter at four o'clock in the afternoon, in the summer at five, an antiphon will be sung with instrumental accompaniment, and on the day itself, there will be High Mass and vespers, and on these three occasions the statue will be unveiled, as it will also be on all feasts of Our Lady during the Masses said at the High Altar. The High Mass in summer will begin at 8.30 a.m. and in winter at 9.30 a.m. Vespers in the summer are at 3 p.m. and in winter at 2.30 p.m.

The principal feast day of this statue is the Birthday of Our Lady, and is celebrated each year on the Sunday following the feast.

After very detailed rubrical ordinances as to the times and manner in which the statue of Our Lady Saint Mary Vulnerata is to be exposed to view, there are instructions for the Sacristan and Prefect of the Church.

2. *The adjustment of lectures, disputations etc. with St Ambrose's College*

By agreement, one public act of disputation in theology every year is allocated to our students. It is the fourth in the series, after three brothers have defended a thesis with the three Masters.

In the public defence of whole treatises, two are by two brothers and the third by a student, throughout the whole year.

This College is free to decide that a student shall not have any public defence in theology apart from the one appointed, after the brothers of St Ambrose have defended.

All this was discussed and arranged with Father Cristóbal de Ribera, provincial, and with Father Padilla, Rector, and Fathers Manuel de Rojas and Sigüenza, professors, and Fathers Funes and Alonso Rodríguez, and so it was put on record.

The conferences of the philosophers in winter from 2 to 3 p.m. and in summer, from May onwards, from 9 to 10 a.m. In Lent from 4 to 5 p.m. This is to be put into the notices, and the subject matter for the public defence by out student is notified by St John's day.

3. *For the first probation of the students who come from England or S. Omer*

When a number of students come together in spring or autumn, it is undoubtedly best that they should undergo probation at the Ribera[1]

---

1. A farm and vineyard by the river on the outskirts of the town.

where the Father confessor of the College can be with them and at his convenience instruct them in all they ought to know before they come to the College to mix with the rest.

It is to be observed that at the beginning, in order that they may not fall ill, the food given to them should be moderate, that they should be kept from drinking too much, and that the wine given to them should be well watered, that during the first three days they should be allowed to sleep as long as they like, and afterwards be allowed eight or nine hours' rest at night until they come to live at the College. Let them dine early and so avoid breakfasts and lunches, except perhaps some light thing in the morning, by way of medicine, such as cherries or oranges, and with this regulation of diet, they will not fall into the sicknesses, as experience shows us they do if they over-eat in the first days, and being alone it will not be difficult for them to realise that this is the right thing for them to do.

When they are well rested they can be given the foundation of the spiritual exercises, and some meditations on sin etc. to prepare them for their general confession, and to throw light on the road they must tread towards their salvation and that of many others.

Afterwards the rules are read to them and they take the oath and are put through the preliminary interrogations, and they are made to hand over any money they have, which will be used for expenses of the mission.

See if they bring books or other things students are not allowed to have in the College, and let such things be taken from them.

During those days they are to be taught the customs of the refectory and the College, how to serve Mass, and to serve and read during the meals. For this there must be read to them the Rules and special observances, and they will learn these things with pleasure if they are told that it is done in order that they may go to the College already well-instructed and with a practical knowledge of everything.

Let the distinctive dress of the students be brought for them to the Ribera, and, if possible, it would be well for them that the first time they go to the College should be to go to Holy Communion on Sunday with the rest and that that act should be their first, and that afterwards they embrace the Superior, Fathers and students, and then go with their prefects to their chambers to rest.

It cannot be said how important are the first impressions they get of the College on entering it. When not more than one or two come, they are placed in rooms apart and the old students have nothing to do with them until they have finished their first probation.

4. *The prescribed form that is observed when the students of this College take their oath*

1. There is sung in choir alternately with the organ the hymn *Veni, Creator Spiritus*.

2. The door of the tabernacle where the most Holy Sacrament of the Eucharist is reserved is opened, and the Rector, vested in surplice and stole, stands on the Gospel side, and the student kneels before the altar and says his oath in a clear voice in the presence of all the students.

3. The versicle and response are sung:

> V. *Confirma hoc, Deus, quod operatus est in nobis.*
> R. *A templo sancto tuo, quod est in Jerusalem.*

and the Rector says the following prayer which is to be found in the missal and is said over the people on the Wednesday after the third Sunday in Lent: *Deus, innocentiae restitutor et amator, dirige ad te tuorum corda servorum: ut spiritus tui fervore concepto, et in fide inveniantur stabiles et in opere efficaces. Per Dominum.*

4. The musical instruments are played and some suitable motet sung.

TRANSLATION OF THE OATH

I, A.B., a student of the English College, Valladolid, considering the divine benefits conferred upon me, and in the first place that He has brought me out of my native country and made me a member of His Catholic Church, and desiring to show myself not altogether ungrateful of God's so great mercy, I offer and engage myself to His divine serviceable attendance, and I swear to Almighty God that I will take Holy Orders and return to England for the preservation and propagation of the Catholic Faith in that Kingdom, and to gain souls for Christ, when, as the rule of this Institute demands, the Superior of the College shall order me in the Lord to do so. Valladolid, A.D. 1582 (*sic*), the — day of February.

This oath lacks what follows: But in the mean time I promise that as long as I shall remain here I will live quietly and peacefully and keep the rules and constitutions of the College to the utmost of my power. This is the formula that ought to be used and is used, and can be found in the book of formulas, folio 6,[1] and it is ordered to be used by those being admitted to this College after six months probation, by Cap 1 numbers

---

1. Serie II, L18.

9 and 10 of the Constitutions[2] signed and sealed by their Eminences Cardinals Borghese and Farnese by order and commission of Pope Clement VIII. And although the last words 'But in the mean time etc.' are not included in the Brief of His Holiness,[3] which includes the oath to receive the priesthood and return to England, he refers to the oath that is taken by those in the College of Rome. See number 13 of the said Bull, which is authentic and a certified copy in the Rector's room, as are also the Constitutions. See number 10 of the said constitution where it says that the formula of the oath, to be taken after the first six months of the probation in order to be admitted to the College, will be placed at the end, and so it is, and at the end of Cap. 7 is found the formula with the words: 'But in the mean time, as long as I shall remain etc.' So that the said students should take two oaths: the first on the first day they enter the College, as is clear from Cap. 1, number 8: the second oath in the same chapter number 9 and 10 of the Constitutions and the complete formula is at the end of chapter 7 of the said constitutions.

5. *Observations on things concerning the Government of the College and students, after consultation with Superiors up to the year 1600*

Fr Robert Persons in a consultation in Valladolid agreed to the following:

The appointment of a servant in charge of the lavatories, to keep them supplied with water and brushes (*estropajos*), and to keep them clean.

The assignment to the servants what they have to sweep of the halls, passages and yards every week, on Wednesdays.

The appointment of someone to fill the holy water stoups every Sunday.

The appointment of two to light the fires, one for the students and the other for those of our Society.

The appointment of someone to have charge of bringing in the barber and calling the students in order, and sweeping up the cuttings.

The appointment of prefects of the places of recreation where the billiards are.

Some student appointed by the Superior will ring the first bell very punctually at a quarter to one, and at the hour will ring for dinner, and the first bell for supper and the supper bell, so that the time for ringing is never late by a single minute without the Rector's permission.

2. CRS, 30, p. 253.
3. CRS, 30, p. 246.

AS REGARDS THOSE OF OUR SOCIETY

Someone to awaken those of our Society, and the students and the serving men.

Someone to pay visits of inspection to morning prayers and mid-day examination of conscience.

Someone to read the rules of their offices to the Brothers and Fathers.

Someone to visit the offices and add to their lists what has been done in that year.

AS REGARDS DOMESTIC DISCIPLINE

Fr Minister appoints each week some Father or Brother of our Society to superintend the distribution of alms at the door keeper's lodge, and to see that the pantry-man and cook always supply it, and that it is given to poor people of the parish nominating twelve persons, and that no women come. On Saturday the bell is rung for community sweeping, and all those of our Company and the students will attend to do the sweeping, and thr Fr Minister will signify to each chamber of students what they have to sweep, and with each chamber he will appoint one of our society to assist them in sweeping. In summer the bell for sweeping is rung when the students come from breakfast, and in winter at 1.30 p.m. and when the bell is rung for sweeping the whole house must be sprinkled and servants appointed to collect the sweepings.

On communion days the first Mass does not begin until a quarter of an hour after prayers, and the bell is rung for communion Mass which will begin promptly at the quarter. This Mass is always said with two acolytes with their surplices and after communion all remain in the church for the space of a quarter of an hour making their thanksgiving, and the bell-ringer signals with a little bell for them to go out, and all leave the church together, and a quarter of an hour later the breakfast bell is rung.

On St Luke's Day and on Easter Sunday, new boots are distributed and others repaired, and new birettas and others repaired to everyone in the College, and the making of boots and birettas is seen to a month beforehand.

In place of gloves a lining of baize is to be put in the cuffs of all the students clothes. During the festivities at Christmas, there is an order from Superiors that there shall be no plays or dances, but ordinary and modest games.

6. Fr Rodrigo de Cabredo, Rector of Valladolid, and Fr Francisco de Peralta, Rector of Seville, approved the following rules

—If, on days when they should go on an outing, they are kept in the house on account of the bad weather or for some other reason, they are given two hours recreation[1] in the morning and two more in the afternoon, and all are obliged to repair to it at the sound of the bell, and no one may be absent without special permission, and without the same they must not go to the places appointed for public recreation.

—The public recreation in the middle of the day lasts for one hour after the second table, and the rest of the time is divided up in various tasks.

—There is a lesson or Greek academy at 9.30 a.m. in the summer and at 10.30 a.m. in winter on all feast days when there is no High Mass, and during the holidays every morning and during the year at such times as the Superiors shall select.

—On Sundays and feast days, apart from those when there is an outing, they can have, in addition to the two public recreations, in the summer afternoons from 5 to 6 and in winter from 4.30 to 5.30, one hour for billiards, and in fine weather they may be given now and then permission to walk out into the country when there will be no disputations and all the College can go out together. Conformable to this the Fr Rector of Seville could do something equivalent in his College so long as it be to some remote part and people from abroad do not have their attention attracted,[2] and in all times of recreation let great care by taken of for the sake edification that noise is not made in the house.

—When they go out into the country Fr Rector will indicate where they are to go, and let great care be taken in this for the sake of edification if they have to pass through the public parts of the city. There must be not less than six or eight who go out, and every time they go out it must be with the permission of Fr Rector, who will not give extraordinary permission unless it were for something urgent and that cannot be avoided, and when they return they must give an account of what they have done.

1. There were two periods of recreation: public recreation, immediately after dinner and supper when all must be together in a public place to chat together — at this time no games were to be played; and ordinary recreation when games were allowed.
2. There was the fear that spies from England might get to know the students by sight and so increase the danger of their being recognised on their return to England. This peril was not so great in Valladolid.

—The warning that was given by Fr Pérez, Provincial of Andalusia, at the visitation of the English College, Seville, that lay people should not be invited to dinners and lunches except on very rare occasions and for serious reasons, and even then in great moderation, must be observed very strictly also in the Valladolid College, and no one is to be invited without the permission of the Rector of the College. Also the rule that invitations of lay people to their farms or estates be not accepted, must be observed strictly in both Colleges.

—In the College at Valladolid there must never be given for breakfast more than bread and wine, except in the case of those who are ill, and during the whole year no one is to be given food in the afternoon except when they go into the country, or when there is some extraordinary reason at the Rector's discretion. But to those who do not drink wine something else may be given with the bread; and especially in the months of June, July and August, so far as is possible they should have fruit for breakfast and not wine. Nor must there ever be any changing of side dish or dessert even if one does not eat what is put before him, except in the case of real necessity; nor must the main dish be changed, except for reasons of health, even though they do not eat it. It is fitting that all this should be observed very exactly also in the College in Seville, without any dispensations, both for the sake of edification and the discipline of the house, and because they are living on alms.

—As regards the dinner of the servants in the College at Valladolid, they are never given side dishes or dessert, and they are allowed for dinner and supper one pound of beef, they are not allowed napkins, and while the portions are being served for the second table they are called by bell to dinner and must all attend with great punctuality, otherwise they get no dinner; and the same person that reads at the second table reads to the servants, and there must be great silence in the refectory; all which should be the rule also in Seville; and it would be well if beneath the students' table cloths there could be put others for the servants that would remain for them when the others are taken off after the first table, and that they should also have their own drinking glasses for greater cleanliness; and the one in charge of the refectory or a server at the second table could see about this, or otherwise as it seems best to the Fr Minister.

—Twice a year the students' summer and winter underclothing is changed, new or repaired, and in addition the one in charge of the clothes room and the Minister, in accordance with their rules, every month will attend to any repairs that may be needed and in this way make it unnecessary for the students to go to the clothes room to ask for anything; and let them be content with whatever is given them. This also ought to be observed in the College at Seville, and the one in charge of the clothes room must give nothing to anyone without the permission of the Fr Minister, and no new clothes or cassocks are to be made without first consulting the Superior.

—It has been agreed that, as regards the clothing and travelling expenses of students who go from one College to another, they should take with them one black cassock and dark clothing which should be sufficiently good to last them at least six months after their arrival at the College in which they are to reside, and if not they shall make them new clothes at the cost of the College where they were and did not provide black clothes; and the travelling expenses are paid by the College that sends such a subject for special reasons that are current in these seminaries as has been agreed, and the Rectors must send them on foot and at the least expense possible, for reasons of edification and poverty, and ordinarily each subject is given three reales for each day and no more, and when they change colleges they must not take any book from the college other than their own papers, breviary and hours-book.

—As regards the cost of the carriage of letters, it has been decided that since the letters that come to Madrid for people in these seminaries from Italy, France, Flanders and England concerns the whole nation and the support of this cause, the expenses should be divided between the two seminaries, and if it be necessary to send anyone there on business, the two Colleges will arrange matters on reasonable lines.

—As regards studies, all those who are found to be incompetent to study scholastic theology are to study moral theology even though they have begun or finished their course of philosophy, and so it must be done in Seville without any dispensation, and such moral theologians must always go to the College of the Society to hear the lecture on cases of conscience and scripture that are read there, and if in the College of the Society there is no such lecture, they must be provided for at home.

—In the admission of servants in the house and the dismissal of those that are there if they are [not?] good there must be much cautiousness, and neither one thing nor the other must be done without the Superior's approval, and in receiving servants it would be well if it were done after holding consultation and procuring information about them from the places where they have formerly worked and enquiring for what reason they left.

—In the College at Valladolid the chambers are swept three times a week. Let the same be done in Seville, and in both College let much care be taken about the cleanliness, arrangement and neatness of the chambers, and once or twice a week let there be a general exercise in cleaning the house at which everyone in the College must assist, and the Fr Minister will see that the servants will sprinkle the house, in summer in the morning and in winter in the afternoon, when the sweeping is to be done, and when the sweeping is over the same servants remove the sweepings immediately.

7. *A chapter from a letter that Fr Persons wrote from Seville to Fr Rodrigo de Cabredo, Rector of this College, on 10 November 1594, about the people who may come to this College from other parts.*

To question as to which College will bear the expense of those who are sent from there as unfit for that College so that this College may receive them or send them to S. Omer, I may say first, if they are unfit people and without the capacity to cope with the studies, in no way is it suitable to send them hither, but with what alms there are they could be given some help and seek further relief as best they may. Secondly, when they are to little grounding like this one whom now your Rev. [wishes to direct hither] it does not seem reasonable to charge this College with his travelling expenses, since it will have to spend so much on him afterwards (either to keep him here or send him to S. Omer) unless that College there give them what alms it can to help them on their way, and as for the rest let them help themselves as best they can. This is what occurs to me here.

The *Diario de Costumbres* contains several versions of the daily timetable but in essentials it remained the same as that described in general terms by Yepes. At one period the scholastic theologians attended their first lecture at 6.15 a.m. in summer and 7.15 a.m. in winter, but by the end of the seventeenth century the early morning period was given up to private study and morning lectures were at 10 a.m. Afternoon lectures were always from 2 p.m. onwards.

There is a memorandum of the special things that have to be prepared each month of the year. This gives instructions as to the celebration of various feasts in chapel and in hall when extra dishes are to be served, and when solemn Matins and Mass are to be sung. A special timetable was in operation when the students went to Portillo in July. The regular visitation of the Provincial to the College assured that these rules were carried out or, if need be, modified to suit new conditions. Judging by the evidence available, the way of life was typical of a Jesuit house of the time. The Spiritual Exercises of St Ignatius formed the basis of the training. For the detailed application one can consult the 437-page MS. from the Seville Archives entitled *Exercitia Spiritualia per annum in Ven. Colegiis Anglici Hispalensis Ad Dei Deiparae Virginis Gloriam* (*sic*). On the title page there is written in another hand '*Pertinet ad C.S. Albani Anglorum Vallisol.*' In their theology the students followed the approved Jesuit authors, and the library possesses two copies of *Veritas Vindicata*, Fr Charles Nocetus' refutation of attacks on such writers as Busenbaum, Conink, Lessius, Lugo, Molina, Tamburini and Viva.

IV

With the coming of the seculars as superiors, new statutes were given in 1770. These were based on the old constitutions of St Alban's (CRS, 30, pp. 252–62) and the statutes of the Colleges at Douai and Paris. They are grouped under the following heads:

Proemium
Cap. I. *De admissione alumnorum*
Cap. II. *De pietate*
Cap. III. *De studiis*
Cap. IV. *De temporis distributione*
Cap, V. *De disciplina*
Cap. VI. *De promotione ad sacras ordines et missione in Anglia.*

The chief differences between the new and the old constitutions are:
(a) The omission of any regulations for the '*camerata*' system whereby students were divided into groups each under the charge of a prefect. This was a Jesuit custom and so no longer had a place in a college administered by seculars.
(b) Special regulations were made for the appointment of a Rector, who had to be an English secular priest chosen by the secular Bishops in England. If by chance there were no Bishops, the choice would be made by the Presidents of the Colleges in Douai and Paris. The Rector on election would have to obtain letters from the Spanish Ambassador in London and present himself to the Supreme Council of Castile. His term of office was six years and was renewable.
(c) Unlike the 1600 constitutions, the 1770 statutes give a detailed daily timetable and we can take it that this was followed from the days of Perry till the upheaval of the Peninsular War:

5.00 a.m. Rise (on Sundays and feast days 6 a.m.)
5.30. To church for meditation, litanies and community mass. After mass return to rooms for study. Philosophers and Theologians are allowed to study in the garden.
7.45–8.00. Breakfast.

8.15–10.00. Lecture.

10.00–11.30. Study.

11.30. Choir practice in church.

12.00. Angelus followed by lunch. During lunch there is reading from the Old Testament, a book of civil or ecclesiastical history, the Roman Martyrology.

Recreation after lunch.

2.00–4.00. Lectures (2.30–4.30 in summer) followed by study.

6.30. Litany of the Saints followed by private spiritual reading.

7.00. Supper. During supper a reading from the New Testament and another book chosen by the superior.

Recreation after supper.

8.45. Litany of Our Lady, examination of conscience, preparation of the next day's meditation, then retire in silence to rooms.

A similar timetable seems to have been adopted with the restoration of the College under Guest. In 1908 Rector Kennedy issued a comprehensive rule book. Some changes had to be made when lectures were once more attended outside the house at the Pontifical Seminary (1910) and when the College ceased to accept juniors (1915). In the Archives there is a typed MS. by John Petit, Edwin Henson's first Vice-Rector, entitled *The Consuetudinary of St Alban's College, Valladolid, being some account of the Rules and Method of Government of St Alban's College, Valladolid*. It dates from the 1920s and is a thoughtful account of the aims and ideals of the College.

B

THE COLLEGE ARCHIVES: A DESCRIPTION

The following account is substantially the same as that which appears in an article in *Catholic Archives*, no. 4 (1984). The Editor's permission to reproduce it here is acknowledged with gratitude.

I

1. Records were kept from the beginning of the College in 1589. There are still extant:

1.1. *Liber Alumnorum*. The Register of students, beginning 1 Sept. 1589 and continuing to the present day.

1.2. *Liber Primi Examinis pro alumnis qui recipiuntur in hoc Collegium*, beginning in September 1592 and ending in 1623. It contains the names and various particulars of students, made immediately upon their arrival, together with an account of the process for preventing undesirable people being admitted to the College.

The *Liber Alumnorum* up to 1862, incorporating the *Liber Primi Examinis*, was edited by Edwin Henson and printed as vol. 30, CRS, in 1930.

1.3. Books of Account: *Gastos* (expenses) and *Recibos* (income). These begin in 1589 and continue right through to the present, but one important volume is missing. Each volume is numbered.

Gastos, 1598–1753, vols 1–5.

Gastos, 1753–67, vol. 26.

Gastos y Recibos 1589–1652, vol. 6. This is the original first book of accounts which contains both income and expenses for the early years. Additional material for the early years can also be found elsewhere in Series II, L13.

Recibos, 1652–1729, vol. 7.

(*Recibos*, 1729–67, is missing.)

There are also *Borradores* (rough notes) for these years:

1644–67, vol. 8.

1662, vol. 10.

1747–60, vol. 16.

Particular account books, Mass offerings, alms and accounts relating to College farms and other property are found in vols 10, 11, 12, 13, 15, 17, 18, 20, 22, 27 and 28.

A new series begins with the administration of the College by the English secular clergy in 1767, and there are 75 numbered volumes for the years 1767–1911. Since 1911 the account books are extant but not numbered.

2. The Jesuits were forced to leave hurriedly in 1767, and when Philip Perry, the first secular Rector, arrived in 1768, he found a whole heap of bound and unbound material in the Procurator's room, and made an inventory of his findings (Press C, shelf 6). In 1768 the three Colleges of St Alban, Valladolid; St Gregory, Seville; and St George, Madrid, were united into the one College of St Alban, Valladolid, which meant that the College now began to acquire materials from these other institutions. Perry was a historian and knew the value of original sources, which he both sought from other places and transcribed. He was anxious to preserve his own records and so the Archives expanded considerably under him and his successors.

3. It was in the nineteenth century when John Guest was administering the College that the first serious attempt was made to organise the Archives.

3.1. Guest catalogued the MSS. and other documents in the archives according to the 25 *legajos* (bundles) then in existence. A description of these can be found in the *Indice de los archivos del Colegio de Ingleses, Valladolid*, pp. 1–94.

3.2. Circa 1855 Guest made further *legajos* which he called Series II (Valladolid). Series I was the already existing 25 *legajos*. Later he formed another collection of *legajos*, which he called Series III, a description of which is to be found in the *Indice*, pp. 237–69.

3.3. He also put together the materials from St George's College, Madrid. Series I (Madrid) comprised 9 *legajos*, and Series II (Madrid) books of account. See *Indice*, pp. 277–93.

3.4. Later the materials from St Gregory's College, Seville, were gathered together. These were classified:

Class 1. 28 *legajos*.
Class 2. Sanlúcar de Barrameda documents.
Class 3. 6 *legajos*.
Class 4. 3 *legajos*.
Extraordinary *legajos* nos. 1, 2, 3, 4.

See *Indice* pp. 297–369.

4. As a result of Guest's efforts, there was now a record of all the materials in the College Archives. Because the labour had taken several years, however, the classification was somewhat complex. At the beginning of the twentieth century, the Procurator Joseph Kelly reorganised all the *legajos* into larger divisions, I–VII and A–H. Individual documents within each *legajo* were numbered, and so by reference to the new index it was possible to know in some detail what the Archives contained. Documents could all be referred to in a similar way, no matter what their original provenance, e.g. Letra B *legajo* 15, no. 2.

5. But there still remained the need to ensure the preservation of the Archives for posterity. Loose papers, even if gathered together, are liable to deteriorate with time. Circa 1940 the Rector, Edwin Henson, broke up the existing *legajos* to form bound volumes. Each volume is bound in leather, a general description and dates are found on the spine, and within each volume is a table of contents, the individual documents being interleaved with blank pages.

5.1. There are 32 volumes of Madrid papers bound in brown leather. (Some of the Madrid papers were published in 1929 by CRS, vol. 29.)

5.2. There are 30 volumes of Seville papers bound in blue leather.

5.3. There are 38 volumes of Valladolid papers antedating 1768, bound in red: twenty volumes known as Series I and eighteen known as Series II. (This nomenclature bears no relation to the old Guest Series I or II.) Another fifteen volumes known as Series III, also bound in red, cover the years 1767–1915; these volumes, however, do not include the Rectors' correspondence for these years. But Henson made typed transcripts of this for the years 1768–1927 and these make up another 17 volumes.

The work is incomplete as Henson was unable to finish binding together all the documents in this way.

6. There are several box files of Henson's own papers, many of them unsorted. But there are 26 bound volumes of official correspondence of the Rectors covering the years 1915–74.

II

Practical advice to anyone consulting the Archives of the English College, Valladolid

The researcher wishing to find materials other than those indicated in 1.1, 1.2 and 1.3 above should proceed as follows:

(*a*) Go first to the Henson bound volumes. Brown for Madrid, blue for Seville and red for Valladolid. On the spine of each volume will be found dates, and a detailed table of contents is inside.

(*b*) If the bound material does not satisfy, then the *Indice*, pp. 101 *et seq.*, should be consulted. There Kelly's catalogue will be found. When you have located the document with Kelly's classification — e.g. Letra B, *legajo* 12, no. 4 — then go to Fr G. Anstruther's schematic index. Here will be found the exact location of the document in the Archive room, e.g. 'Letra B, *legajo* 15 is in Press A, drawer 3.'

As can be seen from the foregoing, the present-day researcher owes much to the labours of those who have gone before. In any living institution the documentation is continually being added to, and hence responsibility for the present is just as much as onus on the archivist as is the preservation of the past. This can present difficulties regarding the classification of the materials, and thus every eighty or ninety years a Perry or Guest or Kelly or Henson comes along and reorganises the collection. There is no comprehensive catalogue to the Archives as they are at present. The *Indice de los archivos* referred to is a bound MS. volume compiled by Kelly and comprising Guest's catalogue and Kelly's own new classification. It also includes Kelly's enumeration of all the books of account. Since Henson did his work, however, it has ceased to be the sole key to the contents, but it will only cease to be of any use in the rather unlikely event of some future archivist completing the task of binding together all the remaining materials.

III

In addition to the Archives there are the Libraries:

1. The 'Pigskin' Library contains 2,883 volumes, all bound in vellum. Most of these are from the original library at St Alban's together with acquisitions from St George's, Madrid, and other Jesuit houses. All

the books are numbered and arranged according to size. There is a card index and a typed catalogue, so it is easy to discover the titles and authors of the volumes as well as their location on the shelves.

2. The Old Library contains the remaining old books with more recent works to fill up the places left by the removal of the vellum-bound volumes. There are 6,765 volumes arranged, numbered and catalogued in a similar way to the 'Pigskin' Library.

3. For everyday use there is a modern working library and resource centre.

4. The contents of the libraries are of interest not only because of the antiquity and wide range of texts in Latin, Spanish and English but also due to the fact that several volumes have passages scored out and deleted as a result of visitations from the ecclesiastical censors.

C

THE COLLEGE MARTYRS AND THEIR PORTRAITS

St Henry Walpole, S.J.	Father Minister, 1593	York, 17 April 1595
St Thomas Garnet, S.J.	Student, 1596–9	Tyburn, 23 June 1608
St John Roberts, O.S.B.	Student, 1598	Tyburn, 10 Dec. 1610
St Ambrose Barlow, O.S.B.	Student, 1610–12	Lancaster, 10 Sept. 1641
St John Plessington (*alias* Scarisbrick)	Student, 1660–3	Chester, 19 July 1679
St John Lloyd	Student, 1649–54	Cardiff, 22 July 1679
B. Mark Barkworth, O.S.B. (*alias* Lambert)	Student, 1596–9	Tyburn, 27 Feb. 1601
B. William Richardson (*alias* Anderson)	Student, 1592–4	Tyburn, 17 Feb. 1603
B. Ralph Ashley, S.J. (*alias* Sherington)	Lay brother, servant at College	Worcester, 7 April 1607
B. Richard (Thomas) Reynolds (*vere* Green)	Ordained at Seville, 1592	Tyburn, 31 Jan. 1642
B. Thomas Holland, S.J.	Student, 1621–3	Tyburn, 12 Dec. 1642
B. Ralph Corby, S.J. (*vere* Corbington)	Student, 1621–5	Tyburn, 7 Sept. 1644
Ven. Thomas Hunt (*vere* Benstead)	Student, 1592	Lincoln, 1 July 1600
Ven. Thomas Palaser	Student, 1593–6	Durham, 8 Sept. 1600
Ven. Roger Filcock, S.J. (*alias* Arthur Nayler)	Student, 1591–7	Tyburn, 27 Feb. 1600
Ven. Robert Drury	Student, 1590–5	Tyburn, 26 Feb. 1607

Ven. Roger Cadwallader	Student, 1593	Leominster, 27 Aug. 1610
Ven. William Southerne	Student, 1598	Newcastle upon Tyne, 30 April 1610
Ven. Edward Morgan (*alias* Singleton)	Student, 1615–17	Tyburn, 26 April 1642
Ven. Thomas Bullaker, O.F.M. (*alias* Tailor)	Student, 1621–2	Tyburn, 12 Oct. 1642
Ven. Arthur Bell, O.F.M.	Student, 1615–8	Tyburn, 11 Dec. 1643
Ven. Edward Bamber (*alias* Reding, Richardson, Wallis, Walsh)	Student, 1625–7	Lancaster, 7 Aug. 1646
Ven. Thomas Whitaker (*alias* Starkie)	Student, 1634–8	Lancaster, 7 Aug. 1646

In addition to the above, the following should be included as Confessors of the faith:

John Maxey, S.J.	Student, 1602	Died in Bridewell prison, 26 April 1617
John Abbot	Student, 1609–12	Condemned to death, 8 Dec. 1641, but reprieved and died in Newgate prison.
Ven. Thomas Downes, S.J. (*alias* Bedingfield)	Student, 1636–7	Died in Gatehouse prison, 21 Dec. 1678
Francis Kemp, O.S.B.	Student, 1602–3	Died in prison, 1642
William Weston, S.J.	Rector, 1614	Spent many years in prison and in exile for the faith. Died 1614

Although not an alumnus, Blessed Thomas Maxfield is connected with Valladolid. He was a Douai priest, but while working in England was closely associated with Doña Luisa de Carvajal. After his martyrdom at Tyburn on 1 July 1616, his body or his remains were brought to Spain, where they were venerated in the family chapel of the Count of Gondomar in Galicia (see CRS, vol. 3, p. 30).

The Portraits

The College possesses the largest existing collection of paintings of the English martyrs.

Philip Perry recorded the paintings he found hanging in the lower gallery (*in peristilo inferiori*) when he arrived in 1768 (Leg. III, Press C, shelf 6). There were sixteen: J. Fisher, T. More, E. Campion, R. Cadwallader, J. Roberts, R. Sherwin, R. Filcock, A. Briant, R. Southerne, H. Walpole, T. Cottam, R. Corby, H. Garnet, F. Page, J. Cornelius, R. Sherington.

In the nineteenth century John Guest copied the inscriptions on the pictures in the gallery (Leg. III, Press C, shelf 6) and these were of: F. Bell, R. Filcock, T. Benstead, E. Morgan, W. Southerne, T. Holland, T. Palaser, W. Weston, T. Tailor, T. Stark, R. Persons, R. Cadwallader, E. Campion, M. Barkworth, W. Walpole, T. Garnet. There are still sixteen, but the names are markedly different from Perry's list, only five being the same.

The pictures in the gallery at the time of writing are as in Guest's list, with the addition of J. Roberts, A. Barlow, W. Richardson, R. Drury, T. Reynolds (*vere* Green). These last five pictures seem to be of a later date since they differ from the others both in artistic style and in the lettering of the inscriptions.

The earliest reference to the portraits of martyrs is in the book of *Gastos* for 1620; it refers to fifteen such being ordered for the College. No further details are given, but this would mean that Holland, Tailor, Stark, Morgan and Bell have to be excluded from the list since they died after 1620. This leaves Weston, Barkworth, Filcock, Benstead, Cadwallader, Palaser, Southerne, Campion, T. Garnet, Walpole and Persons from Guest's list and H. Garnet, Fisher, More, Sherwin, Briant, Cottam, Page, Cornelius, Sherington from Perry's list as the possible subjects of the original fifteen.

The next reference is in the book of *Gastos* for June 1643, where it is stated that two portraits were painted of martyrs who had suffered the previous year. This could refer to Holland and Morgan, who were executed in 1642.

In the Westminster Cathedral Archives (Catalog. Eng. Martyr, no. 9, III) for 1742 there is a reference to portraits of martyrs in the College church. This is the earliest detailed reference to the pictures and of course antedates both Perry's and Guest's lists. It states that on the gospel side in the first chapel there are portraits of Barkworth and Drury; in the second chapel, of Persons, Weston, Benstead and Tailor; and in the third chapel, of Maxey, Bell and Palaser. On the epistle side in the first chapel are Holland and Southerne: in the second chapel Morgan, and in the third chapel Richardson and Stark. In addition to these, there were portraits in the passage near the *portería* of Walpole, T. Garnet, Filcock, Corby, Roberts and Cadwallader. In the refectory were full-length portraits of Campion and H. Garnet. Also in the College there were portraits of Southwell, Cottam, Briant and Page. This makes twenty-six in all.

In 1763 there was in inquiry as to whether the portrayal of *alumni* holding palms in their hands and with angels placing crowns over their heads contravened the ruling of Pope Urban VIII and various decrees of the Sacred Congregation of Rites. Some of these portraits were in the church and others were around the College. A reply was received to the effect that this did not offend against the ruling of Urban VIII (Series II, L12). But we have no indications as to who were the subjects of these pictures.

In 1742 there were in existence all those mentioned by Guest together with others, some of which were mentioned by Perry in 1768. But neither Guest nor Perry mentioned Drury, Richardson or Barlow. Portraits of Drury and Barlow existed in 1742, and form part of the collection today. Of those present in 1714 and mentioned by Guest and still existing today, two could have been commissioned in 1643, namely those of Holland and Morgan. Those of Barkworth, Weston, Benstead, Palaser, Southerne, Walpole, T. Garnet, Filcock, Cadwallader and Campion could have belonged to the original fifteen commissioned in 1620.

In 1985 a local artist painted portraits of St John Lloyd and St John Plessington in the style of the original portraits.

D

RECTORS OF ST ALBAN'S COLLEGE

For the first year of the College's existence from August 1589 to September 1590 its temporalities were looked after by Father Persons and Brother Fabricio Como. In Series II, L11, no. 16, Fr Juan López de Manzano is referred to as the first Rector, taking office on 1 August 1589. But the *Annales* are quite clear that there was no Rector until Persons brought with him from Madrid Fr Bartolomé de Sicilia, who was Rector from 25 October 1589 till 26 November the same year. He was succeeded by Pedro de Guzmán who ruled until 24 June 1590, on which date Juan López de Manzano took office (again?). From this date onwards the succession is clear. All were Jesuits, and except for 1614–17 all were Spaniards.

Juan López de Manzano	24 June 1590–1 Sept. 1591
Rodrigo de Cabredo	1 Sept. 1591–31 Dec. 1594
Gonzalo del Río	1 Jan. 1595–Sept. 1596
Alonso Rodríguez de Toro	Sept. 1596–24 Oct. 1600
Antonio Vásquez	24 Oct. 1600–1 Sept. 1602
Pedro Ruiz de Vallejo	Sept. 1602 (*dismissed 1603 due to the trouble with the Benedictines; Juan de Olmedo took charge of the College in November 1603 but was not officially Rector*)
Diego de Gamboa	20 Feb. 1604–Oct. 1606
Pedro Ruiz de Vallejo	Oct. 1606 (reinstated)–20 May 1607
Juan de Párraces	20 May 1607–25 Feb. 1611
Cristóbal Suárez	Feb. 1611–?
William Weston (the first English Rector)	?1614–9 April 1615 (*died*)
Anthony Hoskins	April 1615–10 Sept. 1615 (*died*)
John Blackfan	?–Nov. 1617
Juan Francisco de Benavides	? 1617–Feb. 1621 (*during interregnum Fr Thomas Sylvester acted as Vice-Rector*)
Francisco González	Oct. 1621–Oct. 1624
Francisco de Aguilar	Oct. 1624–Oct. 1630
Pedro de Ceniceros	Oct. 1630–Dec. 1632

Juan de Oribe	*Often absent, retired because of ill-health, Oct. 1633*
Sancho de Leguizamo	Oct. 1633–Dec. 1633
Hernando Cortés	Dec. 1633–Sept. 1637
Diego Marín	Sept. 1637–Feb. 1641
Juan Díez de Isla	Feb. 1641–Sept. 1646
Francisco Juárez	Sept. 1646–Feb. 1647
Diego de Pangua	Feb. 1647–Aug. 1649 (*during inter-regnum Fr William Sankey in charge*)
José de Ayala	Nov. 1649–Oct. 1652
Ambrosio de Salamanca	Oct. 1652–Nov. 1655
Andrés Antonio de la Oyuela	Nov. 1655–April 1659
Francisco de Liano	April 1659–Oct. 1662
Ignacio de Loyola	Oct. 1662–Feb. 1664 (*died*)
Diego de Montezuma	March 1664–Nov. 1664
Gregorio de Mendiola	Nov. 1664–April 1668
Andrés Reguera	April 1668–June 1669
Bartolomé de Occo	June 1669–April 1671
Manuel de Calatayud	April 1671–Dec. 1679
Fernando de Haro	May 1680–Aug. 1683
Fernando Navarrete	Aug. 1683–Sept. 1686
Teodosio Romay	Sept. 1686–Sept. 1687
Manuel Portocarrero	Sept. 1687–March 1691
Juan de Fuentes	March 1691–March 1694
Domingo de Medina	March 1694–Sept. 1697
Diego Alfonso de Sosa	Sept. 1697–Sept. 1716
Alonso de Zifuentes	Sept. 1716–Sept. 1718
Antonio Ossorio	Sept. 1718–April 1722
Francisco Vicente de la Torre	April 1722–Jan. 1726
Bartolomé Florencio de Torres	Jan. 1726–Sept. 1729
Francisco Nieto	Sept. 1729–Sept. 1731
Juan Bautista Valcarce	Nov. 1731–May 1735
Pedro José Solano	May 1735–Feb. 1754 (*died*)
Joaquín Ignacio de Iturri	*Took charge till May 1755*
Xavier Ignacio de Aguirre	May 1755–Jan. 1762
Francisco Texerizo	Jan. 1762–Aug. 1764

Francisco Torrano	Aug. 1764–Feb. 1767

After the expulsion of the Jesuits the English secular clergy took over the administration.

Philip Mark Perry	1768–74 (*died*)
Joseph Shepherd	1775–96 (*died*)
Thomas Taylor	1797–1808 (*died*)
Richard Cowban	*Took charge till 1813*
William Irving	1813–22 (*died*)
Thomas Sherburne	1822–5 (*during interregnum Thomas Pilling in charge*)
Joseph Brown	1826–38
James Standen	(*In charge till 1845, when John Guest took over*)
Thomas Sherburne	1846–54 (*resided in England while Guest looked after affairs in Spain; when he died in 1854, Guest continued to administer College affairs and was eventually appointed Rector*)
John Guest	1863–78 (*died*)
Charles Allen	1878–1904 (*died*)
William Wookey	1904–6
Thomas Kennedy	1906–11 (*died*)
James Thompson	1911–15
Michael John Burns	1911–24
Edwin Henson	1924–61 (*died*)
David Greenstock	1962–75
John Ryan	1975–84
Ronald Hishon	1984–

E

ST GREGORY'S COLLEGE, SEVILLE

1. Apart from *The Annals of the English College, Seville* (CRS, 14, pp. 1–14), and Martin Murphy's article on the early days of the College in *Archivo Hispalense*, 204 (1984), very little has been published concerning St. Gregory's College. However, materials for a history do exist. At St. Alban's, Valladolid, there are 30 bound volumes of documents as well as some 20–30 books of account, Mass intentions, and other records. At Seville there are documents relating to the College in the Archivo Municipal and Biblioteca Colombina.

2. The College was founded in 1592 through the efforts of Fr Persons and with the support of Philip II, who gave instructions to the Duke of Medina Sidonia to assist to the best of his ability. From the beginning the College relied entirely on alms. There was no fixed income, and even the house it occupied was not owned but rented. This was of set purpose since the King wished it to trust in the faith and piety of the people and Church of Seville. The Archbishop of Seville, D. Rodrigo de Castro y Quiñones on 16 May 1593 gave to the College a *renta de la alcabala* (a sales tax) and there were many other gifts. The Bull of Erection of the College is dated 15 May 1594. In 1595, with an increase in the number of students, it was necessary to move to a new site in the Calle de las Armas, and over the next ten years further property adjoining this site was acquired. The Duke of Medina Sidonia granted water rights, and in 1595 Doña Ana de Espinosa, widow of D. Alonso Flores Quiñones, Captain-General of the Indies Fleet, with her two brothers founded a chapel, giving 13,000 gold ducats for this purpose. She held the patronage and had burial rights as well as having twelve Masses said each week. Philip III continued the support given by his father, and on several occasions charged the Archbishop of Seville to continue to help the English. Permission was given to beg for alms in the Indies (20 Sept. 1620), but already before that date gifts were received from the Archbishop of Cuzco (Peru), D. Antonio de Raya, and there was a legacy from a resident in Potosí (Bolivia). In 1630 the Rector sent books to a Fr Bartolomé Martín Linero of the Order of St John of God, who lived in Panama.

The College buildings were an accumulation of houses on adjoining sites and so it was decided to rebuild. The King contributed to this work which was completed in 1664. It cost 94,153 *reales*, and to raise funds the College sold some property and raised a mortgage which was eventually redeemed.

3. Similar arrangements were made to those in Valladolid. The Rector was a Spanish Jesuit, and the student attended lectures at the Jesuit College of San Hermenegildo. Regular visitations were made by the Provincial of the Province of Bética (Valladolid and Madrid belonged to the Province of Castile). The first Rector (1592–1607) was Fr Francisco de Peralta, who was well versed in English affairs and the author of four works on the English Catholics.

The English Jesuits had been associated with Seville for many years. Father William Weston was a novice there in 1577, and before the College opened there was a strong English presence. This continued despite some opposition. There is extant a document from 1603: *Proving that the English seminary in Seville is not burdensome to the Jesuit province but advantageous and to its honour and good repute*. Among the points made, the following are notable: the three English fathers in the College were able to hear confessions and preach in six or seven languages. During Lent especially, there came to the College French, Walloons, English, Scots, Irish, Flemings and Italians. The fathers exercised a pastoral ministry among the many foreigners in the prisons, galleys and hospitals, and in this they were often helped by the students. Many heretics were converted. In addition to this, English Jesuit fathers assisted their Spanish bretheren in preaching missions in the surrounding countryside. Fr Walpole went to Cadiz, where more than 200 Englishmen were working on the fortifications of the port. It was on a mission to seamen that Dr Stillington died at El Ferrol. Fr Persons worked among English prisoners.

Apart from this, English Fathers occupied important posts in Spanish colleges. Fr Tonson lectured in Cadiz, Fr Johnson was minister at Málaga, and there were English lay brothers in many houses of the Society. The gifts from such as the Duke of Medina Sidonia and the description of Fr Persons by the Bishop of Jaén as another Athanasius have added prestige to the province — a prestige due to the activities of English Catholics at the College in Seville.

4. There is no register of students extant, but the researchers of Edwin Henson in the Seville papers resulted in a provisional list of names. Some of these were published by Albert J. Loomie, S.J., in *Recusant History*, vol. 9, pp. 163–170 (1967–8). Since then, further work has been done in

the College archives and in the Seville Archdiocesan ordination register by Fr Godfrey Anstruther, O.P., the result of which is that there are now 442 names of students for the years 1592–1767 (for the same period the register at St Alban's, Valladolid, contains 605 names). One of the complaints by Campomanes at the dissolution of the Society was that St Gregory's was no longer providing '*becas*' (burses) but relying on '*porcionistas*' (those paying a pension). This is borne out by the records where nearly 500 names of paying guests can be accounted for; these sometimes stayed for only a few weeks, some were children, some were priests — nearly all were Spanish. Whatever criticisms can be levelled at the College in its later years for not providing priests for the English Mission, it was not lying idle but providing some service of hospitality.

5. Like Valladolid, Seville declined in numbers from the mid-seventeenth century onwards. The official yearbook of the Jesuit province of Bética in the 1750s names only two Spanish fathers and two lay brothers as Jesuit residents at St Gregory's. There were complaints from the English in 1645 (*Anglia*, V, 21) and in 1693 (Anstruther, 3, pp. 197–8), but the exact nature of these objections (as an element in College history during this period) has yet to be investigated. A further rebuilding took place in 1761–4, and at the visitation of 8 March 1766 there were two priests, two lay brothers, two student priests and two other students. What students remained at the dissolution were transferred to the Colegio de las Becas.

6. There is extant a copy of an inventory made in 1767 listing the chief effects of the College: paintings, sacred vessels and vestments. In Olavide's proposals for the new uses of the former Jesuit houses in Seville, St Gregory's was designated to become a '*seminario de nobles*'. In 1771 the Medical Society of Seville was given provisional use of the building for its meetings. Although the Royal Decree of September 1767 formally united the three English Colleges of Valladolid, Seville and Madrid into one establishment at Valladolid, the authorities in Seville had yet to be convinced that St Gregory's did indeed belong to the English Catholics and not to the Society of Jesus. Philip Perry, the new Rector at Valladolid, tried unsuccessfully to obtain books from the library at St. Gregory's, but he was able to secure official permission to take seven large chestloads of effects from Seville to Valladolid (2 Oct. 1771). These included the large painting of St Gregory by Roelas which served as the altarpiece. The Medical Society later purchased from the College some of the remaining paintings, which it still possesses. St

Alban's continued its efforts to obtain compensation for the building, and the Medical Society was aware that its own tenure was precarious. It was refused permission to make use of the library, but in 1777 was eventually granted permission to use the chapel. Nevertheless, alterations were made to the house, and the pulpit was removed from the refectory. The property began to deteriorate, part of the garden wall fell down and had to be repaired immediately, and the façade crumbled. However, the Medical Society was able to sell oranges from the trees in the garden for a profit, and the appointment of a '*botánico*' (head gardener?) in 1776 helped to embellish the garden. As the years went on, the Society continued to use the building and acted as though it owned the property. (See Antonio Hermosillo Molina, *Cien años de Medicina Sevillana*, Seville, 1970.)

7. St Alban's, however, never relinquished its claim to the property, but the unsettled state of Spain during the Peninsular War and afterwards with the passing of the mortmain laws, together with the distance of Seville from Valladolid, meant that little was done to further the claim. The Medical Society remained in quiet and peaceful possession. It was in 1908, after the Archbishop of Seville had given the Church (long since closed) to a religious order, that the College renewed the claim. In 1916 a civil court decided that the Medical Faculty (*sic*) had no prescriptive right to the property, but there then arose a dispute as to who was entitled to carry out the sentence, the Ministry of Hacienda or the Ministry of Grace and Justice. In any case, the College did not want to evict the medical students who were then in residence. In 1927 the College lawyer, who had been conducting the case, was killed as a result of a road accident, and Edwin Henson made a special journey to Madrid to get possession of all the documents. Meanwhile the Medical Society moved to another site, and in 1930 the buildings were demolished to make way for the Escuela Hispanoamericana. The church remained standing but was closed in 1933; after the end of the Civil War, in 1939, the Archdiocese of Seville put it at the disposal of the Mercedarian Fathers, who have been there every since.

In 1953 Bernard Malley of the British Embassy in Madrid encouraged his friend Henson to take up the '*Pleito*' once more, and finally in 1965 David Greenstock, who had carried through the negotiations first of all as Henson's Vice-Rector and later as Rector, was able to inform the Nuncio that the College would be indemnified for the expropriation of 1767. The Country House at Las Dos Hermanas, also expropriated in 1767, had been sold and the money put in the State Treasury, but the

College had never received anything; this was to be regarded as '*cosa muerta*'. As to the church of St Gregory: up to 1906 this had been closed with the idea that it would be sold at some suitable time. But in that year the Archbishop of Seville, without consulting the Rector of St Alban's, gave over its use to a religious order. However, there is a document of 1933 which makes it clear that the property does not belong to the archdiocese. The church was closed from 1933 to 1939, and nobody wished to buy it since there was no suitable accommodation for a resident priest, but in 1939 the Archbishop (Cardinal Segura), against the protests of the Rector, once more disposed of the use of the chapel, this time to the Mercedarians. The property, being foreign, has never been included in lists of state property.

F
THE RESIDENCE AT SANLÚCAR DE BARRAMEDA

The origins of the Residence of Sanlúcar are to be found in the presence of English merchants in this outport of Seville at the mouth of the Guadalquivir. It was from here that Columbus and Magellan set out on their journeys of discovery and there is evidence of English traders using the port in those early days. In 1517 Don Alonso de Guzmán, the fifth Duke of Medina Sidonia, Lord of Sanlúcar, gave land and privileges for the establishment of an English confraternity under the patronage of St George. A grant of Henry VIII, which gave it the right to elect a consul for Andalusia, was confirmed by the Emperor Charles V in 1530. The chaplains to this confraternity were appointed with the approval of the Bishops of London, Winchester and Exeter since the merchants were mostly from London, Southampton and Bristol.*

Changes took place in the mid-sixteenth century. With the decline in usefulness of Sanlúcar because of its inability to accommodate the larger vessels then being built, Cadiz and Puerto de Santa María gained in importance. This resulted in rivalry between the English merchants in Andalusia over the election of the consul. However, it was the change in religion in England, the war with Spain and the consequent loss of trade, and the growing sympathy with the English and Irish priests working in this part of the country that led to the next phase in the confraternity's history. On 29 April 1591, in the persons of the consul and seven other English merchants, it made over the property for the founding of a hospice for the benefit of refugee priests and any poor Englishmen in need. There would be a Head (*prepositus*) and chaplains. The business was conducted with the approval and help of the Archbishop of Seville and the Duke of Medina Sidonia, and Cardinal Allen was asked to supply the church and house with sufficient priests. All this took place before the founding of the College of St Gregory in Seville.

The gift fitted in with the developing system of English seminaries in Spain: it could provide accomodation for the increasing number of

---

*For more on the history of the confraternity see Sir Geoffrey Fisher, 'The Brotherhood of St George at S. Lúcar de Barrameda', *Atlante*, 1 (1953), pp. 31–40; Joseph Kelly, 'S. Lúcar de Barrameda', *The Albanian*, vol. 1, no. 4 (1912), pp. 43–9; vol. 2, no. 1 (1912) pp. 47–8; and Gordon Connell-Smith, *Forerunners of Drake*, London 1954.

students, and serve as an assembly point for those leaving for England by sea or arriving in Spain. How far Fr Persons was instrumental in securing the transfer is not clear, but the first superior was Dr Thomas Stillington or Still, who had originally come to Spain to teach at the new College at Valladolid. On 16 November 1596 the Nuncio in Spain, Camillo Caetano, entrusted Fr Persons with the visitation of the hospice, and on 20 May 1600 constitutions and rules were drawn up. Sanlúcar was to give hospitality to English and Irish merchants, and in addition was to assist the other seminaries in Spain by aiding students and priests about to leave for England. St George's had a dual purpose, and the constitutions demanded a discipline for those who were students or priests distinct from whatever applied to the other residents. Philip II gave money to have the church restored, and there were usually three priests in permanent residence. On the death of Fr Persons, the supervision of St George's was given by the Pope to the Jesuit Prefect of the English Mission. In 1614 Fr Francisco de Peralta, the Rector of St Gregory's College, Seville, visited Sanlúcar on behalf of Fr Thomas Owen, the Prefect of the English Mission.

In 1615 there appears the first evidence of controversy concerning St George's. Thomas James, who had been appointed consul in Sanlúcar, objected that without consultation Martín Array had been reappointed superior for a further three years. James made this the occasion for voicing serious complaints about the previous fifteen years of Array's administration; he singled out neglect of hospitality, and expressed doubt as to whether the seminaries had benefited at all from the hospice. It is not clear how far this letter of James reflected a personal grievance — and how far it expressed a commonly accepted view.

It would appear that although it had its own superior, St George's had to struggle for its independence. In accordance with the 1600 constitutions it was closely linked with St Gregory's College, Seville (see Seville account books for 1628, 1640, 1650, 1663 and 1687), and the Rector of that College performed the duties of visitor on behalf of the Prefect of the English Mission. There was an incident in February 1666 when Fernando de Sande, Rector of St Gregory's, claimed his rights of exemption against Antonio Vidapáez who made a visitation on behalf of the Archbishop of Seville. But from 1686, there being no clearly designated visitor, the Archbishop of Seville began to assume that right. Available evidence suggests that, although there was a superior or chaplain looking after the property, there were never as many occupants as in the early years. But the hospice or residence was not simply an appendage of the

English seminaries in Spain. The resident merchants were concerned about its upkeep, and an appeal in 1691 to Cardinal Howard when he was Protector of England resulted in the Dominicans being appointed visitors. This arrangement did not prove successful, and the Archbishop of Seville resumed his visiting on 2 June 1696.

The Westminster Cathedral Archives provide the source for our next information on St George's. The Vicars Apostolic became concerned about its affairs, and in 1727 sent out John Prichard *alias* White, a brother of the Franciscan Vicar Apostolic of the Western District, as coadjutor and successor to the resident chaplain. Prichard found the property in a bad state of repair and the chaplain, Groves, aged and incompetent. There was a fear that if Groves died in office the Jesuits would lay claim to the property. It is not clear how far this was soundly based and how far a reflection of the views of Prichard and the Vicars Apostolic themselves. But Prichard's arrival only served to raise further controversy over the legal and canonical position of the Hospice. Bishop Giffard, the senior Vicar Apostolic who had given Prichard the commission, found that his powers were challenged by the Archbishop of Seville. The matter was taken to Rome, and support was canvassed from Cardinal Davia, the Protector of England. There was a long and complicated case involving the Spanish Cardinal Belluga, then resident in Rome; in the end the Archbishop of Seville said he was not challenging the powers of the Cardinal Protector of England, but only objecting to the nomination of Prichard, who had insufficient pastoral experience. Lawrence Mayes, the agent of the English Vicars Apostolic in Rome, did not proceed further with the case. This occurred *circa* 1737.

However, Prichard's interest remained. It transpired that the real superior of St George's was not Groves — he was only the chaplain in charge; the official *prepósito* was Joseph Hodges, who in 1728 had nominated John Price to act as superior. Price was a sick man, hence his non-participation in the controversy over Prichard. But in 1745 he gave the job to Prichard who, having secured the post, vindicated by his conduct the opinion formed of him by the Archbishop of Seville. He absented himself and, at the request of the local residents, was soon replaced. Price, now recovered in health, was reinstated in 1747. Seven years later the residents petitioned Cardinal Lante, then Protector of England, to renew the mandate of the Archbishop of Seville to visit the residence, since there were renewed fears that the Jesuits would annex the property.

The expulsion of the Jesuits from Spain seems to have had no great effect on St George's; it merely removed a persistent anxiety. For many years there had been scarcely any link between St George's, Sanlúcar and the English seminaries. The chaplains and superiors were secular priests, the local English community continued to have an interest in the hospice, and the Archbishop of Seville was the recognised visitor.

On 1 August 1823 the residents petitioned for the appointment of John Cuthbert as superior. The petitioners were the consul of His Britannic Majesty and four other 'catholic, apostolic, roman' British subjects. They said that the last *prepósito* or Rector was Juan María Fleming, on whose death Don Benito Ramos had been appointed provisionally because of the lack of an English priest. But now there was a suitable candidate, John Cuthbert, a British subject. The petition was to the Archbishop of Seville. It was a period of *sede vacante*, and the Provisor made the appointment which was confirmed by two of the Vicars Apostolic on 23 April 1824.

Cuthbert had ambitious plans for St George's. Having obtained a degree at Seville University, he spent £1,000 on building a new wing for the hospice in order to set up a school. He had about fifty pupils under him and they wore the cross of St George as part of their uniform; they were sons of local inhabitants — Spanish, English and Irish. But at some time before 1846 Cuthbert left Barrameda to go and assist Bishop Hughes, the Vicar Apostolic of Gibraltar; this departure was almost certainly connected with financial troubles. He left a Spanish priest in charge who disposed of some of the property, but on his death Fr Eugene Mulholland persuaded the British consul, Mr Philipps, to present his name to the Archbishop of Seville as the new rector of St George's.

In 1853–9 Fr Mulholland was engaged in money matters, partly as a result of the mortmain laws, and in an attempt to prove the English nature of the establishment. But debts forced him to sell much of the property and the altar plate. He left Sanlúcar in 1859, locking up the church and taking away the key with him. One report said that he went to the Isle of Man, but in 1863 Bishop Scandella of Gibraltar said he was in Seville practising as a medical doctor. Cuthbert was persuaded to resign the Rectorship, and Cardinal Manning, who had now succeeded to Westminster, nominated Luke Edward Beck of the Seville Oratory and a former pupil of Cuthbert as Pro-Rector on 13 December 1865; on 21 September 1866 he was made Rector in Cuthbert's place. When Bishop Vaughan made his visit to the foreign Colleges in 1876, he went to Sanlúcar after visiting Valladolid. He wrote from Lisbon, his next port of call, informing Guest of the state of Sanlúcar and how the church was being served by Don Antonio Pérez who had been appointed chaplain by Beck who had now died. A lawyer Joaquín Honoria was in effective charge of much of the property. In 1877 Guest was given a '*poder*' to administer the property at Barrameda, and a Spanish priest was nominated by him to serve the chapel.

Thus the link between the old hospice of St George and the English seminaries in Spain was reforged. Since the closure of the College in Seville, Sanlúcar had been in effect the concern of the local residents, and by the end of the nineteenth century the need for such a chaplaincy had ceased. But the property now came under the care of the one remaining seminary in Spain, the College in Valladolid. Succeeding Rectors of St Alban's maintained these rights, but for many years the church was not used and the property fell into a poor state of repair. In 1985, however, the Rector visited Sanlúcar and made contact with the local Bishop. An agreement was reached for the Confraternity of Nuestra Señora del Rocio to maintain and use the building. With generous help from the Confraternity, the church was restored and on 28 September 1985 a solemn Mass celebrated its reopening.

SELECT BIBLIOGRAPHY

Archive and manuscript sources

There is a great deal of archive material in Spain, Rome and England which at the time of writing remains unexplored. The Archives of St Alban's College, Valladolid, have provided the basis for the present work, but in addition the following have been consulted:

Leeds Diocesan Archives
    Smith, Penswick and Briggs papers.
Mount Street, London
    Archives of the English Province of the Society of Jesus.
    Xeroxes from Stonyhurst especially *Anglia* II, III, IV, V, VI, VII.
Salford Diocesan Archives
    Bishop Herbert Vaughan, box no. 1.
Scottish Catholic Archives
    Perry MSS.
    Blairs Letters, BL3/262/9.
Ushaw College
    Ushaw College MSS (UCM) III 47, 146. IV 379
Venerable English College, Rome (VEC)
    Scritture 6,9: 6,12: 6,73.
    Liber 1422
Westminster Cathedral Archives (WCA)
    Series A, vols 8, 16, 37, 40, 41, 42, 43.
Old Chapter Archives

Printed documents

Calendar Of State Papers (CSP). Domestic Series, of the Reign of Elizabeth: 1581–90, London 1865; 1591–4, London 1867; 1595–7, London 1869.
Calendar of State Papers, Domestic Series, Addenda. Reigns of Elizabeth and James I: 1580–1625, London 1872.
Calendar of State Papers and Manuscripts relating to English affairs, existing in the Archives and collections of Venice, Vol. VIII: 1581–91, London 1894.
Calendar of Letters and State Papers relating to English affairs preserved in or originally belonging to the Archives of Simancas, Vol. IV: *Elizabeth, 1587–1603*, London 1899.
Catholic Record Society (CRS):
    Vol. 14: *Miscellanea IX*, pp. 1–24: 'Annals of the English College at Seville, with accounts of other foundations at Valladolid, St Lucar, Lisbon and St Omers', contributed by Rev. J.H. Pollen, S.J., London 1914.

Vol. 29: E. Henson (ed.), *The English College at Madrid, 1611–1767*, London 1929.

Vol. 30: E. Henson (ed.), *The Registers of the English College at Valladolid, 1589–1862*, London 1930.

Contemporary printed works

More, Henry, *Historia Missionis Anglicanae Societatis Jesu*, St Omer 1660; ed. and transl. Francis Edwards, S.J. as *The Elizabethan Jesuits*, London 1981.

Owen, Lewis, *The Running Register recording a true relation of the state of the English colleges and seminaries and cloisters in all foreign parts*, London 1626.

Ribadeneira, Pedro de, *Historia Ecclesiastica del Schisma de Inglaterra*, Madrid 1588.

Yepes, Fray Diego de, *Historia Particular de la persecución de Inglaterra*, Madrid 1599.

A Relation of the King of Spayne's receiving in Valladolid in the English College of the same town in August last past, of this year, Antwerp 1592.

News from Spayne and Holland conteyning an information of English Affayres in Spayne with a conference made thereupon in Amsterdame of Holland, Antwerp 1593.

Recebimiento que se hizo en Valladolid a un imagen de Nuestra Señora, Madrid 1600.

Later works directly relating to the College

The Albanian, vols 1–3 (1910–16).

Blackfan, J., *Annales Collegii Anglorum Vallesoletani*, London 1899.

Camm, Bede, O.S.B., 'Jesuits and Benedictines at Valladolid, 1599–1604', *The Month*, XCII (1898), pp. 364–77.

Clifford, C.G. (ed.), 'The Letters of James Standen, 1830', *Ushaw Magazine*, XLVI (1936), pp. 25–47, 111–24; XLVII (1937), pp. 55–62, 205–18.

Esquíluz Ortiz de Latierro, Federico, 'La Fundación del Colegio Inglés de Valladolid', *E.S.*., 10 (1980), pp. 131–77.

Gaffney, W.J., *Elizabethan Students of the English College of St Alban, Valladolid*, privately printed 1981.

Hicks, L., S.J., 'Father Persons, S.J., and the Seminaries in Spain', *The Month*, CLVII (1931), pp. 193–204, 410–17, 497–506; CLVIII (1931), pp. 143–52, 234–44.

Loomie, A.J., and Henson, E., 'A Register of Students of St Gregory's College at Seville, 1591–1605', *Recusant History*, 9 (1967–8), pp. 163–75.

Pollen, J.H., S.J., 'St Alban's Seminary, Valladolid, 1602–1608', *The Month*, XCIV (1899), pp. 248–60

——'English Colleges in Eighteenth Century Spain', *The Month*, CXIX (1912), pp. 190–3.

Taylor, M., *The Scots College in Spain*, Valladolid 1971.

Rios, Romanus, O.S.B., 'The Seville Painting', *Ushaw Magazine*, LXXV (1965), pp. 72–4.

Williams, M.E., 'Philip Perry, Rector of the English College, Valladolid, (1768–1774)', *Recusant History*, 17 (1984), pp. 48–66.

——'English Manuscripts in Scottish Archives: The legacy of an eighteenth-century friendship?', *The Innes Review*, XXXIV (1983), pp. 93–5.

——'The Ascetical Tradition and the English College in Valladolid', *Studies in Church History*, vol. 22 (1985), pp. 275–83.

General works

Of the many works cited in the text the following are the more important.

GREAT BRITAIN

Allison, A.F., 'The later life and writings of Joseph Creswell, S.J., 1556–1623', *Recusant History*, 15 (1979), pp. 79–144.

——'Richard Smith, Richelieu and the French Marriage: The political context of Smith's appointment as Bishop for England in 1624', *Recusant History*, 7 (1964), pp. 148–211.

——'A Question of Jurisdiction: Richard Smith, Bishop of Chalcedon, and the Catholic Laity, 1625–1631', *Recusant History*, 16 (1982), pp. 111–45.

Anstruther, G., O.P., *The Seminary Priests: A Dictionary of the Secular Clergy of England and Wales, 1558–1800*, 4 vols, Great Wakering 1968–77.

Aveling, H., *The Handle and the Axe*, London 1976.

Beales, A.C.F., *Education under Penalty*, London 1963.

Bellenger, D.A., *English and Welsh Priests 1558–1800*, Downside 1984.

Bossy, J., *The English Catholic Community 1570–1950*, London 1975.

Caraman, P., S.J., *William Weston: The Autobiography of an Elizabethan*, London 1955.

Chadwick, H., S.J., *St Omers to Stonyhurst*, London 1962.

Croft, W., *Historical Account of Lisbon College*, Barnet 1902.

Foley, H., S.J., *Records of the English Province of the Society of Jesus*, 8 vols, London 1877–83.

Guilday, P., *The English Colleges and Convents in the Catholic Low Countries, 1558–1795*, London 1914.

Hibbard, C.M., *Charles II and the Popish Plot*, Chapel Hill, N.C., 1983.

Holt, G., S.J., *The English Jesuits 1650–1829: A Biographical Dictionary* (CRS, 70), 1984.

Kenyon, J., *The Popish Plot*, London 1972.

Loomie, A.J., S.J., *The Spanish Elizabethans*, London 1963.

Lunn, D., *The English Benedictines, 1540–1688*, London 1980.

Meyer, A.O., *England and the Catholic Church under Queen Elizabeth*, London 1967.

McCoog, T.M., S.J., 'The Establishment of the English Province of the Society of Jesus', *Recusant History* 17 (1984), pp. 121–39.

Milburn, D., *A History of Ushaw College*, Ushaw 1964.

Payne, Stanley G., *Spanish Catholicism: An historical overview*, Madison, Wisconsin 1984.

Pritchard, A., *Catholic Loyalism in Elizabethan England*, London 1979.

Vaughan, H., *Report of the Conditions of the English Catholic Colleges in Italy, Spain and Portugal*, printed by orders of their Lordships the Bishops of England, Salford 1876.

Williams, M.E., *The Venerable English College Rome: A History, 1579–1979*, London 1979.

SPAIN

Alvarez de Morales, Antonio, *La Ilustración y la Reforma de la Universidad en la España del siglo XVIII*, Madrid 1971.

Aguilar Piñal, F., *La Universidad de Sevilla en el siglo XVIII*, Seville 1969.

Astrain, Antonio, S.J., *Historia de la Compañía de Jesús en la Asistencia de España*, 7 vols, Madrid 1912–25.

Benassar, B., *Valladolid au siècle d'or*, Paris 1967.

——'Valladolid en el Reinado de Felipe II' in *Historia de Valladolid*, vol 3, pp. 71–133, Valladolid 1981.

Domínguez Ortiz, Antonio, *Política y Hacienda de Felipe IV*, Madrid 1960.

Fernández Suárez, J.R., 'Joseph Creswell: al servicio de Dios y de su Majestad Catolica, 1598–1613', *E.S.* (Valladolid), 1978, pp. 47–83.

Hernández, F.M., 'La formación del Clero en los siglos XVII y XVIII' in R.C. Villoslada, S.J., *Historia de la Iglesia en España*, vol. IV, pp. 523–82, Madrid 1979.

Murphy, Martin, 'Los comienzos del Colegio Inglés de San Gregorio en Sevilla', *Archivo Hispalense*, 204 (1984), pp. 3–24.

Rodríguez-Moñino Soriano, Rafael, *Razón de Estado y Dogmatismo Religioso en la España del Siglo XVII*, Barcelona 1976.

Rodríguez Díaz, Laura, *Reforma e ilustración en la España de siglo XVIII: Pedro Rodrigues de Campomanes*, Madrid 1975.

Rodríguez Martínez, Luis, *Historia del Monasterio de San Benito El Real de Valladolid*, Valladolid 1981.

Sarrailh, Jean, *L'Espagne Eclairée de la seconde moitié du XVIIIe siècle*, Paris 1964.

Vera Urbano, Francisco, 'La Consulta de los Católicos Ingleses a las Facultades teológicas Españoles en tiempo de Pitt el Joven', *Anthologica Annua*, 19, (1972), pp. 615–49.

INDEX